Partners of the Empir

Partners of the Empire

The Crisis of the Ottoman Order in the Age of Revolutions

Ali Yaycioglu

STANFORD UNIVERSITY PRESS

STANFORD, CALIFORNIA

Stanford University Press
Stanford, California

Printed in the United States of America on acid-free, archival-quality paper
Library of Congress Cataloging-in-Publication Data
Yaycioglu, Ali, author.
Partners of the empire : the crisis of the Ottoman order
in the Age of Revolutions / Ali Yaycioglu.
pages cm
Includes bibliographical references and index.
ISBN 978-0-8047-9612-5 (cloth : alk. paper)
ISBN 978-1-5036-0420-9 (pbk. : alk. paper)
ISBN 978-0-8047-9838-9 (electronic)
1. Political participation—Turkey—History—18th century. 2. Political
participation—Turkey—History—19th century. 3. Political culture—Turkey—
History—18th century. 4. Political culture—Turkey—History—19th century.
5. Turkey—Politics and government—18th century. 6. Turkey—Politics and
government—19th century. 7. Turkey—History—Ottoman Empire, 1288–
1918. 8. Turkey—History—Selim III, 1789–1807. I. Title.
DR559.Y39 2016
956'.015—dc23

2015028108

Typeset by Bruce Lundquist in 10/12 Sabon

To my late father,
Alâettin Yaycıoğlu,
and my mother,
Rezan Yaycıoğlu

Contents

Preface

I began my research into the history of the Ottoman Empire in the late eighteenth and early nineteenth centuries with the naïve idea that this period was one of the least studied. I was wrong: it is actually one of the most studied periods in Ottoman history. Since the early nineteenth century, Ottoman and European historians and diplomatic observers have written monographs, reports, and articles about the crisis that the Ottoman Empire experienced during the French Revolution and Napoleonic wars. Amid attempts at political modernization and constitutional movements in the late nineteenth century, policy-makers, lawyers, and intellectuals turned to this tempestuous earlier period to find the roots of modernization in the rich repertoire of institutions, episodes, and individuals. During the nation-building process, historians of Balkan, Turkish, and Arab nationalisms sought the origins of their national movements, early modernizers, and founding fathers for their national discourses in the late eighteenth and early nineteenth centuries. Some historians have seen the Ottoman experience in this period as typifying the crisis of the old and the beginning of the modern era. Scholars of the so-called Eastern Question studied this period as a prelude to that of the progressive disintegration of the Ottoman Empire in the early twentieth century. The accumulated literature on this period is therefore massive, appearing in all languages of the Ottoman lands, along with many European ones.

Although this period of the Ottoman Empire is one of the most studied, it has also been one of the least understood in its entirety. Despite the vast literature, the many archival sources, and the scholarly work done on this period, I have often found studies of major themes—such as regional developments in the Balkans, Turkey, and the Arab world; the rise of provincial notables; the transformation of Ottoman institutions; military and fiscal reform; and the context of diplomacy and war—handled separately. I have come to believe that thinking about these problems separately prevents us from seeing the complexities of the Ottoman order, its institutional umbrella, and the interactions and connections among various actors in the empire. In this book, I seek to explain the transformation of Ottoman institutions, regional formations, and the global context as an integrated phenomenon.

Stanford Shaw's *Between Old and New: The Ottoman Empire under Selim III, 1789–1807* (1971), certainly the most comprehensive work on this period so far, is still shaping the way many historians see this period: as a battle between old and new. I met Professor Shaw in Ankara in 2006 just before he passed away. Although we did not have the opportunity to chat about his book, my tone as an overconfident graduate student allowed him to sense that I wanted to reappraise his work. He was not at all annoyed. On the contrary, he complained that no scholar had tried to rewrite the history of this period in a larger scheme since his book had come out. I took this as sincere encouragement.

In this book I approach the Ottoman Empire in this transitional era from a new perspective. In the first place, I argue that its inhabitants had multiple options, some old, but most new. Often they combined the old and the new. This time of crisis was rich with possibilities of agendas, programs, coalitions, conflicts, and settlements. Many of these fell by the wayside, of course, thus becoming less relevant to scholars interested in finding the roots of the institutions and experiences of our own time.

Second, I contend that a multiplicity of actors—individuals, households, and collective actors with their own agendas, calculations, and capacities to change the status quo—participated in the Ottoman transformation. The battle was not between old and new, state and people, elites and the crowd, center and periphery, Muslims and non-Muslims as monolithic blocs. Rather, many battles and coalitions took place between various groups and interests in a messy political landscape. Instead of telling readers about the parties that participated in a particular battle, I therefore examine patterns of political action, the making and unmaking of coalitions, forms of building and losing power, expressions of public opinion, and how order was maintained and agreements were reached.

This book is by no means a comprehensive study that deals with every Ottoman problem, region, and episode in this era. My main interest in this study is to analyze the transformation of institutions, discourses, and political culture and to situate important individuals, collective actors, and events in this transformation in the Ottoman Empire. Since completing the book, I have become even more strongly convinced that we need more discussion and research on how the Ottoman world entered the nineteenth century of modernization and globalization. Today, it is vital for scholars and intellectuals who think and care about the Middle East and the Balkans to realize that people in these regions tried a variety of solutions, deploying a range of institutional restructuring and vast imaginations to confront the challenges before them. Eventually, as in each transformative age, winners and losers emerged, there were continuities and ruptures, some options were taken up and others abandoned. Considering some of these in an integrated way in the Ottoman context and within the larger framework of the age of revolutions, this book is, first and foremost, an invitation to new discussion on how people participated in an age of radical change on the eve of nineteenth-century modernity in the Ottoman world.

Partners of the Empire was written with the help, support, guidance, encouragement, and inspiration of many institutions and people. I was privileged to work in various archives and libraries. I would like to thank the employees of Harvard's Widener Library, Stanford's Green Library, Princeton's Firestone Library, the Prime Ministry Ottoman Archives and Topkapı Palace Museum Archives in Istanbul, the Orientalski Otdel kim Narodna Biblioteka "Kiril i Metodiï" in Sofia, the Gazi Husrev-beg library in Sarajevo, the Haus-, Hof- und Staatsarchiv in Vienna, and the Archives du Ministère des affaires étrangères in Paris. My special thanks go to the Stanford Humanities Center for organizing a manuscript review workshop for this book.

I am endlessly indebted to Cemal Kafadar, my teacher, supervisor, and mentor. For many years, he has been an indispensable guide and inspiration. I am grateful also to Halil İnalcık, Özer Ergenç, and Engin Deniz Akarlı, teachers with whom I have worked closely and learned Ottoman history and to Aron Rodrigue and Joel Beinin for their guidance, support, and friendship during the past four years at Stanford. I would also like to thank Keith Baker, Molly Greene, Avner Greif, Hakan Karateke, Alexander Key, Nancy Kollmann, Christoph Neumann, Oktay Özel, Şevket Pamuk, Richard Roberts, Baki Tezcan, Robert Travers, Caroline Winterer, and Fatih Yeşil for reading my manuscript at different stages, either partially or in its entirety, and sharing their valuable comments and criticisms.

Over the years, I have benefited from the ideas, guidance, and criticism of many teachers, colleagues, and friends. Among many, I would like especially to thank Hakkı Acun, Seven Ağır, Virginia Aksan, Mehmet Arısan, Tuna Artun, İlker Aytürk, Karen Barkey, Halil Berktay, Hülya Canbakal, Annette Coşkun, Charles Donahue, Beshara Doumani, Muhittin Eren, Boğaç Ergene, Nilüfer Duygu Eriten, Dimitri Gondicas, Rachel Goshgarian, Rossitsa Gradeva, Antonis Hadjikyriacou, Şükrü Hanioğlu, Mehmet Kalpaklı, Leyla Kayhan, Seyfi Kenan, Ilham Khuri-Makdisi, Michael Kimmage, Hakan Kırımlı, Elias Kolovos, Hulusi Lekesiz, Nuray Mert, Alan Mikhail, Gülru Necipoğlu, Erol Özvar, Evgeni Radushev, Veysel Şimşek, Yannis Spyropoulos, Tristan Stein, Himmet Taşkömür, Umut Uzer, the late Gilles Veinstein, Fikret Yılmaz, İpek Yosmaoğlu, Patricia Young and Sibel Zandi-Sayek. I would like to express my gratitude to the late Celalettin Çapanoğlu, and other members of the Çapanoğlu family, for sharing their memories about the family's history with me.

My colleagues in the History Department (and other departments) at Stanford University have been highly supportive and collegial during my writing of this book. I thank them all. But I am particularly grateful to Paula Findlen, Kären Wigen, Jennifer Burns, James Campbell, Gordon Chang, Robert Crews, Estelle Freedman, Martin Lewis, Mark Lewis, Norman Naimark, Yumi Moon, Priya Satia, Edith Sheffer, Matt Sommer, Laura Stokes, Jun Uchida, Amir Weiner, Steven Zipperstein, Monica Wheeler, Shahzad Bashir, Kabir Tambar, Burçak Keskin-Kozat, Burcu Karahan, Kristen Alff, Fırat Bozcalı, Rebecca Gruskin, Ali Karamustafa, Michelle Kahn, Demetrius Loufas, Uğur Peçe, and Vladimir Troyansky. I would like to express my gratitude to Umran İnan, the president of Koç University, and Scott Redford, former director of the Research Center of Anatolian Civilization at Koç, for their support during my time at Koç and RCAC at different stages of the completion of this book. Very special thanks to my fellow historian and editor Daniela Blei and to Peter Dreyer, copy editor for Stanford University Press. Both helped me express Ottoman facts in a comprehensible way to the broader community of historians. Thanks also to Kate Wahl, editor-in-chief at Stanford University Press, who has a great vision for the humanities and social sciences.

During my time in Turkey, my cousins Sevil Baltalı-Tırpan, Tuluğ Tırpan, Sevgi Karay, Hayri Karay, Almıla Karay, Deniz Coşkun, Meliha Coşkun-Yıldar, Canbek Yıldar, Yasemin Biricik-Tüjümet, and my childhood friend Tunç Başaran always looked after me.

I can scarcely express my thankfulness to my love, wife, and colleague Patricia Blessing. She was always by my side while I was completing this book. She tolerated my frustrations, read every single line, thought together with me, and made this book hers. Without her, it would have never existed.

My final words of thanks here are for my late father, Alâettin Yaycıoğlu, and my mother, Rezan Yaycıoğlu, who believed that I would produce something meaningful after many years of study, in graduate school and subsequently. I hope I have met their expectations. My father, who had devoted his life to doing good work as a civil engineer and an intellectual, learned that this book had been accepted for publication just before he died. I miss him but know that we shall meet again. I dedicate this book to him and to my mother, with whom I hope to share much more beautiful time in this life.

A Note on Transliteration
and Exchange Rates

In transliterating Ottoman Turkish, Arabic, and Persian technical terms, I have been guided by the *International Journal of Middle East Studies*. Place-names and other proper names are, however, given in their modern forms. Terms that have entered English usage, such as kadi, agha, or pasha, are given their English spelling unless precise transliteration is required for clarity. The exchange rate of British pound sterling to Ottoman *ġuruş* was 1:8 in 1800 and 1:19 in 1808.

Partners of the Empire

Introduction

During the age of revolutions between 1760 and 1820, like many polities around the world, the Ottoman Empire experienced a series of institutional shakeups, political crises, popular insurrections, and different attempts at settlement. The old order was collapsing and possibilities for a new order emerged. Old institutions vanished. New institutions were tested and contested. Istanbul and cities and regions in the Balkans, Anatolia, and the Arab lands became political theaters where various actors struggled, collaborated, and competed over conflicting agendas and opposing interests. Examining some of these episodes, actors, and institutions, this book describes the transformation of the Ottoman Empire in this radical age.

In the historical literature, scholars of the Ottoman Empire have treated this period as the first major phase of Westernization and administrative reform under Sultan Selim III, which failed after turmoil struck in 1806 and 1808. According to the mainstream view, the delayed process of reform was restarted in the 1820s under Mahmud II.[1] My book shows that the history of the empire in the late eighteenth and early nineteenth centuries was far more complex than a story about failed Westernization. During this era, the Ottoman Empire offered a diverse repertoire of reform agendas, institutional restructuring, political discourse, and shifting coalitions, which cannot be reduced to conflicts between East and West, or old and new. These binaries are misleading for grasping the empire's multifaceted transformation. As we shall see, Western and Islamic patterns were intertwined, and there is no easy way to juxtapose them. Competition in this period took place, not only between the forces of old and new, but also and even more so, between different actors and agendas, many of which can be classified as new. This book presents a multilayered picture of the Ottoman Empire in the age of revolutions that goes beyond the existing binaries.

Examining the complex nature of the empire, I focus on various themes, institutions, and actors in the Ottoman center and the provinces. But this book also offers a broader argument. During this period, it shows that the

Ottoman polity experienced a turn from a vertical empire, in which the imperial elite sustained claims to power through a hierarchical system, to a horizontal and participatory empire, in which central and provincial actors combined to rule the empire together. Throughout the eighteenth century, through formal and informal contractual relations, provincial notables became consolidated as an essential component of state. Provincial communities formed new participatory mechanisms in public administration with their leaderships and became active participants in governance. These two structural changes were entangled with a reform program by the Ottoman imperial elite that pushed military and fiscal reorganization in the late eighteenth century. Reform came at the expense of various groups, especially the janissaries, a giant socio-military organization whose members had accumulated privileges and rights throughout the previous two centuries and had come to control public opinion in Istanbul and other cities. As a result, shifting coalitions and alliances among reformist elites, the janissaries, provincial notables, and communities appeared. These groups sought to control the state and negotiated different agendas of order, reform, and restoration. In 1808, an alliance of reformists and provincial notables came close to changing the imperial order for good into a partnership based on mutual trust, security of life and property, and military-administrative reform. But this attempt remained partial. The empire continued its journey to build a new order in the nineteenth century.

This experience was a result of institutional and political developments, as well as structural changes and contingencies that mirrored developments in other polities around the world. In the age of revolutions, other polities experienced similar crises, but employed different solutions. Some of these solutions succeeded, while others failed, or were reoriented and renegotiated. One response of the Ottoman elites to crisis was partnership. It helped the empire surmount challenges to its survival, while precluding dismemberment. Later the empire would take a different course, resuming a vertical structure. The Ottoman nineteenth century was to a large extent a story about state modernization, centralization, and bureaucratization. New practices and institutions that were tested during this period endured, however, and the legacy of actors who played a transformative role in the age of revolutions continued to shape Ottoman political culture throughout the nineteenth and early twentieth centuries through different channels. In this respect, the Ottoman experience in the age of revolutions was about different versions of top-down (or bureaucratic), contractual (or constitutional), and participatory (or democratic) experience, which should be understood in their political and institutional contexts and not simply as analogues of modern categories.

Each chapter in this book presents its own autonomous argument. Chapter 1, which is heavily based on the current scholarship in the field of Ottoman history, offers a brief sketch of the Ottoman world in the eighteenth century and examines the New Order, a set of reform agendas proposed by the Ottoman imperial elite to resolve military and fiscal crises. Some of these reform agendas threatened segments of society, particularly those that endorsed the political claims of the janissaries. I argue that neither the New Order nor the opposition were monolithic groups, but rather large coalitions with branches in the provinces, diverse positions, and various interests. Chapters 2 and 3 shift our focus from the center to the provinces. In chapter 2, I discuss the nature of the relationship between the provincial elite and the empire in the late eighteenth and early nineteenth centuries. I argue that throughout the eighteenth century, provincial notables came to act as fiscal, administrative, and military entrepreneurs who engaged in formal or informal contractual relations with the empire. These contractual relations were based on offers, acceptances, rejections, and counteroffers in a volatile arena, without the formal security of contract, status, property, and life. Some provincial notables joined the coalition of the New Order, while others acted with the opposition. The process gradually produced a new order of notables, by which the empire was run through partnerships between the central and provincial elites. Chapter 3 analyzes the ways in which provincial communities responded to changes in the eighteenth century. I argue that while the central administration was disconnected from the provinces and outsourced authority to provincial notables, provincial communities developed bottom-up mechanisms to manage fiscal and administrative matters under the supervision of elected or communally nominated notables. Instead of reversing this participatory and electoral process and launching a centralizing policy, the central administration institutionalized bottom-up collective actions. In the new provincial order, collective action became a source of legitimacy. Provincial communities were becoming political actors—sometimes at expense of notables—in governance.

The book's first three chapters thus present analytical and thematic discussions of the institutional transformation of the Ottoman order (or orders) and how the imperial elite, notables, and communities experienced and shaped this transformation in the late eighteenth and early nineteenth centuries. Chapter 4 shifts to a narrative history of the events that took place between August 1806 and November 1808. Stories from previous chapters converge in chapter 4, where I focus on the popular opposition to the New Order led by the janissaries, shifting coalitions between provincial and imperial elites, growing politicization of Ottoman communities, and the interimperial story of the Napoleonic wars and wartime diplomacy. This narrative style enables me to highlight a process that consisted of multiple episodes, contingencies, shifting alliances, and dead ends. Confronted with a janissary-led popular revolt in 1807, the New Order collapsed and the prior order was restored. This triggered a political coalition between the elites of the New Order and a group of provincial notables for a coup d'état to restore the New Order. This coalition manifested itself in a constitutional synthesis of the New Order and the order of notables, embodied in a document called the Deed of Alliance, which envisioned a new imperial regime based on partnership, security, stability (rather than volatility), and trust among elites. Chapter 5 presents a textual analysis of the Deed of Alliance. Close reading of the text, combined with commentary, is followed by a discussion of the document's reception in modern history and its place among other constitutional texts from the age of revolutions.

Partners of the Empire thus operates on several levels. While supporting its overall argument, each chapter tackles a number of specific issues, such as military-fiscal reform, provincial notables and their political and economic power, communities and collective action, the politicization of the masses and urban riots, the making of a constitutional document in Ottoman political culture, and war and diplomacy in the age of revolutions. Interconnected themes, episodes, and individuals emerge in each chapter despite the diversity of topics and genres. Readers will, for example, encounter and reencounter the city of Ruse, the events of 1807 and 1808, life-term contracts or apportionment, the reformist sultan Selim III, the leading provincial notable Mustafa Bayraktar, and the pro–New Order preacher Ubeydullâh Kuşmânî.

Since *Partners of the Empire* engages with diverse questions and themes in many locations, it takes advantage of a wide array of sources in various genres and languages. In addition to growing scholarship in different languages on the period, documents from local and central Ottoman archives in Turkey and Bulgaria, some published but most unpublished, provide the bulk of source material for my story. I also rely heavily on narrative sources, chronicles, and histories, as well as on European (French, Austrian, British, and Russian) diplomatic archival sources. Keeping in mind the focus and length of the book, I mention only a limited number of the many sources I have gathered and studied over the years. At several points, I discuss the nature of my primary sources.

A PROGRESSION OF REVOLUTIONS
OR AN AGE OF PLURAL REVOLUTIONS?

Readers will gather from the title of this book that one of my objectives is to place the Ottoman Empire in the age of revolutions. Throughout my story, I explore how Ottoman history contributes to our understanding of that age as a global phenomenon, and in turn, how our discussions of the age of revolutions contribute to our understating of the role in it of the Ottoman Empire. The Ottoman Empire experienced challenges that were common to many polities in the late eighteenth and early nineteenth centuries. Ottoman responses sometimes resembled events in other parts of the world, but in other cases did not. My main objective is not to place the Ottoman Empire apologetically in the framework of the established historiography of the American and French political revolutions and the British Industrial Revolution without taking historical specificities into consideration. Rather, I understand the Ottoman experience in the age of revolutions in its own way and on its own terms. But this book also conceives a broader framework for the age of revolutions, in which episodes, patterns, and themes in North America, Britain, France, and the Ottoman Empire; but also in Haiti, Russia, Iran, Burma, Mexico, and other regions shared a common global experience. Thus, events in disparate places had similar, comparable, and commensurable characteristics, which were, moreover, interconnected.

R. R. Palmer's path-breaking 1959 book *The Age of the Democratic Revolution* presented the revolutionary period as transnational.[2] Palmer explored connected phenomena in Europe and the Atlantic world, suggesting that the boundaries of democratic revolutions extended to Poland, but not beyond. Many historians, following Palmer, have focused on a transnational revolutionary age, examining developments from Central Europe to the Americas. Historians of the Muslim world have only contributed to this oversight. Bernard Lewis, in his seminal works on the impact (or lack of impact) of the French Revolution on the Ottoman Empire, argued that the ideas of the French Revolution impinged on the empire but collided with civilizational walls that divided Islam from the West.[3] As I mentioned earlier, this period, according to many historians, was when the seeds of Westernization were sowed. According to this narrative, Ottoman Westernization was military and administrative, not social or democratic. Ottoman intellectuals were thus mostly indifferent to the French Revolution, according to Lewis.

In this narrative, the Ottoman Empire makes a brief appearance in the age of revolutions during Bonaparte's invasion of Egypt from 1798 to 1799. Many historians consider this Napoleonic moment the beginning of the "modern" period in the Middle East. This short interval triggered unexpected developments in Egypt that resulted in the rise of Muhammad Ali and his radical transformation of Egypt in the early nineteenth century. In this account, the Ottoman Empire, including Egypt, constituted another world, distinct from Europe's revolutionary change. The top-down characteristics of the modernization reforms of the Ottoman sultans in the Balkans and Anatolia, or Muhammad Ali in Egypt, were not compatible with the revolutionary era's democratic ideas and bottom-up movements.

The main impact of the American and French revolutions on Ottoman political culture was that it gave rise to the nationalism of Christian Balkan peoples. Starting with the Greek War of Independence in the 1820s, Balkan nations under the influence of revolutionary ideas separated themselves from the Ottoman Empire. According to this argument, the French Revolution's only effect on Muslims was the rise in the late nineteenth and early twentieth centuries of the Young Turks, the Ottoman constitutionalists, in opposition to the despotism of Sultan Abdülhamid II. Their constitutional revolution in 1908, and revolution in Iran in 1906, were Muslim versions of the French Revolution, ending sultanic despotism. Revolution thus finally arrived in the Ottoman lands 119 years after the revolutionary events of 1789 in France. Republicanism came even later, with the foundation of the Republic of Turkey in 1923, which relegated the Ottoman Empire to the dustbin of history.[4]

This narrative was based on a peculiar version of world history, which depicted revolutionary changes as the progression of a certain universalist framework, shaped by the Enlightenment, that promoted the rights of the individual, the market, and public sovereignty against the privileges of the old order. This progression began with the American and French revolutions and the fall of the ancien régime in France in the late eighteenth century (or, for some historians, with the Glorious Revolution of 1688 in England). Revolutionary currents thus moved across the earth's surface, region by region, during the nineteenth and twentieth centuries, arriving in the Ottoman Empire after a century's delay. The Marxist version of this global narrative of revolutionary progress argued that the journey of revolutions was radicalized by the Russian Revolution of 1917, marking an ontological shift from bourgeois to proletarian. This process continued with the Xinhai Revolution of 1911, ending the Qing Empire, followed in 1949 by the Chinese Communist Revolution. Other versions of revolutions continued to spread throughout the world, exploding at different times with different characteristics in India (1947), Egypt (1952), Algeria (1954), Zanzibar (1964), Iran (1979), Eastern Europe (1989), and again in Egypt (2011), among others.[5]

As some have suggested, the late eighteenth-century revolutions never came to an end. The nineteenth and twentieth centuries, and even the current century, have witnessed revolutions of different types, all of which had roots in late eighteenth-century Europe and America to some extent. As Keith Baker argues, the French Revolution changed the meaning of the word *révolution* from *any* abrupt change to *a particular type* of abrupt change, with a universal and world-historical script expected and followed in different corners of the world. As David Armitage shows, after the American Revolution, the idea of national sovereignty became contagious, so that every nineteenth- and twentieth-century collective ethno-national group was expected to declare it.[6] But this revolutionary progressionism should not prevent us from asking whether in the late eighteenth and early ninetieth centuries there existed a broader context for abrupt, dramatic institutional change and deliberative searches to form new orders with wider social bases. The American and French cases were perhaps only two versions of such episodes that unfolded in different corners of the world.

Instead of engaging with the global history of revolutionary progression from advanced to "late" societies, some historians have recently generated another debate on the concurrent history of revolutions on a global scale in the late eighteenth and early nineteenth centuries. Franco Venturi planted the seeds of contemporary discussions of the global age of revolutions in his massive survey, *The End of the Old Regime in Europe, 1768–1776* (1979).[7] Venturi suggests that the radical changes that ended the old order first appeared, not in western Europe, but further east, on the Ottoman-Russian-Polish frontiers in the entangled Hellenic, Slavic, and Islamic cultural zones. In relocating the roots of the revolutionary age from west to east, Venturi masterfully illustrates that connections between Europe, the Ottoman Empire, Russia, and Poland were so profound and lively in the late eighteenth century that it is impossible to write their histories on separate pages.

Recently, several historians have proposed a wider scope of analysis and have explored the notion of a global or plural age of revolutions.[8] In *The Birth of the Modern World* (2004), C. A. Bayly provides a map of converging revolutions occurring in different parts of the world, from Burma to Haiti and from the 1760s to the 1820s. Some of these revolutions were connected by similar political or philosophical agendas and variations of Enlightenment. But most were not. Each political, legal, and intellectual culture responded to similar crises in its own way. According to Bayly, however, at some level these responses—occurring in the same stormy global context—were connected, comparable, and commensurable. A historian working on a specific case by considering broader patterns, dynamics, and perceptions must thus confront these generalities.[9]

What exactly were these global patterns, generalities, and connections? In the eighteenth century, global interactions increased as a result of intensifying mobility and the increasing circulation of commodities and ideas through trade networks and diaspora communities. However, after the consolidation of colonial empires, especially the British and French, interstate (interimperial) competition reached a global scale, which was responsible, to some extent, for a "world war" between 1756 and 1763 in many corners of the world. Other empires also deepened and expanded their rule. Russian power reached inner and central Asia. The Qing Empire moved westward and swallowed Xingjian, Tibet, and Mongolia. The Spanish Empire reestablished itself in Latin America and the Philippines. The Ottoman Empire conquered Crete, reconquered the Peloponnese, and captured Caucasia, formerly part of Safavid Iran. Under Nader Shah, Iran expanded toward India. At the same time, extinction threatened many polities. The Mughal Empire was stuck between Iran and the British and French empires and their proxies. Poland disappeared after its partition by Russia, Austria, and Prussia. Ottoman expansion in the early eighteenth century was dramatically curtailed by Russia, which moved toward Ottoman-dominated lands bordering on the northern Black Sea and annexed Crimea.

Imperial expansion, long-distance military campaigns, and prolonged wars led to a dramatic increase in the need for military reform, including expensive military technologies and new organizational patterns for disciplined and drilled standing armies. Soaring military expenditures, wars, and constant military reorganization pushed states to extract more resources from their people, provinces, or colonies. These pressures led to fiscal reforms and the introduction of new financial instruments for internal and external borrowing. Military and fiscal reform often brought with it new reform agendas to discipline urban and rural populations or social reforms to curb different forms of opposition. Various reform agendas were disseminated not only through publications and trade networks, but also by military and fiscal experts who sought employment in foreign countries.

Reform agendas triggered a wide range of responses and unrest, sparking riots and rebellions in many places. Separatist movements were sometimes successful, but also triggered new expansions and consolidations of state rule or imperial control. Amid the turmoil, new possibilities for negotiations and coalitions between ruling elites and other groups emerged. Some coalitions that controlled the state apparatus expanded through co-optation, while others shrank through new exclusions. These negotiations and coalitions gave birth to unprecedented settlements and ways of envisioning the political order by reconfiguring rights and privileges. Ideas and attempts to change the order triggered codifications. The state was both successful and unsuccessful in dealing with opposition. In different regions, these developments brought about profound institutional changes that reconfigured everything from the social order to the meaning of life, in a process we generically call "revolution."[10]

Focusing on the Ottoman context, this book examines several of these themes and episodes that contribute to a comparative history of crisis, reform, and revolution in the late eighteenth and early nineteenth centuries.

My purpose is to show how Ottoman political culture produced possibilities for reform of the empire in an epoch when reform was increasingly understood as inevitable, and how various groups—with their own agendas, priorities, and calculations—challenged or became part of reform politics. The book also highlights historical connections, since most of these episodes took place, not in an isolated Ottoman theater, but as an integrated part of Eurasian politics, economies, and war. In this period, the internal and external affairs of the state were not clearly separated, sovereignty and territoriality were constantly renegotiated, and national or royal loyalties split and shifted. Ambitious projects for regime change were on the table.

Comparative and connected history can help us identify and analyze both similarities and differences, as well as points of convergence and divergence. Although this book does not present a particular argument about the Ottoman Empire's convergence with or divergence from Europe, it can contribute to these discussions. It examines various institutions and practices that are crucial to understanding political and economic performance, such as contracts, negotiations, participation, trust and accumulation of wealth, risk and volatility, and order and violence. These categories of analysis help us understand the comparative history of economic development and institutional transformation. Debates about the institutional origins, not only of development and underdevelopment, but of authoritarianism and democracy in the West, the Islamic World, and East Asia are put in comparative perspective by my contention that during the age of revolutions, the Ottoman Empire tested shifting from a vertical to a horizontal state, and from a volatile hierarchical order to a stable order of partnership and participation.[11]

THE HISTORIOGRAPHY OF OTTOMAN DECLINE, CRISIS, AND REFORM

The history of the Ottoman Empire was long told in terms of its fifteenth-century rise, sixteenth-century grandeur, seventeenth-century stagnation, eighteenth-century decline, and (unsuccessful) nineteenth-century reform, followed by its collapse in the early twentieth century. In this Gibbonian rise-and-decline narrative, the period between 1770 and 1820 was presented as an initial attempt and failure at Westernization and the era of one of the Ottoman Empire's worst crises before World War I. Efforts at reform and Westernization were curbed by various powers, first by the janissaries, acting in conjunction with conservative forces such as the ulema (Islamic scholarly class), and to a certain extent by provincial notables, who represented a centrifugal reactionary and feudal power. Conventional historical discourse, which emerged during nineteenth-century bureaucratic modernization and twentieth-century nation-state building, failed to grasp the complexities of this earlier period of crisis. For Turkish historiography, the janissaries and the coalition of provincial notables targeted the modernizing state. In Balkan and Arab historiography, provincial notables and janissaries tightened the Ottoman-Turkish yoke, operating against local people according to the tyrannical and arbitrary rules of a feudal order. Paradoxically, the rule of the notables was instrumental in fostering national awaking, since under their rule, the provinces were separated from the Ottoman state, preparing the ground for the national movements and nation-building processes that followed.[12]

Since the mid 1960s, historians have revised this "decline and breakdown" narrative from many perspectives. Albert Hourani's work on the politics of notables opened new avenues for studies of the provincial elite. Hourani depicted notables in the Arab lands, not as feudal oppressors, but as local elites who gave voice to the interests of local people against the empire, inasmuch as they were incorporated into local politics and the economy.[13] Halil İnalcık, who modified his work on imperial decline from the 1970s, argued that the military and fiscal transformation of the seventeenth and eighteenth centuries gave birth to new provincial elites who promoted a process of decentralization, but not disintegration, of the empire.[14] Avdo Sućeska illustrated how in the eighteenth-century Balkans, local communities and notables were involved in reciprocal relationships through various legal and fiscal instruments.[15] These three pioneering historians, while revising the old narrative, show that the eighteenth and early nineteenth centuries were not a period of total breakdown for the Ottoman Empire, but of multifaceted transformation that introduced new actors, institutions, and relationships.

After the 1970s, studies of the Ottoman long eighteenth century followed three tracks: (i) regional studies, (ii) military and fiscal transformation, and (iii) political culture and the politics of reform. Since the 1980s, writings on regional settings, families, and economies have enriched the perspectives introduced by Hourani, İnalcık, and Sućeska. A vast literature has emerged on Arab,[16] Anatolian,[17] Balkan,[18] and Greek[19] provincial centers, notable families, and networks in the eighteenth and early nineteenth centuries. Nevertheless, the imperial context is not adequately problematized in these studies, and the modern boundaries of post-Ottoman countries and divisions between the geographical zones of the Middle East, Anatolia, and the Balkans are assumed. Recent writings on central Anatolia, Mosul, Jabal, Nablus, Egypt, and Cyprus illustrate the limits of Ottoman imperial control, the consolidation of regional political economies and their connections to interimperial economic zones, and the transformative role played by provincial notables in provincial societies as new centers of the empire.[20] While focusing on the local level, these scholars problematize local, regional, imperial, and global perspectives, showing their intersections and interactions through various relationships and institutions.

Beginning in the 1980s, a number of studies have examined the institutional transformation of the Ottoman polity from a tributary empire to a fiscal-military state with far-reaching financial and administrative institutions. Meticulous work on the expansion of tax-farming as the dominant fiscal mechanism,[21] research on its structural implications in the rural economy,[22] and studies of the new fiscal regime under the Ottoman New Order[23] were further developed by various historians. These scholars suggest that new fiscal transformation based on outsourcing provincial units and internal borrowing increased private entrepreneurial attitudes and nexuses that fostered imperial integration through fiscal entrepreneurs.[24] Recent studies of macroeconomic performance in the Ottoman world and the gradual appearance of the market economy in the eighteenth century have not only rescued economic analysis from the framework of fiscal history, but have also qualified and quantified the argument that the eighteenth century was not a period of economic decline.[25] Despite the growing literature on Ottoman fiscal institutions and economic performance in the eighteenth and early nineteenth centuries, however, the majority of these studies are not interconnected with political developments, but operate in the relatively isolated fields of fiscal and economic history.

Other scholars have shown interest in the transformation of political culture and public life in the Ottoman world in the seventeenth and eighteenth centuries. The notion that these two centuries should be understood, not in terms of structural decline, but rather in terms of transformation, with losers and winners who endorsed different political agendas and historical discourses, has recently gained acceptance.[26] Historians have recently responded to Cemal Kafadar's invitation to understand the janissary rebellions as social movements that resulted from the new forms of sociability in public life, the politicization of urban communities, and their integration into economic life.[27] In the seventeenth and eighteenth centuries, some scholars argue, the Ottoman Empire produced a new political society, autonomous from the dynasty and the central imperial establishment, through new economic and political claims that signified a second phase of the Ottoman Empire. Earlier studies of the Ottoman reforms of the late eighteenth and early nineteenth centuries, which analyzed the politics of reform as a battle between old and new and East and West,[28] had already undergone reevaluation by scholars who provided a more intricate picture of Ottoman reform and Westernization. Specifically, these historians have uncovered agendas mobilized by internal dynamics and complex cultural encounters and social movements.[29] A new generation has shown that the New Order's reforms amounted to much more than military reorganization. Instead, these scholars have illustrated that the New Order was a set of agendas with political and social components that became a disciplinary mechanism to reshape the social order in the early nineteenth-century Ottoman world.[30] Studies on how various public opposition movements and moral economies in the urban space reacted to disciplinary reform politics throughout the eighteenth and nineteenth centuries support this argument.[31]

While engaging in dialogue with these evolving literatures, *Partners of the Empire* departs from them on methodological matters and in terms of focus and scale. First, it examines themes and problems—generally treated as separate phenomena by scholars in the field—in an integrated format, around a process: crisis, transformation, reform, revolution, and settlement in the Ottoman Empire in the age of revolutions. Themes such as fiscal transformation, military reform, the rise of provincial notables, the consolidation of collective action and public opinion, political radicalism and violence, and constitutional settlements are, I argue, analytical components of the same accelerated transformation. Second, the level of analysis in this book is the empire, rather than a particular region or the transformation of central government. Therefore, I shift the focus, by zooming out and zooming in, from the provincial level to the regional, from the regional to the imperial, from the imperial level to the theater of Istanbul, and from there on to the global politics of the French revolutionary and Napoleonic period.

In this respect, I analyze connections as well as autonomous developments and the local, imperial, and interimperial contexts. Clearly, I am unable to focus on every region and event. Rather, I have chosen to represent specific cases, some of which are representative, and others unique, and examine these moments in different regions in comparative fashion. I do not dismiss the importance of local and regional realities. Rather, I propose looking at these local realities in tandem with the imperial and interimperial contexts to examine how various levels of activity interacted with one another. By doing so, I suggest that the relationship between the empire and the provinces is not a binary story about center and periphery. In my account, the Ottoman Empire appears as a relatively integrated unit, entangled through ties, institutions, and relationships that were continuously renegotiated by many actors. Integration was neither necessarily imposed by the center nor fully controlled by it.

Recently, two books have set new agendas for the transformation of the Ottoman Empire in the seventeenth and eighteenth centuries. In *The Second Ottoman Empire* (2010), Baki Tezcan argues that a new political society came into being as a result of early seventeenth-century social and political crisis. Constant struggles among the old imperial elite and new social and political forces, including janissary affiliates and the learned, gave birth to a strong society positioned against the conventional elites of the central state and maintaining claims to economic resources and political rights as well as new cultural and legal orientations. Tezcan calls this process "proto-democratization." It gradually changed the institutional structure of the empire; hence, Tezcan argues, we can refer to the new regime as the Second Empire. The eighteenth century was more or less a continuation of the Second Empire with some new actors, namely, provincial notables, who became empowered and enriched with the fiscal institutions of the Second Empire.[32]

In *Empire of Difference* (2008), Karen Barkey proposes a comprehensive framework for the Ottoman imperial system and its transformation.[33] In the eighteenth and early nineteenth centuries, Barkey argues, two major developments occurred: "the empowerment of the political" and the consolidation of networking society. The former pertains to the politicization of urban space through janissary-led public dissent, while the latter refers to the rise of fiscal nexuses, based on fiscal contracts and tax-farming. In Barkey's analysis, neither trend, each of which developed separately from the other, became a viable alternative to Ottoman modernization. Eventually, in the nineteenth century, the Ottoman state was able to suppress dissent and eliminate networking society through centralizing policies and bureaucratic modernization.

Although *Partners of the Empire* very much shares the general arguments of Tezcan and Barkey, it offers a different take. I agree with Tezcan and Barkey that in the seventeenth and eighteenth centuries there was a profound transformation in the empire. New actors came into being from different segments of the Ottoman society in the center and provinces. They developed new claims on economic resources and political life. Meanwhile, the central organization, based on a top-down hierarchy of the servants of the state and sultanate, if not marginalized, came to terms with new actors, realities, and institutions. The Ottoman state in the seventeenth and eighteenth centuries had more *partners* than the Ottoman state in the sixteenth century both in the center and provinces. However, this "new" social and political order, gradually developed in the seventeenth and eighteenth centuries and based on an "empowered political" and "network society," did not bring long-term stability. Urban riots, regional rebellions, peasant unrest, violence committed by state agents or local notables, massive confiscations, and the elimination of different groups after a certain time of wealth accumulation were natural components of this period. In fact, the imperial elites and growing fiscal bureaucracy, janissary affiliates, enriched and empowered provincial notables, the learned, and different religious groups criticizing the ruling elite did not agree on a persistent settlement in the seventeenth and eighteenth centuries. Yet the empire did not collapse and the contained volatile system created its own dynamic of endurance and balance of power among the power groups. The unbearable crisis came from the outside. The relatively stable period between 1730 and 1768 ended with the Ottoman-Russian war of 1768–74. The war left the Ottoman Empire with an immense military and fiscal crisis, which had a potential to transform the crisis of existence. In the late eighteenth century, the Second Empire, as Tezcan calls it, was coming to an end, having sustained a crisis similar to what other early modern polities experienced.

In the late eighteenth century, although there was no agreement in Ottoman political society about the nature of reform, there was consensus that some sort of reform was inevitable. Yet there were many questions to be answered. Who would be the partners of reform? Who would be the members of the alliance? Who would be included in or excluded from the new order? Would the janissaries intend to be part of the process, and, if not, were they to be ignored or sacrificed? Would provincial notables be in or out? If they were to be included, what role would they play in the new order? Would they be free contractors or servants of the state? What would their relationship to provincial communities look like? Would state officials closely administer the provincial communities as much as possible, or would provincial notables take on this task? Or would the communities govern themselves through elected leaders? If so, then, how would the state monitor the provinces? What kind of deal should the empire conclude with the actors to keep them loyal or at least to prevent them from menacing peace and integration? All these questions were on the table in the late eighteenth century, and there were no simple answers. Similar queries came from janissaries, provincial notables, and leading members of the communities who knew that reform was inevitable and that they would be smart to develop strategies to decide under what conditions they would be a part of reform coalition or against it.

This book argues that in the late eighteenth century, the Ottoman Empire tested three competing alternatives to reform the imperial order and preserve a relatively integrated and operational system. First, there was a reform agenda that was based on top-down reorganization through bureaucratic and military centralization and disciplining the military, and gradually society. I call this alternative "the new order of empire." The second alternative was based on a partnership between imperial and provincial elites, not only through fiscal relationships, but also through political and constitutional ties. I call this alternative "the order of notables." The third alternative was based on bottom-up mechanisms, such as collective participation in fiscal and administrative management, public opinion, and electoral processes, which I call "the order of communities." These alternatives were all enmeshed in the larger agenda of reform. The three orders—horizontal based on partnership, top-down based on military-bureaucratic hierarchy, and bottom-up based on public opinion—echoed the aristocratic, monarchic, and democratic forms in the ideal terms of classical political philosophy. In the age of revolutions, the Ottoman Empire tried and tested different combinations of these three alternatives. In 1808, when my story culminates, partnership between central and provincial elites triumphed when it came to military reform and new mechanisms of trust and security against volatility. Hence the title of my book: *Partners of the Empire.*

CHAPTER I

Empire

Order, Crisis, and Reform, 1700–1806

If I deserve in this world throne and might,
Serving people would be a pure delight.
May God uphold the religion of Islam.
Collapsing then rebuilding, one calls it *devrān*.[1]

Selim III

On April 7, 1789, following the death of his uncle Abdulhamid I
(r. 1774–89), Selim III (1761–1808) was enthroned in Istanbul as the
twenty-eighth Ottoman sultan. Selim was also a poet and composer; he
wrote the quatrain that appears above as an epigraph not long before
he became sultan.[2] The Turkish word *devrān* variously means "times"
and rotations in time, periodic movements of stars, circuits, and revolutions.[3] In Ottoman and Persian literature, astronomy, and political
writing, it signifies the cyclical nature of time.[4] Selim associated *devrān*
not only with a cyclical process but also with collapse and rebuilding.
It resonates with "revolution" as the term was used in seventeenth and
eighteenth-century Europe, meaning changes wrought by the collapse of
social orders and the building of new ones.[5] Selim aspired to fulfill his
mission—namely, to serve the people—in a time of collapse and rebuilding. "The constitution [*tab'*] of the state is disordered," he wrote in the
same poem, "give, my God, your cure for it."

Selim became sultan when the Ottoman order was in profound crisis.
During the long war against Russia, from 1767 to 1774, Ottoman
armies were humiliated, exposing the incompetence of Ottoman military administration. The war resulted in the loss of Crimea, a strategic
and prestigious province. The 1774 Treaty of Küçük Kaynarca between
the two empires left the Ottomans with an unbearable economic burden. Fiscal institutions fell short of deriving the necessary resources

from the provinces to pay compensation to Russia or the salaries of
enlarged military units. Following the war, fiscal pressures and internal
unrest shook provinces in the Balkans and Arab lands. In 1786, another war began against the Russian and Austrian empires. This war,
which was raging when Selim was enthroned, only worsened the existing problems.[6]

Despite the crisis, Selim bet on optimism in his poem. *Devrān* signified
not only collapse, but also rebuilding. Known as a young prince with a
reform agenda, he aspired to serve the people, transforming disorder into
order. His optimism carried a tone that differed from the attitude that the
decline in order was preordained, a foregone conclusion.[7] Selim's aspira-
tion to serve the people reflected a new orientation. In traditional imperial discourse, God entrusted the people to the sultan, who was ordained
to rule them. Selim reoriented this relationship. He joyfully desired to
serve the people. The choice of the word "people" (*nās*) was perhaps
a deliberate choice, giving a sense of universalism. It sounds as though
Selim aspired to serve humanity.

Many in the Ottoman Empire hailed Selim's reform agenda. Galib
(1757–99), a renowned poet and a sheikh of the Mevlevi order, burnished
Selim's image as a servant of the people, describing him after his enthronement as *müceddid*—a concept applying to those who came into the
world with a divine mission—"for the earth and religion."[8] The term had
been used of earlier Muslim rulers since the medieval period.[9] This time it
echoed the Niẓām-ı Cedīd, the "New Order," or reform movement that
Selim patronized. The Mevlevi Sufi order, to which Selim belonged, was a
network influential with the reading public in Istanbul and other cities.[10]
The Mevlevis crafted the public image of Selim as a sultan who had come
to renew the order of the Ottoman Empire. His reputation as a reformist ruler also took hold abroad. His correspondence with Louis XVI in
1786 was not a secret. As a fellow prince, living in the Topkapı Palace,
he asked the king of France for advice on military and fiscal reorganization.[11] A number of royal French military experts had already been
in the Ottoman Empire, working with Ottoman officers to reform the
military establishment. However, just a couple of months after Selim's
enthronement in Istanbul, turbulent events unfolded in Paris, preparing
the ground for Louis's demise. The meeting of the Estates-General led
to the assault on the Bastille. These events epitomized dissolution and
renewal in many regions of the world, an age of revolutions. In another
line of Selim's poem, he virtually evoked that global moment by referring
to Judgment Day:

Since the entire world is in decay,
Let the balance be reset one day.[12]

I. THE OTTOMAN WORLD

When Selim was enthroned, the Ottoman Empire was more than four hundred years old and one of the world's largest polities. Neighboring the Austrian/Habsburg, Russian/Romanov, and Iranian/Qajar empires, the Ottoman lands encompassed most of the Balkans and Greece, Crimea (until 1774), Anatolia, Kurdistan, and the Arab lands, as well as islands in the eastern Mediterranean such as Crete and Cyprus. The empire's population totaled roughly thirty million.[13] Ever since Mehmed II had conquered the capital of the Eastern Roman Empire in 1453, Constantinople (or Istanbul) had been the seat of the Ottoman dynasty and center of its empire. In the late eighteenth century, Istanbul, with its hinterland, counted 600,000 inhabitants, and was one of the world's most crowded metropolises.[14] Although urban life was lively in Istanbul and other major port and inland cities, most of the empire's population lived in rural areas. Sunni Islam was the dominant religious orientation of the ruling elite, but the Ottoman world housed communities of the three Abrahamic religions—Islam, Christianity, and Judaism—with their sectarian and denominational variations. Ottoman Turkish was the primary language of the Ottoman state apparatus, though Arabic, Greek, and Armenian were used throughout the empire as ecumenical written languages, and more than twenty other tongues were spoken and written in different communities.[15] Multiple forms of urban, rural, littoral, and pastoral life further diversified this dizzying religious, ethnic, and linguistic mix.[16]

Ottoman provinces, cities, and communities were integrated into the empire in different ways. Historically, the Ottoman center established tight institutional and political control in Anatolia (extending into Bilad al-Sham, or Greater Syria) and Rumelia (the Balkans). Wallachia and Moldavia, Bosnia, the Morea (Peloponnese), Kurdistan, the provinces of Baghdad and Basra, Egypt, Yemen, the Hejaz, and other regions contiguous to the central lands were relatively autonomous, with diverse institutional formations and ties to the administration. The central administration developed mechanisms to keep these distant provinces integrated into the empire. Sometimes, it maintained a small but effective military presence in strongholds or co-opted regional elites. Crimea, Algeria, Tunis, the republic of Dubrovnik, and Montenegro were vassal polities with their own ruling dynasties or oligarchies.[17]

Despite the diversity of the Ottoman Empire, transportation networks created considerable physical integration. The Ottoman capital and provinces were linked by a web of old land, river, and sea routes, many used by earlier empires. On intercity roads, which the Ottomans maintained and upgraded, hundreds of inns, storage houses, and barns served travelers, merchants, caravans, and imperial officers. Along the roads, there

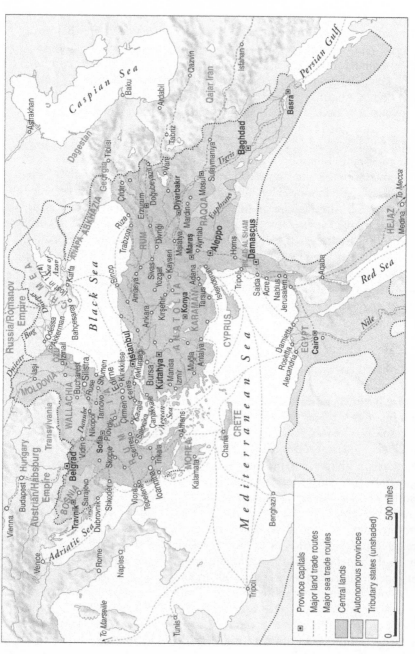

Map 1. The Ottoman Empire in the eighteenth century. The author and Philip Schwartzberg / Meridian Mapping.

were checkpoints and post-houses, where horses were readily provided for dispatch riders. Robbers and bandits were regular participants in Ottoman intercity traffic. The center assigned the tasks of securing and maintaining roadways to local communities with tax exemptions, or it outsourced the work to local notables.[18]

The Ottoman Empire was a land, river, and sea empire. Istanbul was the imperial capital, but also a port city, built on the Bosporus, the strategic sea passage connecting the Sea of Marmara to the Black Sea. Other port cities, such as Izmir, Salonika, Acre, Sidon, Alexandria, and Basra, were not only hubs and customs stations but also sites where inter-imperial merchant communities thrived. The Danube was the key water-way linking eastern Europe to the Balkans, and the Balkans to the Black Sea. Istanbul depended on this route for its grain, which was supplied from Bulgaria and Wallachia. The Nile connected sub-Saharan Africa to the Ottoman Mediterranean, while the Euphrates and Tigris tied Indian Ocean trade routes to Ottoman Mesopotamia.[19]

Natural barriers, such as rivers and mountain ranges, formed the bound-aries between the Ottoman Empire and the Austrian, Russian, and Iranian empires. Local militias and units sent from the center manned for-tresses along the borderlands. Traders and diplomatic emissaries crossed borders at these checkpoints, paid tariffs, and presented their papers to guards. But other actors—pastoral and peasant communities with cul-tural and economic ties to neighboring empires, migrant rural workers, smugglers, political refugees, and fugitives—were always present too, cir-cumventing the borders. Bordering seas proved even more difficult for the Ottoman authorities to control. Piracy was an enduring challenge, and captives and merchandise seized from the merchant ships of other states kept diplomatic missions in Istanbul busy, as they did their counterparts in other imperial capitals.[20]

According to Charles Maier, the defining features of empire are two-fold. First, conquest and the subjugation of diverse peoples and lands by a conquering elite. Second, a political regime based on an unequal relationship between the ruling elite and ruled subjects.[21] If we accept this definition, we can refer to the Ottoman polity as an empire. However, unlike colonial empires, that of the Ottomans was not structured as a hierarchical relationship between a mother country (or "metropole") and conquered and colonized distant lands and peoples. Rather, it resembled the Roman Empire, with a contiguous body and a center associated with the imperial capital, Istanbul. Ottoman elites called the lands under their authority the Ottoman, or Well-protected, Domains (*Memālik-i 'Os̠mānī* or *Memālik-i Maḥrūse*) and the polity, which elites constituted with a set of institutions and a hierarchy of officeholders, the Exalted State (*Devlet-i 'Aliyye*). The central pillar of the polity was the Ottoman dynasty (*Āl-i 'O<u>s</u>mān*), which had founded and ruled the empire from the fourteenth century on without interruption or competition. Since its establishment, except for a short interregnum in the early fifteenth century, when four Ottoman princes became vassals of the Turco-Mongol conqueror Tamerlane, an Ottoman sultan had always occupied the pinnacle of the state. Until the seventeenth century, Ottoman princes became sultans as a result of internal competition, including civil wars and fratricide. In the early seventeenth century, fratricide gave way to primogeniture among male heirs of the family. When Selim III was enthroned, there were only two other princes, his cousins Mustafa and Mahmud.[22]

The Ottoman sultan, who also held other titles, including padishah, khan, and caliph (referring respectively to the Persian, Turco-Mongol, and Islamic traditions), was considered an omnipotent sovereign who received his authority from God. The Ottoman elite sometimes depicted the sultan as the spearhead of Holy War (*ġazā*) and leader of holy warriors (*ġāzīs*), or as a messianic figure who came to power during an apocalyptic breakdown to reorder the world. Sometimes the sultan represented a caliph, God's shadow on earth, the leader of all Muslims and servants of the holy cities Mecca and Medina. Or he appeared as a leader with a spiritual mission to renew the affairs of religion and earth, as in Galib's attribution of this role to Selim III. A tacit agreement was thought to exist between God, the sultan, the sultan's servants, and the people (or subjects). God entrusted his subjects (*vedī'at'u-llah*) to the sultan, who in turn entrusted his servants—the viziers, governors, and other officeholders—with their rule. The sultan was meant to punish his servants if they acted unjustly and unlawfully. However, if the sultan acted unjustly, there was no formal institution to punish him. God would punish an unjust ruler in the afterlife.[23]

Traditional Ottoman politics did not include formal limitations of the sultan's authority. He was without a partner or institutional and formal limitations such as estates or diets. His legitimacy as a sovereign power sprang from two different roots, Sharia (Islamic law) and Ḳānūn (corpus of sultanic law and imperial customs). Sharia "was universal, immutable, divinely revealed and hence spiritually supreme" law, Cornell Fleischer writes. "Ḳānūn was regional, amendable, and created by human reason."[24] In Ottoman political language, "religion and state" (*dīn ü devlet*) were often used together as a single term to reflect this dual nature of the source of authority. Even though he was not bound by formal laws, as were most of the other absolute monarchs of the early modern world, Ottoman elites and the public expected the sultan to abide harmoniously by Islamic law and imperial customs, as well as to consult with dignitaries and the learned as the ruler and protector—or, as Selim III defined himself—the servant of the people. Despite that, the relationship between Islamic law and Ḳānūn was not static and free from tension. Islamic law was often seen as protecting life and property against the menace of sultanic seizure and executions. Moral and religious critiques of the sultan and sultanic authority by various circles sometimes resonated strongly in different segments of the society. Palace politics and factionalism among imperial elites and in the military establishment often restricted sultanic power. Most of the time, sultans' mothers, sisters, brothers, wives, concubines, cousins, and sons-in-law acted as leaders of or protagonists in competing factions. Urban rebellions led by the janissaries in alliance with various segments of the society, including religious scholars, preachers, guilds, merchants, and migrant workers, not only regularly challenged authority, but also gave rise to new legitimacy claims on the social and political order. Regional unrest and uprisings by peasants and nomads in the seventeenth and eighteenth centuries imposed further restrictions on the sultan's authority.[25]

Elites, Imperial and Provincial

If it is a necessity to grant a vizierate to somebody from the provinces, one should look at his fame.

Ali Pasha of Canik[26]

The ruling people in the metropole were not a national body but a web of imperial and provincial elites organized around the Ottoman dynasty, military, and fiscal bureaucracy and/or established in the provinces or attached to the center through different offices, deals, and statuses. Unlike in many European and Asian polities, there was no hereditary office that passed automatically from one generation to the other in Ottoman statecraft. Despite this fact, various households managed to monopolize positions in the imperial establishment across multiple generations. Family lines, a patronage system, and references were key for a young man seeking to launch a career. Slavery persisted as an important instrument by means of which the Ottoman elite acquired, trained, and employed young men in the military and bureaucracy. And elites with slave or humble backgrounds were as much inclined as others to construct bureaucratic dynasties after the consolidation of their positions as high-ranking officeholders.[27]

Military and administrative careers began in the lower ranks and culminated in viziership. Heading the empire's limited number of viziers was the grand vizier, who was chief of the military and bureaucratic establishment. Provincial governors of various ranks (including that of vizier) and leading military commanders came after the grand vizier. High-ranking governors holding the title of vizier enjoyed not only great prestige as primary representatives of the sultanic authority but also substantial revenues collected in their provinces. The decrees (*buyruldu*) they issued under their seals were the second most authoritative imperial documents after sultanic decrees (*fermān*) in provincial governance. Governors and their retinues traversed the empire, accompanied in times of both war and peace by commanders and admirals appointed for special military and administrative missions, with different ranks and titles.

Istanbul's fiscal and diplomatic bureaucracy was detached from the imperial household and expanded as an autonomous bureaucratic body throughout the seventeenth and eighteenth centuries. Ottoman bureaucracy had its own hierarchical orientations and technical expertise. The transition from a polity based on the imperial household to one based on the bureaucracy coincided with the semantic transformation of the word *devlet* from a generic term meaning "power and good fortune" in the earlier period to one signifying governmental apparatus and, eventually, from the seventeenth century on, a "state" ruling over a people in a specific territory.[28] Over the centuries, Ottoman bureaucracy developed a discourse envisioning a special role for the Ottoman state in world history as an enterprise conquering lands, bringing justice, and establishing a worldwide peaceful order. This discourse of "world empire" continued to exist, even though the empire became more and more a territorial state, with clearer notions of external borders, in the latter part of the eighteenth century.

Many families in Istanbul and the provinces specialized in Islamic law and contributed members to the learned hierarchy, or ulema, from which *kadi*s (judges), muftis (legal consultants), and professors of law and theology were appointed. The grand muftis who headed the learned hierarchy, also known as *Şeyḫ ül-İslām*, were chosen from major ulema families in Istanbul, which monopolized key judicial and professorial positions for generations. Although many families dominated the ulema career lines, young Muslim men of humble origin nevertheless found opportunities to acquire an education in imperial or provincial colleges and join the hierarchy. The majority of the imperial elite were Muslims, but it also included Christians. Greek Phanariots, members of the old Greek families of Istanbul, some with roots dating back to the Byzantine Empire, belonged to the administrative elite and enjoyed special ranks and statuses.[29]

The Ottoman provinces were contested zones between imperial elites who were directly connected to the center and provincial elites, who were entrenched in their localities. In the fifteenth and sixteenth centuries, the Ottoman center's new land regime had effectively marginalized the pre-Ottoman provincial elites' power base in the central provinces.[30] By the seventeenth century, the declining revenues of governors and petty members of the provincial armies pushed some provincial governors to rebel against the center, building power bases and constituencies among landless peasants and unemployed urban crowds. Violence, known as the Celali rebellions, flared up in the first half of the seventeenth century, shattering the provincial order in Anatolia and Syria.[31] In the eighteenth century, as a result of institutional changes discussed in chapters 2 and 3 below, the Ottoman state was readier than ever to accept provincial notables into the imperial establishment. Provincial notables became key actors in district and city and rural hinterland administration, estate management, and gradually in every field of governance. By acquiring imperial titles, a growing number of local strongmen rose from ancillary positions to the highest echelons of the imperial elite throughout the eighteenth century, expanding their regional zones of influence by adding offices and contracts to their portfolios. Some captured governorships and some even became viziers.[32]

The Ottoman system did not recognize hereditary nobility except for a couple of vassal dynasties and certain titles referring to descendants of the Prophet Muhammad, such as *sayyid* and *sharif*.[33] In conventional imperial discourse, which persisted during the reign of Selim III, military and bureaucratic officeholders were seen as servants (*kul*) of the sultans. In the patrimonial system of the fifteenth and the early sixteenth centuries, the household and the state were integrated, and servants of the sultan were also considered members of the imperial household. As a result, officeholders were stripped of private rights vis-à-vis their benefactors, the sultans. This *kul* doctrine permitted the sultan to revoke offices without compensation, to confiscate officeholders' wealth (since it derived from service through the sultan's grant), and, in extreme cases, to order executions without judicial process, often with just a generic legal opinion (*fetvā*), mainly from the grand mufti.[34] The culture of the Ottoman elite was made volatile by sultanic power over the wealth and life of officeholders. Elites could rise in status without noble descent but also ran a high risk of suddenly losing everything, including their lives.

In the seventeenth and eighteenth centuries, this patrimonial system gradually gave way to a new bureaucratic establishment in the center and the proliferation of elite households in Istanbul and in the provinces. Despite the growing number of elite households, who were able to transmit their wealth from one generation to another through political negotiations, the sultan's ability to take the property and the lives of officeholders endured until the mid nineteenth century. The volatility of the imperial sector for individuals serving the empire as office- or contract holders continued to characterize the Ottoman order. In fact, Abdülhamid I and Selim III vigorously applied confiscations to ameliorate the constant fiscal pressures on the central administration, while new ideas to abolish this imperial instrument emerged.

The property and lives of members of the learned classes, merchants, and ordinary subjects, Muslim or non-Muslim, were generally considered to be under the protection of Islamic law. Thus many families specializing in learning and trade were able to maintain their wealth for many generations more than elites operating in the military and administrative sectors. Nevertheless, sometimes the boundaries between these two kinds of elites are difficult to draw. As we shall see in chapter 2, many elite families were involved in various areas of cultural and economic life. Decisions concerning business and political partnerships between the imperial and provincial power elite, ulema, merchants, and financiers often determined their fate.

Provincial Order

Ayntab, Malatya, [and] Zu'l-Kadriye, which were subprovinces in Maraş Province, were sometimes granted as *mālikāne* [life tenancies] and sometimes seized by the state and granted to the governors.

Ottoman imperial edict, September 1720[35]

The Ottoman Empire was predominantly an agrarian society. Peasant and pastoral communities constituted the majority of the population. Peasantries were organized in a variety of ways, from small conjugal families who worked a strip of arable land with a pair of oxen to large clans that collectively cultivated contiguous fields. Demographic fluctuations, scarcity of labor, and peasant displacements as a result of bad harvests or political instability were common themes in the Ottoman rural economy. This is why, in the eighteenth century, the central administration rigorously tried to settle nomadic communities in rural areas and turn them into peasants. The Ottoman land regime, which was consolidated with legal syntheses of Ottoman jurists in the sixteenth century, defined most cultivated lands as state-owned domains (*mīrī*). The land regime rigorously restricted private ownership (*mülk*) to urban property and orchards in and around cities. Estates connected to charitable foundations called *waqf*s constituted around 15 percent of all arable land. According to the sixteenth-century legal synthesis, which largely prevailed until land reforms in the second half of the nineteenth century, peasant households on *mīrī* lands were hereditary tenants, free to organize production and transfer lands to heirs or others. In this order, the elites collecting surplus were beneficiary officeholders or contractors rather than landlords or fief holders.[36]

The beneficiary officeholders in the provinces collected taxes in cash, kind, or labor from administrative units of different sizes (*tīmār* and *ze'āmet*) assigned to them, in return for military service, which included attending military campaigns with their retinues under the command of provincial governors. *Tīmār* and *ze'āmet* holders often had administrative and revenue collection authority over a village (or set of villages) with attached arable lands and farms. Their administrative and security authority over their zones did not include any judicial power, which rested with kadis appointed by the ulema. In the sixteenth century, the holders of *tīmār*s and *ze'āmet*s supplied great numbers of provincial equestrian troops, which were mobilized in a hierarchic fashion for seasonal military campaigns. Throughout the seventeenth century, however, these troops were marginalized in battle by changes in military technology, which favored infantry equipped with firearms over mounted archers wielding swords. In the eighteenth century, *tīmār* and *ze'āmet* holders did not disappear but became absentee landholders and/or the leaders of ancillary troops who provided logistical services to the imperial armies during war. They often outsourced their revenues and jurisdiction over their zones to middlemen.[37]

Governors of different ranks with short-term tenure often moved from one province to another accompanied by their households and armed retinues. Their revenues were often collected by their deputies (*mütesellim*) from their *ḫāṣṣ*—various agricultural or urban units, spread out in provincial zones under their administration. Centrally appointed governors were one of the main pillars of Ottoman administrative integration, with centrally appointed kadis representing the judiciary. In wartime, armed groups of peasants and urban dwellers known as *sekbān*, *sarıca*, or *levend*, commanded by local military leaders, sought to be included in the retinues of governors. Although the boundaries between local *sekbān* and bandits were often not very clear, *sekbān*ship became a career for many young men looking for ways to climb the military ladder. As we shall see in chapter 2 in specific cases, during the eighteenth century, provincial strongmen collected *sekbān*s around them and competed to win imperial positions, such as deputy governorships at first and then, gradually, governorships.[38]

In addition to the benefices held by the provincial military elite, members of the dynasty and imperial elite held revenue units as sinecures simply by virtue of their status or pedigree, without supplying any service. These grandees managed units and communities attached to them through proxies and local contractors. Similarly, imperial waqfs had agricultural units spread across the empire. The waqf administration managed these units and collected revenues, often through local contractors and subcontractors. Furthermore, in various regions, some units were defined as separate urban or rural revenue divisions (*muḳāta'a*), which included mines, workshops, and customs. The state either outsourced (*iltizām*) these divisions to contractors (*mültezim*) with short-term revenue collection rights or managed them directly through salaried supervisors. Contractors collected revenues in these enterprises, remitted the amount agreed on in their contracts to the state or primary holders, and kept the rest as profit.[39]

As in other early modern polities, limited revenues reached the central government in the Ottoman Empire. A majority of the surplus collected in the name of the state was either spent locally on military or administrative needs or extracted by officeholders and contractors for their military-administrative duties and profits. The regular and irregular taxes collected from peasant communities, with different agents and contractors, constitute a long list. The tithe, criminal and murder fines, bribe money, and other regional taxes and fees were listed in the provincial land codes. Poll taxes (*cizye*) levied on non-Muslims were collected directly by the center, by salaried agents or contractors. Often, priests in the Greek Orthodox ecclesiastical hierarchy acted as *mültezim* in the process of poll tax collection.[40] In the seventeenth century, other direct taxes, called *'avārız* and *nüzūl*, similar to *taille* in France, increased the central administration's direct share of the overall surplus. Governors collected irregular aid taxes (*imdādiye*) in cash or kind from provincial communities to maintain their households and troops. In addition to regular and irregular levies, the central administration directly bought crops or cattle from peasant communities below market price. This practice, called *mubāya'a*, was regularized in the eighteenth century. For peasants, such enforced procurements proved an increasing burden, while for Ottoman governors, they were the main source for provisioning the imperial capital and troops. Peasant communities marketed the rest of their agricultural surplus in the urban centers of provincial districts to the local population and sometimes at regional fairs to broader markets. Under the constant threat of famine, the central authority tended to limit exports of agricultural products, yet there were always legal or illegal ways, such as smuggling, of exporting crops and avoiding high tariffs.[41]

In the earlier period, Ottoman land codes included detailed records of taxes and taxable households. However, throughout the seventeenth century, these numbers lost their validity with demographic changes and inflation. In the eighteenth century, taxes were increasingly collected as lump sums through negotiations with imperial and local officers, contractors, and urban and rural community leaders at district (*każā'*) courts under the supervision of judges (kadis). In addition to paying taxes, communities had the duty of performing services for the empire locally, such as maintaining roads and the postal service, or financing state agents passing through. In the absence of updated tax registers, some provincial notables incurred lump-sum expenses and taxes on behalf of the community and managing public affairs. The community met notables at judicial courts, settling accounts to apportion lump-sum burdens on taxpayers and delivering aggregate amounts, with commissions, to notables who made expenditures on the community's behalf. In this process, judicial courts were transformed into local assemblies at which public deeds and budgets were deliberated. In many localities, taxes, the shares of governors and imperial officeholders, as well as other public expenditures, were collected through this apportionment mechanism. Gradually, as we shall see in chapter 3, these practices, which developed organically, were formalized by the state and gave rise to new provincial politics, in which some local notables known as *a'yān* (hereafter ayan), competed to secure support from their communities to win managerial positions.

Another important eighteenth-century structural change was the contraction of the benefice system and the expansion of contract-based tax-farming. Beginning in the 1700s, as a response to fiscal pressures resulting from the long wars with the Habsburgs, hundreds of large and small revenue units, mainly agricultural estates under the jurisdiction of provincial governors and members of the cavalry army, were seized by the center, reassessed by fiscal experts, and rented to financiers and entrepreneurs, whether by auction or not, under life-term contracts known as *mālikāne-muḳāṭaʿa*. Under this arrangement, the state outsourced provincial revenue units—and the communities attached to them—as immune (*serbest*) enclaves (i.e., protected from the intervention of governors or other authorities, except the judiciary) to semi-private entrepreneurs, who were also given administrative jurisdiction in these zones. In some provinces in eastern Anatolia and the Arab lands, enclaves with *mālikāne* status were bundled and granted to superintendents (*voyvodas*) who were responsible for coordination and revenue remittance between the enclaves and the central administration. As the epigraph to this section shows, the statuses of some units constantly changed from *mālikāne* to benefice and back. The designers of this reform anticipated that holders of the enclaves, invested in their units, would protect communities and increase productivity, and therefore revenues. *Mālikāne* holders were generally members of the imperial elite or provincial notables who had the financial capacity to participate in auctions, who obtained references and guarantors from among the dignitaries, or who had the political power to oblige the center to grant a *mālikāne* in negotiations.[42]

As a result of this process, the central administration diverted assets from imperial and provincial elites to the central state in the first decades of the eighteenth century. Most *mālikāne* holders, instead of settling in their units, outsourced them to local contractors, which created a market for local notables, who developed proficiency in managerial expertise, revenue collection, and remittance. Privatizing governance within these *mālikāne* zones coincided with the expansion of commercial agricultural estates, known as *çiftlik*, in various regions, such as western Anatolia,

Thessaly, and Macedonia. Immigrant agricultural workers from lost territories and settled nomads often fostered this process by providing extra labor. However, the burgeoning commercialization of agriculture did not lead to large-scale agricultural tracts. In many regions, small free peasantries continued to represent the essential unit of rural social formation, while life-term contracts for revenue collection did not transform into private ownership of land units.[43]

Urban Life, the Janissaries and the Networks

The community of that town were as a whole from the janissary class [*zümre*].
BOA: HAT 1788

Throughout the eighteenth century, we see the steady increase of urban populations.[44] Traditional manufacturers and local merchants, organized into guilds, continued to be important collective actors in the urban economy and in urban politics. However, the growing number of newcomers in the cities seeking new opportunities confronted the guilds' monopolies in urban markets. New managerial local notables also challenged the guilds' leadership. Changes in urban governance and economy overlapped with state-sponsored projects that bypassed the guilds, creating new workshops and factories in different sectors, such as textiles, iron, and paper. We also see such attempts by private entrepreneurs in the provinces. These entrepreneurs sometimes sent plans for workshops or factories, with samples of the products manufactured, and requested permissions, tax exemptions, or financial support from the central government. Despite such attempts, the Ottoman Empire continued to depend heavily on imports of manufactured goods from Europe and India, especially of luxury goods, ironware, and, increasingly, textiles.[45]

The janissaries, the most visible actors in Istanbul and some provincial cities, were well integrated with the guilds and often involved in the rural economy in the hinterlands of their cities. Thanks to their ability to act together as a collective and their organic connections to different segments of Ottoman society, janissary affiliates were also political actors, influencing or shaping public opinion. While their acquaintances and political allies within the imperial elites and factions made the janissaries key actors in politics, their organic ties to urban guilds and merchants, as well as the lower class of urban laborers, porters, rowers, peddlers, beggars, bachelors, and city gangs, enabled them to set agendas, mobilize people, and stir up crowds. In many ways, the janissaries linked the highest and lowest segments of Ottoman urban life.[46]

As indicated by their Turkish name, *yeniçeri*, which means "new troops," the janissary corps was founded as a new, salaried infantry equipped with firearms in the mid fourteenth century. The janissaries were the central component of the slave military (*ḳapı ḳulu*), who were under the direct command of the Ottoman dynasty. The corps was originally constituted predominantly of conscripted young non-Muslim men, who were taken as a levy (*devşirme*) from Christian peasantries, converted to Islam, trained as soldiers, and deployed in Istanbul and the provinces. The barracks and camps where janissaries trained and organized were called *ocaḳ*, literally, "the hearth," which symbolized the ceremonial meals shared with the sultan and the janissary corps' intimate relationship with the Ottoman imperial house. The corps had a patron saint, Hacı Bektaş Veli, a religious thinker in thirteenth-century Anatolia and the legendary founder of the Sufi order known by his name, the Bektaşiye. Rituals built around the cult of Hacı Bektaş provided members of the corps with spiritual affiliations that coalesced into military prowess.[47]

By the seventeenth century, the janissary corps had lost its earlier character as a small professional infantry unit. Long, multiseasonal wars and the spread of firearms in battle gradually diminished *tīmār*-holding provincial cavalry and boosted the role of the janissaries (and mercenaries equipped with firearms) in Ottoman warfare. As a result, the janissary corps grew with the influx of new recruits. This expansion of the corps coincided with the disappearance of the *devşirme* system. Janissaryhood became a promising career path or social-military status for many young Muslim men, many from humble backgrounds, including urban migrants who had left their villages for the cities. They voluntarily applied to chiefs and other high-ranking commanders for admission to the corps. Janissary recruits received salaries (*esāme*) and/or other social benefits from the state for performing military duties. By the eighteenth century, the janissaries of Istanbul and its hinterland, who totaled over 100,000, had become a massive socio-military grouping.[48] There were also thousands of janissary affiliates in the empire's provincial cities. These provincial janissaries had their own conventions. When a new governor was appointed to Bosnia, for instance, the janissaries of Sarajevo ceremonially met with him. At this meeting, the commander of the Sarajevo corps presented a list of individuals with janissary status to the governor, who would then distribute various favors.[49]

The regulations pertaining to the janissary corps often complained of the janissaries' integration into the urban and rural economy. "A janissary should not be acquainted with another craft," a seventeenth-century janissary regulation prescribes. "This is against the law. If a janissary earned forty piasters a day from his other profession, he would not serve as a janissary."[50] However, the integration of the janissaries into the empire's economic life by reason of their privileged statuses and prestige as the sultan's intimate *ḳuls*, was a natural process. The same regulation complained that there were people who dressed and behaved like janissaries in the provinces without having that formal status.[51] Gradually, janissaryhood became not only a formal status to be acquired from the state or the corps, but also a social and cultural claim to that status by thousands of men who were not necessarily regular, wage-earning members of the corps.

From the early period, despite their formal *kul* status, janissaries were able to develop a contractual relationship with sultans. Sultans tried to secure the loyalties of janissary chiefs through financial and political deals. Leading factions in the central establishment—princes, dynastic women, viziers, high-ranking bureaucrats, and ulema—built alliances with the corps according to political calculations, which sometimes included dethroning the existing sultan and enthroning their favorite. Attempts to abolish the corps (or rumors of attempts) instigated revolts. Some of these mutinies resulted in the depositions of sultans, even their executions. In 1622, Osman II (known as Osman the Young), who was believed to be committed to abolishing the corps, was deposed and killed in a janissary-led revolt. As we shall see in chapter 4, which discusses the events in 1807 and 1808 that resulted in the fall of Selim III, some of these revolts altered the dynamics of imperial politics by giving rise to new actors who emerged victorious from rebellions, while eliminating others.[52]

The metamorphosis of the janissary corps from an infantry of slave soldiers into a massive socio-military grouping or class (*zümre*) with social status and privileges changed its relationship to the masses. In most revolts, janissaries developed popular claims, often transcending their corporate interests, and were perceived as protectors of the old order, laws, customs, and sometimes the rights of commoners. They developed the capacity to mobilize urban crowds. They built alliances with other parts of the military establishments, as well as with urban guilds, new migrants, irregular workers, and city gangs. Revolts gave birth to a script, a pattern of collective behaviors and rituals, such as the removal of the cauldron of the mess kitchens from the hearth, assembling with camps in the Hippodrome, or collectively asking for fatwas from the muftis for the elimination of targeted bureaucrats. These scripts, while transforming rebellion into political theater, also disciplined crowds and curbed violence. The corps gradually came to combine the characteristics of an army motivated by esprit de corps, a corporate bloc whose agenda was to enhance and preserve social and economic benefits secured from the state, and a political party able to translate its claims into a common language of rights of the people.[53]

The rise of the janissary corps as a sociopolitical power with agendas beyond its corporate interests is part of a larger story about the consolidation of new public realities in urban life. In the seventeenth and eighteenth centuries, Istanbul and other Ottoman cities functioned not only as administrative and commercial centers, but also as the setting for new forms of public life. While religious spaces such as mosques, Islamic colleges, Sufi lodges, churches, and synagogues continued to serve as centers for collective gatherings, new lay public spaces, such as coffeehouses, taverns, and barbershops, fostered new forms of sociability. Political colloquies (*devlet ṣohbeti*) among commoners in these public spaces often frustrated the ruling elite, especially in times of political crisis and social duress. Over 8 percent of coffeehouses in Istanbul were reportedly owned by the janissary affiliates in 1792.[54] Coffeehouses (or outdoor coffee gardens) became loci of opposition in times of crisis. The state tolerated coffee spaces not only because they offered revenue, since coffee consumption could easily be taxed, but also because the state could monitor and register activity contained in these spaces.[55]

While elite gatherings known as *meclis*—where men and women (often separately) read poetry, performed music, debated, and dined—continued to proliferate in private mansions, street life produced different kinds of social entertainment. In addition to the religious festivals and spectacles sponsored by the dynasty and imperial elite, urban inhabitants gathered at shadow theaters and other public venues to watch theatrical shows by individual performers called *meddāḥ*, where political and cultural satire was part of the repertoire. Sultanic enthronements, parties celebrating princely circumcisions, sermons by charismatic preachers, the funerals of important men and women, public executions, and festivities in the month of Ramadan during both the day and the night were arenas of sociability, politics, and performance in Istanbul and provincial cities. Given the limited number of presses able to print in the different Ottoman languages and alphabets, the circulation of affordable printed books was not yet a key factor in shaping public opinion. Until the late nineteenth century, handwritten books and pamphlets dominated written life. However, the circulation of information through oral media, by storytellers, singers, reciters, and preachers, functioned in social spaces, provided information, and nurtured public opinion.[56]

New forms of sociability did not necessarily foster security. Stability declined in provincial towns, especially in the Balkans, in the second half of the eighteenth century. Growing numbers of irregular troops who had armed themselves in wartime subsequently became *sekbān*s or *klephts* (Greek irregular armed bands). Failing to find patrons, they often dispersed as vagabond bandits. In the late eighteenth century, Muslim and Christian irregulars, known as *kırcalı*s or *dağlı*s (mountaineers), created serious problems of security and disorder, sometimes spreading terror, while at the same time constituting a pool of armed men available for hire by provincial communities for protection or by provincial notables as private militias. As we shall see in chapter 3, some leaders of these groups established their own patronage over small communities by making different claims, including their janissary affiliation. At the same time, urban dwellers were collectively granted janissary status in many places, including Vidin in northwestern Bulgaria, Bolu, and Erzurum, in return for rendering communal services such as providing security in frontier areas or mountain passes. The spread of firearms among urban and rural communities in the late eighteenth century alarmed the central authorities. One report from a governor to Sultan Abdülhamid I explained:

Although it is the communities' obligation to obey the viziers, they did not. If a vizier goes to a locality, dwellers meet him with rifles. As in the time of the grand vizier Köprülü Mehmed Pasha [1578–1661], the state should collect firearms and convey them to the imperial arsenal. Only after that, will it become clear who is a subject and who belongs to the military class.[57]

The spread of firearms and security problems, together with new collective fiscal mechanisms in various cities, led some provincial notables and their partners to establish control over communities. Notables assumed these roles with the formal or informal nomination of the communities, or they imposed themselves with the help of their armed retinues and perhaps the backing of other strongmen in the region or in Istanbul. The commercialization of the office of the judiciary (kadis) enabled local learned men to capture proxy-judge positions and participate in these local coalitions. In the second half of the eighteenth century, reports sent to Istanbul about the state of provincial cities complained that notables established little "republics" (*cumhūr*) and had become autonomous entities.[58]

In the eighteenth century, despite the growing security issues, Ottoman cities were by no means isolated from intellectual and cultural trends in Europe. The *échelles du Levant*, French subjects who constituted a distinctive commercial community as the result of multiple trade agreements that dated back to the sixteenth century, exemplify the Euro-Ottoman connection. Gradually, the Euro-Ottomans began intermingling with Christian and some Muslim segments of the Ottoman elite in the transcultural milieu of Istanbul and other port cities.[59] This coincided with an increase in the number of European military experts employed by the Ottoman administration. Many wrote memoirs, some of which became bestsellers in Europe.[60]

The vibrant exchange of information between Europe and the Ottoman Empire gave rise to what Ian Coller calls the "East of Enlightenment," namely, a lively intellectual interaction within European commercial and diplomatic circles and other groups clustered around them in the Ottoman world.[61] This not only shaped ideas about the Ottoman World in Europe but also became instrumental in disseminating European ways in the Ottoman Empire. We should understand the East of

Enlightenment in relation to other enlightenments in the Ottoman world. In the eighteenth century, Ottoman Greek and Armenian networks, which tied together the European and Ottoman markets through diasporal connections, developed their own transimperial republic of letters. A vivid learning culture, known as the Greek Enlightenment, flourished under the patronage of the notable Greek Phanariot families, as well as of various European academies. The Greek Enlightenment linked intellectual activities in Vienna, Paris, Saint Petersburg, Padua, and the Ionian islands with the Ottoman-Hellenic centers in Istanbul, Izmir, Athens, Iaşi, Bucharest, and Jerusalem. Various Greek intellectuals, scholars, and engineers, who constantly traveled across the Ottoman, Russian, Austrian, and Venetian empires, conveyed European discussions on various fields to the Ottoman lands. The translation campaign from European languages into Western Armenian by the Mekhitarists, the Catholic Armenian network, spread across the Armenian intellectual community in the Ottoman World.[62]

But it was not only Hellenic and Armenian transimperial networks that experienced the vibrant intellectual and political climate of the Age of Enlightenment. Recent discussions of eighteenth-century logic, cosmology, cartography, geography, mathematics, and engineering among Muslim intellectual circles, as well as the proliferation of libraries and publication activities, have pushed some historians to reconsider the rigid boundary or binary between the Western Enlightenment and Islamic traditions. Along these lines, intellectual historians have recently come to reexamine figures like İbrahim Müteferrika (1674–1745), the founder of the imperial printing house and a polymath who published extensively, from geography to political philosophy; Esad Efendi of Ioannina (d. 1731), a neo-Aristotelian Muslim philosopher who connected the Hellenic Enlightenment circles with Muslim intellectuals; and İbrahim Hakkı of Erzurum (1703–80), the writer of a massive cosmology, *Ma'rifetnāme* (The Book of Gnosis), in which he combined post-Copernican astronomy with mysticism and mustered subtle moral criticisms of new economic attitudes.[63] If we understand the Enlightenment, not as an exclusively secular tradition of radical transformation, but rather, according to David Sorkin's broader interpretation, as linking religious and secular scientific conceptions,[64] it would not be misleading to define the cultural, intellectual, and scientific vitality of the Ottoman eighteenth century, with all its variants, as the Ottoman Enlightenment.

From Economic Stability to Contraction

From the 1740s on, following the conclusion of new commercial treaties, France became the Ottoman Empire's most important trading partner, outstripping the Austrian Habsburg Empire, England, the Dutch

Republic, Russia, Venice, and Iran in that respect. Mughal India was still a major trading partner, too, providing Ottoman consumers with textiles, spices, and other luxury goods, sometimes through the British East India Company or Armenian trade networks based in Iran. Jewish trade networks centered in Livorno were active in cities with a substantial Jewish population, like Salonika, Aleppo, and Izmir. Merchants of Dubrovnik, an autonomous republic under Ottoman suzerainty, were still actively trading in the Adriatic with special privileges from the Ottoman administration to export livestock and crops from Bosnia. European merchants built diaspora communities, like the French-speaking _échelles_, in Ottoman port cities. These communities, with their local Greek, Armenian, and Jewish brokers, were deeply integrated into different sectors. Notable Muslim families in the provinces provided foreign merchants with protections and connected them to local producers and markets. In the eighteenth century, as some intellectuals and bureaucrats advocated protectionist measures for local manufacturing, measures against exportation were relieved. Cotton produced in Macedonia and western Anatolia gradually found its way into European markets. Duties collected on cotton for export increased 300 percent between 1720 and 1800. Cotton was followed by wool, mohair, wax, oil, rice, wheat, dried fruit, and soap. In the eighteenth century, the Ottoman Empire was still the world's main supplier of coffee.[65]

Economic historians have suggested that the Ottoman economy steadily grew or at least experienced a relative stability during the first three quarters of the eighteenth century. The end of long and expensive wars fought in the late seventeenth century; territorial gains (Crete in the 1670s; the Peloponnese, regained from Venice in the 1730s; and Caucasia, captured after the fall of the Safavid Empire in the 1720s); a population increase; better climate conditions following the Little Ice Age; improvements in transportation; and technological innovations in mining and manufacturing may have contributed in varying degrees to economic improvement. Institutional changes in land tenure with more secure lifelong contracts, which encouraged investments in the agricultural sector, combined with growing domestic and interimperial trade. New consumption patterns, epitomized by the so-called Age of Tulips (1703–30) emerged, when conspicuous consumption and relative prosperity in Istanbul and other major centers became visible. New cities in the first half of the eighteenth century, such as Nevşehir (New City) founded by the grand-vizier İbrahim Pasha; Yozgat founded by the central Anatolian notable family, the Çapanoğlus; and Sulaimaniye founded by a Kurdish notable clan, the Babans, illustrated not only capital accumulation by imperial and provincial elites, but also growing regional trade that required new markets.[66]

By 1760, economic and political stability had come to an end. Between the 1760s and the 1810s, the Ottoman Empire faced several crises. Military defeats by Russia and Austria in 1768–74 and 1786–92 coincided with internal mutinies and insurrections in Greece, the Balkans, Egypt, and Arabia. For now, it is sufficient to point out that Russia's annexation of Crimea (1774–82) signaled that the partition of the Ottoman Empire, like Poland's, was imminent. Military defeat was accompanied by sharp economic and fiscal decline. When Selim came to the throne in 1789, military setbacks were accompanied by economic contraction. Rising inflation and poor harvests compounded efforts by a desperate central government to find cash to finance expensive wars and compensation payments to Russia. Mutinies flared in various regions in the Balkans, Syria, Egypt, and Arabia and developed into profound security problems for provincial communities. Pressing security matters increased the cost of provincial governance for the center and the leverage of provincial notables, who gradually amassed sizable military power. We shall see the implications of these crises in different Ottoman regions in chapters 2 and 3.[67]

The fiscal crisis during the Russo-Ottoman war of 1768–74 pushed the central government to initiate new fiscal measures.[68] The government levied war taxes on *mālikāne* holders and issued imperial edicts to curb extravagant consumption by dignitaries of the central authority.[69] Furthermore, it took actions to decrease the number of janissaries collecting salaries from the Ottoman Treasury.[70] Inspectors were sent to determine overexploited tax sources.[71] The central government asked for loans even from the sultan's personal treasury.[72] The Küçük Kaynarca peace treaty that concluded the war of 1768–74 imposed extra burdens on the Ottoman Treasury. Under the treaty, the Ottoman Empire was expected to pay an indemnity of 7.5 million *ġuruş* (4 million rubles), half of the empire's budget, to Russia in three installments. Meanwhile, Wallachia and Moldavia's annual taxes were to be reduced.[73] But there were other reasons for fiscal pressures, such as military reforms. Intensifying fortification along the borders, new benefits for provincial governors who lost stipends, and payments to foreign military experts continued to increase. Plans to renovate the Ottoman navy and to institute a modern artillery corps proved particularly costly.[74]

In 1784, the imperial Divan agreed on applying to the sultan of Morocco for a loan. During Selim's reign, the state attempted to obtain loans from the Netherlands and Spain. These initiatives failed, however.[75] The center's attempts to reorganize the provincial order were sometimes productive, sometimes counterproductive. In many regions, the state equipped local communities and notables to manage taxation, public finance, security, and infrastructure maintenance using local mechanisms and without direct interference from the center. This policy of decentralizing fiscal administration reduced the state's burden. However, efforts to eliminate some provincial notables and divert their wealth to the center through confiscations led to greater instability and volatility in the provincial order, but also empowered some provincial notables who consolidated their power and wealth at the expense of others. Attempts to eliminate *mālikāne* contracts failed, since the fiscal administration could not come up with a feasible solution for managing hundreds of agricultural units without contractors. In 1775, a creative way out of growing budget deficits was proposed, called the *eshām* (shares). Estimated annual profits from various tax sources were divided into shares as state bonds and sold off to investors for life terms. In this system, the state borrowed from small investors. Unlike in the *mālikāne* system, non-Muslims and women were allowed to purchase shares. The *eshām* system enlarged the pool of financiers on whom the central government could rely, but it hardly ended the fiscal crisis. Instead, some believed that it only increased the risk of dragging the empire into a perpetual debt circle.[76]

When Selim ascended the Ottoman throne in April 1789, like other monarchs of the late eighteenth century, he faced the challenge of intensifying military and fiscal reforms to ensure a competitive army and navy, equipped with new military technology. This military restructuring required functional revenue collection in the provinces and a borrowing system. However, Selim and his associates were unsure as to how to reorganize. While the European models with which the Ottomans were familiar offered alternatives, the new cadre in Istanbul were uncertain that they could change the established order. The Ottoman Empire was a vast, complex structure, with claimants on its resources as various as the military, officeholders, contractors, financiers, borrowers, and recipients of privilege. Any reform would produce winners and losers, challenging vested rights, statuses, expectations, and hopes. Therefore, any reform would require coalitions able to manage the opposition. Any coalition called for a process of give and take, concessions, and negotiations. In 1789, the main questions were: what exactly the reform agenda would contain (how radical it would be); what players were to be included or excluded (and eliminated) in the new order; and what the methods or ways of inclusion and exclusion were to be.

II. THE NEW ORDER

Following Selim III's enthronement, his supporters and the leaders of other reform-minded factions captured key bureaucratic and military positions. Nonetheless, Selim's was not a monolithic bloc. There was scant

agreement on the reform program among the members of the new ruling elite, who came from different backgrounds and represented different factions. In May 1789, soon after the enthronement, Selim invited
bureaucrats and commanders, the learned, and some foreign military experts to a consultative assembly to deliberate about the reform program.
Throughout the eighteenth and early nineteenth centuries, in addition
to regular meetings of cabinet members (*dīvān*), consultative assemblies
(*meclis-i meşveret*) convened by sultans or grand viziers, with a large
turnout of members of the imperial elite, became a recurrent practice.
These assemblies were, beyond their consultative functions, grounds for
legitimizing decisions through consensus and collective responsibilities.[77]

While Selim was convening the consultative assembly, another meeting, attended by commanders and janissary leaders who had been fighting
the Russians, took place in Shumen in central Bulgaria. Saying that they
refused to continue fighting because of supply problems, the janissaries
effectively went on strike. Attendees at the Shumen meeting advised Selim
that a janissary army could in any case not stand up to the disciplined,
well-drilled Russian forces.[78] The Shuman assembly and the disobedient
attitudes of the janissaries alarmed some in Istanbul about the urgency of
military reform. Selim asked participants in the consultative assembly in
Istanbul to freely express their thoughts about the predicament facing the
empire and possible remedies.[79]

We do not have minutes of the consultative assembly. However, we
know that after the deliberations, the sultan verbally asked for written
statements. "I wrote this report after the verbal decree of the sultan asking everyone [who attended the meeting] to write down their thoughts
about religion and the state so that reasonable thoughts would be taken
into consideration and the rest would be left aside," noted Mehmed
Şerif, one of the leading fiscal bureaucrats. "Now I am writing down
my thoughts in brief. Later, I shall write them down in detail."[80] Like
Mehmed Şerif, many grandees submitted their statements over the course
of the year. Some of these statements were collected and compiled by
Selim's associates, providing a repertoire of ideas about the nature of the
Ottoman order, its crises, and possible remedies.[81] Meanwhile, Ottoman
ambassadors to Vienna, Saint Petersburg, and Berlin wrote long memoranda about the military and administrative systems in the countries they
visited and possible lessons for the Ottoman Empire. They submitted
them to Selim and members of the imperial elite with other reform pamphlets. In the early 1790s, Istanbul became a fertile site for the proliferation of reform ideas.[82]

Reform statements in the late sixteenth and seventeenth centuries
hailed the empire's formative period, around 1450 to 1550, as a model.
The old order and conventions were used as reference points. These early

statements were framed as historical discourse, stressing the ongoing decline of a once-perfect order, a fictive golden age. According to this discourse, the deterioration of old glory was prevented only through restoration, rather than renovation. Were these references to an idealized old order subtle rhetorical strategies presenting new political agendas and inevitable changes as customary norms? Or were these historical references simply manifestations of innate traditionalism among imperial elites? The answer is debatable.[83]

In the eighteenth century, the relationship between old and new underwent reorientation. Beginning in the early 1700s, terms such as "new" (*cedīd, nev*), "renewing" (*tecdīd*), "innovation" (*īcād*), "fresh" (*tāze*), and "invention" (*iḥtirāʿ*) become more noticeable, not only in political writing, but also in literature and architectural and urban discourse. The circulation of new ideas, technologies, styles, and commodities as a result of intensifying commercial, diplomatic, and intellectual encounters with the outside world generated aspirations to adopt unfamiliar practices. The growing sense among some elites that the times necessitated new arrangements gave legitimacy to the new order(s). Gradually, the Ottoman elite grew readier, as Shirine Hamadeh puts it, "to free itself from the weight of the canon and revealed a changing disposition toward both tradition and innovation."[84]

Defining Crisis, Proposing Reform

"Old conventions should be fixed up, if possible. If not, they should be changed to accord with the rules of time," the author of one reformist proposal presented to Selim asserted.[85] Another pamphleteer and one of the previous ministers of the fiscal bureau, Hacı İbrahim Efendi, wrote: "corruption and deterioration found their way into the order of the state like a incurable disease, which spread through entire branches and the arteries of the sultanate. Therefore the order of the state and people need surgery, as in medicine."[86] Enverî Efendi was less radical. He argued that reform should be a gradual (*tedrīcī*) process, to minimize the damage to vested rights accumulated in the old order over decades. "Some of these maladies were 150 years, some 100, some 50 years old. They came into being gradually, so they should be corrected gradually."[87] Enverî was responsive to groups whose interests might be threatened by reform.

The most heated debate among authors of the statements emerged over what we might call the military crisis. There was general agreement among authors that the Ottoman military machine, which had suffered humiliation against Russia and Austria since 1767, should be reordered. The common critique was that the janissaries had overexpanded as a result of growing numbers of commoners acquiring janissary status. For the central government, this created an unbearable fiscal burden. But an equally important problem was the social profile of the janissaries. According to one of the authors of the reform statement, as a result of a long peaceful period before 1767, some janissaries had developed interests in trade and agriculture. Janissaries who were involved in such activity were not only untrained but also unwilling to go to war and fight on the battlefield; instead, they looked after their businesses.[88] The remedies proposed in the reform statements were diverse. Some suggested ridding the corps of those who lacked military skills through comprehensive inspections; others recommended the imposition of new training techniques; still others advised signing collective contracts with janissary leaders to stop accepting commoners into the corps. No one openly proposed the immediate abolition of the corps. Although the janissary corps was the target, pamphleteers were careful not to disparage them. Some mentioned the vested rights of members of the corps, others the janissaries' glorious past.

The most radical proposal concerning the military crisis was to create a new army parallel to the janissaries. The irony was that in Turkish the term "janissary" (*yeniçeri*) also means "new army," or rather "new soldiery," referring to the innovative nature of that corps as a standing regular army that was an alternative to the *ġāzī* warriors and cavalry hierarchy in the fifteenth century. The new "new army" would be called the *Niẓām-ı Cedīd*, literally the "New Order," this time rendered in Arabic. *Niẓām-ı Cedīd* combined newness with orderliness. The New Order would later become a generic term for the reform movement in general. The new army would be organized according to the new military science (*fenn-i* or *'ilm-i 'askerī*) of Europe. Soldiers were to be recruited from Muslim peasants, particularly those uncorrupted by urban economic life (*gözü açılmamış köylüden*).[89] They would drill regularly, which would keep them disciplined and fully loyal to the sultanate. As one of the pamphleteers wrote, "the essence of drilling and disciplining is the base of loyalty."[90] Soldiers and commanders were to be hierarchically ranked and organized into regiments. They were not to be part of civil and economic life as the janissaries were. A disciplined army that had undergone "scientific" military training was further strengthened by the expansion of an already modernized artillery and other fields of military engineering, as well as cartography, mathematics, and world history.

Mouradgea D'Ohsson, an Ottoman Catholic Armenian dragoman (interpreter) at the Swedish embassy in Istanbul and author of a massive French-language survey of the Ottoman Empire, proposed that the empire should invite military officers from Europe to develop new military schools, with courses ranging from engineering to astronomy and from geography to naval sciences. Ottoman Muslim and Christian students should be trained together. As the universal language of military science,

French should be the medium of instruction, and students should wear uniforms as a mark of discipline.[91] For some, however, military discipline was to be enforced with religious discipline. Mehmed Hakkı, a military bureaucrat who served in both the army and the fiscal bureaucracy, recommended that, as part of their military training, soldiers should study the writings of the sixteenth-century orthodox Sunni scholar Birgivi to systematically learn about their religion.[92] According to Ebûbekir Râtıb Efendi, the former Ottoman ambassador to Vienna, warfare was becoming a science; it required drilling and discipline (*ta'līm ve terbīye*) in addition to (and eventually in place of) valor and courage (*şecā'at ve cesāret*).[93]

Even if drilling and discipline could replace valor and courage, however, what of money? What was the relationship between war and finance? Ali of Canik, a military commander and the founder of a provincial notable family, the Canikli dynasty in Black Sea Anatolia, wrote: "[W]hen the war against the Muscovites started in 1767, Sultan Mustafa Khan [r. 1757–74] thought that he could carry on the war with money alone. What was the result of disbursing all the coins in the Treasury and ignoring glory and valor? Our state could not be administered with fortune [*māl*] alone."[94] Despite arguments among Ottoman military elites that one should not make simple associations between war and money, the Ottoman fiscal elite was convinced that fiscal and military reforms were two sides of the same coin for eighteenth-century polities: what today we call the military-fiscal state. Increasing state revenues through tax reform, budgetary discipline, and austerity measures were immediate suggestions by pamphleteers to bring the fiscal crisis to an end. Warning the administration against draconian budgetary measures, however, Mehmed Şerif maintained that revenues collected from producers should not be kept in the Treasury. Rather, administrators should allow the circulation of the money in the market. Only in this way would production grow and wealth increase. This policy, he continued, would also ameliorate relations between the state and the people.[95]

This pro-market proposal for the domestic economy did not resonate with international commercial practices. The Ottoman economy's constant trade deficit vis-à-vis Europe and India generated an outflow of silver and gold from the empire. In fact, protectionist trade policies to initiate development of domestic industry had been proposed by several Ottoman intellectuals since the mid eighteenth century, including Ahmed Resmî Efendi (1700–83), a Cretan Ottoman diplomat who wrote extensively on new patterns of diplomacy, and Süleyman Penah Efendi (d. 1785).[96] Among the pamphleteers of the New Order, Sun'i, the secretary of the grand vizier, urged the fiscal administration to limit the consumption of imported luxury goods to reduce the chronic deficit in the empire's balance of trade.[97] Mehmed Emin Behiç, a leading reformist in the New Order party, completed his longer pamphlet about the reform program later, openly advocating protectionist policies. Behiç went beyond trade policy to limit luxury goods, but proposed that the administration sponsor imperial elites to help them invest in certain industries, such as iron, cotton, and paper, and export manufactured goods abroad. Behiç's proposal of protectionism for industrial development explicitly reoriented traditional Ottoman trade policies that encouraged imports and discouraged exports.[98]

The reformists did not solve the puzzle of whether the fiscal crisis would be alleviated by the free market, austerity measures, or protectionist policies. Perhaps a more immediate problem concerning the fiscal crisis was revenue collection from agricultural units. The *mālikāne* system was introduced in the early eighteenth century in a reform program, as Mehmed Şerif wrote, "with the expectation that the *mālikāne* holders would maintain their units as their private orchards and gardens and provide the poor peasants with seeds, so that the Islamic lands might become more prosperous by the day."[99] But Mehmed Şerif argued that *mālikāne* holders preferred outsourcing their units to local subcontractors, who had short-term interests. Subcontractors neither invested in the units nor protected the producers. When *mālikānes* were expected to increase protection and productivity, the system devastated agricultural farms and overexploited farming communities. Furthermore, the center could not trace vacant units after their holders died. The central administration was not able to monitor provincial conditions and left their administrative control to provincial notables. Many remedies were proposed: gradual elimination of *mālikāne* contracts; closer and more efficient management; limiting the profit margins of contractors and subcontractors; and reorganizing *mālikāne* zones to end complications owing to overlapping authorities and blurred boundaries.[100] The dilemma, however, went unresolved. Some proposed that *mālikāne* contracts should be granted to local notables who had economic and social capital in the provinces,[101] while others remained skeptical about the delegation of authority through contacts.[102]

The place of provincial notables in the imperial order was in fact one of the key questions facing the Ottoman imperial elite. Would the provincial elite be included in the Ottoman imperial establishment by granting offices and allowing them to ascend imperial hierarchies? Or would they be excluded from the system as much as possible to prevent them from accumulating wealth and power? Perhaps they would remain as contractors and community leaders, without acquiring imperial offices and becoming part of the central establishment? Advocates of these three options appear in the reform pamphlets. Süleyman Penah Efendi, an influential bureaucrat and an early pamphleteer who examined tensions between Greek communities and Muslim Albanian notables in the Morea in the 1770s and 1780s, was unambiguously against the incorporation of local notables into the state apparatus at every level. His clear position was that the state should be run by its servants, governors, and centrally appointed intendants, who were unconditionally loyal to the sultanate. Muslim and Christian provincial elites should be restricted to limited areas in provincial governance as much as possible, since they were neither loyal to the state nor impartial and just to the communities.[103] Koca Yusuf Pasha, the grand vizier at the time when Selim convened the consultative assembly, was also skeptical of provincial elites. He thought, however, that the notables were the only group capable of handling provincial affairs and should therefore be allowed in the provincial order, but under the close watch of the center to prevent them from committing injustices when dealing with fiscal matters on behalf of communities. Mehmed Şerif and others proposed that the Ottoman provinces could not be governed without provincial notables and important families, such as the Karaosmanoğlus of Manisa and the Çapanoğlus of Yozgat, who had the ability to divert resources from the provinces. Both the empire and communities needed these wealthy and powerful men, who knew local conditions, to handle public expenditures and manage matters on the ground.[104]

Mehmed Hakkı, one of the high-ranking scribes, suggested that he preferred centrally appointed administrators, rather than local notables, to manage the affairs of the districts. But he knew that replacing the local managers (ayans) with centrally appointed administrators would create confrontations between the center and the provincial communities. On the other hand, Firdevsi Emin, a deputy at the Bureau of Foreign Affairs, proposed that through systematic examination the state should select provincial notables with janissary backgrounds, or from well-established old families, who had good reputations among the communities as reasonable, considerate men, and delegate the affairs of the districts to them. If Firdevsi Emin was for the consolidation of a system of hereditary leadership by certain notable families in the provincial order, Hacı İbrahim Efendi, one of the ministers of the fiscal bureau, went even further. He proposed that not only district affairs but separate revenue units (*mukāṭaʿa*) should be entrusted to communally accepted local notables.[105]

Clearly, reform was also about where the Ottoman state ended and where society began. Should the state include provincial notables or should it be constituted entirely of imperial elites, bureaucrats, and high-ranking members of the learned hierarchy centered in Istanbul who shared certain cultural ties and styles? What about wealth accumulated in the hands of the officeholders, grandees, and provincial notables? Since the institutionalization of the *mālikāne* system in the early eighteenth century, there had been a spreading conviction that security of property, office, and life was essential for the political and social order. Security gave officeholders and entrepreneurs the incentive to invest in their estates, to make them prosperous, and to protect the local communities. At the same time, security was good for the overall economy, since it would promote the accumulation of wealth. Süleyman Penah Efendi, who was against the provincial elites, was openly critical of executions and confiscations. "Order," he wrote, "is by no means possible with executions, exiles, and confiscations, but only through [the] art [of governance]."[106] Mehmed Şerif suggested that officeholders, particularly governors, should be able to feel secure. They should not be dismissed without good reason, and their wealth should not be confiscated. If they accumulated more wealth, this would be beneficial to the empire, since they could supply more effective military force if they were rich.[107]

However, in the early 1790s, amid the uncertainties of wartime and the administrative-fiscal crisis, the reform pamphlets did not propose total abrogation of confiscations and executions. In the late eighteenth century, confiscations were still seen as a sometimes necessary—if undesirable— mechanism to extract revenue accumulated in the provinces by officeholders and contractors. This was likewise the case with executions. The right to put an end to the life of an officeholder not only symbolized the supreme authority of the sultan over his servants, but also was seen as a threat in the hands of the center against the officeholders and provincial notables, over whom the central authority had no real control.

Perhaps more important, since the beginning of the eighteenth century, while the boundaries between servant of the state and notables of the provinces blurred in the business of governance, so did wealth acquired from a public office or private endeavor. Provincial powerholders, who acted as contractors or as district ayans, accumulated wealth through their various activities, from tax collection to managing public finance, not as centrally appointed administrators but most often as profit-driven entrepreneurs involved in the business of governance. Despite that, as we shall see in chapter 2, the center continued to confiscate the wealth of such contractors, like that of officeholders, without clearly differentiating between public revenue and private wealth. The state sometimes carried out confiscation directly by an officer sent from the state, sometimes by delegating (selling) confiscation rights to third parties acting as confiscation entrepreneurs. Any attempt to dissolve this old convention had to come from the provincial notables. There was such an attempt in 1808, as we shall see in chapters 4 and 5.

Although the boundaries of state and society, public and private, were unclear, when the provincial notables were concerned, the reformists nonetheless developed an agenda for the state to order certain aspects of society in general. Among some reformists, there was some degree of consensus that the state should closely monitor urban spaces frequented by migrants and bachelors and other sites where unruly groups convened, such as hostels, coffeehouses, barbershops, wharfs, and city streets. These measures were not old. However, as Betül Başaran illustrates, a new discourse became evident in this period, emphasizing disciplining (*terbiye*) society in line with the interests of the state. *Terbiye*, or disciplining society, was seen as an alternative to the discourse of *maṣlaḥa*, or minimizing tensions and maintaining social peace through negotiation, accommodating demands, and collective engagement.[108] Atıf Efendi, one of the chiefs (*re'īs efendi*) of foreign affairs, not only reported on radical incidents in France and the diplomatic implications of these events, but also evoked the need to discipline the streets of capital cities. He depicted the *yaḳoben* (Jacobins) as the source of disorder and eventually, revolution, drawing implicit parallels with Istanbul's riffraff.[109]

Behiç devoted a chapter to the issue of how to discipline Istanbul's vagabonds. The population of Istanbul, according to him, should be regularly counted; riffraff and regular city dwellers should be meticulously separated; travelers were to be granted passports, which were to be registered; a city magistrate was to be appointed to police the population; city gates were to be carefully watched; and immigrants from other cities were to be registered and, if possible, sent home. Property owners and all properties were to be recorded with the help of imams; residents could only move to another neighborhood after receiving the city chief's permission; the names of deceased persons were to be immediately submitted to the city chief to be recorded; bachelors staying in bachelor hostels, and the rooms in the hostels, were to be recorded; and spies should be dispatched to various neighborhoods to collect information about shops, workshops, and the area. Furthermore, neighborhood residents and members of guilds were to be bonded to surety contracts liable for one another's actions, while visitors entering the city were to declare personal information, including where they were from, their lodging arrangements, and how long they planned to stay in the city. These measures, intended to control, monitor, and discipline urban space, implied that reform would not be limited to military and fiscal measures. For some, society was an inseparable part of the reform agenda.[110]

In sum, although there was agreement among most of the imperial elite on the need for institutional reorganization to end the military and fiscal crisis, there was hardly any consensus on how to carry out this reorganization. Would it be radical or gradual? Would this process be top-down or negotiated? Would it be market-friendly or impose harsh budgetary measures? Would it be inclusive (including the janissaries and provincial elites) or not? In spite of these uncertainties, a distinctive language of reform began to surface in the 1790s. The terms for "newness," *cedīd* (new) and *tecdīd* (renewing), mingled with signifiers of order (*nizâm*), ordering/regulating (*tanzīm*), regimented (*tertīb/tertībli*), aligning (*rābıṭa*), disciplining (*terbiye*), repetitive drilling (*ta'līm*), and being well educated (*mu'allem*). The new orderly military discourse challenged the cultural and economic codes of the janissaries, whose martial culture prized individual courage and valor. But a challenge greater than the janissaries emerged. Most members of the corps were fully integrated into the urban economy and civil life. Accordingly, reform discourse extended beyond the confines of military and fiscal matters. It sought to regulate and discipline urban life through various forms of enlisting, registering, demarcating, and employing collective surety mechanisms to marginalize unruly riffraff, the unemployed, and immigrants in the urban space.

The New Army, 1792–1807

Starting in 1792, the reform party, which was clustered around Selim's patronage, began taking action. The reform program began with the old military order. Under the new regulations, *tīmār* holders were summoned to their provincial centers for thorough inspection. The statuses of absentee *tīmār* holders were cancelled, and others belonging to acting holders were reorganized under the coordination of district commanders (*alaybeys*), who, according to the new regulations, were to be elected by *tīmār* holders in each province. Governors were given new leverage to expand their armies, with contributions from local communities under their jurisdiction. Selim praised the janissary elders in imperial decrees, saluting their glorious history as intimate servants of the Ottoman dynasty. The janissaries were guaranteed regular salaries. In return, the administration asked them to learn new military tactics and the use of state-of-the-art rifles. Regulations promulgated by the imperial Divan pertaining to artillery, grenadiers, sappers, and the navy enhanced the reform agenda for these favored corps.[111]

These measures to rehabilitate the old military establishment did not block a more radical step, namely, constituting a disciplined new army under the name of the New Order, which was organized according to French, Austrian, and Prussian models and financed by a New Treasury. Shortly before the conclusion of the peace treaties with the Habsburgs and Russia in 1792, a small regiment under the command of the grand vizier began training under the supervision of French infantry officers. This small regiment was quickly transformed into a small army. In 1797, it counted 2,536 men and 27 officers. By 1801, the figures had grown to 9,263 men and 27 officers, and by 1806, there were 22,685 men and

Der Sultan ertheilt begleitet von den Grossen des Reichs, bei der Heerschau des neuorganisirten Fussvolks der Massoums und Cambaraiss, den Paschen Befehl.

Figure 1. Sultan Selim III and attendants, mounted at left, inspect New Army infantry. Hand-colored engraving, 1806, artist unknown. Reproduced by permission of Anne S. K. Brown Military Collection, Brown University Library.

1,590 officers.[112] The administration charged some governors with special missions to draft soldiers from the Anatolian peasantry. Some provincial notable families who saw the enthronement of Selim as an opportunity to consolidate their power by joining the New Order campaigns, for example, the Çapanoğlus and the Karaosmanoğlus, played a critical role in the draft in their regional zones. Chapter 2 offers a close examination of these zones. Provincial communities who contributed soldiers to the New Order were granted certain tax exemptions.[113] Some communities declared that they volunteered to send soldiers to the New Army and be attached to the New Treasury.[114] In 1800, after a small Ottoman regiment successfully confronted the French in Egypt and Syria, the reaction to conscription and official attempts to create a disciplined, well-drilled army became excited. This small accomplishment allowed the administration to present the New Army to the Ottoman public as the solution to long-standing military problems.

The reformists portrayed the New Army not only as an alternative to the old military establishment, consisting of provincial *tīmār* holders, armed retinues of governors, and the janissaries, but also as its antithesis. In the barracks in Istanbul, repetitive drills enabled soldiers to act together as part of a larger, impersonal war machine, rather than as individual fighters graced with valor, courage, and good reputation. The bodies of soldiers, who were trained to be part of a symphonic totality in a new rhythm of exercise, were decorated with blue and red uniforms. These uniforms functioned as the visual component of the ceremony of power, showing anonymous young men in an integrated regiment, rather than robust fighters wearing diverse, colorful costumes, tattoos, and the insignias of their affiliations with their corps. A new military band used drums to coordinate collective movements of the regiments during drills and battle. Synchronized loading and firing drills were pedagogically carried out, with detailed time measurement. Janissary sports, such as hunting, the game of jereed, archery, and wrestling, were replaced with athletic exercises that trained soldiers to act as a group, from marching to building human towers. Soldiers were addressed by their first names; ranks; and the names of their regiments, villages, and fathers rather than by nicknames that signified personal reputations.[115]

The regulations for regiments, which were spelled out in elaborate charts, diagrams, and timetables, systematized military drills and codified the new military regime, not in terms of historical conventions, like the laws of the janissaries, but as universal rational coordinates. The New Order's leadership was comprised of hierarchically ranked officers who were responsible for their teams, under the command of superiors. Officers were promoted according to seniority and education, unlike the *alaybey*s, who were elected by *tīmār* holders or janissary elders, who

served as natural leaders of the corps under the often-nominal authority
of the janissary chief appointed by the sultan. The state carefully watched
promotions, regulations, and drills through inspectors (*nāẓır*), who were
separately appointed as watchdogs to guarantee the army's unconditional
loyalty to the state. But the designers of the New Order also sought the
public's approval. According to one military engineer, drills gave New
Army soldiers greater physical and mental agility. These young men were
now ready to carry out the necessary maneuvers and "impressed spec-
tators with the movements they achieved en masse." This encouraged
young Muslims to join the new troops. These achievements elicited the
"admiration of the public" and "general approbation."[116]

The New Order by no means espoused an agenda counter to or free of religion. On the contrary, this project promoted religion and was promoted
by religion at the same time. As Fatih Yeşil suggests, the reformists situ-
ated the New Army within an Islamic framework as well as a European
one. Religious discipline was to mentally motivate and spiritually coordinate soldiers.[117] Military drills, which enhanced physical and collective
discipline, were supplemented by specific religious training with imams
from orthodox texts, such as those of Birgivi, for mental discipline. While
European military sciences (*'ilm-i ḥarb*) were the reference point for the
designers of the new system, the mosque congregation, praying together
in an orderly way behind their imams, as a "clamped wall," was another
inspiration of the New Army, whose soldiers were taught to act as though
under the discipline of a stopwatch.[118] By suppressing the self (*ıṣlāḥ-ı
nefs*), mental training based on religious texts helped make soldiers docile parts of a hierarchical order. The orthodox religious education given
soldiers of the New Order in the new baroque mosques in Üsküdar under
the supervision of imams contrasted with the rituals of the janissaries,
who met haphazardly in wooden lodges under the spiritual leaders of the
Bektaşi order, where elements of Sunni and Shi'a Islam, and even Christianity, were combined in syncretic ways. Offices connected to the New
Army were called jihad offices (*me'mūriyet-i cihādiye*).[119]

The New Army's Islamic teaching emphasized collective action by the
congregation as a spiritual disciplining tool, or even an ideology. But in
many ways, the New Order was an Ottoman experiment for adopting,
but also negotiating and interpreting, European military practices. Engineers and medical doctors, ranked according to the new regulations,
became an integral part of the new military order as technical experts.
Artillery, grenadiers, and sappers, in addition to the navy, with the
new Naval Academy and Arsenal, were seen as the military sectors that

perfected the New Order. A new engineering school and medical center built in the Imperial Arsenal invited European engineers and doctors to impart knowledge as professors and experts. Ottoman military reform offered opportunities for men to acquire and share expertise in military sciences, military architecture, and medicine. Many European experts, including royalists who had fled the French Revolution, and many technical envoys, freelance military engineers, and inventors from Prussia, Russia, Austria, Spain, Sweden, and Britain found positions in the Ottoman New Order as advisors of the New Army or, less often, as professors at the schools. Acquisitions and translations of technical books made the latest writings on European military science available in the library of the Imperial School of Engineering.[120]

Military engineers in the late eighteenth century shared a common vision of military reform, regardless of their political or national loyalties. Writing about the New Order in his book *Révolutions de Constantinople*, the French émigré and military engineer Antoine Juchereau de Saint-Denys, who was hired by the Ottoman administration as an expert in fortification and artillery, stated that his loyalty was to his mission as an engineer who believed in military reform, "free from his political orientation."[121] Ottoman military engineers, graduates of the new military schools, employed the global discourse of scientific military order. The reformist bureaucrat Mahmud Raif proudly presented Ottoman achievements to European military engineers' "republic of letters" in his *Tableau des nouveaux règlements de l'empire ottoman*, published in 1798 by the New Imperial Engineering School in Istanbul.[122] Seyyid Mustafa, a military engineer and professor of mathematics at the military college, sought to share the Ottoman experience with his European fellow military engineers in his autobiographical *Diatribe de l'ingénieur Séid Moustapha*:

> The pleasure of seeing the sciences cultivated in all regions of the world is every philosopher's grand passion. Hence, I attempt this small piece of writing with this double aim: to show my gratitude to the masters of the [military] arts from whose books I have acquired the little knowledge that honors me and to present a brief sketch of the present state of the military arts and military engineering in these [Ottoman] lands, and of the felicitous reforms that they have experienced in a small amount of time.[123]

In sum, the New Army was a disciplined army, but it also promised an agenda for a new life, which resonated globally in the age of revolutions. This was an orderly, coordinated, precise, punctual, mechanical, and regularly monitored kind of life. In the 1790s, however, the New Order was still predominantly a military program. It would take at least another fifty years for the reform programs to frame society in the Ottoman Empire (and Egypt), and the Ottoman state introduced comprehensive city planning, compulsory schooling, epidemiology measures, surveillance, and border monitoring only in the second half of the nineteenth century.[124] Yet even in the early 1800s, there were pilot projects aiming at a new life.

New Space, New Life

Barracks built for the New Army in Istanbul in Levent in the 1790s and at Selimiye in Üsküdar in the 1800s were full-fledged military compounds, housing facilities from hospitals to religious centers to fill the days and nights of soldiers and officers and keep them from having recourse to the city's civil services and structures. Starting in 1800, new barracks were built in Anatolia based on the Selimiye prototype, which was designed as an orderly alternative to agitated, sprawling Istanbul. In the Selimiye complex, roads were laid out in a grid, and there were underground sewers. The military barracks were integrated with residential buildings, a shopping center, educational units, religious compounds (including a mosque), public baths, a well, a library, a printing house, and textile and gunpowder factories. In this pilot project, military order, trade and manufacturing, and socio-religious life were seen as sharing common features. Merchants and shopkeepers working for the New Order were free from intervention by urban janissaries. They were granted privileges and registered according to regulations. Their industrial projects aimed to meet the needs of the New Army, in particular, guns and clothing. Through these urban projects, the New Army facilitated a new life.[125]

The New Order was not only a reform project, but also a style of living and an elite identity. While the regime had an agenda to discipline unruly Istanbul, with its bachelors, immigrants, and janissaries, the elites of the New Order were gradually leaving the city for new developments. In the early eighteenth century, Istanbul's upper and upper-middle classes started to build houses on the Golden Horn and the Bosporus, and a register of these seaside mansions compiled between 1798 and 1803 shows that many of their owners, both Muslim and non-Muslim, were in one way or another connected with the New Order.[126] Still, the regime developed an agenda to discipline its own elite. The new social life that developed in these affluent zones, with gender and religious mixing, pushed the New Order to promulgate regulations laying down gender and religious codes of sociability.[127]

The new polite society of Istanbul began to prefer living in these coastal suburbs, rather than tumultuous, crowded Istanbul, and some members of the dynasty built baroque sea palaces along the Bosporus. Istanbul became attractive to European architects and designers, who, like European military engineers, were looking for new job opportunities. The architect and painter Antoine-Ignace Melling (1763–1831), who lived in Istanbul for eighteen years, designed and furnished palaces, gardens, and kiosks for Selim, his sister Hadice Sultan, and others. After embarking on a new career in Paris as a landscape painter for Empress Josephine in 1803, Melling published a book on picturesque Istanbul and the Bosporus for European readers, depicting the life of the imperial elites and gentry of the Ottoman Empire under the new regime.[128] As we shall see in the next chapter, some provincial notables closely followed and adopted these trends in the capital. If the New Order was about drill and discipline, it was also about new forms of politeness and new habits of consumption.

The New Fisc and the New Order Coalition

What about the new fiscal order? In March 1793, a new revenue treasury, İrād-ı Cedīd Ḥazīnesi, was constituted to finance the military and administrative reforms.[129] Revenues collected from sale taxes and customs duties on alcoholic beverages, cotton, fleece, gallnut (tree galls used in the manufacture of ink and dyes), and mohair, which the administration considered lucrative items, were transferred to the New Treasury. But a more critical measure was taken to divert revenues from rural estates under the jurisdictions of benefice and *mālikāne* holders. The administration intended to abolish some *mālikāne* and *eshām* leases and to transfer these provincial revenue units to New Treasury managers. The first step in this direction was to seize fiscal units whose annual revenue exceeded certain amounts and whose holder had died. However, this attempt triggered opposition from *mālikāne* holders and their subcontractors over cancelling *mālikāne* contracts.[130]

While the attempt to transfer *mālikāne* units to the New Treasury was not fully successful, the fiscal administration was able to seize hundreds of vacant *tīmār*s and assign them to the management of the New Treasury after reassessing their value.[131] Instead of managing these units through directly appointed supervisors, the New Treasury outsourced them to powerful imperial and provincial elites known to support the reforms. As a result, the majority of *tīmār*s came under the control of a handful of men. According to Yavuz Cezar, in 1795, one third of *tīmār*s and *ze'āmet*s were controlled by seven grandees from imperial and provincial elites.[132] In 1804, officials conducted an extensive inspection.[133] The inspection found that 3,575 *tīmār* units were registered throughout the empire. Of these, 2,047 units appeared vacant; that is to say, their holders did not appear at inspections. These latter *tīmār* units were granted as *emānet* or farmed out to be supervised by a few imperial grandees and regional powerholders:

> Abdi Bey, who as *emin* supervised 243 units in several mining centers in Karaferya, Siverek, Çar, Ergani, Malatya, and Maraş

Kadı Abdurrahman Pasha, the governor of Konya, who acquired 356 units in the sub-province of Konya

Alaeddin Pasha, the governor of Erzurum, who acquired 498 units in the province of Erzurum

Hacı Ahmed Agha (Karaosmanoğlu), the intendant of Aydın, who acquired 66 units in Aydın

Kösepaşaoğlu Hafız Ahmed Agha, who acquired 63 units in Divriği, Sivas, Arabgir, and Çorum

Tepedelenli Veli Pasha, the son of Ali Pasha, who acquired 20 units

İbrahim Pasha, the governor of Rumela, who acquired 136 units in Avlonya/Vlorë, Elbasan, and Shkodër

İsmail of Ruse, who acquired 75 units in Siliste and Nikopol/Niğbolu

Hacı Mehmed Emin Agha, the intendant of Diyerbakır, who acquired 273 units

Cabbaroğlu Süleyman Bey, who acquired 284 units in Bozok, Menteşe, Sivas, and Kars-Maraş

Tayyar Pasha, who acquired 320 units in Trabzon, Kara Hisar-ı Şarki, and Canik

Karaosmanoğlu Hacı Hüseyin, who acquired 65 units in Saruhan

Karaosmanoğlu Ömer, who acquired 21 units in Karasi[134]

The government's institutional limits and the New Army's urgent financial needs pushed the fiscal administration to collaborate with the empire's strong and wealthy men, not just for the task of drafting soldiers, but also for financing the reform. This conflicted with some of the reformists' initial idea of creating a centralized fiscal administration through direct taxation and management of revenue units with centrally appointed officers. Instead, the Treasury outsourced hundreds of former *tīmār*s and *ze'āmet*s to a group of notable men with contracts and made them partners of the New Treasury and the New Order.

As the next chapter explains, this list could also be understood as a coalition of the New Order, consisting of imperial grandees and provincial notables linked by fiscal ties. Those who were not included in this coalition were threatened by political marginalization and/or economic elimination through confiscations, since revenues collected from confiscations also provided the New Order with resources. Paradoxically, the consolidation and expansion of the New Army would challenge this coalition in the long run, since it would empower the central military bureaucracy against provincial elites. In other words, the coalition of the New Order had its own internal contradictions. It provided new financial and political opportunities for various notables who acted as fiscal and administrative contractors of the New Order; but it also challenged them, since the consolidation of the New Army would empower a centralized military, fiscal, and administrative bureaucracy against provincial notables.

As Stanford Shaw illustrates, between 1792 and 1807, the New Order party was by no means a stable alliance. At its center were dynastic and military/bureaucratic circles. Küçük Hüseyin Pasha and his wife, Esma Sultan (Selim's cousin), were supported by the navy. Yusuf Agha, the former head of mines and later the steward of Mihrişah Sultan (Selim's mother), was supported by Mihrişah herself and by Anatolian notables, including the Çapanoğlus. Members of the fiscal bureaucracy gathered around İzzet Mehmed. Some officers of the New Army clustered around Kadı Abdurrahman Pasha. These individuals rose as leaders of various factions that competed and collaborated to control the key positions in the center and important revenue sources spread out in the provinces. Many affiliates of the religious orders, such as the Nakşibendiye and Mevleviye, which were integrated into the Ottoman bureaucracy openly supported the New Order (except the Mevlevis in Konya—the spiritual center of the order and the hometown of its founder, Mevlana Celaleddin Rumi—who kept their distance). Opposition came from the Bektaşiye, an order historically entrenched in the janissaries. Many individuals and groups, including members of the imperial establishment, constantly switched from pro- to contra-reform stances.[135]

Provincial notables such as Tayyar Pasha and İsmail of Ruse, left the New Order coalition at different points. As we shall see in chapter 2, Tayyar left around 1804 as a result of his competition with the Çapanoğlus over Amasya province. He called on other provincial families to establish an alliance to stop the New Order. Ismail left in 1806 when Selim sent Kadı Abdurrahman Pasha to build up the New Army in the Balkans, which threatened Ismail's autonomous zone in Danubian Bulgaria. Ali Pasha of Ioannina and his son Veli Pasha negotiated vigorously with the center for new deals, contracts, and offers to strengthen their control in western Greece. Notables who were out of touch and not in the empire's fiscal and administrative nexus adopted anti–New Order positions. Osman Pazvantoğlu, a magnate in Vidin who rose quickly from a humble background to become a regional and interimperial actor between 1792 and 1804, mobilized masses and janissaries against the New Order party, which he blamed for corruption and disloyalty to old imperial conventions. Clashing Serbian notables and janissaries in Belgrade led Selim to act on behalf of Serbian notables, suppressing the janissaries of Belgrade. This decision only increased tensions. Pazvantoğlu provided safe haven for the Belgrade janissaries, as well as other dissenters, and signaled that a fight between the New Order and a coalition against it was imminent, as chapter 4 explains.

The New Order and anti–New Order factions were amorphous coalitions of imperial and provincial elites with diverse political calculations. Different groups in Istanbul, provincial communities who were willing to send men to the New Army, others who resisted doing so for various reasons, and religious networks were integrated into the bureaucracy or the janissaries. But internal actors were not the only group to play a crucial role in the polarization of imperial politics. European powers were also heavily involved in the Ottoman New Order controversy. Factions within the reform party in the center were allied with European diplomatic circles. The party led by Küçük Hüseyin Pasha had France's support, while the Yusuf Agha party was allied with the Russians and the British. The party headed by İzzet Mehmed remained neutral. Foreign diplomats, military missions, and foreign engineers employed by the Ottoman state, merchant networks collaborating with foreign powers, and some non-Muslim Ottomans under their diplomatic and commercial services participated in these coalitions. Wars and diplomacy after the French Revolution put France on one side and a coalition of Russia, Britain, Austria, and Prussia on the other. Each side was actively involved in Ottoman politics to gain the advantage over the other. Jacobin diplomats representing the new French republic developed friendships with the janissaries, while French émigrés and British military experts became actively involved in building the New Army after the French Revolution.[136]

Still, Selim's pro-French sentiments did not dissipate until after the French expedition to Egypt in 1798. The rapprochement between the Ottoman Empire and the Russian-British coalition against France resulted in an Ottoman-Russian joint campaign to capture Corfu and other Ionian islands from France in 1801. Following the Campo Formio Treaty of November 1797, France ended Venetian control of the islands, eliminated the pro-Venetian oligarchy, and established a pro-French republic. The Ottoman-Russian alliance was successful in capturing the Ionian islands and gave birth to a conservative republic with support from the islands' pro-Russian notables, who gained Ottoman-Russian protection in 1801. During this turbulent period of Ottoman foreign policy, the pro-French party in Istanbul lost credit. After Napoleon became emperor of France, however, the pro-French party regained its strength. Napoleon's vigorous attempts to create an alliance with the Ottoman Empire (and Qajar Iran) against Britain and Russia and his support of reform projects changed the dynamics in Istanbul.[137]

Between 1802 and 1806, the Ottoman Empire—not only Istanbul but also its provincial cities—was a battleground between Napoleonic and British-Russian diplomacy to enroll the Ottoman center and regional magnates such as Ali Pasha of Ioannina, Pazvantoğlu of Vidin, and Muhammad Ali of Cairo in their coalitions against each other. Diplomatic crises were generated by Ottoman recognition of Bonaparte's title as emperor; the status of the Dardanelles; the status of Serbia after Serbian notables rebelled against the Belgrade janissaries; and whether Ottoman Wallachia and Moldavia were to be governed by pro-French or pro-Russian voyvodas. Selim timidly decided in 1806 to move the Ottoman Empire away from the Russian-British coalition and toward France, having been influenced by General Horace Sébastiani, who had been sent on a special mission by Napoleon to secure an Ottoman-French alliance. Russia occupied the Romanian principalities, and a British fleet passed through the Dardanelles, anchored in front of Istanbul, and trained its cannon on the city. These events, which turned into a siege, would trigger an anti–New Order revolution, led by an auxiliary janissary unit, as we shall see in greater detail in chapter 4.

Defending the New Order, Refuting the Populace

By 1806, tensions between the New Orderists and individuals and groups voicing anti–New Order sentiments became increasingly apparent in both Istanbul and the provinces. But for now, let us look at two texts, written around 1805 and 1806, aimed at defending the New Order against its growing opposition. Koca Sekbanbaşı's pamphlet *Hülasât ül-kelâm fî redd il-aʿvâm* (Concise Statement to Refute the Populace) helped sway public opinion in favor of the New Order.[138] We do not know who Koca Sekbanbaşı was. His name, however, seems like that of a senior janissary officer, or perhaps a janissary chief. According to one historian, a committee commissioned by leaders of the New Order, perhaps Selim III himself, might have written the text to counter the negative attitudes of ordinary people to the New Order. Perhaps it was thought that a janissary pro-reform voice would be more effective in doing so, and the pamphlet was meant to show that not all janissaries were against reform. In any case, the author declared that he had written it to help ordinary people understand (*aʿvâm-ı nâsın tefhîm etmesi için*) the virtues of the New Order and, as the title implied, to refute public denigration of the reform.

The pamphlet was written in everyday language, like a conversation between ordinary people. The author quoted questions and remarks made against the reform in coffeehouses, barbershops, and taverns and then rebutted them in a polemical manner. Not only were the janissaries against the New Order, since they were afraid that the New Army would slash their salaries and render their corps obsolete, but, according to the author, ordinary people (*aʿvâm*) also spoke freely against the New Order without knowing much about current conditions in the Ottoman Empire and beyond. They attributed all the empire's problems to the New Order, from the turmoil in the Balkans and Arabia to that in the wider world.

"Such disturbances are not happening only in France," Koca Sekbanbaşı declared. "In India, China, Arabia, Iran, and in the New World, disorder and terror [are] not absent. So do you think that our New Order is behind all these [turmoils]?"[139]

After sketching public opinion on the streets of Istanbul, the author compared the old and new armies. The old was slow, while the new was quick (*serī'*) in loading and shooting, attacking and defending; the old was undrilled and clumsy, while the new was robust (*dinç*). The old was not uniformed, and thus disorderly (*karmakarışık, perākende*), while the new was uniformed and orderly, like a watch (*kurulmuş sā'at gibi*). The old was open to manipulation by foreign spies, while the new was well controlled and self-contained, so that spies could not infiltrate it. The old was based on individual valor, whereas the new was based on the coordination of the group (*yek-hey'et üzere*). This explained why the old army had been bested by the Russians since 1767 and why the new one had been successful against the French in Egypt and against bandits in the Balkans. The new way (*tavr-ı cedīd*) had therefore been substituted for the old (*tarz-ı kadīm*).[140]

Koca Sekbanbaşı then refuted the complaints of ordinary people about new economic burdens owing to the reform. Since the new taxes were in great part collected from wine consumption, he argued, the Muslim public would be largely unaffected. Revenue units outsourced to provincial notables to finance the reforms would be recovered. These were not granted forever, and they were to be returned to the Public Treasury of Muslims (*beyt ül-māl-ı müslimīn*).[141] Clearly, public opinion against the New Order went beyond the concerns of the janissaries, who had only their own corporate interests in mind. Rumors that revenue units in the provinces were to be allocated to small groups of elites in the name of financing reform had sparked more negative sentiment toward the New Order party. Koca Sekbanbaşı was not only explaining the sound reasons for military reform, but also trying to fix the public image of the New Order.

Koca Sekbanbaşı's pamphlet was written to encourage favorable public opinion about the New Order and perhaps to quell possible outbursts from the street against the reform and the ruling party. However, there were other groups, aside from commoners, that needed convincing—in particular, the learned, including the ulema. A more scholarly and morally oriented defense of the New Order came from Ubeydullâh Kuşmânî, who was not a central political figure but a preacher. Originally from a small town with a considerable Tatar population in Udmurtia in central Russia, and probably connected to the Nakşibendi order, Kuşmânî traveled to various Ottoman lands and countries under Russian control, probably in the Caucasus and Central Asia, where Nakşibendism was rejuvenated. He gave public sermons in Istanbul and wrote pamphlets to advocate on behalf of the New Order and the efforts of Selim and his supporters around 1806. Members of the New Order possibly sponsored Kuşmânî's mission. But en route from Abkhazia in 1805, Kuşmânî was captured and faced allegations that he was a spy for Tayyar of Canik, then a leader of the anti–New Order coalition in Anatolia. As a result, he became a political refugee in Russian-controlled Crimea. It appears that Kuşmânî had been under surveillance by the central administration before he became a popular preacher in Istanbul. He was released by the order of Selim III.[142]

Between 1806 and 1808, Kuşmânî proved himself an outspoken advocate of the reform and for Selim. Adopting a polemical tone, he was a kind of New Order activist.[143] In his *Zebîre-i Kuşmânî fî ta'rîf-i nizâm-ı İlhâmî* (Letter of Kuşmânî Explaining the Order of İlhâmî), a polemical text in Turkish with Arabic and Persian quotations from the Qu'ran, Hadith, and Persian dictums and poetry, the erudite Kuşmânî put forward a defense of Selim's New Order. (İlhâmî is Selim's pen name.) Kuşmânî's defense differed from Sekbanbaşı's. He provided a manifesto from a moral and religious perspective. Kuşmânî made a case for the new military order based on discipline and drill as scientific necessities of jihad (*'ilm-i cihād*) and thus religious obligations (*farż-i żarūrî*). The New Order was to augment the science of Holy War (*'ilm-i cihād*). In the way that Kuşmânî formulated it, as disciplined, learned, and coordinated military action, the science of Holy War resonated differently from prac-tice of *ġazā*, the traditional ethos of Ottoman military culture, which was religiously motivated warfare that cultivated heroism and voluntarism. Opponents of the New Order were not only ignorant, idle riffraff, but also people in religious disarray. New military techniques included the innovations of infidels, but this was no reason to refuse them. On the contrary, Muslims were obligated to learn and adopt these innovations and put them to use in jihad. Kuşmânî praised Selim as the patron of the New Order, for teaching his people that military science was a religious and moral responsibility. He had created new institutions and a new dis-ciplined, well-drilled army to accomplish this religious and moral duty.[144]

Kuşmânî was engaged in polemics with the janissaries. Commoners and the learned gathered around the latter to discredit Selim's moral and Islamic claims, but Kuşmânî condemned the janissaries as confused, mud-dleheaded, and ignorant and accused the learned around them of hiding the truth from commoners. Some janissaries worked at groceries, others as porters. Most were idle, which depleted public wealth (*beyt ül-māl*) since these janissaries received salaries without delivering services. Kuşmânî juxtaposed the new soldier's discipline and drills with the idleness and ignorance of the janissaries. Training the body (*terbiye-yi beden*) was not only a military duty, but also a task that enabled individual worship. "A human, without being disciplined/trained [_terbiye olmadıkça_], is like an unfinished thing." The idleness of the janissaries (and their opposition to drill) prevented them not only from being good soldiers but also from fulfilling their purpose as Muslims and even as human beings. Kuşmânî's critique, in this regard, often became overly polemical. He addressed the janissaries as "the side of dishonor" (_ṭaraf-ı bī-şeref_) and a "detestable crowd" (_gürüh-ı mekrūh_), who, he added, were mocked in every corner of the world, as he had seen in his travels.[145]

Behind this critique was subtle anti-traditionalism. Kuşmânî attacked the traditional symbols of the janissaries. He contended that there was no reason, for instance, to believe that Hacı Bektaş, a patron saint of the janissaries, had actually been involved in the foundation the corps. "Did he [Hacı Bektaş] give a deed to you?" Kuşmânî mocked the janissaries. Their attribution of holiness to Hacı Bektaş as the prophet of the corps was similar to Jewish and Christian false claims about the prophets Moses and Jesus, Kuşmânî asserted.[146]

But he went a step further in his anti-traditionalism and challenged the traditionalists, contending that there was no reason why one should follow one's predecessors in every case. He explained that it was incorrect to say, "our precursors acted like this, [so] we should act likewise," since good or evil deeds committed by people in previous eras were their responsibility, not ours. Old was not necessarily legitimate by virtue of its age.[147] These anti-traditionalist contentions were supported by his argument that renovation was not only inevitable but also a necessity. Likewise, it was an obligation of the sultans, not to let the people go their own way, but to intervene in the social order and change it according to the necessities of the time. Kuşmânî cited a verse from the Qur'an: "but you may hate a thing although it is good for you, and love a thing although it is bad for you."[148]

Kuşmânî's argument culminated with him making the case for _ictihād_, or legal reasoning, to extract a rule from the original sources of Islamic jurisprudence. He argued that there was debate over whether there was no longer a _müctehid_, namely, a legal authority with the capacity to extract new rules. Perhaps there was no _müctehid_ to originate a new legal school (_mazhab_), since legal schools had been established centuries ago, but in every age, there should be _müctehid_ to find necessary answers to contemporary problems (_müctehid-i bi'l-mes'ele ber-mukteżā-i ḥāl_).[149] Kuşmânî thus argued that the New Order was first and foremost a religious necessity to be authorized through ictihād.

In the nineteenth century, Islam became a modern political discourse and shaped Ottoman and later Turkish political culture, Kemal Karpat asserts. In this process, the Nakşibendi network, extending from Central Asia and India to the Balkans, had a central role. This view challenges some modernist historians who see political modernity as anti-religious or nonreligious. In fact, religion became an essential component of the reform discourse. The roots of this transformation, what Karpat calls the politicization of Islam, lie in the controversy over the New Order.[150] As we shall see in chapter 5, legal and moral concepts derived from Islamic tradition provided not only a framework for the reform to discipline individual and society, but also a constitutional scheme to reintegrate the Ottoman Empire based on contract and partnership.

CONCLUSION: THE (NEW) ORDER OF STATE

The Ottoman New Order aimed to establish both a well-drilled, disciplined new army and a new fiscal, political, and social order. As Michel Foucault writes:

It may be that war as strategy is a continuation of politics. But it must not be forgotten that "politics" had been conceived as a continuation, if not exactly and directly of war, at least of the military model as a fundamental means of preventing civil disorder. Politics, as a technique of internal peace and order, sought to implement the mechanism of the perfect army, of the disciplined mass, of the docile, useful troop, of the regiment in camp and in the field, on maneuvers and on exercise. In the great eighteenth century states, the army guaranteed civil peace no doubt because it was a real force, an ever-threatening sword, but also because it was a technique and a body of knowledge that could project their schema over the social body.[151]

In this respect, the Ottoman experience was not very different from those of other eighteenth-century polities in the Age of Revolution. The experience of the New Order in the 1790s and the early 1800s expanded from the Ottoman center to the provinces, and in Egypt under Muhammad Ali in the 1820s and 1840s, as Timothy Mitchell and Khaled Fahmy show, it really took hold and profoundly transformed the social, military, and economic order.[152] However, in Istanbul and the heartlands of the Ottoman Empire, in the Balkans and Anatolia around 1800, the ability of the New Order to effect such change was limited, first, because there was still no agreement about all aspects of the reform program among the elites, and, second, because the opposition, which was more visible around 1805, was expanding and had strong moral claims.

Depictions by Koca Sekbanbaşı and Kuşmânî of the opposition to the New Order as ignorant, self-interested janissaries and the urban mob clustered around them may be misleading. There were groups and individuals, both in the center and provinces, who were against, critical of, or distanced themselves from the New Order for various reasons and on different occasions. The New Army threatened the vested salaries and

privileges of thousands of men who had acquired janissary affiliations
and were invested in these statuses. Thousands of migrants in Istanbul
were also threatened by attempts to oust them from the city, where they
sought to begin new lives. The New Order also confronted various provincial communities that resisted recruitment of the new troops (although
some communities declared collective willingness to be part of the new
project). Many provincial notables benefited from the reform's fiscal opportunities, since dozens of *tīmār*s and immune revenue units under the
jurisdiction of the New Treasury were outsourced to them. But others,
such as Pazvantoğlu of Vidin (until 1805) and Tayyar Pasha of Canik
(after 1804), were excluded from this larger coalition, and threatened
with confiscations and eliminations. Establishing new armies directly connected to a small group in the center also intimidated provincial notables,
even those who were fiscal partners of the New Treasury, especially after
the center decided to build camps for the new troops in the provinces.
This triggered massive resistance in Edirne in the summer of 1806, as we
shall see in chapter 4. Beginning in 1805, economic conditions in Istanbul worsened because of difficulties in obtaining Balkan wheat, owing to
challenging security conditions. The quality of bread deteriorated and the
price of meat rose.

    Therefore, by 1806, one did not necessarily need to be a tenacious
traditionalist or anti-reformist to participate in the opposition to the New
Order. The small minority that commanded a new army thus isolated and
independent of social life, customs, and conventions would acquire immense power over the society. The janissaries, on the other hand, were integrated into social and economic life and had evolved within the existing
social and economic system. They were perceived as both natural components of Ottoman society and defenders of existing morals, markets, and
rights. Thus, for some, as we shall see in chapter 4, to defend the janissaries was to defend collective values, conventions, and rights against those
who wanted to eliminate them. Opposition to military discipline, drill,
and uniforms thus did not only mean opposing a new military order;
it also defended the autonomy of Ottoman society against far-reaching
radical changes by a small party, the New Order, which, some believed,
undermined existing rights and claims.

    The New Order was seen as a small reformist group that not only
belittled the conventions of thousands of people affiliated with the old
order and janissary claims but also monopolized resources and enriched
its leaders at the expense of others. The "[w]ealth and splendor [of the
New Orderists] pricked the eyes of the public like a thorn," the historian
Cevdet Pasha wrote, commenting on the general sentiment in the streets
of Istanbul toward the ruling elite.[153] "Between the accession and deposition of Selim Khan, [the New Orderists] . . . conquered the state . . . and

ruined the entire country," the anti–New Order author Ebû Bekir Efendi wrote in his history.[154] He harshly attacked the ruling party as a small, corrupt group and condemned the elite for provocatively attempting to bring about a confrontation between the janissaries and the New Army without seeking another solution for reform.

It thus seems that, as with other contemporary reform projects, the success of the New Order depended on its capacity and willingness to mobilize a large coalition. The success of Peter the Great and the failure of Louis XVI were the two examples best known to Ottomans. By the early nineteenth century, it was not clear whether the New Order would be able to mobilize a workable coalition for reform by negotiating with or eliminating the available actors, such as the janissaries and provincial notables, or whether the growing anti–New Order bloc would be able to mobilize the public for a revolt. The latter turned out to be the case. How the New Order collapsed and how other options emerged are discussed in chapters 4 and 5. Now, accompanying readers out of Istanbul, I shall take a closer look at two major actors in the story of the empire: the provincial notables, who appear in chapter 2, and its provincial communities, which are examined in chapter 3.

CHAPTER 2

The Notables

Governance, Power, and Wealth

Provincial people generally do not apprehend the honor of the
sultanate.

Süleyman Penah Efendi (1769)[1]

In 1809, at a critical stage in the Ottoman-Russian war, with the Ottoman
Empire urgently in need of funds to pay and supply its armies fighting on
the Balkan front, the Imperial Divan (council of state) recommended a
personal appeal from the sultan to four eminent provincial strongmen for
financial support. The deputy grand vizier submitted its proposal to the
young sultan Mahmud II, who had ascended to the throne a year earlier
after the fall of Selim III in May 1807:

[Given the wealth and affluence of] Ali Pasha of Tepelenë [Tepedelen in southern
Albania], Mehmed [Muhammad] Ali Pasha, governor of Egypt, the Cabbarzades
[Çapanoğlus], and the Karaosmanzades [-oğlus],[2] each has the capacity to send
. . . thousands of *akçe*s [silver coins]. In fact, they owe their wealth to the Exalted State. For that reason, in such a [troubled] time, it is obviously incumbent
upon them to help [the Exalted State]. However, because of their temper, if their
assistance were to be requested through ordinary sultanic orders, they would
make several excuses to escape sending it. Thus it would be [more prudent] if
your Majesty were to write special letters to each without informing the servants
of the state of these letters. In these letters, if Your Majesty were to express his
judicious imperial opinion, and to ask in his own imperial hand if they would
"send that amount of *akçe*s to my imperial abode, to be spent in the army's campaign, which is to expel the enemy of our faith that is attacking the empire from
various sides," if these letters were to be enclosed together with imperial decrees
and conveyed to each of them by palace stewards, and if the money were to be
requested in similar fashion, it is very likely that each would show urgent obedience to sultanic orders and deliver the necessary amounts. Sending that kind of
letter to servants of the sultanate will not damage the glory [of the sultanate].

Previously there were occasions on which such aid was requested. We cannot think of any alternative to obtaining money from outside sources.[3]

This account shows the ways in which the members of Ottoman imperial circles viewed magnates in the Ottoman provinces in the early nineteenth century. Ali Pasha, also known as Ali of Ioannina, a native of Tepelenë, was governor of Ioannina in northwestern Greece. His authority extended to various regions in southern Albania, the Peloponnese, and central Greece. Muhammad Ali, an Albanian and a native of Kavala near Salonika, came to Egypt as a warrior with an Ottoman Albanian legion to fight against the French during the turmoil of Bonaparte's invasion in 1798–99. After various unexpected developments in Cairo, he became governor of Egypt in 1805 and established his control there. These two men autonomously controlled two strategic Ottoman territories on opposite sides of the eastern Mediterranean. But they also stood—at least formally—at the highest level of the imperial pyramid of governors, which ranked them hierarchically. Ali of Ioannina and Muhammad Ali of Egypt held the title "pasha" and were entitled to display banners with three horsetails, the insignia of their vizierate and governorship. But the Karaosmanoğlus and the Çapanoğlus, dominant households of western and central Anatolia respectively, did not act as governors. These families built zones of influence, without belonging to the imperial hierarchy, by acquiring various offices, deals, and contracts. While Ali and Muhammad Ali acted individually as imperial governors, the Çapanoğlu and Karaosmanoğlu households collectively consolidated power and wealth in large regional zones. Despite the disparities between their formal standings, the Ottoman state treated these individuals and families as magnates who built power and accumulated wealth in four primary regions of the empire: the Balkans, western and central Anatolia, and Egypt.

These magnates and their families had to be treated carefully. They could be expected to supply the necessary funding only if the sultan personally asked for the money as a favor. In warning the sultan that servants of the state—such as governors, generals, bureaucrats, palace dignitaries, chiefs of the janissaries, and others who were not rooted in the provinces, but directly connected to the imperial center—should not be informed of the letters to be sent to these magnates, the deputy grand vizier acknowledged a division between the imperial and provincial elites. The sultan's informal personal approach to these powerful provincials, as conveyed by his letters to them, might potentially disturb the dignitaries of the central state, to whom it might seem inappropriate.

Mahmud II, who had just become sultan a few months earlier, might well have considered this treatment humiliating as well. In asking for financial support in personal letters, he approached the provincial magnates as equals or partners in negotiations. The deputy grand vizier assured

Mahmud that such negotiations were not unknown in recent history, and that these developments would not damage the glory of his sultanate.

Throughout the eighteenth century, individuals and families in various localities in the Ottoman empire, from the Balkans to Egypt, consolidated power, accumulated wealth, built headquarters, and formed regional zones of influence. While imperial elites connected to the central establishment or to military and bureaucratic hierarchies were marginalized in provincial governance, these provincial magnates acquired offices and contracts from the empire, becoming governors, deputy governors, ancillary contractors, or collectively nominated or elected district managers. By holding these offices and contracts, these provincial notables not only integrated themselves into the institutional apparatus of the empire, but also monopolized taxation, public finance, policing, provisioning, conscription, and other imperial and public services in the business of governance in the Ottoman provinces.

In this chapter, I focus on the relationships and interactions between the powerful notables and the Ottoman state in the late eighteenth and early nineteenth centuries. My aim is to illustrate the way provincial magnates were incorporated into the Ottoman Empire and how they became part of the Ottoman establishment. This process, I argue, gave birth to a new order of notables, in which provincial magnates were not servants or bureaucrats of the sultan or of the state organized in a top-down, hierarchical fashion. Rather, I suggest, they came to act as administrative, fiscal, and military entrepreneurs, whose relations with the Ottoman establishment were based on ongoing deals, negotiations, and a process of give and take. The magnates sometimes agreed with the orders they were given and sometimes turned them down. Sometimes they offered services and asked for favors; or they received them, rendering services in return. In other words, they were engaged with the empire, not as *servants*, but as *servicers*.

These new provincial elites also differed from the nobilities we know in Europe and elsewhere, which were clustered as corporate bodies with hereditary rights and privileges. In the Ottoman Empire, with the exception of dynasties in distant provinces that were integrated in the empire with special vassalage arrangements, such as Crimea (until 1774), Bosnia, Kurdistan, the Caucasus, and the Hejaz, such magnates did not enjoy their offices and contracts as hereditary rights. Their status, wealth, and even their lives were in potential jeopardy, since according to old conventions, the Ottoman sultan reserved the right to dismiss officeholders, revoke contracts, and even confiscate property and order executions without judicial process. Ottoman provincial magnates were not only entrepreneurs, but also active risk takers and risk managers in a volatile imperial sector.

In the following pages, I discuss how these provincial grandees consolidated themselves in the Ottoman provinces and how they were incorporated into the Ottoman imperial establishment; how they operated through negotiations and deals; how they built regional zones and accumulated wealth; how institutional and political insecurity and volatility shaped their actions. We shall also see how some of them actively participated in the political controversy over the New Order's military and fiscal reforms. And how some magnates discovered new possibilities and considered breaks with the empire in the turbulent political and diplomatic environment of the age of revolutions and the Napoleonic wars. I seek to map the limits to their capacity to act independently in this turbulent global age.

The discussion that follows does not resemble a prosopographic analysis seeking to include all powerful individuals and families in a systematic way. Rather, I focus on various themes and problems that help us understand the order of notables and provide comparative examples. This eclecticism is not without logic; I am particularly interested in families and individuals who played roles beyond the regional setting and participated in the imperial political theater of the late eighteenth and early nineteenth centuries.

HOUSEHOLD, CITY, AND DYNASTY

It is virtually impossible to provide a complete picture of all the Ottoman Empire's provincial elites in one chapter. From Bosnia to Egypt, and from Albania to eastern Anatolia, each region gave birth to different forms of elite, resulting in great diversity. Some of these individuals and families had pre-Ottoman roots. Others originated during Ottoman times, whether from among the local population or from Ottoman elites who settled in various provinces and became localized. Some built power and wealth through activities in commerce and crafts. Others used cultural capital as people of learning. Others emerged through activities in the business of governance. Not all were Muslim. Greek and Serbian notables also built power and wealth in their respective localities. But the institutional framework of the Ottoman Empire allowed only Muslims to ascend to certain levels of office and status in the business of governance. These magnates were integrated into the administrative and military apparatus of the empire through different mechanisms, deals, and terms. They provided order and security, collected taxes and revenues, managed public affairs and finance, conscripted soldiers and militia, and participated in wars. The Ottoman institutional framework provided them with statuses as provincial governors, contract holders, or district managers. Other than governors, however, the Ottoman system did not hierarchically rank these individuals by status and office as in European and Russian tables of ranking nobility.

If we examine how provincial magnates organized their enterprises, we often see a patrilineal family at the nucleus—a unit of kin related by blood, marriage, or adoption—bound by a sense of common political enterprise. Sometimes, the family was the conjugal group of a leader father, his wives (for Muslim notable families, generally more than one wife), concubines, sons, and daughters. But more often, the central kin group was a consanguine agnatic clan that included several conjugal families attached to each other through bonds of kinship and a leading charismatic figure, a paterfamilias. First- or second-generation notables tended to act as a conjugal family. With figures like Ali Pasha of Ioannina and Muhammad Ali of Egypt, we do not observe large clans. Rather, a charismatic leader was the founder of the enterprise, and his sons and grandsons were his followers. The Çapanoğlus, the Karaosmanoğlus, the 'Azms, and the Rişvanzades, who had established themselves in a few generations, were large family structures with multiple conjugal families knitted together. The centrality of the patrilineal family in provincial power-building was reflected in the use of clan names ending in -oğlu or -zāde, both meaning "son of" and indicating the founding father of the family, such as Karaosmanoğlu, the son(s) of Osman the Black.[4] Despite the dominant role played by men, women often played important roles, whether as mothers, wives, widows, or concubines. Marriage was often a device to ally households, or to co-opt a subordinate man into the family. The widows of charismatic family heads might be key actors in decision-making about family strategy.[5]

Typically, the grandee family was surrounded by a household, generically known as *kapı halkı* (the people of the gate), which included dozens, sometimes hundreds, of retainers such as domestic servants, concubines, and eunuchs in the inner household and secretaries, treasurers, and stewards in the outer household. The term *kapı* signified the administrative nature of the notable households, mimicking the name of the Sublime Porte (*Bāb-ı'Ālī*), the symbolic gate between the outer (administrative and military) and inner (privy chamber, including the harem) realms of the Ottoman imperial household. Armed bodyguards or militias under the command of captains constituted the household's third layer. It was always possible to move up in the layers of the household, and even to become part of the central family through marriage or adoption. As Jane Hathaway illustrates for eighteenth-century household-formation among Egyptian grandees, the household might be considered a family-centered institution to which individuals, including slaves, could be attached

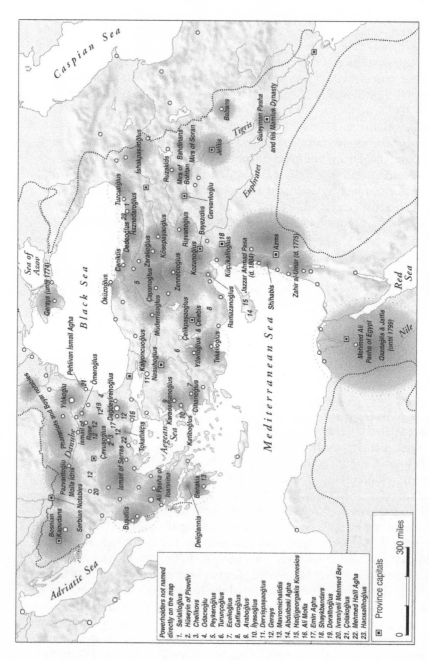

Map 2. Leading provincial powerholders and their regions of influence. The author and Philip Schwartzberg / Meridian Mapping.

Powerholders not named
directly on the map
1. Sarialioğlu
2. Hüseyin of Plovdiv
3. Chelikovs
4. Odacıoğlu
5. Peykeroğlus
6. Turuncuoğlus
7. Ecelioğlus
8. Gaffaroğlus
9. Araboğlus
10. İlyasoğlus
11. Dervispaşaoğlus
12. Gerays
13. Mevromichalidis
14. Abdülbaki Agha
15. Hadjigeorgakis Kornesios
16. Ali Molla
17. Emin Agha
18. Shaykbandars
19. Doralthoğlus
20. İvraniyeli Mehmed Bey
21. Çolakoğlus
22. Mehmed Halil Agha
23. Hacısalihoğlus

■ Province capitals

0   300 miles

Caspian Sea

Black Sea

Sea of Azov

Adriatic Sea

Aegean Sea

Mediterranean Sea

Red Sea

Nile

Tigris

Euphrates

Gerays (until 1774)

Bosnian Kapudans
Serbian Notables
Pazvantoğlu
Molla İdris
Phanariots and Bosnians
Yılıkoğlu
Çavuşoğlus
Ömeroğlu
Pehlivan İsmail Agha
İsmail of Ruse
Daddevirenoğlu
İsmail of Serres
Tokatlıcıs
Katıboğlus
Karaosmanoğlus
Çitanoğlus
Nasuhoğlus
Kalyoncuoğlus
Okuzoğlus
Canikilis
Haznedaroğlus
Tuzcuoğlus
İshakpaşaoğlus
Dedeoğlus
Zaralıoğlus
Çapanoğlu
Köprüpaşaoğlus
Müderrisoğlus
Zennecioğlus
Rişvanoğlus
Çalıkpaşaoğlus
Kozanoğlus
Bayezidlis
Gervanlıoğlu
Ruzakids
Mirs of Bahdinans
Bohtan
Mirs of Soran
Jelilis
Babans
Süleyman Pasha
and his Mamluk Dynasty
Yılanlıoğlus & Çelebis
Tekelioğlus
Ramazanoğlus
Küçükalioğlus
Cezzar Ahmad Paşa (d. 1775)
Zahir al-Umar (d. 1775)
Amits
Shihabis
Mehmed Ali Pasha of Egypt
Qazdağlis & Jalfis (until 1799)
Deligiannis
Ali Pasha of Ioannina
Benakis
Busatis
Danube

though patronage relations, known as *intisāb*, and into which they could be gradually co-opted at different levels.[6]

Provincial strongmen erected residential buildings of different kinds with annexes for administrative and soldierly purposes. The most striking examples were palaces. In Ottoman architectural history, scholars working on palaces generally focus on imperial residences, especially the Topkapı Palace in Istanbul.[7] Palace architecture commissioned by notables in the provinces has been ignored in the wider scheme of Ottoman patronage and relegated to the realm of local vernacular architecture. Perhaps the earliest example outside Istanbul is the Khan Palace (Hansaray) in Bakhchysarai (Bahçesaray), the capital of the Crimean Gerays, erected in the fifteenth century by the Geray dynasty, which had special status thanks to its Chinggisid ancestry. After its total destruction, the Khan Palace was rebuilt by the Gerays in the 1740s.[8] Throughout the eighteenth century, other notable families who did not have such pedigrees but were able to consolidate power and wealth also built palace-like residential complexes for large households in the localities where their power was centered. Ali Pasha's palace in the Castro in Ioannina, İshak Pasha's palace at Doğubayazıt, the Çapanoğlu palace in Yozgat, the Haznedaroğlu palace in Ünye (Ordu), and the 'Azm palaces of Damascus and Hama are important examples of such complexes.[9]

The main characteristic of these provincial palaces was the juxtaposition of residential and administrative functions as two sections of private and public life, which were organized around different courtyards, divided by walls. The complexes were stretched with several annexes for administrative and soldierly functions, stables, and perhaps a small prison. A mosque, commissioned by the family, was often connected to the palace or erected in the vicinity (or both), sometimes in combination with a household cemetery. Both the palace and mosque featured inscriptions that glorified the family and references to the Ottoman state and dynasty. Some complexes were located in the city, such as the 'Azm palace of Damascus, and others in the vicinity of the city, such as the İshak Pasha palace at Doğubayazıt. In both cases, walls or natural cliffs protected the notable households from enemies, brigands, and even the central state. John Macdonald Kinneir, a British diplomat and geographer en route to Persia, stopped in Yozgat, where Süleyman Bey, the leader of the Çapanoğlus, hosted him in the family's palace in 1813. Kinneir wrote in his diary:

The palace is a very extensive building, divided into suites of apartments, long galleries, and different courts and gardens, all of which are surrounded by high walls. It is built of brick and wood, only two stories high, and covers an immense area in the centre of the town. The apartments of the prince and his sons were painted and gilded and richly furnished; there were four state chambers, one at each corner of a long and handsome gallery, lighted by large glass windows—a red room, a yellow

room, a brown room, and a room of variegated colors. On one side of the apart-
ment, where his highness generally received company, I perceived a small organ,
and a number of clocks and watches, which made so great noise that it was difficult
to hear a person speak in a distant part of the room. A small door at the other end
led into the cabinet of the Chakbook bashi, or master of the pipes, a closet com-
pletely surrounded with long amber-headed pipes, many of which, I was informed,
were valued at five or six thousand piasters. The apartments of the haram I was not
of course permitted to enter; but, according to [the family's French medical] doc-
tor's account, they far surpassed, in splendor and magnificence, those I had seen.
. . . The palace occupies a large space in the centre of the town; and a handsome
mosque had been lately erected of hewn stone in imitation of St. Sophia.[10]

Kinneir was mesmerized by the lavish style and collections of goods
and merchandise from different regions for conspicuous consumption.
Dizzying traffic around the palace—the result of dozens of visitors, officers, messengers, and tradesmen who arrived each day from different
parts of the empire, mostly from Istanbul but also from beyond the Ottoman territories—might explain the palace's diversity of materials and
styles. Imitations of Istanbul were accompanied by strong local references. The Çapanoğlu buildings housed wall paintings representing panoramic scenes of their urban center, Yozgat. This preference for localism,

Figure 2. İshak Pasha Palace, Doğubeyazit, Turkey, 1685–1784.
Josephine Powell Collection, Courtesy of Special Collections, Fine Arts Library,
Harvard University.

while reaffirming the connections of the buildings with the visual memory of the Yozgat area, also served the self-aggrandizement of the family, the city they built, and the region under their control.[11]

The architectural and material culture that sprang up around the households of the provincial powerholders fascinated European observers who visited their headquarters. The French painter Louis Dupré, known for his depictions of scenes from the Greek revolution, was among them. During a visit to Epirus in 1819, Dupré also painted Ali of Ioannina and his household and bodyguards, as well as views of Ioannina showing the city's inhabitants and ancient ruins. The cover of this book showing Ali Pasha's grandsons İsmail and Mehmed is one of Dupré's paintings. The two young men, wearing elaborate Ottoman silk garments with fur collars and sleeves and turbans of the local type, are represented sitting comfortably on a rustic wooden terrace. Bejeweled pistols are stuck in their gilded cummerbunds, reminding viewers of the immediacy of violence and martial life in the Ottoman provincial world. They hold long tobacco pipes, like their grandfather, who was famous for smoking tobacco from long pipes. This suggests a family habit spanning the generations. Despite the elaborate garments of the two, the outdoor space where they are sitting is haphazardly decorated with a plain curtain and pillows spread on the floor. Overall, the image, while including some elements of the splendor common in orientalist painting, emphasized the simplicity of provincialism.[12] Some years before Dupré's visit, during their stay at Ali Pasha's headquarters in 1811, Baron Broughton and his close friend Lord Byron had met these two grandsons of Ali's when they were children. In a room containing panoramic depictions of Istanbul, Mehmed and İsmail showed Broughton and Byron elaborate watches and other ornaments. Broughton mentions that the two boys spoke both Albanian and Greek and were now studying Ottoman Turkish under tutors from Istanbul. They were being prepared to rule the region in the Ottoman fashion. Dupré and Broughton, through depictions of Ali's grandsons, captured the image of a dynasty under construction.[13]

Although most provincial magnates were acquainted with Ottoman imperial conventions and Ottoman Turkish (the imperial language) to some extent, only some were native speakers of Turkish.[14] Biographical dictionaries and local architecture and memory, songs, and histories record their ties to urban space.[15] When members of a notable family built residential-administrative complexes, they also reorganized urban spaces with new walls, mosques, Sufi lodges, public libraries, military compounds, and infrastructural works.[16] An outsider setting up as a strongman in a region needed to erect a secure mansion for his household first and then a few communal buildings to show his generosity and public spirit. An early nineteenth-century biography of Pehlivan İbrahim

telling how he established his local power through architectural patronage exemplifies this process:

He was settled in a village named Kuzgun [today's Antimovo near Silistra in Bul-
garia]. He started to build a mansion for himself and his men. In a short time, he
completed the mansion, with sixty-two rooms. Three thousand cavalrymen could
be camped in its yard. Then he built a fine school. He appointed teachers. Then
he built a mosque and installed in it imams who could read and write. Prayers
were held with a congregation five times [daily] in the mosque. . . . Then he built
walls around the mansion to protect himself, with seventeen towers. And then he
acquired eight farms around the village. . . . Then he acquired concubines. . . .
Then God gave him two sons.[17]

Architectural and infrastructural patronage helped a magnate consolidate leadership among the local people, who became his primary constituency, as well as guarantee (and increase) his prestige in the center.
This was why, for instance, a report submitted to the central government
concerning the affairs and deeds of Jazzar Ahmed Pasha to lobby for a
promotion in Istanbul included a section on the fortress and mosques he
had commissioned, in addition to an account of his military capacity.[18]
Provincial magnates commonly employed architects for such projects. But
they also provided a wide range of other employment opportunities in
their towns for scribes, military experts, as well as literati from Istanbul
or elsewhere in the Ottoman Empire or ouside it. In the late eighteenth
century, the prominent poet Ebû Bekir Kânî complained that he could
no longer find a generous patron in Istanbul. His friends, Kânî said in an
autobiographical poem, advised him to go to Ruse, where "the notables
of the city would take care of him."[19]

We find different patterns in the relations between notables and their
towns and urban communities. In Yozgat, the Çapanoğlus constituted
the town's founding family; they had no competitors.[20] Elsewhere the
dominant household was *primus inter pares* among other notable families with historical local roots. These families had long-term matrimonial
and business relations with other notables in the business of governance
or those who specialized in a particular learning or trade. In Damascus,
for instance, relations between two families, the 'Azms and the Muradis,
provided an example of partnerships over several generations. The
'Azms, who monopolized the business of governance and the Muradis,
who patronized Islamic learning, united their political, economic, and
cultural capital on different occasions as two distinctive houses of the
city.[21] In other cases, magnates who constituted a distinctive group came
from outside as a part of an empirewide network, such as the janissary

corps, or an ethnic and ethno-religious network and settled in the localities as military-administrative entrepreneurs. They acted as an oligarchy, detached from local civil society and other notable families. Similarly, the Albanian Muhammad Ali Pasha in Egypt, the Bosnian Jazzar Pasha in Acre, the Georgian households in Egypt and Baghdad, the Crimean Gerays in Ottoman Bulgaria, and Greek Phanariots in Wallachia and Moldavia built up power bases in different provinces and were not fully assimilated with other local elites.[22]

By and large, Ottoman interconnectedness provided these administrative entrepreneurs from different parts of the empire with possibilities to find opportunities as outsiders in regions far from their hometowns. There was a good chance that, after a generation or two, "outsider" magnates would be localized through matrimony or partnerships and become integrated into local customs, memories, and languages.

According to many historians, both Islamic law and Ottoman imperial conventions constituted obstacles to the continuity of powerful wealthy families for generations in the Ottoman Empire. While the Islamic law of inheritance gave a clear mandate for the division of the patrimony among male and female heirs after the death of the paterfamilias,[23] the Ottoman imperial order guaranteed hereditary privileges only for office, contracts, and status, with some exceptions. Despite these institutional constraints, many families in the Ottoman provinces were able to develop strategies to keep power, wealth, and status within the family for transmission to the next generation. In Muslim societies, one of the earliest strategies for many families to preserve wealth for their progeny was transforming assets into family waqfs, or endowments for the public good under the protection of Islamic law, while transferring some of the assets to family members as annuities. Recent studies illustrate that there was a proliferation of family waqfs in the eighteenth-century Ottoman Empire.[24] Likewise, some households bypassed the Islamic law of inheritance by reaching collective decisions for a new family head, who formally or informally controlled the household's wealth as joint patrimony through entail arrangements.[25] But perhaps the most important strategy for office-holding families was to negotiate with the central government to reach a political and/or financial deal by which the center agreed to renew offices, contracts, and deals for heirs. In the eighteenth and early nineteenth centuries, thanks to such negotiations, several families were able to keep their deals with the empire for generations and accumulate power and wealth in the Ottoman provinces despite the lack of institutional guarantees.

The consolidation of multigenerational notable families resounds in the political terminology of the period. The Persian word *ḫānedān*, meaning "household" in a generic sense, came also to signify notable households in a city, region, or province with dynastic continuity. In imperial

documents dealing with Rumelia and Anatolia, the term *ḫānedān*s refers to notable houses, testifying to a new empirewide reality: the consolidation of new centers clustered around notable households in the
provinces.[26] As Christine Philliou shows, the Greek Phanariot families
of Istanbul were also called *ḫānedān* in official and semi-official texts.[27]
Meanwhile, several families produced their genealogical trees, emphasized their notable lineages, and designed family banners.[28] Did the expansion of the term *ḫānedān* signify a tacit acknowledgement that the
Ottoman dynasty was no longer the only dynasty in the empire? Ottoman
formal or informal documents contain no explicit acknowledgement that
provincial "dynasties" were equals to or peers of the Ottomans, with the
possible exception of the Crimean khanate.[29] The term *ḫānedān* was an
acknowledgment that some provincial units were notable families who
were deeply rooted in their localities. Despite institutional insecurity that
threatened the continuity of these families' power and wealth, the term
ḫānedān recognized the dynasticization of provincial elites independent
of a particular status bestowed by the sultan.

This recognition went hand in hand with the appropriation of some old
honorific titles, such as "chief gatemen of the Sublime Abode" (*dergāh-ı
'ālī ḳapıcı başısı*) and "chief of the imperial stable" (*mīrāḫūr-ı evvel*). Originally, these titles connoted the *outer* circle of the imperial palace.[30] Now,
the sultans granted them to members of provincial *ḫānedān*s who were
not formally in the Ottoman imperial hierarchy as viziers or governors but
rendered services to the empire with ancillary offices and contracts thanks
to their local power.[31] These titles symbolized the extension of the sultan's
might in the provinces. But they also functioned as a new titular mechanism to connect local notables to the empire and, symbolically, to the sultan and his palace in an alternative web that differed from formal imperial
hierarchies of governors, judiciary authorities, and janissaries and holders of religious honorific titles, such as *seyyid* or *şerīf*, which were used
to proclaim ancestral connections to the Prophet Muhammad.[32] Unlike
the term *ḫānedān*, which applied to both Muslim and Christian notable
families, these titles were granted only to Muslim notables. Throughout
the eighteenth century, such honorific titles were granted with greater frequency to provincial magnates regarded as belonging to the imperial web
of provincial notables, helping them acquire other positions.

OFFICES, CONTRACTS, AND DEALS

"Whenever an important matter arose, [imperial grandees] were forced
to transfer it to the hands of a powerful person from a local community.
Gradually, local notables were becoming responsible for all matters in

the provinces, which were taken out of the hands of the governors," a late eighteenth-century Ottoman bureaucrat reported.[33] This was a typical complaint from some members of the imperial elite in Istanbul, who observed that while provincial elites amassed power and expanded their control, imperial elites were marginalized in governance in the Ottoman provinces. Throughout the eighteenth century, several individuals and families with local backgrounds won offices and contracts in the provinces that covered administration, taxation, management, policing, provisioning, public finance, and conscription. This was a structural process in which individuals and families unconnected to the palace, military, and administrative hierarchies or the households of imperial grandees, but closely connected to local dynamics, were integrated into the apparatus of the Ottoman state in the Balkans, Anatolia, and the Arab provinces. The social base of the Ottoman ruling apparatus was being transformed. Provincials were integrated into the Ottoman establishment; the dichotomies between imperial and provincial, military-administrative and civil, and the ruling and the ruled, once key parameters of the empire's order, were now renegotiated.

In the eighteenth and early nineteenth centuries, the Ottoman institutional structure offered provincial notables various possibilities and venues to participate in governance.[34] At the district level, several notables supervised the public affairs of the district—that is to say, a town and its rural hinterland—on behalf of the district community. As discussed in the next chapter, the Ottoman government called these notables operating at the district level ayans (if they were Muslims) and *kocabaşıs* (if they were Christians). Ayan and *kocabaşı* were generic terms for notables, but in the late eighteenth century, they came to mean offices that were held by collective nomination of the district community. The empire was not, however, neatly divided into districts under ayans and *kocabaşıs*.[35]

In different provinces, the central administration farmed out large and small revenue enclaves (villages, towns, or sometimes entire districts) to fiscal entrepreneurs for short or, increasingly, life-term contracts known as *mālikāne*, with immunity (*serbestiyet*) from fiscal and administrative interventions by other officeholders.[36] Some of these holders were local notables, who acquired their units either through auctions or in lieu of administrative services. They were present in their units to carry out administration, management, and revenue collections. A majority of the others, however, were absentee holders. Grandees of the empire, active and retired palace employees, bureaucrats, governors, and leading members of the learned hierarchy in particular often purchased *mālikāne* contracts of revenue units in the provinces without so much as visiting their units, which they often assigned to local subcontractors and managers.

As a result, chains of contracting, from the center to small local units, functioned as fiscal nexuses that attached entrepreneurs to one another through financial contracts and deals. The estates of male and female members of the Ottoman dynasty, as well as units under the jurisdiction of imperial charitable foundations (waqfs), were similarly contracted out to local managers, generically known as *voyvoda*s. In different regions, numerous small estates and *mālikāne* enclaves were bundled together and transferred to the supervision of superintendents, called *voyvoda*s or *muḥaṣṣil*, who were supposed to coordinate administration, revenue collection, and remittances.[37]

At the higher level, the provincial governors often put their jurisdictions in the hands of local deputies, or *mütesellim*s, who often acquired their offices through financial deals with the governor. The central government and governors sometimes preferred the highest bidder or those they believed had the capacity to maintain security and order. After a local notable and a governor agreed on a particular deal, the governor issued a letter to the communities in his province: "I have appointed Kalaycizade Mustafa Agha, who was exemplary among his peers, as deputy governor. Regard him as your deputy governor, let nobody interfere in his business, and deliver all required dues to him. . . . And you, the deputy governor, will collect our revenue from the communities . . . and deliver it to me."[38] These appointment letters were intended to be read aloud in the kadi courts of the province's central town in the presence of community leaders, where the deputies informed the communities of the deal reached with the governor. "I have acquired this deputy governorship with a contract [*iltizām*], paying a high down payment. You should now assist me in collecting dues,"[39] a deputy governor announced to community leaders, making the financial arrangement between the governor and his deputy a public matter.

In various provinces, mainly in the outer reaches of the empire, such as Epirus, Albania, Damascus, Sidon, Çıldır, Baghdad, and Egypt, some local magnates were able to capture governorships, the highest status.[40] Each notable individual or family had its epic stories of rise from a provincial background to the highest echelons of the Ottoman imperial hierarchy. Some offered military and administrative services or revenues to the empire in times of crisis, and in return, lobbied for a governorship.[41] Some entered the patronage of existing governors by becoming part of their households through matrimonial relations and then eliminated their patron and established rule.[42] Others rose from a petty military office after performing a critical military service and securing reference letters from key figures among the imperial elite.[43] Still others curbed political turmoil, repressed a rebellion, or mobilized local communities and had them declare their collective consent or support to the central government.[44] In each story of such an ascendance, provincial magnates negotiated with the central government, directly through representatives in Istanbul, or indirectly through supporters in different factions of the central establishment. In extreme cases, rebellion was a way of negotiating one's rise in the empire.[45]

To this list, various short-term, ad hoc contracts and missions must be added. The center often asked provincial grandees of different statuses to recruit troops for the army; to participate in campaigns and provide provisioning and logistics; to capture outlaws; to oust dismissed officeholders, and to confiscate the assets of deceased ones on behalf of the state; to buy crops from rural communities at a fixed price in lieu of taxation; or to mediate between local communities and the imperial offices. Either these short-term, ad hoc contracts and missions enabled them to make a profit or they obtained other political or social benefits from the center. Some provincial notables collected various long- and short-term offices, contracts, and deals, acquiring the ability to operate in multiple sectors of governance.[46]

In sum, by the end of the eighteenth century, local notables who operated at different levels, held different offices, and engaged in different deals dominated governance in the Ottoman provinces. As a result, while the officeholders who were connected to the imperial center by sociocultural background, training, and personal allegiances were marginalized, others with provincial backgrounds and only conditional loyalties consolidated their power. But the localization of governance was only one of the structural trends that changed the dynamics of the Ottoman provinces. The other was the monetization of governance. As we have seen, since the mid seventeenth century, offices had increasingly been contracted out in the Ottoman provinces. Provincial units formerly granted as benefices for administrative and military services were now assigned under long- or life-term contracts. As Ariel Salzmann illustrates, entrepreneurs ranging from absentee holders to local managers and subcontractors constituted various complex fiscal nexuses connecting provincial units to the central establishment.[47] The empire was reintegrated through these fiscal ties, and provincial administration became a business.

The third development was the increasing role of the provincial communities, or what I call the expansion of collective action. As we shall see in the next chapter, in many provinces, the district communities were more and more active participants in the administration, approving or disapproving their budgets and electing or dismissing their managers. Many notables needed to secure the formal consent of the district communities in order to function. As a result, notables competed to secure collective endorsement. District communities were divided into factions, and governance was politicized.

Localization, monetization, and politicization of provincial governance reoriented the strategies and priorities of provincial notables. They developed expertise, not only in the management of provincial tax units and the ability to mobilize local resources, but also in intrinsically financial matters. They hired fiscal bureaucrats and professional scribes for managerial and financial purposes. Many of them worked with financiers and moneylenders. And many needed to be responsive to local communities. At least in theory, ayans and *kocabaşıs* acquired their offices through collective nomination. But voyvodas, deputy governors, and holders of the estates, among others, needed to consider the collective action of the communities in their zones. Even governors had to take a collective petition endorsing or protesting against a candidate into consideration as either an asset or a deterrent.

Ali Pasha of Ioannina and Muhammad Ali Pasha of Egypt were governors; İsmail of Serres and İsmail of Ruse were ayans; the Karaosmanoğlus monopolized deputy governorships in several subprovinces in western Anatolia; the Çapanoğlus held Yozgat as a *mālikāne*. In addition to their primary offices, they all made several other short- or long-term deals with the state or other primary holders.[48] Several individuals and groups might be involved in these negotiations and deals between the magnates and the central government. But the official representatives of the grandees in the center, known as *kapı-kethüdāsı*, or Porte-stewards,[49] and their moneymen, known as *ṣarrāf*s, were arguably two of the key factors. Porte-stewards, who were appointed by the center with the approval of magnates, or by the latter with the approval of the center, acted as caretakers of the business of provincial magnates, as well as imperial governors, in the central bureaucracy.[50] For many educated men in Istanbul who did not have posts in the Ottoman bureaucracy, being the Porte-steward of a provincial strongman was a fine option.[51] They dealt with official correspondence and remittances between the center and their patrons, as well as doing all kinds of paperwork.[52] They presented the offers of their patrons to the state and participated in auctions for contracts. Depending on the level of trust between them and their patrons, they might act either as political advisors, reporting to their patrons on developments in Istanbul, or as brokers seeking to maximize the commissions from transactions, or both.[53]

The *ṣarrāf*s, that is to say, moneylenders, who were usually Jewish, Armenian, or Greek, provided credits for the magnates in their business of governance. In the Ottoman fiscal system, contract- and officeholders often worked with financiers, who provided not only loans but also surety if the contract- or officeholder failed to pay his dues to the Treasury. Often the state granted an office or contract after the person who would hold it secured a financier as a surety. In the seventeenth and eighteenth centuries, these moneymen were organized into a guild in Istanbul, with regulations and limited openings for new members.[54] There were also financiers in the provinces, some of whom had business partnerships with those in Istanbul. Provincial grandees worked with both central and provincial financiers, who sometimes operated as a network across the empire—sometimes even beyond it—by extending different credit markets. Often, the partnership between the financiers and magnates went beyond financial relations. Like the Porte-stewards, the financiers lobbied in Istanbul on behalf of their partners to obtain lucrative offices and contracts with favorable terms for them and to block cancellation of any office or contract. Some went beyond their roles as financiers and lobbyists and rose to be important political actors in their regional setting or even at the imperial level.[55]

Acquisition and transmission of offices and contracts was always contingent upon new negotiations, offers, and deals. Most notable families, especially those who held strategic offices and lucrative contracts directly from the state, had to renegotiate terms with the state after the death of the family's primary officeholder. In a volatile office market, there was constant competition among provincial actors hoping to capture and retain offices or to add new ones to their portfolios and transmit them to the next generation. To acquire and/or keep offices, provincial notables simply offered the best financial deal to the center; or sought to convince decision-makers that they could offer the best military, fiscal, and administrative services. Meanwhile, they established alliances with imperial elites in Istanbul and local actors in their regions, while eliminating competitors. Collective petitions from local communities in favor of a magnate were considered important assets. The strongest well-connected grandees collaborated with foreign powers to put pressure on the Ottoman administration to appoint or keep them in certain positions. In the most dramatic cases, as described above, magnates defied the central authority and rebelled as a means of negotiation with the center for better offices, greater glory, and more revenue sources.

While provincial grandees competed to capture, maintain, and multiply their offices, the central authority also negotiated with them for services and deals. During wars or/and financial crises, the state offered new opportunities in the office market, while its bargaining power diminished. Between 1770 and 1820, when the Ottoman center desperately sought the financial, administrative, and military support of provincial magnates on many occasions, the central administration often persuaded provincial magnates to take part in governance and military campaigns by granting higher offices, additional revenue units, and lucrative contracts with short- or life-term arrangements. When the imperial Divan frantically asked Mustafa Bayraktar, ayan of Ruse, to accept the governorship of

Silistra and organize a militia in the region to oppose the Russians in 1807, he negotiated and agreed to do so only after the Tarnovo district was also granted to him as an additional revenue source.[56] Stormy times provided opportunities to become integrated into the empire on favorable terms. For some, however, additional offices were not necessarily favorable. "We heard that you have some concerns as to whether you will be granted a vizierate when you reach the imperial army or whether an inappropriate service may be asked of you," the imperial Divan informed the Karaosmanoğlus' Hasan Bey, who had been asked to guard the Dardanelles against a possible British attack. The center granted him Aydın district, a region that produced high revenues. Noting that Hasan was reluctant, the administration guaranteed that no unwelcome service would be imposed on the family. "You would not be appointed to a position that is not appropriate for your situation."[57]

From the perspective of the imperial authority, the *formal orders* of the sultan could be in practice *informal offers*. At the beginning of this chapter, we saw that Mahmud II was advised to send personal letters to provincial magnates *asking* for financial aid, in addition to formal decrees *ordering* them to send revenues. The discrepancy between informal and formal relations between the state and provincial grandees enabled the latter, depending on their bargaining capacity, to negotiate sultanic orders without formally rejecting them. The center tried to remove Jazzar Ahmad Pasha, the governor of Sidon, to Erzurum, to prevent him from consolidating his power in Palestine. "However," the Divan noted, "whether he will go to Erzurum or turn down this appointment is not known."[58] In long letters to the imperial Divan, Jazzar explained, without explicitly rejecting the offer, why he should not be removed from Sidon. He stated that he had just cracked down on Zahir al-Umar, the magnate of Acre, and would reestablish Ottoman rule in the region.

Such negotiations—a process of give and take, offers, acceptances, and rejections—were often carried out with the decorum of the imperial hierarchy. Letters using the templates of imperial and bureaucratic discourse traveled back and forth. So did personal letters expressing gratitude or voicing open rebuke or even protest. In Greece, Ali Pasha of Ioannina was given Trikala, a province in Thessaly, which would open up new avenues for Ali's regional expansion. When, in 1809, the central administration removed Trikala from his jurisdiction, Ali protested in a personal letter to the grand vizier: "Since I have mobilized my sons and so many of my soldiers for the imperial campaigns, and I was not at any fault, this decision hurts me greatly. Since it was natural to expect gratitude from the grand vizier, the removal of the said subprovince from our jurisdiction caused excessive sadness."[59] After this letter emphasizing his disappointment, Ali was offered the position of commander of the Danubian army in 1812. He declined.[60]

Third parties who offered favorable financial deals or services to detach offices from their holders were often involved in these formal or informal negotiations. In *mālikāne* contracts, which were sometimes acquired through formal bids or political deals, interference by third parties was quite common. Since the early eighteenth century, Abdurrahman of the Rişvanoğlu clan had held the Malatya intendantship as a *mālikāne* like his father and grandfather before him. In 1813, the new governor of Sivas, Pehlivan İbrahim, known as Baba Pasha (mentioned above who built a large headquarters with a massive walled mansion, mosques, and schools for the community in Kuzgun), challenged the Rişvanoğlus. In his reports to the central government, Baba Pasha stated that upon his appointment as governor of Sivas, he had visited *mālikāne* units in Malatya and testified that the communities complained of the Rişvanoğlus' rule. Baba Pasha recommended that the central administration revoke Abdurrahman's contracts and lobbied in Istanbul to acquire the Malatya intendantship for himself. The grand vizier supported Baba Pasha, arguing that the Rişvanoğlus had difficulties paying annuities to the Treasury. Baba Pasha had the financial resources and was well connected to the imperial elite, but when his case was presented to Mahmud II, the sultan declined the proposal on the basis that the Rişvanoğlus had made a considerable down payment for the contract. The Treasury would be burdened if the deal were revoked, since this down payment would have to be returned to them. Seeking to protect the financial credibility of the Ottoman state, Mahmud II suggested that Malatya could not be managed from Sivas, since the distance was considerable. Eventually, the Rişvanoğlus were able to keep the Malatya intendantship under their control. But the family failed to pay annuities and remained indebted to the Treasury.[61]

These sporadic episodes illustrate formal and informal negotiations and how different actors fashioned offers and counteroffers. Various central or provincial actors could be involved when a lucrative strategic office and contract in a particular region was at stake. In these games, various calculations, political and economic priorities, and concerns about trust, reputation, and credibility were involved, offering different roles for different actors in different circumstances. In sum, acquiring an office or contract in the Ottoman provinces was not so much a bureaucratic, top-down process as a matter of formal or informal bargaining, whether open or tacit; of negotiations, give and take, offers, counteroffers, and rejections. Those in the business of governance, both local notables rooted in their regions and imperial governors who moved throughout the empire from one region to another, needed to be familiar with the strategies of their competitors and partners in their regions as well as in Istanbul.

The power of many leading provincial families and individuals in the business of governance was centered in a town and its rural hinterland. But some went beyond their localities and constructed regional zones of influence, over which they exercised both administrative control and political or economic power. Between 1770 and 1820, some magnates were able to build regional zones of unprecedented size. Usually, these magnates expanded these zones by acquiring additional offices and contracts. Sometimes one individual acquired more than one office. Or various members of the same family acquired different offices and expanded the family's influence throughout a particular region. The most powerful and well-connected magnates eliminated competitors, often by appropriating their wealth and status (with or without the authorization of the state), or incorporated them into their power zones through different partnerships and/or patronage relations. Grandees might lose offices for several reasons, including dismissals, confiscation by the central state, or interference by competing individuals or families. The Ottoman provincial order witnessed a dizzying traffic in offices, and the boundaries of zones of influence constantly shifted.

The Region of the Çapanoğlus: A Regional Contractor

The Çapanoğlu house under Süleyman Bey provides one of the most remarkable examples of expansion. Before Süleyman's time, members of the family had established themselves in Bozok (now Yozgat) province in central Turkey, building from scratch the city of Yozgat, where they ruled as deputy governors for many years from the early eighteenth century on. In 1782, the death of Mustafa, the oldest family member, triggered new negotiations, since the central government in Istanbul used the threat of imperial seizure of an officeholder's estate as a negotiating tool to raise revenues. Despite the opposition of the grand vizier, however, Mustafa's brother Süleyman was able to reach a deal through key members in the government: if the state did not confiscate his brother's wealth, Süleyman would pay 1,900,000 *ġuruş* in compensation to the Treasury. In return, he asked to inherit his brother's wealth and a *mālikāne* contract for Bozok. Faced with financial pressures after the Ottoman-Russian war,

the central government accepted this offer and granted Bozok to Süleyman in 1782, making him holder (*mutaṣarrıf*) of the subprovince for life,
with full administrative authority.[62]

Süleyman was not, however, able to pay what he had promised. By
1785, he had paid only two-thirds of the total, which created a crisis
between the family and the government. In 1786, the central administration decided to organize an intervention in Egypt to put an end to
civil strife among the magnates there. This presented an opportunity for
Süleyman to recoup his debt. When he promised to contribute to the military campaign financially and with an armed division, not only was his
debt repayment postponed, but he also acquired a neighboring province,
Çankırı, to help the finance his recruitment. The Ottoman-Russian war
of 1787–92 was an opportunity to reach more deals by offering different
services to the state. The center asked the Çapanoğlus to organize provisioning and recruitment in Anatolia for the imperial campaign. In 1788,
when the family contributed three thousand soldiers, Süleyman added
the deputy governorship of Ankara province to his portfolio. He also
acquired contracts to collect taxes from nomadic tribes and to administer
various mines scattered throughout the region. The family expanded its
managerial and administrative expertise under Süleyman.[63]

Selim III's enthronement in 1789 further improved relations between
the family and the center. In 1790, Süleyman personally attended the
campaign in the Balkans. Selim III honored him with an imperial title,
chief of the imperial stable, and Abdulfettah Bey, his son, who stayed
in Bozok, became a chief of the imperial Gate. The Çapanoğlus enthu-
siastically supported Selim's New Order. Süleyman obtained several
short-term contracts for revenue collection, estate management, military recruitment, and fiscal reorganization. However, the main challenge to the Çapanoğlus came from the north. The Canikli family was
influential both in the central government and in the Black Sea region
of Anatolia. One reason for the controversy was Amasya province, a
strategic area connecting central Anatolia and the Black Sea. Its center,
the city of Amasya, was a prestigious town and had been the seat of the
crown princes in the sixteenth century. The Caniklis long held Amasya,
with different titles. As a result of Süleyman's service in the Balkan campaign against Russia and the Caniklis' failure on the Caucasian front,
Selim III decided to remove Amasya from the Caniklis and grant it to
the Çapanoğlus in 1791. In the absence of Tayyar, the chief of the Canikli family, who became a political refugee in Russia, this move opened
the Black Sea region to the Çapanoğlus. A couple of years later, however, when Tayyar was pardoned and returned to the Ottoman lands,
Amasya was removed from the Çapanoğlus and once again granted to

the Caniklis. While the central authority balanced its policies between the two families through this give-and-take process, the Çapanoğlus were allowed to expand in the south. In 1794, when Süleyman acquired the subprovince of Tarsus, becoming its deputy governor, the family's zone of influence reached the Mediterranean coast.

Political alliances, formal or informal patronage relations, and business partnerships were as important as acquiring additional offices and contracts for expansion for the Çapanoğlu family. An episode in the central Anatolian province of Konya in April 1803 illustrates regional expansion through patronage relations. Kadı Abdurrahman Pasha, one of the leading architects of the military reform, was appointed governor of Konya.[64] Several estates in central Anatolia were granted to him to finance his army-building efforts.[65] But the people of Konya opposed this appointment and expelled the governor from the town. Abdurrahman's humiliation alarmed Istanbul. The imperial Divan asked Süleyman, whose political influence extended over central Anatolia, and who had also already managed several estates in the region, to arbitrate between the community and the governor.[66] Süleyman sent a representative to Konya and negotiated with the city's notables, particularly the leaders of the Mevleviye Order, which had been the dominant religious and social association in Konya, the seat of their saintly founding father, Jalal al-Din al-Rumi (1207–73). Eventually, the people of Konya agreed to allow in Governor Abdurrahman, who bound himself by deed not to harm them (*Ḳonyaluyu incitmemek*) and to leave Konya as soon as his mission was complete.[67] The state thanked Süleyman for protecting the honor (*nāmūs*) of the sultanate. But he was also protecting the rights of the community of Konya against the New Order. This episode would raise his prestige both in the eyes of the central government and among local communities in his regional zone of influence.

The big move came in 1805. The Çapanoğlus' fervent support for the New Order, their conscription activities for the New Army, growing influence in central Anatolia, and Tayyar's opposition to the new regime convinced the central government once again to grant the subprovince of Amasya to Süleyman, who acquired its deputy governorship, along with those of Tokat and Zile, in 1805. At the same time, his younger son, Celaleddin, was appointed governor of Sivas with a high rank.[68] This put almost the entire central Anatolian province under the control of the Çapanoğlus and led to armed conflict with the Caniklis. In 1805, the two families fought, and the central administration backed the Çapanoğlus. When Tayyar was declared an outlaw, the Çapanoğlus expected to acquire the lands along the Black Sea coast under the control of the Caniklis. One strategy the family pursued to convince Istanbul was to let the central government believe that local communities were not willing to accept a governor from outside. When the Canik subprovince was granted to Yusuf Ziya Pasha, an imperial grandee, the communities allegedly complained to the Çapanoğlus, declaring that they had not consented to the appointment. Süleyman heralded Istanbul as the protector and spokesman of the local people, announcing their unhappiness with (*dilgīr*) Yusuf Ziya, and encouraging the central administration to appoint an intendant sympathetic to the poor (*fukarā'-perver*), implying himself.[69] Süleyman followed similar strategies in the south. Despite the resistance of the Kozanoğlus, the major household controlling Tarsus and the Cilicia region along the Mediterranean coast in southern Anatolia, the family acquired Tarsus province. Meanwhile, Süleyman established alliances with local leaders and nomadic communities in the Taurus Mountains that were at odds with the Kozanoğlus. Süleyman invited the heads of notable local families into his court, honoring them with robes and granting deputy positions to represent the family in the region. The incorporation of Tarsus into the Çapanoğlu zone was celebrated as an epic moment in *The History of the Menemencioğlus*, a mid-nineteenth-century family history. The Menemencioğlus were one of the houses that entered Süleyman's network in the southern wing of the Çapanoğlu zone.[70]

The Çapanoğlus' expansion was blocked after the janissary-led popular coup in Istanbul that ended the New Order. After Selim was dethroned and his nephew Mustafa IV became sultan in 1807, Tayyar was pardoned; the new sultan took Amasya away from the Çapanoğlus and granted it to the Caniklis. A couple of months later, Tayyar was invited to Istanbul and asked to act as deputy grand vizier. Meanwhile, Celaleddin Çapanoğlu was dismissed as governor of Sivas and presently appointed governor of Diyarbakır in southeastern Anatolia, far from the family's central zone.

As we shall see in great detail in chapter 4, however, a countercoup led by Mustafa Bayraktar and his New Orderist allies resulted in the death of Tayyar and once again presented the Çapanoğlus with new possibilities. Karahisar (1808), Kayseri (1810), Kırşehir (1811), and Aleppo (1813) were all allocated to Süleyman or his son Celaleddin.

Süleyman was one of the most successful regional magnates of his time. He skillfully negotiated with the center and local actors, employing all available mechanisms: financial deals, services, contracts, and local politics. The central administration, for its part, benefitted from Süleyman's expansion, inasmuch as he offered it generous payments, military service, and his prestige and influence in the region, where he had established

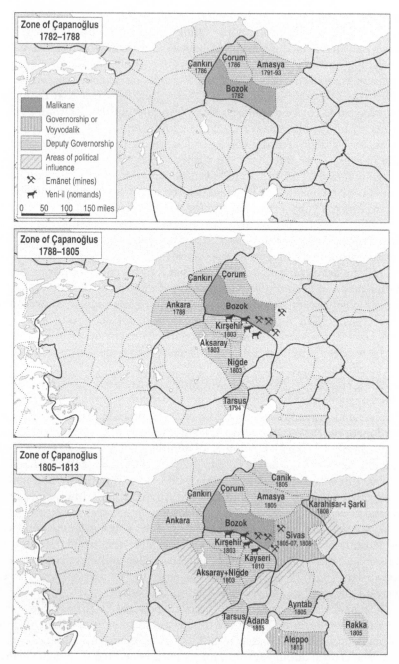

Map 3. The territories of the Çapanoğlu family (1782–1813).
The author and Philip Schwartzberg / Meridian Mapping.

bonds of trust with local actors in his zone of influence.[71] Following Süleyman's death in 1813, however, the new sultan, Mahmud II, declined to reassign his offices and contracts to members of the Çapanoğlu family, and its domain abruptly shrank back to Yozgat.

Ali Pasha of Ioannina: The Vernacularization of Governance

For a comprehensive analysis of the inner functioning of the regional zones, we should examine a wide range of sources such as local histories, literary works, popular accounts, and material and architectural culture. Among these sources, perhaps the most important and least well known are documents that were produced by the scribal bureaus of great provincial powerholders. Some of these magnates, such as Ali Pasha of Ioannina, established their own bureaucratic and scribal institutions, which paralleled the imperial administrative apparatus and were not under the central administration's surveillance.[72] Unlike imperial records, the documents produced in the scribal bureaus fostered vernacular conventions in the regions in both language (Greek in the Balkans and Arabic in the Arab provinces) and format. These documents constitute alternative archives of Ottoman provinces ruled by regional strongmen, illuminating their inner workings.

The archives of Ali Pasha of Ioannina, a former *derbendci agha*, or guardian of the passes, in the Pindus Mountains, are among these rare records.[73] Starting in the 1790s, Ali Pasha and his sons Veli and Muhtar built a regional zone of influence along the shore of the Adriatic from Epirus in Greece to southern Albania. In the late 1790s, the family expanded northward when Ali became governor of the province of Avlonya (Albanian Vlorë), strategically located on the Adriatic coast. In 1799, the central administration granted Thessaly to Ali as well to provide security of passage there and rid the region of bandits. Ali was subsequently made governor of all of Rumelia, enabling him to acquire additional revenues and territories in the Balkans, but his tenure in that office was short. The family later lost Thessaly but kept control of the Adriatic coasts of Greece and Albania for two decades, with an increasing role in the Adriatic, amassing substantial wealth from agricultural estates and trade. Its power endured until 1822, when Mahmud II eliminated Ali and his children after a long, bloody siege of Ioannina.

The documents in Ali's archives reveal that his regional expansion was based on delicate deals, strategies, and negotiations, not only with the central government, but also with various local leaders, networks, and communities in his region, who were constantly complaining, proclaiming their loyalty, or seeking to negotiate or renegotiate their terms of agreement with him. Ali's officials in the city of Ioannina responded to their petitions and sent inspectors and sometimes troops to protect or coerce the locals. His sons Veli and Muhtar, who lived in different sub-provinces under the family's jurisdiction; agents scattered across his territories; and his factors in Istanbul contributed to the endless stream of dispatches.

This archive consists of documents primarily in Greek, the vernacular language of Ali's zone of influence, with significant Turkish and Albanian interpolations. His scribal bureau, while using Ottoman Turkish in Ali's formal correspondence with the imperial authorities, used Greek (we can call this style Ottoman Greek) in his correspondence with local communities and members of his network. The format of the petitions by the communities differed from those produced in the kadi courts or other areas of Ottoman officialdom. When Ali acquired a provincial unit from the center, he appointed representatives or deputies (*vekīl* or *mütesellim*) to act on his behalf. Often these representatives hired local militias who accepted Ali's patronage.[74] Ali's financial representatives, who acted as fiscal officials as well as creditors, circulated within the zone to facilitate complex fiscal transactions and revenue collections with ayans, *kocabaşıs*, and other community headmen.[75] His officials frequently communicated with localities in his zone and received collective petitions from them, such as this one submitted by the village of the Kokosi (part

Figure 3. View of the Southeast Citadel (Its Kalé) at Ioannina, Greece, with the Fethiye Mosque, commissioned by Ali Pasha, ca. 1795. Author's photograph.

of the present-day province of Almyros in Thessaly, Greece) on September 4, 1794:

Your most glorious, sublime, prosperous pasha, our lord, we, your servants, the old and the young subjects of [the village of] Kokosi humbly kneel in front of your highness, and we kiss your noble hand and your footprints and plead to God—we do this night and day—to increase your prosperity/statehood [*devlet*] and to give you a long life, and to grant you the noble desire of your heart as you wish and even more so, amen, so that we, your servants, can have you as a great mountain to lean on whenever we are in need. With our humble letter we come first to kneel in front of you, as is due, and second, to reveal to you, if you are enquiring, about Mahmud Bölükbaşı, whom you have sent to us; we have been well, and our orphanhood has passed peacefully and quietly; and we plead to your highness again to let him stay with us for the next six months with your good command. Moreover, we plead [with you] to let him stay with us because we have known him, we and all the orphans, and he rules for the benefit of the poor, and the poor pray for you day and night. . . . [We request] that you write to him to protect our households. Know [this], too, our efendi, from your messenger who has gone to all the provinces where the bandits are hiding and where this affliction is taking place. That is all, and may your years be many and good, from God, amen—

Your servants and well-wishing elders of Platani, Sourpi, Koffi, and the rest of the villages:

We kneel.[76]

Between the lines there was negotiation between the community and Ali. In return for protection, the community consented to be part of Ali's network and paid tribute to him in an area where bandits and other imperial officers competed with his authority. Ali offered protection to various towns and villages in return for open deals and had members of the community declare loyalty to him. He also concluded contracts with neighboring notables, so that communities under the protection of Ali Pasha were not imprisoned or punished by others.[77] The communities offered money or services to remain under Ali's protection. "In return for his protection against the *tīmār* holders, we cede our village to Ali Pasha as [part of] his lordship [*ağalık*] with [a payment of] two hundred *ġuruş* and [additional] dues [for highway security]," one community stated.[78] While this community offered a deal in exchange for protection from other officeholders or exemptions from certain fees, in other cases, notables of a community asked for revenue from Ali Pasha to integrate their locality into Ali's realm.[79] In these deals we hear statements from the headmen of the communities who declared themselves servants or friends of Ali.[80] Becoming incorporated into Ali's zone, accepting his protection, patronage, and/or friendship, did not end negotiations. The door was always open for new deals, especially concerning payment arrangements and tax collection. In 1803, several villages in Florina in northwestern Macedonia concluded agreements with Ali regarding taxes and dues to be collected. One such reads: "We, the inhabitants of Gornizovo, have agreed with our most sublime vizier *efendi* to give his highness the above portion of the produce of our land." The village also offered him shares of the wheat, barely, rye, oats, and grapes they cultivated.[81] Such agreements between Ali's agents and local headmen illustrate the ongoing transactions and negotiations that took place in his zone.

These deeds and deals should not suggest the absence of coercion and violence. On the contrary, while Ali could coerce those who rejected his patronage, communities might present him with threats to leave their lands, rise against him, or complain about him to the central administration, as in 1802, when the notables of Chebelovo complained of Ali's policy favoring neighboring villages and threatened to break away.[82] Communities discontented with Ali's rule not only had recourse to the Ottoman kadi courts and imperial authorities in neighboring provinces but could directly petition Istanbul.[83]

Ali's allies in Istanbul aided him by providing information both about the market in offices in the imperial city and about grievances that the central government received. In 1797, for example, Stefanos Misios, a member of the Phanariot elite and Ali's close associate and head of his lobby in Istanbul, advised him in a letter on how to retain his position as guardian of the passes in the Pindus Mountains.[84] A rival had made a higher bid for the office, and Stefanos recommended that Ali increase his offer to the Treasury. Stefanos also advised Ali to seek better relations with local communities who paid their taxes to the guardian of the passes, since ongoing complaints provided an excuse for the center to take the office away from Ali and give it to the challenger.[85] Such delicate relations between Ali, local actors, and the central administration pushed Ali to expand his connections with different groups and networks to enhance his control over his zone. To this end Ali became involved in the politics of the Greek Orthodox Patriarchate in Istanbul, lobbying for various appointments in his region.[86]

Tirsinikli İsmail of Ruse: Patronage and Alliance

In addition to acquiring offices and building coalitions with communities and local powerholders, generating trust and concluding patronage-based alliances played an important role in regional expansion. In Danubian Bulgaria, İsmail of Ruse built his zones through collective alliances and patronage relations. İsmail—dubbed Tirsinikli in allusion to his home village, Tirsinik—was ayan of Ruse.[87] In accordance with the office of ayanship, he was not appointed from the center in a top-down fashion and he did not purchase his position and territorial units in a contract deal. Rather, he was elected by the local community to govern the district of Ruse. Beginning in 1800, İsmail consolidated a zone of influence in the region by placing several individuals under his patronage as the ayans of neighboring districts. Many local notables became "friends" of İsmail, among them his close associates Mustafa Bayraktar and İbrahim Pehlivan.

Pehlivan, for instance, came to the region in 1798 to participate in the siege of Vidin, a city under the control of Osman Pazvantoğlu, a rebellious powerholder, and remained there with his men, looking for a patron. According to one account, after some tension between İsmail and Pehlivan, İsmail was informed of Pehlivan's military and organizational abilities. Noting his courage and the way that he amassed men around him, İsmail "fell in love" with Pehlivan's audacity. On İsmail's invitation, they met in Ruse, talked, embraced each other, and became intimate friends, like "father and son." Pehlivan became a member of Tirsinikli's faction or team (*Tirsinikli ṭaḳımı* or *ḥavādārı*).[88] İsmail started gathering local men, like Pehlivan, around him, getting his men elected in different district ayans, and expanded his zone. A report sent by an imperial inspector concerning İsmail's activities in 1804 notes:

> İsmail Agha has captured control of districts in Deliorman and Dobruca regions, which had been under the control of Yılıkoğlu Süleyman. He placed [his men] Pehlivan in Dobruca, Gavur İmam in Hacıoğlu Pazar, Hüseyin Agha in Umur Fakih district, and Uzun Agha in Topçu district as ayans. Then he invited them to Ruse and bestowed robes of honor on them.[89]

Through this network of elected ayans in northeastern Bulgaria, İsmail would defeat Yılıkoğlu, his main regional competitor. However, İsmail's regional consolidation alarmed Istanbul, and he was warned not to interfere in the business of surrounding districts. This prompted İsmail to write to Selim III in self-defense, arguing that he had taken the initiative in eliminating bandits and establishing order in the region; moreover, he said, he did not impose his men on local communities, but sought popular approval for his nominees: "My lord, my struggle with these rival notables is just because I [have tried to have appropriate men] go to the places where they would serve. . . . From among the notable families of Şumnu, el-Hac Mahmudzade el-Hac Mehmed Ağa, who was the choice of the community, was appointed ayan. The former ayan of the Cuma district, el-Hac Ali Ağa, was sent [by me] to oversee the matters of Cuma as before, only with the unanimous will of the people of Cuma."[90] İsmail built his territory, not through acquisition of offices, contracts from the state, or from other primary holders, but through complex political engineering, mobilizing local communities so that they elected his protégés as district administrators. Even after his death in 1806, as an Ottoman report stated, the Tirsinikli faction continued to dominate eastern Bulgaria, now under the leadership of one of his followers, Mustafa Bayraktar.[91]

I have discussed three distinctive models of regional expansion. In Çapanoğlu's case, expansion was accomplished by acquiring additional contracts and offices. In Ali Pasha's case, expansion was carried out through acquiring offices; but the underlying mechanism was to build, alongside the system, a parallel institutionalization of officialdom in vernacular administrative culture. In İsmail's case we see a provincial magnate expand his zone through collective declarations of local communities and by engineering informal alliances and bonds of trust with client local leaders and liege men. In all three cases, however, acquiring additional offices, creating bonds of trust and patronage relations, and gaining the collective backing of communities were strategic. In these zones, local structures such as cultural institutions and networks and the power relations of different groups sometimes complemented and sometimes competed with the imperial institutions. Managed by the power-holders, this interaction between the local and the imperial constituted what Ariel Salzmann calls "government in the vernacular."[92] From the spatial point of view, rather than being territorial divisions of enclosed, exclusive, cohesive authority or sovereignty claims, these regional zones were amorphous, variegated, mosaic-like spaces, composed of overlapping regulatory configurations occupied by multiple actors. Other actors always competed or shared power with provincial grandees in their zones. Competition and/or patronage relations between regional magnates and local heads were common. Multiple officeholders also functioned in these zones, including the kadis representing judiciary authority, tax collectors, and military recruiters, who were independently authorized by the central administration.

These three cases by no means represent all possible regional formations developed under provincial notables in the Ottoman Empire in the late eighteenth and early nineteenth centuries. For a more comprehensive analysis of the spatial configurations of local powerholders, one should add case studies of regional zones organized under large tribal clan networks like Rişvanoğlus in central Anatolia[93] and the Bedirhan clan in Kurdistan;[94] of intertwined commercial and agricultural areas under the patronage of prominent Greek families such as the Benakis and Deligiannis in Peloponnese;[95] of the overlapping zones of the various tribal Circassian and semi-pastoral Nogay networks in the Caucasus; and of charismatic Shiite notables, such as the Shiabis in Lebanon.[96] In these examples, one finds different political mechanisms, spatial characteristics, ethno-religious and economic adherences, and alliances linking localities to form regional influences. In all these different spatial formations, we should also consider overlapping claims and enclaves of local, transregional, imperial, and sometimes interimperial actors.[97]

CAPITAL, WEALTH, AND PORTFOLIO

Comparing the leading provincial magnates shows that they accumulated wealth through a variety of activities in what I call the business of governance. These activities ran the gamut from tax and revenue collection to estate management, and from extending credits to communities to participating in the provisioning of Istanbul and the imperial army. Most grandees, especially those who had strong connections to the Treasury, concluded short-term deals with the state, sometimes through formal auctions, but mostly based on a combination of financial, administrative, and military services. Personal connections and lobbying the Istanbul bureaucracy helped them acquire these short-term contracts. But we also see the situation in reverse. Sometimes the central government tried to impose these services on provincial magnates against their wills. These short-term activities concentrated around three main fields: provisioning the army or the capital (*i'āşe*); buying crops for the state at fixed, below-market prices (*mübāya'a*) from producers, mainly peasants; and confiscating the property of dismissed officeholders or inheritances of deceased individuals whose property was seized by the state (*müşādere*). These activities required tough financial management, as well as scribal expertise in fiscal matters. Provincial magnates therefore employed fiscal experts, some trained in the central bureaucracy.[98]

As briefly mentioned before, we observe a proliferation of agricultural estates, generically called *çiftlik*, under the direct or indirect management of provincial grandees in Macedonia, Bosnia, Epirus, and western and northern Anatolia in the eighteenth century. Çiftliks were agricultural units consisting of arable land and a peasant community living in a village. In most cases, a building complex with a mansion, storehouses, small or large tracts of land for stock raising, and a well were attached to the estate. Beginning in the second half of the century, local magnates came to hold large numbers of such estates granted them by the central administration or other primary holders. Some had hundreds of such agricultural units throughout their regional zones and beyond. By the early nineteenth century, as we saw in chapter 1, hundreds of *tīmār* (agricultural units held as benefices of provincial cavalry) were transformed into *çiftlik*s after being assigned by the New Treasury to provincial notables such as the Karaosmanoğlu of Manisa, Ali Pasha of Ioannina and his sons, the Kösepaşaoğlus of Divriği, İsmail of Ruse, the Çapanoğlus, and Tayyar of Canik.[99] When grandees acquired these *tīmār*s, some built close patronage relations with peasants. They provided seeds, credits, necessary equipment, and animal power, and engaged in sharecropping (*müzāraʿa*) with peasant communities. Some collected revenue or crops in kind as a tax without becoming involved in the cultivation process. In several cases, magnates organized the marketing of crops produced by peasants to foreign and domestic merchants or state commissioners.[100]

Perhaps the biggest challenge in these multifarious tax and revenue collection processes was providing bottom-up revenue extraction. In most cases, contractors and communities were not prepared to pay taxes on schedule. Creditors included not only communal administrators but also governors and contractors as well as subcontractors such as intendants and deputy governors. District kadis recorded these debts and credits in the court registers as deeds. Since actors in these nexuses might not have the cash to remit to representatives at higher levels, when higher office-holders outsourced their jurisdictions to contractors, they carried debt on a regular basis. Consequently, we see a constant debt cycle and vibrant credit activities in the taxation process, from the center to the village level. Magnates involved in such financial relations also extended loans to private individuals in addition to communities, and they constantly sought loans from other individuals. Provincial grandees therefore often had partnerships with moneylenders, who served not only as links to credit markets but also as financial and fiscal advisors.[101]

Some magnates were involved in regional and international commerce. However, in most cases, they did not act as merchants but as facilitators or superintendents of mercantile activities. In doing so, they sometimes established partnerships with peasants and established monopolies over the products of some peasant communities. Buying products below market price, they sold them to foreign merchants. They provided transportation by financing and protecting caravans and markets in their zones. Many of them also provided real estate for merchant communities. The Çapanoğlu zone covered trade routes in central Anatolia and several hub cities, such as Tokat and Kayseri. The Çapanoğlu family actively interacted with merchants operating along the east-west and north-south Anatolian trade routes.[102] İsmail of Serres, who controlled numerous lucrative estates in Macedonia, also had patronage relations with merchants in Salonika, a key port city in the eastern Mediterranean. İsmail and his son Mahmud were major players in cotton production in late eighteenth-century Macedonia through their patronage of estates throughout the region and partnerships with the foreign and Ottoman merchants settled in Salonika.[103]

Similarly, the Karaosmanoğlus controlled the agricultural hinterland of the Aegean port city of İzmir, with which they had strong ties. While commissioning several hubs for merchants in Manisa and İzmir to rejuvenate Aegean trade, the family developed connections with French and Dutch merchants operating in the region. In the eighteenth century, the family settled Greek and Albanian agrarian communities from Greece in various depopulated rural estates in the Manisa region and rejuvenated cotton production there.[104] İsmail of Ruse not only oversaw the provisioning of Istanbul with meat and wheat from the Danubian region with partner families but also helped local producers and merchants participate in regional export markets.[105] Zahir al-'Umar and Ahmad Jazzar transformed Acre into the main hub of Levantine trade and were heavily involved in French and British trade networks in the region. Both clashed with local merchants who challenged their monopoly policy.[106]

Mustafa Bayraktar and Manuk Mirzayan: Debt and Credit

A glance at the wealth of Mustafa Bayraktar, who accumulated immense capital in less than three years, offers a demonstrative case for understanding the nature of wealth formation and the debt/credit nexus. Mustafa Bayraktar was a minor ayan of Razgrad (Hazargrad) in Danubian Bulgaria and a follower of İsmail of Ruse until 1806. After İsmail's death in 1806, the community of Ruse elected Mustafa Bayraktar ayan of Ruse, a more important district on the Danube. He rose rapidly in the imperial hierarchy, first as governor of Silistra province, covering northeastern Bulgaria, then as intendant of Tarnovo, a rich district in central Bulgaria, and finally as commander of the provincial army on the Danubian front during the Ottoman-Russian war.[107]

Mustafa Bayraktar's main partner in his rise was an Armenian moneylender named Manuk Mirzayan. Manuk, who was originally from Ruse, started his career as a merchant in Danubian Bulgaria and Wallachia and a real estate speculator in Bucharest in the late eighteenth century. In 1795, he approached İsmail of Ruse, who desperately needed credit for his expenditures as the ayan of Ruse. In a short time, İsmail and Manuk became close associates. Manuk operated in the silk, wool, cotton, tobacco, honey, and spice trades in the Danube basin under İsmail's protection, with international connections. Partners of his attended fairs as far away as Leipzig, and he built a large inn for merchants visiting Bucharest. He established close connections in Russian markets through Constantinos Ipsilantis, the Phanariot governor of Wallachia. With İsmail, he also acquired contracts for the provisioning of Istanbul with wheat, which enabled him to become an important member of an Armenian financial network in the early nineteenth century. When İsmail of Ruse was killed on his farm in 1806, Manuk and Mustafa Bayraktar agreed to work together. Manuk lobbied through his acquaintances in Istanbul for Bayraktar's appointment as ayan of Ruse. With the loans Manuk provided, Bayraktar was able to make a substantial offer to the state for the inheritance of his late patron, İsmail.[108] After the inheritance was granted to Bayraktar, Manuk went to the region, traveled with this associate, and recovered 400,000 *ġuruş* owed to İsmail.[109] İsmail's confiscated wealth was Mustafa Bayraktar's starting capital.

As we shall see in chapter 4, with the fall of the New Order, Bayraktar became the leader of a party known as the Friends of Ruse and of some provincial magnates. The party initiated a conspiracy and coup in Istanbul, which carried Bayraktar to the post of grand vizier, the highest rank a provincial powerholder had ever reached. In this process, Manuk Bey continued to be Mustafa's main business and political partner. After the coup, Manuk was appointed first as the intendant of Moldavia and then as the chief dragoman, a primary office in Ottoman foreign affairs. Bayraktar's brief grand viziership ended a couple of months later, in mid-November 1808, when he was killed in a janissary-led popular riot. Manuk fled to lands controlled by the Russian Empire with considerable cash. Later, he continued his career as a businessmen and diplomat in the Russian context. After Bayraktar's death, the imperial Treasury confiscated his property, selling some of his immovable properties in the market. Other properties were transferred to the Treasury or to various officeholders. Fiscal bureaucrats prepared a detailed record of his inheritance in 1809.[110] According to these accounts, Bayraktar had considerable wealth in kind, cash, and receivables. He also possessed substantial debt. Here is a summary of his estate:

- Provisions, which were transferred to the new grand vizier: 18,152.5 *ġuruş*
- Slaves and concubines in his household: 38,775 *ġuruş*
- Personal clothes: 3,584 *ġuruş*
- Armor and military equipment used in his private retinue: 12,249 *ġuruş*
- Horses and livestock: 32,827 *ġuruş*
- Saddles and other horse supplies: 67,815 *ġuruş*
- House supplies from his mansions: 2,470.5 *ġuruş*
- Jewelry: 25,049 *ġuruş*
- Miscellaneous: 5,152.5 *ġuruş*
- Receivables: 1,391,741.1 *ġuruş*
- Debts: 908,048 *ġuruş*

Excluding his debt, Bayraktar's receivables from communities and individuals constituted more than 87 percent of his total wealth. However, 56.8 percent of his wealth was tied up in debt. Analyzing his receivables and debt illustrates a debt-credit nexus. He had made loans to various merchants and military and administrative officeholders. According to the inheritance register, he had receivables from various individuals and communities. Some of these were authorities or contractors; others were ayans who represented their communities. Some had obtained credit from Bayraktar for their businesses. The ayans of Balchik, Topçu, and Shumen, the deputy governor of Silistra, and the customs director of Ruse were all indebted to Bayraktar. All operated in Bayraktar's regional zone and were supposed to collect revenues from their units or constituent communities and deliver Bayraktar's share. Meanwhile, the communities of Razgrad, Kazanlak (Kızanlık), Tarnovo, and Svishtov (Ziştovi) were indebted to Bayraktar as collective entities, not as individual representatives. Bayraktar had considerable debts (but still less than his receivables) to various individuals, including Armenian moneylenders and Greek, Armenian, and Muslim merchants. Some were regional financiers; others operated transregionally in Ottoman markets from Bulgaria to Egypt. Bayraktar had received credits from these moneylenders and provisioning from merchants for his household and militia.

Portfolio Entrepreneurs

How should we conceptualize the multifaceted "business" enterprises of the provincial magnates? Like the *zamīndār*s of seventeenth-century Mughal India, who developed operational expertise in administrative, fiscal, and commercial fields as semi-public and semi-private entrepreneurs,[111] Ottoman provincial magnates allocated their investments and managerial operations to various fields, from taxation to loan extension, confiscation to provisioning, and estate management to facilitating trade. In their diverse portfolios, the business of governance and public finance (credits extended to other contractors, officeholders, and communities) was the main sector in which they accumulated wealth. In this respect it would not be wrong to define provincial grandees as entrepreneurial contractors with large portfolios in the business of governance who did deals through bids, negotiations, bargains, and offers in a volatile imperial sector. In the business of governance, however, magnates also took risks. They could lose invested capital, for instance, without collecting more revenue from a unit under their jurisdiction than they had paid the state to acquire it. They had a considerable chance of loss when extending loans to a community or acquiring a contract to organize the provisioning of the imperial army, especially in time of war and instability.

VIOLENCE, DISSENT, AND SEPARATISM

In the Ottoman provincial order, administration and violence were two sides of the same coin. In the late eighteenth and early nineteenth centuries, in different parts of the Ottoman Empire, violence, insecurity, and fear were parts of everyday life. Wars with Russia, Austria, Britain, and France profoundly influenced the social and political landscape. But it was not only the wars that fostered military activity and violence. The empire was transformed into a space of overlapping battlegrounds by the rising ferocity of irregular troops known as *kırcalı*s or *dağlı*s who failed to find patrons in the Balkans; the unresolved conflict between the janissaries and the Serbian notables in Belgrade; Bosnian notables known as *kapudan*s, who increasingly employed bands of peasants; unruly nomadic groups in southern Anatolia who resisted being settled; the Wahhabis in Arabia, a religious cult that developed into a revolutionary movement; and various unruly provincial grandees who preferred to negotiate with the empire by rebellion rather than by means of offers and counteroffers.[112] The increasing violence made vaguer the boundaries between legal and outlaw, negotiation and insurgence, loyal and rebel. Under these conditions, an administrative entrepreneur or officeholder might need to command armed bands, such as a militia or even an army, which called for close acquaintance with recruitment strategies and military practice. Sometimes, magnates' military organizations produced their own codes of honor, family banners, regional styles, and uniform clothing. It was common for magnates' military detachments to be trained by captains, Ottoman or foreign, hired from a growing international pool of military experts during the revolutionary and Napoleonic wars.

In general, magnates drew military power from four different sources. The first consisted of existing Ottoman forces in the provinces connected to the central government, such as janissary units in the towns and dispersed cavalry units in the countryside. Communities in the zones of the magnates were the second. Conscription activities expanded when Selim III unleashed the New Order program, beginning in the 1790s.[113] The Çapanoğlus and the Karaosmanoğlus mediated regional conscription campaigns under some grandees, and these efforts had the potential to trigger popular unrest.[114] The third source consisted of mercenaries and gangs. In wartime, provincial communities were regularly asked to form detachments or hire troops, equip them with firearms, and send these forces into battle. Groups fleeing battles that scattered in the provinces organized as brigands, known as *levend*s, under charismatic leaders, called *ṣāḥib-i cumhūr* and *ser-cemīyet* (leader of a group or collectivity) in Ottoman documents. As a result of the growing market for freelance mercenaries, some bandit leaders became power entrepreneurs, looking for patrons or communities to hire them.[115] The fourth way to build an armed force in a regional zone was through client magnates who acted with the patron magnate, either under his supervision (*māʿiyyet*) or in an alliance (*ittifāk*). Regional webs helped magnates mobilize thousands of armed groups under the command of client grandees, without maintaining troops.[116]

Tayyar of Canik, 1785–1807

From among the many examples of armed-force building in the Ottoman Empire, let me focus on the notable Canikli family of northern Anatolia, mentioned above in connection with the Çapanoğlus.[117] The Canikli house, which was founded by one of the leading generals of the Ottoman imperial army during the Ottoman-Russian war of 1768–74, the renowned Canikli Ali Pasha (1720–85), had controlled the governorship of Trabzon and the surrounding regions since 1774. The family's competition with the Çapanoğlus for regional leadership caused a major crisis in 1802, when Tayyar began collecting military forces from several settlements and built a network in northeastern Anatolia against the Çapanoğlus and Selim III's New Order.[118] Before he was again declared an outlaw, the central administration asked Hüseyin of the Cihanoğlus, the intendant of the neighboring town of Gümüşhane, to send a detailed report about Tayyar, the sources of his power, and whether he had acquired the support of notables and communities in the region. In his report, Hüseyin reviewed Tayyar's regional power base:

Tayyar's soldiers were basically collected from districts in the region. In other words, he has very few Ottoman soldiers ['*Osmānlı ʿaskeri*]. He had some affiliates, such as Denebaş, Yakmazoğlu, Cihhetoğlu, and Kadı Çırağı, and they have settled in some districts like ayans. In total, he must have one to two thousand cavalry [under his direct command]. Otherwise, his troops are composed of infantry collected from the districts. If necessary, he summoned them under the command of other powerholders [who acted with him]. When he says come to where I am, troops from the communities, peasants, and laborers gathered around him. However, their obedience to him depends on their fear. I think that if they heard that the Exalted State had issued an order against him, they might take sides against Tayyar. They would not want their regions to be wiped out by the state, and in fact they were seeking peace. Everyone knows that no one can go against the state. However, Tayyar Pasha controls them with tricks and artifice. . . . Tayyar is in fact a capricious man and not one of those who are inclined to fight. The person who commands his soldiers is his steward, Lütfullah Agha. His cousin Hasan Bey is a very skillful and courageous man. Tayyar takes him in his entourage when he goes into battle. In fact, it is Hasan Bey who seduced Tayyar Pasha [into such acts].[119]

Tayyar provides an example of how a provincial powerholder built a military force from local resources against the military reforms of the Ottoman central government and fashioned his rebellion with larger ideological claims. The military reforms asked provincial magnates to recruit soldiers from the communities. Tayyar militarized their regional zones with local militias and former janissaries who were at odds with the New Order. Many influential individuals, such as the mufti of Tokat, were reported to be followers (*ṭarafdār*) of Tayyar.[120] When Selim declared Tayyar an outlaw, the central government warned local notables in the region not to join him and declared that amnesty for Tayyar would no longer be possible.[121] Tayyar responded by banning peasants in his zone of influence from being recruited by the New Army. His men defied agents dispatched from Istanbul.[122] Tayyar sent papers to local communities asking them to resist recruitment to the New Army and not to pay taxes to the new Treasury.[123] He sent envoys to the Çıldıroğlus and other grandees in eastern Anatolia and offered alliances against the New Order and the Çapanoğlus.[124] Meanwhile, several communities rose up, expelled governors sent from the center to their towns, and declared loyalty to Tayyar.[125]

In the fall of 1806, when Tayyar fled to the Russian Empire for a second time,[126] Selim III fell following the janissary coup in Istanbul. In early 1807, during the armistice, the Russian emperor, Alexander I, asked the Ottoman state to pardon Tayyar.[127] After the fall of Selim III and the New Order, he was pardoned. The new sultan, Mustafa IV, invited Tayyar to Istanbul and offered him the position of deputy grand vizier in the restoration government. This development troubled the Çapanoğlus, since the consolidation of Tayyar's power in Istanbul would threaten their influence in Anatolia. Süleyman, the leader of the Çapanoğlu family, declared that as long as Tayyar was alive, the notable Anatolian families would not cross the straits to the Balkans to join the imperial army.[128] In the summer of 1808, Tayyar was dismissed and stripped of his rank after controversy with leaders of the janissary coup in Istanbul. He went to Rumelia and joined Mustafa Bayraktar, but was later killed in a conspiracy.[129]

Tayyar's career was extraordinary, from his role as a member of a notable family in the Anatolian Black Sea region to his political dissent from Selim III and the New Order, and from his political refugee status in Russia to his rise to deputy grand vizier of the restoration government in Istanbul. His career illustrates the range of possibilities during this turbulent period for provincial actors who had the capacity to mobilize military resources in their regions and play a role on an imperial and even interimperial scale. As Karen Barkey illustrates, in the early modern Ottoman Empire, the boundaries between legal and illegal, lawful and unlawful, were permeable.[130] In fact, rebellion could serve as a form of negotiation for a higher office, greater glory, and wealth. In the stormy period between 1770 and 1820, several provincial magnates, like Tayyar, were on the border between legality and illegality, gratification and rebellion, glory and disgrace. Perhaps the best example of a transition from rebel to vizier was Pazvantoğlu of Vidin.

Osman Pazvantoğlu: Rebellion, Separatism, and Amnesty

Osman Pazvantoğlu started his career as a janissary chief in Vidin, a strategic city on the Empire's Danubian Bulgarian western front.[131] From the early 1790s on, Pazvantoğlu consolidated his leadership in the region. His involvement on behalf of his janissary comrades during the conflict between Serbian notables and Belgrade janissaries created tensions between him and the New Order. "The center will abolish the janissaries of Vidin. My effort is for you [for your protection]," Pazvantoğlu declared to the janissaries in the region. The center considered this behavior disobedience, and Gürcü Osman Pasha, an imperial commander, attacked Vidin, but Pazvantoğlu managed to resist the assault. Istanbul pardoned him through the mediation of the janissary elders in Istanbul, who became guarantors (*kefil*) for their comrade. In return for his compliance, Selim III appointed Pazvantoğlu intendant (*muḥaṣṣıl*) of Vidin.[132]

But Pazvantoğlu was soon declared an outlaw once again after he implied that he was not satisfied with this offer, that he wanted the governorship and would continue to support the rebel janissaries of Belgrade. While he gathered local mercenary leaders around him, the center tried to mobilize major grandees in the Balkans who were known to be loyal to the New Order. In 1798, a massive siege of Vidin, under the command of Grand Admiral Küçük Hüseyin Pasha, in which Ali Pasha of Ioannina participated, together with forces sent by the Karaosmanoğlus and the Çapanoğlus, failed. This victory gave Pazvantoğlu a reputation throughout the empire and beyond as one of the main challengers of Selim III's New Order. In June 1798, the administration closed several coffeehouses in Istanbul and elsewhere in which stories about Pazvantoğlu circulated.[133] According to an Austrian diplomat, peasant communities in the Balkans saw him as their liberator from the new military and fiscal measures.[134] Regional storytellers lauded him in popular epics written in Bulgarian as a hero who could not beaten by the empire.[135] Pressed by the New Orderists, however, the janissary chiefs in Istanbul withdrew their support for Pazvantoğlu while he was expanding his zone of influence and becoming a regional leader, declaring, "this wicked man shames the janissaries . . . we accept neither him nor those who join him."[136]

En route to Istanbul, the French consul general at Ioannina, F.-C. Pouqueville, recorded a song sung by a "young Turkish sailor" in which Pazvantoğlu proclaims himself "the dog of the Grand Signor" (i.e., the sultan), who barks "only at his ministers."[137] As in the song, Pazvantoğlu sent messages that he was not a rebel but a loyal servant of the sultan and the sultan's mother (who held important estates in the region). He was a victim of ill-intentioned New Orderists, he argued, who had prevented him from getting what he merited. In 1799, an emissary, Hüseyin Agha, was sent to Vidin to settle the case with Pazvantoğlu. In the emissary's report we hear Pazvantoğlu's voice:

My request and wish from my masters [in Istanbul] is only to be decorated with the rank of vizierate [the highest-ranking governorship]. [. . .] [If I am made vizier,] I will serve with full loyalty and enthusiasm and demonstrate my obedience. If my masters illuminate me with the rank of vizierate, let them order me to go against the mountaineer brigands. Or let them order me to go to Greece for the imperial campaign. I shall entrust the city of Vidin to a shrewd man and proudly go to that place in accordance with the order. With the help of God, I shall perform my service rightfully and with loyalty. If my wish cannot be granted within a few months, to satisfy my poor heart, for the present, I ask [at least] to be raised to the rank of head of the gatemen of the imperial abode and deputy governor of Vidin.[138]

Pazvantoğlu thought that he deserved to be the only authority in Vidin, where he had established political and military control. He offered the state a deal. Hüseyin Agha, in his negotiations with Pazvantoğlu, voiced the state's position:

The Exalted State would not grant you horsetails [i.e., a governorship or viziership] just like that. Unless you pursued the path [of that career] and deserved it, you would not acquire it. Why not acquire the rank of chief of the gatemen, and later, if the state grants you a governorship, accept it? After a time of service, you might have the right to assume this noble status. Otherwise, the granting of a vizierate to the chief of a local militia has never been known to happen, or [even] been suggested.[139]

In April 1799, however, when the imperial Divan debated Pazvantoğlu's request, some members argued that he could be granted the vizierate.[140] Bonaparte had just occupied Egypt, and the Ottoman administration was desperate to end the disturbance in Vidin. Selim III decided to give Pazvantoğlu what he wanted, granting him the vizierate, appointing him military governor of Vidin, and giving him the subprovince of Niğbolu (Nikopolis) as a source of revenue as well.[141]

But this was not the end of the story. From that point on, Pazvantoğlu began playing another game, this time an interimperial one, soon becoming an important actor in Napoleonic Europe in alliance with Mehmed

Cengiz Geray, a member of the Geray dynasty. Cengiz Geray was a different kind of powerholder. He was not an upstart like Pazvantoğlu, but a member of the most prestigious house in the Ottoman Empire after that of Osman, thanks to his Chingisid ancestry.[142] When Mehmed Cengiz Geray was declared an outlaw by the center following a controversy about the status of his estate, like many others, he fled to Russia and spent several years in Moscow as a political refugee. Upon his return, Pazvantoğlu invited him to Vidin. Pazvantoğlu and Geray developed an ambitious plan and sent it to the French Republic and Bonaparte, who had just become first council. Pazvantoğlu proposed helping the French partition the Ottoman Empire. If France attacked the empire, Pazvantoğlu would cooperate on the condition that the French government pledged to grant him and Cengiz Geray a province where they could rule in peace under the protection of French law. If the French government chose to preserve the Ottoman Empire as it was, Pazvantoğlu promised to cease all hostilities against the Ottoman state, provided the French government requested that it pardon him. Pazvantoğlu gave his word to be faithful to the French Republic and serve its aims, as long as these did not conflict with Islam.[143]

This episode illustrates the ambitions of Ottoman regional magnates in the age of revolutions. By entering into partnership with Geray, with his strong trans-Ottoman connections, Pazvantoğlu hoped to participate in the remaking of Eurasia. He united his organizational, economic, and military might with Geray's domestic and international prestige, or what Devin DeWeese has called "Chinggisid charisma."[144] In this episode, where we see Napoleon and Genghis Khan in the same symbolic context, it becomes evident how the politics of Ottoman notables overlapped with the radicalism of the age of revolutions. When Pazvantoğlu's proposal reached Paris, the French Republic and the Ottoman Empire were about to conclude a peace treaty. But Pazvantoğlu also asked the French to help obtain amnesty from the sultan if the French opted to make peace with the Ottoman Empire. Pazvantoğlu was pardoned and confirmed as governor of Vidin, again with high rank.

When Pazvantoğlu died in 1805, in the absence of hereditary office, a fresh crisis arose over who would rule in Vidin. The central administration considered appointing another governor from the imperial elite or placing Pazvantoğlu's son Ali in his father's seat, although he was only thirteen years old. The notables of Vidin gathered, sealed the chests containing Pazvantoğlu's coins and papers, and wrote a collective petition to the Divan, asking the state to entrust the affairs of Vidin to Ali, under the guardianship of Molla İdris, Pazvantoğlu's old comrade and treasurer.[145] This petition was not, however, accepted by some of Pazvantoğlu's followers, who rejected İdris. Despite the disagreement, successful lobbying by the İdris party persuaded the Divan to appoint İdris governor of Vidin. İdris became İdris Pasha. Pazvantoğlu's patrimony (including his debts and receivables) was transferred to İdris, who married Pazvantoğlu's widow. Ali, Pazvantoğlu's son, escaped the city, went to Istanbul, and started a new life under the protection of some of Pazvantoğlu's friends. This was the end of Pazvantoğlu rule in Vidin and the start of the era of İdris of Vidin.[146]

As we have seen, the Ottoman central government did not exercise a monopoly over governance or organized violence. It did not have a monopoly over diplomacy either. There had often been regional actors in the Ottoman Empire who bypassed the central administration, established diplomatic relations with the outside world, and pursued their own foreign policies. Magnates whose regional zones were close to borders or in coastal areas developed close ties to broader regions outside the Ottoman territories. They both hosted foreign diplomatic missions, merchants, moneylenders, and military experts and sent emissaries, brokers, and spies to various centers, including some capitals of foreign powers. Some found safe haven through trans-Ottoman connections and became political refugees. In some cases, these magnates obtained pardons requested and mediated by foreign rulers.[147]

The most fascinating episodes occurred when some regional power-holders participated in grand negotiations and alliances with the great powers in the stormy diplomacy of the revolutionary and Napoleonic years. Between 1801 and 1807, Ali Pasha of Ioannina opened diplomatic relations with the French and British over the Ionian Islands.[148] Ali's active involvement in Adriatic diplomacy and achievements in Ottoman Greece and Albania increased his reputation in European circles and even in popular culture, where the orientalist fantasy of an exotic Muslim "despot" ruling the lands of ancient Greek civilization took hold. Ali, who was aware of this fabricated depiction, deliberately used this image in his diplomatic missions.[149] When Mustafa Bayraktar was the commander of the Danubian front in the Ottoman-Russian war of 1806–8, he offered Tsar Alexander an alliance against Napoleon and promised him an Ottoman army.[150] His secret diplomacy with Russia during the Ottoman-Russian war concluded in a cease-fire and helped him initiate his coup in Istanbul to reinstate the New Order. These episodes illustrate that some regional magnates acted as autonomous political actors in European politics. They negotiated in the context of the new realities of the empire, of their regional settings, and of the world. When old regimes collapsed and new grand designs appeared, they took the stage in the international arena, bringing with them their own agendas, calculations, and strategies.

DEATH, CONFISCATION, AND WEALTH TRANSFER

What happened when Ottoman regional magnates died? As we saw in chapter 1, the Ottoman system did not grant life-term or hereditary offices and contracts. However, the lack of institutional security went beyond that. It did not guarantee the property or the lives of the holders of offices or contracts themselves. According to conventions that had endured since the reforms of Mehmed II (r. 1451–81), members of the administrative and military elite were considered slavish servants (*kuls*) of and were devoid of private rights vis-à-vis the sultan. According to this convention, the wealth accumulated in the hands of these men was gained from the benefices granted by the sultan for their service to his state. Therefore this wealth belonged to the state or public (*mīrī*). After the demise of a *kul*, his patrimony could be seized by the state or granted to another servant (including the heirs of the deceased) in return for another service or deal. Wealth could also be seized during the life of the officeholder, if his office was cancelled for some reason. The central administration often organized public auctions to liquidate the confiscated movable properties of officeholders. Debts and receivables were handled as well. The public authority collected the receivables and was liable to pay the debts of the person whose wealth was confiscated. The state could assign humble annuities to the male or female heirs of officeholders whose wealth was seized. The Ottomans called this confiscation process *müṣādere* or *mīrīce/mīrī içün żabṭ*, that is seizure for/by the public authority. More controversially, moreover, the sultan could execute an officeholder with or without judicial process for his alleged wrongdoings, failures, or injustices committed. Most of the time, a generic legal opinion (*fetvā*) from the grand mufti would provide adequate legal and religious legitimization. In Ottoman terminology, such executions were known as *siyāseten ḳatl*, which could be translated as political or sultanic executions. Hundreds of high-ranking officeholders, from grand viziers to provincial governors, and many more lower-ranking bureaucrats, tax collectors, and members of the janissary and cavalry armies were executed and their wealth sequestered by the Ottoman state.[151]

Imperial executions and confiscations were conventions that only applied to servants of the sultan and the state, that is to say, to the officeholding and administrative and military elites. Members of the learned hierarchy (ulema) and civilian subjects were traditionally exempted from such executions and confiscations. These conventions represented the symbolic absolute power of the sultanic authority over members of the Ottoman state, rather than rules to be applied on every occasion. Often the central administration used this prerogative as an instrument for negotiating with wealthy officeholders. The threat of execution and confiscation boosted the central influence over agents of the state. Executions were more common in times of political crisis, civil strife, and military defeat. We see an upsurge in confiscations during fiscal crises and fewer confiscations as the state's revenues grew. Between 1770 and 1820, as a result of fiscal and political crisis, these practices intensified. By the end of the eighteenth century, according to a new formulation, anyone who accumulated wealth as a result of public matters (*serveti beytü'l-māldan olmağla*), regardless of the nature of the office or contract, qualified for imperial seizure. The administration asked officeholders and notables to report affluent people (*eshāb-ı servet ve yesār*) who had passed away for consideration of seizure.[152] This new configuration increased the risks for provincial actors operating in the administrative and fiscal sectors, while at the same time offering new opportunities.[153]

Although seizure of provincial wealth was a great source of income for the Treasury, it was difficult, costly, and even risky to confiscate a local powerholder's property, even after his death. Since these individuals were profoundly entrenched in their local worlds, local groups and the households of deceased persons often resisted confiscation.[154] Sometimes, resistance took the form of skirmishes between provincial forces and imperial agents. In different cases, the family members buried cash and valuables in different spots to hide them from the authorities.[155] The central administration often lacked sufficient information about the deceased person's debts and receivables.[156] Settlement processes for debts and receivables could take months or years and were not only long and complicated but also costly. Some individuals indebted to the deceased simply disappeared. Others showed up in court with fabricated documents alleging that they had claims on the inheritance. In such cases, the center preferred to avoid tension and complications and made a transfer to one of the deceased's heirs if the deceased's family was willing to "buy" the inheritance from the state by offering quid pro quo such as new services.[157] These offers to the state as compensation were a type of inheritance tax. Such deals enabled several families to maintain their wealth and status for generations, while allowing the Ottoman administration to avoid the hassle of the confiscation process.

However, there was always a possibility that third parties would offer a better option for seizing property in the name of the state. Magnates who acted as confiscation entrepreneurs developed expertise concerning confiscations and information techniques. They employed fiscal experts who were able to prepare intricate paperwork for complex accounting settlements. Some, like the central administration, sent spies and agents to learn about elderly or wealthy individuals who might soon pass away, so that they could propose that the state confiscate their property. Others used this confiscation right as a political strategy to suppress or eliminate competing families. The central administration preferred to delegate confiscation rights to these individuals and avoid involvement in local conflicts, minimizing the cost and receiving compensation in advance. Through these delegations, the state also avoided the risk of dealing with the inheritance, particularly in cases when the deceased had more debts than receivables. In fact, for confiscation entrepreneurs to acquire confiscation rights was also to engage in risk analysis. Before confiscation, it was not easy to anticipate the particular amount that would be seized and the value of receivables and debt in this person's budget. Only after settlement in court where debtors, creditors, and other parties were present did the details of the accounts become clear. In any case, for the central administration, transferring such wealth to a third party by granting him the right of confiscation in return for a payment (*muḥallefāt bedeli*) was a strategy to maintain order in the provinces by minimizing the risk and transaction cost. As a result of this policy, intricate negotiations took place between the state and individuals who made offers for the wealth of deceased persons.[158]

The Confiscation of Jazzar Ahmad Pasha's Inheritance

One of the most contentious confiscation processes during this period began in 1804, following the death of Jazzar Ahmad Pasha, who had been governor of Sidon for more than twenty years.[159] Jazzar's immense patrimony was spread from Damascus to Beirut and from Jerusalem to Gaza. Numerous individuals and communities were involved in the inheritance settlement, because Jazzar held hundreds of revenue units in his zone. He had also been involved in debt and credit relations with many communities and individuals during his long tenure. The central authority had showed an interest in Jazzar's immense wealth prior to his death. In fact, in 1796, rumors about his health created anxiety in Istanbul and among other magnates in the region who were interested in seizing his wealth on behalf of the sultan. When Jazzar appeared, declaring that he had not died, the central administration stopped the investigation into his wealth. Jazzar was well acquainted with the confiscation process. He was actively involved in seizing the inheritances of three major figures: Zahir al-Umar of Galilee, Ali al-Kabir of Egypt, and Muhammad al-'Azm of Damascus. Jazzar's contract as confiscator had helped enrich him.

When Jazzar died in 1804, one of his close associates, Süleyman, was appointed governor of Sidon. However, although the central administration had earlier assigned Pazvantoğlu's patrimony to Molla İdris, along with his office; when the latter replaced him, it was unwilling either to transfer Jazzar's patrimony, in toto or partially, to Süleyman. The fiscal administration wanted to transfer the entire inheritance to the imperial treasury. Ragıb of Damascus, a fiscal bureaucrat, was chosen as an expert to settle the inheritance. For months, Ragıb examined documents, consulted Jazzar's moneylenders, and met individuals and communities who were debtors or creditors. Eventually, Ragıb sent a detailed report to Istanbul. But when the settlement process began, the state was unable to seize the receivables. The debtors were not cooperating. Several individuals came to the courts claiming they had already paid their debts to Jazzar during his lifetime. Officers sent by the central administration did not have adequate information about local transactions or the capacity to settle intricate debt and receivable claims.[160]

Ragıb's mission to confiscate Jazzar's immense wealth was a legendary episode. According to a popular story circulating in Istanbul in those days, after he was appointed as a confiscator, he tried to find Jazzar's buried treasures with magic and talismans. He also brought tens of experienced sappers and dredgers from Istanbul to Palestine. However, the result was disappointing. Ragıb failed to uncover the silver and gold coins supposedly buried in various sites in Acre and Sidon. Invoking the notorious stereotype of North Africans' unsuccessful treasure-hunting, people ridiculed him after he failed to unearth Jazzar's fabled trove by referring to him as Ragıb al-Maghribi [i.e., the North African] *defîne-güşâ* [treasure hunter] instead of Ragıb al-Shami the Damascene.[161]

One problem was that Süleyman and Ragıb disagreed over the items listed in the inheritance. As the new governor of Sidon and a former henchman of Jazzar's, Süleyman still controlled most of his master's wealth. Ragıb, however, intended to maximize the items he could substantiate, not only because this would increase his commission but also because he had been ordered to do so. Eventually, the center was able to confiscate only a small portion of the list prepared by Ragıb. Meanwhile, several individuals showed up in Acre and Istanbul for their receivables from the inheritance. Not only did the locals ask for their receivables, but the British merchant Richard George claimed that he had loaned Jazzar a substantial amount for the construction of the fortress of Acre during the French attack. George submitted deeds. Ottoman subjects, foreign merchants, and moneylenders also lined up before the Ottoman fiscal administration with different claims over the inheritance.[162] Meanwhile, constant rumors about Jazzar's uncovered wealth reached Istanbul, and the Treasury sent new experts to prepare new reports. Endless investigations added little to the amounts already secured.[163]

The confiscation of Jazzar Pasha's inheritance was an unsuccessful process on the part of the center, which was able to secure only a little of his reported wealth. However, since the bequest was confiscated by the state, the Treasury was liable to pay debts to claimants who could prove what they were owed. The fiscal bureaucracy was rigorous in substantiating debt to private individuals. The Treasury paid these debts in installments for several decades. We do not know what happened to Jazzar's treasures. Very likely, the reports of it were misleading. Or perhaps the cash, jewelry, military equipment, and even a number of ships remained in the hands of Süleyman, Jazzar's successor.

The Ottoman administration's determination to confiscate the patrimony of deceased holders of offices and contracts, as well as competition among notables to seize the wealth of their peers, contributed to the volatility of the Ottoman imperial sector. The assumption that the wealth of the holders of offices and contracts derived from their public (*mīrī*) service, and that the Treasury therefore had the right to confiscate their possessions after they died, endured until 1839. This pushed many families to develop strategies to negotiate the preservation of their wealth and status with the central administration. Nevertheless, after each death of a rich person, the heirs of the deceased and the authorities started negotiations, often with the involvement of third parties. This insecurity, on the other hand, offered new possibilities for others. Like the transfer of offices and contracts, the transfer of wealth was a significant component of the Ottoman business of governance. A rich man's death was the beginning of a new life for someone else.

CONCLUSION: THE ORDER OF NOTABLES

I have analyzed different aspects and illustrated episodes of how some notable individuals and families in the provinces operated in the Ottoman Empire. I argue that as a result of military, administrative, and fiscal transformations throughout the eighteenth century, provincial strongmen and their families who were not part of the imperial establishment participated in governance, becoming essential components of the imperial apparatus. By the late eighteenth century, the Ottoman state and imperial elites were becoming dependent on the collaboration of these provincials in taxation, policing, management of public services, and drafting soldiers. They were incorporated into the Ottoman state by acquiring offices to collect taxes, managing public deeds, providing order and security, and assembling regional militias made up of local men. Some of these offices were short-term, some life-term, and others included limited rights to collect taxes. Some came with a package of full jurisdiction, a wide range of revenues, and immunity from the intervention of other officeholders. Governorships (and sometimes deputy governorships) and life-term contracts came directly from the central administration, by appointment or contract. Several ancillary offices were delegated by absentee primary holders, and some administrative positions at the district level were filled by popular consent through nomination and elections in local communities that were approved by the state.

With these diverse offices, contracts and deals, the notables not only consolidated power bases in the localities; they also accumulated wealth from revenue they extracted from urban and rural units under their jurisdiction. Many were creditors to local communities and private individuals and were actively involved in estate management and commercial agriculture. The wealth they accumulated enabled them to expand their governmental portfolios in the business of governance and commission palatial residential complexes, fortresses, and public works in their localities. More powerful notables expanded their authority beyond their localities and created regional zones of influence. In these regional zones, they nurtured patron-client relations, partnerships, and alliances with subordinate notables, communities, and networks. The most powerful ones established parallel bureaucratic machinery, with scribal bureaus specializing in vernacular languages, as well as sizable regional armies through recruitment and alliances with local mercenaries.

In fact, some of the patterns that we have discussed in this chapter had been encountered before the eighteenth century. In the fifteenth century, in the episode of the regional rebellion of Skander Beg (1443–68) in Albania, we see an early example of a regional noble with an aristocratic pedigree (in this regard very different from the notables of the later period) who was first coopted by the Ottoman regime, then rebelled, and subsequently negotiated with the Ottoman Empire, as well as with other powers, including the papacy.[164] Albanian nationalists would later see Skander Beg as a national hero who rose against Ottoman rule, like Ali of Ioannia.[165] In the late fifteenth and seventeenth centuries, we see many episodes of unruly and rebellious powerholders and governors who tended to establish regional bases and sometimes were coopted by, sometimes negotiated with, and sometimes fought against the central administration of the Ottoman Empire, such as the Canbolatzades of Kilis, today in southeastern Turkey, or the Ma'ns of Chouf, today in Lebanon.[166] In many ways, the order of notables was deeply entrenched in the Ottoman imperial system from the beginning, as in many of other imperial systems. However, what happened in the eighteenth century was not only a proliferation of some old, but mostly new, regional notables in almost every corner of the empire, but also propagation of various new formal and informal institutions, examined above, which enabled them to be systematic parts or partners of Ottoman governance, without whom the empire would have become ungovernable.

Despite that, however, the Ottoman imperial sector did not provide them with any institutional guarantees. In principle, the Ottoman order did not recognize any hereditary rights to offices. The sultan could dismiss any officeholder and revoke any contract. Even life-term contracts could be cancelled if a third party made the state a more favorable offer. Furthermore, according to old imperial conventions, after the death of a powerholder, the state could confiscate the wealth he had accumulated. In extreme cases, the sultan might execute such a person without judicial process. Under this volatile institutional order, without formal guarantees of office, wealth, and life, magnates and the state were constantly engaged in negotiations. The central administration sought to reward regional powerholders as servants who rendered it services and loyalty, but it also developed strategies to prevent them from gaining too much power in their local bases, which might challenge the central government, by tacitly or implicitly threatening them with elimination. In return, magnates developed strategies to acquire offices, retain them, expand them, and transfer power and wealth consolidated in the business of governance to the next generation. The state formally or informally offered deals, and magnates constantly negotiated these offers, accepting or rejecting them, or extended counteroffers. After the death of a magnates, negotiations started anew. These negotiations were open to third parties, who interfered with the bids. In severe cases, negotiations included threats from the state and rebellions by magnates. In this volatile imperial sector the provincial powerholders acted as neither hereditary nobility nor bureaucrats, but as fiscal, military, and political entrepreneurs and active risk takers.

The central administration and provincial powerholders, however, did not constitute monolithic blocks. There were always competing coalitions within the central state and the provinces. These divisions also fostered alliances between certain factions in the center and in the provinces. Communities often participated with collective petitions that supported or protested against the magnates or the central government. At the higher levels, foreign actors interfered in the Ottoman political theater, explicitly or implicitly collaborating with magnates and factions in the center. These activities intensified in the late eighteenth and early nineteenth centuries when the Ottoman center and various provinces were polarized between the New Order—with its agenda of fiscal and military reform—and public opposition led by the janissaries. This was also a period of war and shifting coalitions between the Ottoman Empire and Russia, Austria, France, and England.

Competition, struggle, and insecurity were the main characteristics of the Ottoman order, but so were collaboration and the process of forging alliances and trust. What were the possibilities and limits for a broader, transregional elite alliance, bridging various actors from the center and the provinces, to foster a more stable order? Douglass C. North et al. argue that when competing elites agreed that it was in their collective interest not to compete but to collaborate, they could create incentives to establish coalitions and recognize each other's privileges, including statuses and property rights.[167] Such a coalition would create access to resources for elites and political and institutional stability. For various reasons, however, such a coalition to transform the imperial order was difficult to achieve in the Ottoman Empire in the late eighteenth and early nineteenth centuries.

Firstly, the Ottoman system did not provide institutions, such as diets or assemblies, for magnates to communicate and deliberate with one another, and in the vast geography of the empire, negotiations between regional grandees and the central administration took place mostly on a regional scale, not across the empire. There was no empirewide deliberation or negotiation platform for the notables. Simply put, the large geography of the empire did not allow for such an empirewide mechanism. Secondly, this volatile system, while challenging established magnates seeking to hang on to their status and wealth, provided new opportunities for upstarts. Especially during the late eighteenth and early nineteenth centuries, when political and economic instability dramatically increased with wars, unrest, and fiscal crisis, new actors who entered the business of governance found new venues to consolidate power and wealth at the expense of old practices. Confiscations, in particular, provided a favorable environment for upstarts, who often found opportunities to seize status and wealth from the deceased. Instability fostered social mobility.

Thirdly, the institutional limitations of the Ottoman Empire made it unable to recognize provincial magnates as equal political partners. Although the Ottoman state constantly negotiated and built horizontal ties with regional powerholders, the central establishment did not formally recognize them as actors with the capacity to deliberate on an institutional basis. Despite real circumstances, those in the business of governance were formally servants of the sultan and state. In the document cited at the beginning of this chapter, Mahmud II was advised to write informal requests to provincial magnates asking for financial support in addition to formal orders. There was a discrepancy between the formal and informal empires. Even if the Ottoman state did not have the power to enforce the formal empire based on vertically and hierarchically ranked servants who were fully and unconditionally loyal to the sultan, there were no political or ideological conditions to change this formal order and institutionalize a new one. This was why the sultanic right to order confiscations and executions was not revoked until the 1830s, although they were hardly applied in every case.

For many members of the Ottoman establishment, the consolidation of grandees in their regions for long terms was just a temporary reality during a time of crisis. Şanizade Ataullah, an Ottoman historian and intellectual, summarized this view in the official chronicle he wrote during the early reign of Mahmud II. According to Şanizade, provincial magnates consolidated power "by seizing the public lands, killing men, confiscating property, collecting private armies, and unlawfully seizing and occupying a piece of the Exalted State's land."[168] Şanizade categorically rejected the institutional possibility of partnership between regional magnates and the state, granting them hereditary rights to their offices, wealth, and status. Despite these obstacles and resistance, as we shall see in chapters 4 and 5, such an alliance was almost achieved in September and October 1808, during a political vortex that shook the entire empire, when Mustafa Bayraktar and his allied New Orderists successfully led a coup in Istanbul, summoned the chiefs of notable families to Istanbul for an imperial assembly, and initiated an imperial settlement for a new imperial order. We shall see how this effort collapsed. But first let us continue our journey through the Ottoman provinces and see in the next chapter how the communities there experienced this volatile order.

CHAPTER 3

Communities

Collective Action, Leadership, and Politics

Important matters and the affairs of the districts are to be handled
by those elected by the communities.

Ottoman imperial edict, 1768

Chapter 2 discussed the provincial notables in the volatile institutional
and political environment of the Ottoman Empire. In this chapter, I shift
my focus to the empire's provincial communities. I argue that in the eighteenth and early nineteenth centuries, we see an institutional consolidation of several bottom-up collective practices in public administration and
finance in the central provinces of the empire. Provincial communities
started to settle their fiscal accounts, elect and dismiss the administrators who managed their public matters, and assume responsibilities in
relations with the center. They became active participants in provincial
governance and politics. In the beginning, such practices flourished as
local dynamics that were autonomous from state's direct intervention.
But gradually the Ottoman central authority regulated, formalized, standardized, and institutionalized these local participatory patterns in a provincial reform program. Increasingly, collective participation became a
required component of the Ottoman provincial order.

The central administration promoted these participatory mechanisms
to facilitate taxation, governance, and public finance at the district level.
The conviction grew in the minds of some Ottoman reformists that, when
it came to provincial governance, these bottom-up mechanisms operated
more effectively and fairly than top-down administration and taxation by
imperial agents and contract-based deals by fiscal-administrative entrepreneurs and provincial magnates. This conviction, which echoed physiocracy in France and Spain in the eighteenth century, was based on the

assumption that the interest of the empire and the provincial communities could be harmonized if the communities participated in governance and contributed to the imperial order.

Conventionally, historians have depicted the Ottoman Empire as an omnipotent power that imposed institutions on passive or unruly local communities. Accounts of provincial communities as collective actors have depicted them as either passively enjoying justice granted to them or resisting injustices imposed by the state. According to this narrative, until the late nineteenth century, provincial communities were not effective actors in political processes, decision-making, and governance unless they either abandoned their lands and immigrated or simply rebelled.[1] By this account, as the Ottoman central authority progressively lost its leverage in the provinces and the power of provincial notables grew, local communities became trapped between the oppression of the Ottoman state and the provincial magnates. Only after Western-inspired top-down municipal reforms, following the Tanzimat edict of 1839 and the inauguration of the first imperial parliament in 1876, did the some communities—and only urban ones—come to take part in politics and governance through electoral and other collective participatory mechanisms.[2]

I challenge this convention and suggest that rather than being stuck between passivity and resistance, provincial people participated in politics and governance in different ways in the eighteenth and early nineteenth centuries, long before modern municipal and parliamentary reforms. I do not propose that individuals in the Ottoman Empire were citizens equipped with the rights of popular sovereignty. We do not observe a viable republican option fostering ideas of popular sovereignty in the Ottoman lands in this period. However, in the late eighteenth and early nineteenth centuries, an age of popular revolutions around the globe, Ottoman political and administrative culture produced alternatives of collective participation in local administration, taxation, public finance, and other public affairs. Gradually the central administration promoted collective participation, settlement of public accounts through communal deliberation, and electoral practices. In fact, I suggest that there was profound continuity between patterns of collective participation and democratic experience in municipal politics in the Ottoman lands in the eighteenth century and the later parliamentary process in the nineteenth and early twentieth centuries.

This chapter discusses district administration as it came into being in the late eighteenth century, and how the communities and community leaders who acted as district administrators/managers interacted; the ways in which the Ottoman center tried to reform district administration and how the principle that those notables who formally managed district affairs "should be elected by the local communities" was consolidated. I offer examples from different localities and examine how these electoral practices and other collective and entrepreneurial actions took place. The chapter concludes with a short analysis of approaches and agendas among Ottoman bureaucrats regarding the participatory role of the communities in the Ottoman provincial order.

DISTRICT ADMINISTRATION

Ruse, 1806

Let me begin with an episode of a fiscal settlement, or apportionment (*tevzi*), that took place in Ruse (Rusçuk), a city on the Danube in Bulgaria. In 1806, representatives of the community of Ruse and İsmail Agha, the ayan of Ruse district, met in the city's court to settle expenses İsmail had incurred on behalf of the district community.

This is the register of expenses of the city of Ruse and its district, covering six months, from Rūz-ı Ḳāsım 1219 [October 26, 1805] to Rūz-ı Ḫıżır 1220 [April 23, 1806]. The expenses were incurred by İsmail Agha of Tirsinik—the ayan of the district, . . . for the affairs of the district, the poor, and the subjects, as their representative and on the condition that he be reimbursed. In order to settle the accounts, the notables of the community, imams of the neighborhoods, some members of the community, imams of the villages, and some of the villagers, in person and as representatives of their people, convened at the court and agreed on the entries in the accounts one by one. [After the settlement the] accounts were accepted and approved by everybody, and with public agreement reached in the court, everybody pledged [to carry out the apportionment and to deliver the amounts due to İsmail Agha].[3]

Ruse, a strategic city on the Danube, was also a major hub of Danubian and Black Sea trade and central to supplying Istanbul with grain from Wallachia and Moldavia. İsmail—a powerholder originally from Tirsinik, a village in southern Ruse—established his power in the district in the 1790s. After the community of Ruse elected him as ayan, he played a major role in political developments in the broader region.[4] Between October 1805 and April 1806, İsmail made payments on behalf of the community (*fukarā' ve rā'iyyete bi'l-vekāle*) and recorded his spending in an account book. To settle accounts, notables of the city and villages came to court in person as representatives of their quarters and villages. Each expense was examined in court proceedings. After a settlement was reached, community leaders unanimously approved the accounts and pledged (*müte'ahhid*) to collect shares from taxpayers in their constituencies in their neighborhoods and villages and deliver the aggregate amount to İsmail. The register of expenses listed the amounts incurred by İsmail:

5,500 *ġuruş*: to the men of İbrahim Pasha, the governor of the Rumeli provinces, concerning the Tokatlıkcı incident

150 *ġuruş*: to Ebû Bekir Agha, who went to meet the messenger of the governor of Rumeli, for travel expenses

2,500 *ġuruş*: to the messenger who came from the Exalted State with robes of honor awarded by His Majesty to İsmail Agha because of his services in the Tatarcıklı incident

50 *ġuruş*: to the messenger of Palaslı Mehmed Pasha, the governor of Silistre . . .

3,750 *ġuruş*: to the French consul for his expenses during his stay in Ruse and for horses delivered to him . . .

2,800 *ġuruş*: to the men sent from different managers in the region concerning important matters

1,380 *ġuruş*: six months' wages for the commander of the armed forces [*serdār*] of Ruse

120 *ġuruş*: maintenance of the assistant of the commander . . .

5,000 *ġuruş*: expenses of Mehmed Pasha, the governor of Silistra, during his stay in Ruse . . .

5,000 *ġuruş*: the expenses concerning the gifts sent to [various grandees] in Istanbul . . .

10,600 *ġuruş*: wages of the heads of corps and standard-bearer for six months

Total: 60,642 *ġuruş*

6,064 *ġuruş:* six months' interest [due to İsmail of Ruse]

[Expenses of the court transaction]

2,000 *ġuruş*: fee given to the kadi

150 *ġuruş*: fee given to the steward of the kadi

220 *ġuruş*: fee for the scribe, service man, and guards of the court

[Total]: 69,056 *ġuruş*

120 *ġuruş*: rent for the court building from Rūz-ı Hıżır 1219 to Rūz-ı Ḳāsım 1220

220 *ġuruş*: allowance to the governor of Vidin for the year 1218/1219

+ _____

69,396 *ġuruş*

8,634 *ġuruş*: subtraction of the share of the villages of Chernova, which is an imperial estate

Total: 60,722 *ġuruş*

The bulk of the items listed in the account book pertain to the expenses of messengers and imperial agents during visits to Ruse. Another portion includes the stipends of the security forces, local janissaries, and commanders of the city's citadel. Rent for the court building comprised another expenditure. Other expenses were related to taxes collected for various imperial grandees in the region. The Ruse district contributed to the allowances of the commander of Vidin, a neighboring city. In the end, İsmail Agha claimed a charge (*fa'iz*) of 10 percent (6,064 *ġuruş*) of the total amount (60,642 *ġuruş*) he had spent during the six months. Fees for the kadi and court were added to the aggregate amount. Other items, which were to be paid separately by villages operating with a different fiscal status, were deducted from the net total. In the third section of the register, we see how expenses were allocated within the district:

> The aggregate amount, 60,722 *ġuruş*, is now apportioned among the neighborhoods and villages of the Ruse district. . . . divided into 326 *rub'* [quarters, as allotment units]. . . . Each *rub'* corresponds to 186 *ġuruş* and 30 *pāre* [cents]. In the city of Ruse, as has been the custom, the *rub'*s of the imperial estates within the city were subtracted from the share of the community. Therefore, their *rub'*s correspond to 140 *ġuruş* and 30 *pāre*. Accordingly, this was the endorsed [apportionment] register delivered to İsmail Agha in the court.

> Cami-yi Cedid neighborhood, 21 *rub'*; Hacı Musa Müsellem neighborhood, 10 *rub'*; Hacı Musa—Ermeniyan neighborhood, 11 *rub'*; Kara Mustafa neighborhood, 9 *rub'*; Arık Ramazan neighborhood, 7 *rub'*: Kayık neighborhood, 9 *rub'*: Mahmud Voyvoda neighborhood, 2 *rub'*; Mesih neighborhood, 2 *rub'*; Cami-yı Atik neighborhood, 2 *rub'*; Bacanak neighborhood, 1 *rub'*; Kuyumcu neighborhood, 1 *rub'*; Tuna neighborhood, 12 *rub'*. Total: 88 *rub'*

> The villages in the Bala region . . .

> Total: 139 *rub'*

> The villages in the Zir region . . .

> Total: 102 *rub'*

The court translated the total amount into an apportionment matrix (*rub'*), indicating shares rather than the sum to be paid. Those who attended the meeting deliberated as to how to determine the *rub'* and apportion the total expenditure to neighborhoods in the city of Ruse and villages in the broader Ruse district. In the end, community leaders from the neighborhoods and villages of Ruse pledged to deliver the amounts to İsmail. A few weeks later, the community leaders convened again with İsmail in the Ruse court, this time to determine the aid taxes (*imdādiye*) due to the governor and how to apportion them in the district.

This record kept by the kadi of the Ruse district is typical of a widespread practice in the central provinces of the Ottoman Empire in the

late eighteenth and early nineteenth centuries. In Ottoman administrative
terminology, the apportionment was called the *tevzī'* and the associated
documents, which included lists of expenses, apportionment matrixes,
and the community's endorsement, were called the *tevzī' defteri* (apportionment book).[5] Such apportionment practices were central processes
in district administration. The provincial communities handled the taxes
and dues they paid to the empire and other public expenditures through
this process. The key figure in this practice was the ayan, in this case,
İsmail Agha, who acted as administrator/manager and patron-creditor
of the district.[6]

The Transformation of Ottoman District Administration:
From Lump-Sum Taxation to Public Financing

The origins of apportionment settlements coincided with the deterioration of the traditional Ottoman tax regime. As we saw in chapter 1, the
traditional tax regime of the Ottoman Empire arose in the fifteenth century and was fully developed and widespread in the central provinces in
the sixteenth century. It was primarily based on provincial codes (*ḳānūn-
nāme*) and detailed census registers (*taḥrīr defters*), which were prepared
after periodical surveys. These codes and censuses meticulously itemized
each tax-paying household (*ḥāne*) in the provinces, as well as fixed taxes
and dues that these households were to pay in cash or kind. By bundling
these tax-paying households in villages, towns, and cities, the central administration created benefices of different sizes (*ḥāṣṣ, ze'āmet,* and *tīmār*),
which the sultan bestowed on officeholders, ranging from petty cavalry
commanders to provincial governors, who comprised the administrative
and military hierarchy in the provinces. In return for revenues collected
from their benefices, the sultan's servants rendered military and administrative services to the state. The servants acted as provincial administrators and commanders of the seasonal provincial cavalry armies, which
stood ready to be mobilized during imperial campaigns.[7]

As several historians have illustrated, from the mid seventeenth century
on, this regime deteriorated as a result of structural changes. Persistent
inflation, following the influx of silver from the Americas into the Ottoman lands, dramatically devalued the fixed taxes paid by households.
Meanwhile, changes in military technology obliged the Ottoman state to
expand its standing army, particularly the janissary corps, at the expense
of the irregular provincial cavalry. The Ottoman state instituted new
taxes (*'avārıż* and *nüzūl*), directly collected by the central government
from the provincial communities, to pay for the larger standing army and
military investments such as building fortresses in the borderlands on the
western and eastern fronts.

The catastrophic wars against the Habsburgs between 1683 and 1699 not only revealed that most of the Ottoman cavalry was obsolete but also drove the central fiscal administration to find new instruments to extract more resources from the provinces. The Treasury accordingly seized hundreds of benefices and estates that were either assigned to cavalry units or unclaimed and rented them to fiscal and administrative entrepreneurs on short- and long-term contracts to raise money. This created a major problem for provincial governors. They lost their cavalry units and thus needed to create small armies and hire mercenaries. At the same time, the incomes that the governors collected from their provinces diminished. In response, the governors levied irregular taxes and fees in the form of an emergency tax, called the aid tax (*imdādiye*), from provincial communities, and after a while, the Ottoman state regularized this tax.[8]

These briefly sketched interconnected changes had major institutional implications for the Ottoman provincial order. One of the most significant repercussions was the expansion of lump-sum (*maktū'*) tax collection. In the absence of updated registers and reorganization of the cavalry hierarchy that oversaw revenue collection, the central administration and provincial governors were unable to collect taxes and dues in fixed amounts from tax-paying households. Both the central administration and provincial governors therefore began imposing taxes and fees in lump sums on the provincial communities. This system was already used to collect the poll tax (*cizye*) levied on non-Muslims.[9] Beginning in the late seventeenth century, we see this lump-sum collection at every level of the tax and revenue collection process. Officers, tax collectors, and fiscal entrepreneurs asked provincial communities to deliver aggregate amounts and left the collection and apportionment process to community leaders. Community leaders then collected taxes in accordance with local and intercommunal dynamics, negotiations, and processes. These leaders delivered total amounts to the authorities under the supervision of district kadis. Gradually, not only regular taxes but also irregular and sporadic imperial fees and expenses, such as the cost of postal services and of provisioning visiting officeholders, were collected the same way. Moreover, in addition to imperial taxes, dues, and expenses, other public expenditures pertaining to the public good and the interest of local communities were collected in similar fashion.[10]

Lump-sum tax collection presented community leaders, petty officeholders, and local notables with new financial possibilities. Some who were wealthy or had the capacity to obtain credit from financiers took the initiative individually or with partners, incurring taxes and expenses in advance as entrepreneurs and patron-creditors on behalf of the community. These local notables and patron-creditors, generically termed ayan by the Ottomans, after paying public expenditures, met with other community leaders at the district courts under the supervision of the kadis. In these meetings, the ayan and leaders who claimed to represent the community settled accounts. The ayan presented documents and witnesses to explain expenses and demanded service fees or interest. If the community leaders agreed with the accounts, the assembly deliberated on how to apportion the aggregate amount among town neighborhoods and villages. After reaching agreement, the representatives went to their constituencies, collected their shares, and paid the ayan. Gradually, in several regions of the central provinces, most taxes, imperial fees, services, and other public expenditures were collected using these apportionment settlements between district ayans and community representatives.

The District and the District Court

The spatial context of the apportionment practice was the district (*ḳażā'*), a primary administrative unit consisting of a central town and its rural hinterland.[11] Its defining institution was the kadi court, a principal institution of the provincial order since the fifteenth century, which was supervised by a kadi, or judge, appointed by imperial diploma from the hierarchy of college-educated Islamic lawyers and scholars, the ulema. In the eighteenth century, the Ottoman Empire comprised approximately six hundred districts of various sizes.[12] In much of the literature on Islamic legal culture, the kadi courts are treated as judicial or notary bodies.[13] In the eighteenth-century Ottoman provinces, however, the kadi courts, in addition to judicial and notary functions, served as public spaces where representatives of the communities congregated to settle public expenditures, as well as to deliberate, negotiate, vote, register, and pronounce on other public affairs. The resulting documents prepared by the kadis and their scribes according to the standard legal and administrative template of the empire, and then bound and kept as codices, not only gained validity in the institutional context of the empire but also functioned as the local archives of the districts for private and public transactions, legal cases, and notary documents.

At the same time, the kadi court was a channel for the central authority to communicate with local communities. "When an imperial edict arrives from the state, the kadi summons the notables and dignitaries, the hajjis, the leading merchants, the imams, and the preachers to the district court," a late-eighteenth-century Ottoman bureaucrat wrote. "As they are the representatives of the community, the edict was read before them. They expressed their loyalty with due ceremony and did the sultan's will."[14] It is obvious that reading imperial decrees aloud to community leaders at the provincial courts was one the most effective ways in which the empire (often the sultan himself) spoke directly to Ottoman subjects. The kadi court was also a platform for communities to communicate directly with the imperial administration and their sovereign. For those speaking different Ottoman languages—vernacular Turkish, Greek, Serbian, Albanian, Bulgarian, Arabic, Kurdish, and others—the kadi court allowed for translating collective petitions, not simply into Ottoman Turkish, but also into the Ottoman bureaucratic format. One of thousands of collective petitions prepared at the courts to be sent to Istanbul begins: "The learned and the virtuous and the imams and the preachers and the nobles and chiefs and standard-bearers and the elders and the Muslim subjects and the non-Muslim subjects of the city of Ruse and its district, all together came to the court and declared . . . ";[15] the kadi court was a space where the empire spoke to the communities and the communities to the empire, with the kadis translating between them.[16]

District Community Representation and Leadership

In Ottoman administrative terminology, a district community was called *ḳaża' ahālīsi*, which is to say, people (*ahālī*) of the district (*ḳaża'*), comprising the central town and its rural hinterland. These communities, the populations of which varied from a couple of thousand to tens of thousands, were not necessarily cohesive. Taxes and public charges, which were to be apportioned throughout the district, were to cover the entire district community. However, there were always internal conflicts, partisan divisions, or competition within the district communities between different groups, such as merchant and professional associations clustered around urban guilds, peasantries, nomadic tribes, kinship groups, or households. Often, some groups and individuals claimed to be entitled to pay less, while others may have been obliged to pay more because of their distinctive fiscal and administrative statuses.[17]

The district communities were not socioreligiously cohesive collectivities either. Most of them had multiconfessional or multi-ethno-religious compositions consisting of Muslim, Christian, and Jewish subgroups concentrated in different neighborhoods of a particular city or across villages. In general, when it came to civil matters, these religious subcommunities constituted autonomous groups. Their leaders were expected to supervise collection of the poll tax (*jizya*) levied on non-Muslims, generally as a lump sum. However, at the district level, the community was a multiconfessional entity. The district community was therefore a group of people with a common interest who had the capacity to act together as a political constituency in a shared administrative space regardless of their internal tensions and diversity. The authorities considered such tensions and diversity manageable through the process of deliberation and negotiations in the kadi court. The deliberation in the court attuned the members of the *ahālī* to a common public interest.

Representation in Ottoman provincial assemblies was flexible, ad hoc, organic, fluid, and communal. Depending on the meeting's subject, the sociopolitical structure, the administrative status of the district, and the attendees at the court varied. In the case of Ruse, it was "the notables of the community" who were the voice claiming to represent the public interest of the district. Most of the time "notables" (ayan or *vucūh*) was not a fixed category in terms of status or numbers, but rather a generic, negotiable term referring to the community's natural leaders. Strongmen, wealthy or respected individuals, religious leaders (imams, priests, and rabbis), some title- and officeholders, members of prominent families, and representatives of craftsmen and tradesmen all belonged to the category of notables of the community. Generally, these natural leaders gained their status through the internal dynamics of the district community without formal electoral procedures or nominations.[18]

We may expect there to have been alliances, partnerships, and factionalism among the notable leaders operating at different levels within the district (or beyond) and conflicts of interest between the notables and different segments of the district communities. Muslim notables were considered the primary group in the district, claiming to represent the entire community, even if Muslims were a minority there. Christian and Jewish notables' names generally appear at the end of lists of local notables in kadi court documents.[19]

Factionalism and internal divisions within the community were intended to be minimized by applying the principle of unanimity (*ittifāk-ı ārā*). Unlike some early modern and modern assemblies based on the principle of majority rule, in the Ottoman assembly courts, notables of the community were expected to reach unanimous consent in their decisions. Since no detailed procedure existed for designating representatives of the community attending the court assemblies, the unanimity principle was more justifiable than majority vote. It is not easy to substantiate whether there was kinship between the Islamic legal principle of a consensus of Muslims (*ijmā' al-ummah*) and the Ottoman administrative principle of unanimity.[20] However, as Susan Reynolds observes of medieval European assemblies, unanimous decisions provided greater legitimacy in premodern societies without well-defined procedures for representation. According to this principle, the community was to reach consensus through a process of negotiation. After unanimous agreement was reached, it was imposed on the entire community.[21]

In traditional Ottoman provincial governance, the term *ayan* referred to the natural, primarily Muslim, leaders who represented the community vis-à-vis the central authority.[22] From the mid eighteenth century on, however, *ayan* acquired another meaning aside from the conventional one. It also came to mean *an* individual (in the singular in spite of its Arabic syntactical plural form) who was formally and individually responsible for public affairs in a district community. As we have seen in the case of İsmail Agha, the ayan incurred public expenditures on behalf of the community and bore responsibility for the community's public works, protection, and security. In return for this service, he earned income in the form of a commission. And as we shall see in the coming pages, from the 1760s on, the central administration issued several edicts to regularize how such ayans were designated. According to these edicts, a would-be ayan needed to obtain an unanimous nomination or vote of consent from the district community. After a kadi court had endorsed the unanimous nomination, the grand vizier would then recognize the man as the ayan of the district.[23]

Public Expenses and the Matrix of Apportionment

As we saw in the case of Ruse, an ayan incurred public expenditures on behalf of the district community and met twice a year at the kadi court with his district's community leaders to settle accounts. After the ayan and the community leaders agreed on the accounts, they apportioned the aggregate amount of expenses within the district. What types of expenses were incurred by ayans? A comparative analysis of apportionment accounts in the central provinces shows that irregular aid taxes (*imdādiye*), which were paid to provincial governors (or their deputies), are the commonest entries.[24] Next came postal service expenses; security and road maintenance; provisioning the households or retinues of governors; dues to imperial agents visiting or passing through the district; and the expenses of diplomatic missions passing through or established in the district. Debts from earlier settlements were also listed in the account books' balance sheets. Another common item was the contribution of the district communities to provisioning the imperial army or the capital with grain.[25]

Generally, historians examine the expenses subject to the apportionment process as taxes and dues paid to the empire, rather than for communities' own public needs. This assumption should be reappraised. In the apportionment registers, communities often differentiated between expenses for important matters of state (*umūr-i mühimme*) and for the affairs of the district community (*umūr-i vilāyet* or *meṣāliḥ-i ʿibād, umūr-i fukarāʾ ve reʿāyā*) as two distinct sets of public expenditures.[26] The juxtaposition referred to a separation between imperial and local/communal goods.[27] But it is not always easy to differentiate the business of the state from the business of the community. The expenses of the postal service, messengers, or the security of the roads between cities might be considered benefits for both the community and the empire. In Edirne, expenses related to the water system repairs are in the *tevzī'* registers. However, in Ruse, İsmail Agha paid for the city's water system out of his own pocket, treating it as a waqf.[28] In fact, in the eighteenth and early nineteenth centuries, as in other Muslim polities in medieval and early modern times, the apportionment system in the Ottoman Empire increasingly complemented the customary waqfs financing public works through charitable endowments by imperial grandees and rich provincials.[29]

In principle, community leaders decided the apportionment by unanimous agreement in the court settlement according to criteria such as precedent, the populations of neighborhoods and villages, and the incomes and property of taxpayers. According to an Ottoman bureaucrat in the late eighteenth century, the representatives of the district and notables (*iḫtiyārları ve vucūḥ-ı ḳavm*) should come to the court and the expenses should be read aloud, one by one. Everybody should be informed of these expenses. Then the aggregate sum should be "justly" apportioned in the presence of all. After the kadi sealed the register, the expenses were collected from the community in accordance with the local conventions (*ḳaʿide-i belde*) and people's capacity.[30] Other documents indicate that the community carried out the apportionments "in accordance with previous practices,"[31] with guidance from "men of knowledge,"[32] "with the rules of the districts," and "with unanimous agreement . . . by notables, dignitaries and the community" (*cümle ittifāḳıyla . . . bi-maʿrefeti'l-aʿyān ve'l-eşrāf ve'l-āhalī*).[33] There might be different apportionment patterns in different districts.[34] These patterns changed not only the collective dynamism in the court assemblies but also urban and rural politics in general. In any case, such apportionment allowed considerable liberty to local notables and community leaders who claimed to know previous applications and who were able to persuade and/or coerce communities to pay the assigned amounts.[35]

The apportionment system treated district people as a *community* with common interests, sharing collective burdens according to income or economic capacity, rather than privileges or religious identities. The key criterion in becoming a taxpayer in the apportionment process was being a holder of private property or of a usufruct over arable land (*emlāk ve ʿarāżiye mutaṣarrıf olanlar*). This rule was to be applied regardless of one's status as a military or administrative officeholder, peasant, urban dweller, Muslim, or non-Muslim.[36] While anyone holding a property (as private property or in the form of usufruct) was required to contribute to district expenses, each household was to contribute justly and proportionately according to its capacity. However, it was the community, not the state, that would decide the matrix of apportionment, what was just and proportionate.[37] Although apportionment was a collective process led by representatives of the communities, each apportionment had its losers and winners, decided through complex negotiations within the community and between the community and outside entities, including the central state, that had an interest in the process. The Sarajevo imam Molla Mustafa, who witnessed an apportionment in that city in 1772, described grumbling by different groups in his diary:

> The tax [*taksīṭ*] was apportioned according to conventions [*usūlünce*]. The share of the city of Sarajevo was 1.080 guruş. . . . As a formality they [the kadi and other authorities] asked the city community whether the community had consent or not. The ignorant populace complained about [this amount]. But the tax was firmly demanded, since it was the sultan's request and it was wartime. When a letter from the sultan was received [by the community of Sarajevo] asking for the names of those who would not pay their share, the community stopped complaining.[38]

Public Finance and Credit/Debt

Ayans were not only administrators managing public affairs but also patron-creditors who were paid fees or interest in lieu of services.[39] After accounts were settled and community leaders approved the expenses before the kadis, the *tevzī'* registers functioned as legal loan contracts, which included receivables and payables between the ayans and the community. The next step was to collect and pay balances to creditors. Frequently, however, debts were not closed in settlement but transferred to the next assembly.

Discussing the political role of the credit culture in late medieval Marseille, Daniel Lord Smail writes: "Credit, in short, was a form of power, whether it arose voluntarily or circumstantially."[40] In the Ottoman case, too, extending credit to a community was not only a business deal. It was also a communal and political action. As a patron-creditor who managed public affairs using his private power and wealth, an ayan also established his leadership by providing a public service. According to the common convention, ayans had to be wealthy, powerful men (*ṣāḥib-i iḳtidār*) able to advance the necessary amounts and protect the community.[41] In the collective petitions of the communities, therefore, the credit capacity of the ayan and his patronage of the community were cited simultaneously. One reads: "Whatever is apportioned to us through the mediation of the Sharia court is our liability. We are all obliged to pay our debts to him [the ayan]. And from now on, whatever he disburses, he shall be our ayan by our will, and we shall be obliged to pay his disbursements back to him. We have had debts to him and no receivables from him."[42] Such collective declarations registered during the apportionment settlement illustrate that the community's willingness to accept someone as an ayan was also related to his capacity to advance a public loan to them.

Clearly, the financial capacity of the ayan was contingent on finding available credit from the financial market. This is why most ayans worked with other moneylenders (*ṣarrāf*) to pay the expenses of the communities in advance.[43] The financial relations of Jewish moneymen with the janissary corps and other grandees of the imperial elite are well known in Ottoman economic history. Far less is known about the consolidation of the Armenian and Greek financial web in the Balkans and Anatolia in the eighteenth century. Typically, the Armenian and Greek financial network was active in that era in the credit market used by provincial ayans. Manuk Mirzayan, an Armenian moneylender from Wallachia, whose connections stretched from Russia to Austria, is a striking example. As we saw in chapter 2, Manuk became the primary moneylender to İsmail Agha of Ruse. But his role was not limited to the financial sector; he also functioned as İsmail Agha's political and diplomatic advisor, supervising his connections in Istanbul and Russia.

The apportionment process had various scales. The governors (or deputy governors if the governors were absentee holders, as was generally the case) of subprovinces and provinces claimed several tax items and dues, including irregular aid taxes (*imdādiye*), from local communities in their provincial units. Each district bore its share of the total taxes levied on a province. Conventionally, ayans handed over their districts' shares to representatives of the governor or deputy governor who visited the districts during tax season. Sometimes district ayans participated in person or through their representatives in large provincial assemblies held in the kadi court of the central district of the province. Hence, we often see a chain of apportionment processes from the provincial to the district level.[44]

Beneath the district level, the representatives of towns, neighborhoods, or villages who pledged to pay their constituencies' shares to the district ayan could also serve as creditors for their own constituencies. Studies by Sokrates Petmezas and Demetrios Papastamatiou, who worked in local communal archives in Morea and Thessaly, provide us with rich sources about loan contracts between notables, in this case, Greek notables, known as *kocabaşıs*, local communities, and district ayans.[45] The local archives illustrate the financial dynamics and the credit mechanisms at levels below the kadi courts.[46] As a result, some individuals could simultaneously be creditors and debtors within a chain of credit and debt relations from the governor's level to the district and from the district level down to neighborhoods and villages.

Prota Matija Nenadovic, an early nineteenth-century Serbian intellectual who transmitted stories learned from his father, recounts an episode that took place between Muslim janissaries and Serbian peasants: "Such an agha [a janissary chief] took a few retainers, went into whatever village he liked, called the peasants together and said to them: 'Raja [Subjects], I am a chief and a son [servant] of the sultan; give and admit that you belong to me and I will defend you from any sort of oppression, and whoever of you has no money to pay his tribute, I will give it to him as a loan."[47] Receiving a loan from a notable brought with it the risk for the communities of a cycle of debt and peonage, or the use of laborers bound in servitude because of debt.[48] However, it was not only the communities who were vulnerable in these relations. When İsmail of Ruse died soon after the *tevzī'* episode discussed above, he was about to go bankrupt, since the community of Ruse had not paid him what they had pledged to pay him in the *tevzī'* settlement.[49] The risk was mutual.

Accountability and Accountancy

The communities were not passive constituencies that simply enjoyed the generosity of credit-extending notables or became trapped by them. In principle, the ayans were accountable to the community. The apportionment settlement was a public arena where the ayans had to substantiate the public expenses they claimed to have incurred with documents and witnesses in the court assembly. Hundreds of cases recorded in the Ottoman archives illustrate that tough negotiations and disagreements between district ayans and community representatives about the accounting process were commonplace. Ayans were frequently blamed for listing expense items that they had not really incurred, or that were not supposed to appear in the account books. If expenses were not approved in court, then the assembly was transformed into a legal tribunal mediating between the ayan and the community, and the kadi turned from supervisor of a district assembly into a judge. These collective tribunals mediating between ayans and the communities made the courts legal theaters where parties presented contrasting stories and provided witnesses. When cases could not be settled in the district courts, it was common practice for the central administration to send an inspector to supervise the settlement of a case.[50]

Court settlements of disputes or inspectors sent from Istanbul were just two of many mechanisms sponsored by the empire to coordinate relations between ayans and communities. From the 1770s on, the state started to interfere in district apportionment by centrally auditing account books. An imperial edict dated 1784 states: "the apportionment accounts will be copied from the court records and sent to the Exalted State, where they will be examined, and if there are unsubstantiated items contrary to the directions, the ayan of that district will immediately be punished."[51] The center ordered district kadis to send the account books to it for audit and approval twice a year. According to a decree sent to the kadis of districts in Anatolia and Rumelia in 1791, ayans proposed apportionment accounts for obscure expenses without clearly identifying them. At the end of six months, the account books would be sent to Istanbul for a central audit. If fiscal experts discovered obscure items, these would have to be repaid by the kadis who signed the account books and the ayans who claimed them.[52] The regulations illustrate the policy of the Ottoman state, not only of preventing ayans from overcharging local communities, but also of monitoring district administrations and intervening if necessary.

How did the financial experts in Istanbul check these items and on what basis? Central bureaucrats double-checked the validity of local expenses against various parameters, considering whether they were dubious, uncertain, or duplicated. Often the center requested reports from various experts or from officeholders who knew the local conventions.[53] "I examined the expenses [in the case of Salonika] one by one," a bureaucrat charged with auditing account books from Rumelia recorded. After summarizing the amounts levied on the communities in different categories and classifications, he wrote that the superfluous items were "substantiated with the reports of the experts [*erbāb-ı vukūf*]" in that city. Then, he itemized the expenses to be removed from the account registers and decided for a reduction (*tenzīl*).[54] The fiscal bureaucracy had the final say, and there was no way to appeal the process. A total reduction for the entire district or a partial reduction pertaining to the share of a neighborhood, professional groups, or a village was possible. Reductions hurt ayans and benefitted communities.

Auditing of apportionment accounts by the fiscal bureaucracy could be considered a component of the reform agenda for regulations and centralization in the late eighteenth century. Most of the time, however, the scrutiny of fiscal experts in Istanbul was a formality rather than an effective audit.[55] Although the central audit mechanism was not sufficient from a purely auditing perspective, still it helped the central state make itself felt by communities in the provinces. It was also a way for the central bureaucracy to update its data on provincial realities ranging from fiscal capacity and demographics to property conditions.

How widespread throughout the empire was the apportionment system? To answer this question, we need a thorough analysis of fiscal practices in different provinces. As examples from the court records below indicate, we can conclude that this mechanism was common in the central provinces in the Balkans and Anatolia. Arguably, the system was not as common in districts that were granted as *mālikāne* in toto, where the *mālikāne* holder had an exclusive prerogative and immunity. In these units, we expect to see various forms of estate management in which the *mālikāne* holder or his subcontractor administered fiscal units more closely without needing election by the community or a formal apportionment system with collective participation. But both large and small *mālikāne* units either participated as separate divisions to pay their shares in the apportionment of larger zones in which they were located or were exempted in toto from contribution to the aggregate amount to be paid by the taxpayers in those zones. For instance, Bozok, which was held by the Çapanoğlus, did not participate in the apportionment process for the province of Rum as a whole in the court at Sivas, which was the provincial capital, where Bozok was one of the subprovinces. This was because the Çapanoğlus had been granted fiscal privileges making them immune to provincial fiscal jurisdiction.[56] Overall, the apportionment system was arguably less common in regions where large units, districts, subprovinces, or entire provinces were granted as *mālikāne* to provincial notables in eastern Anatolia, Baghdad, and Damascus.[57]

The total share of revenues collected through the apportionment system in the Ottoman economy as a whole is also unknown in certainty. As I have already argued, revenue collected through the apportionment system included not only some taxes but also communal expenditures. It is therefore virtually impossible to come up with a precise number for the share of the provincial sector in the imperial economy without analyzing every apportionment document, since the budgets in the central treasury would not reflect these figures. But using calculations based on an incomplete number of apportionment documents, Yavuz Cezar has suggested that taxes and dues collected through apportionment solely from the central Balkans (1,574,000 *ġuruş*) amounted to more than 10 percent of the Ottoman state's total revenues in 1784 (14.7 million *ġuruş*).[58] If so, provincial public financing by means of apportionment constituted a sizable portion of the Ottoman imperial economy.

COMMUNITIES, AYANS, AND THE EMPIRE

So far, I have outlined how public affairs were managed through apportionment in the central provinces of the Ottoman Empire in the late eighteenth and early nineteenth centuries. Now let me examine a series of edicts issued by the Ottoman central administration from the 1760s to the 1790s. These edicts, which were part of an ongoing agenda to reform provincial governance, were released just before the Ottoman-Russian War of 1768–74 and continued under the New Order in the reign of Selim III (1789–1807). The primary goals of the edicts were to improve the regulatory capacity of the central authority in the provinces and the collection of taxes, dues, and services from district communities, especially in the time of war, and to reduce the growing number of complaints by provincial communities about arbitrary taxation by officeholders and notables. In doing so, instead of empowering centrally appointed officeholders, the Ottoman central state expanded, consolidated, and formalized bottom-up collective arrangements. The edicts equipped provincial communities with the capacity to approve or disapprove apportionment by district courts and to elect or dismiss their ayans, who managed public deeds and acted as patron-creditors. The edicts were aimed to redesign provincial governance by reinforcing collective participation. But perhaps more important, this policy gave rise to a new discourse in which communities were presented as the essential source of power and authority in provincial order.

Reform of district administration was ushered in by Grand Vizier Muhsinzade Mehmed Pasha during his first tenure (1765–68) under Mustafa III (1757–74).[59] According to Yuzo Nagata, before his tenure as grand vizier, Mehmed Pasha was actively involved in the restoration of Ottoman institutions in the Peloponnese, which was retaken by the Ottomans in 1715, following thirty years of Venetian rule (1682–1715). During this mission, Mehmed Pasha observed widespread discontent among provincial communities. In many districts, some powerful figures imposed themselves as administrators and creditors without the consent of the local people. Some of these men had paid the provincial governors to authorize them. Many complained about these self-appointed ayans. Mehmed Pasha developed a new perspective on reforming district order, and when he became grand vizier, he put this into practice. The program aimed to integrate the collective voices of the communities into the operation of provincial governance and prevent higher officeholders and communal notables from acting arbitrarily. Noting the situation that needed to be corrected, the sultanic edict of 1766 that established the new norms stated:

The district ayans go to the governors and ask for letters of appointment. In return for large amounts of their money, the governors then grant letters appointing them as ayans. When those who snatch up these letters arrive in their district, they deceive the kadis, declaring, "I have paid this amount for the letter of appointment as ayan," triple the apportionment account, and collect this from the community. In so doing, they devastate the abodes of the poor and roast their livers with the fire of oppression. My subjects already have great difficulty paying the taxes levied by my imperial orders, [and this additional burden] further harms and injures them. . . . From now on, governors or kadis will by no means issue letters of appointment or certificates of ayanship. If the community comes to you [kadis] and asks you to appoint somebody as [their] ayan, make sure that he is faithful, upright, and committed to the protection and well-being of the community, and [check] whether his good qualities are testified to and known by the general public. Then impartially report on the situation to my grand vizier, who is my representative with full authority. The grand vizier too will verify whether this person whom the community requests as their ayan possesses the reported qualities. After all these [things] are definitely substantiated, the grand vizier will inform the governors of the appointment by official letter. This person is then appointed ayan in accordance with the will [of the community].[60]

The central administration thus intervened on behalf of the local communities, decreeing that ayans were to be nominated only after the collective decision of the district. And, as with the Treasury's decree that district accounts be settled by central auditing, it proclaimed its right to check and either approve or veto the collective choice.

In September 1768, a long and costly war between the Ottoman and Russian empires began. During the war, which continued on several fronts until 1774, the district ayans, who were able to mobilize provincial resources at the grassroots level, proved vital in providing logistical support and provisioning to the Ottoman forces. The central authority increasingly requested the ayans' assistance in collecting extraordinary dues, organizing grain provisions, and recruiting soldiers from their localities. War conditions pushed the Istanbul administration to make modifications in district administration. Toward the end of 1768, imperial edicts were sent to the provinces to amend the process of ayan elections. The 1768 edict declared: "In the districts and settlements in my empire the appointments of the ayans should be carried out by appointing individuals on whom the communities agree and whom they elect [*'ale'l-umūm ittifāḳ ve iḥtiyār eyledikleri*]." The edict reiterated that members of the imperial hierarchy should not intervene in the process: "appointing an ayan through a higher order [*emr-i 'ālī*] is outlawed." Bottom-up authorization, the edict explained, enabled "district affairs [to be handled] with the community's voluntary compliance [*muḥtār-ı ahālī*]."

This was a clear statement on the part of the imperial administration that the participation of the communities in choosing their own ayans would facilitate the handling of public affairs. Therefore, it was not enough for the ayans, who were mighty and wealthy, to act as generous patrons. They also needed to acquire the community's consent. "In some districts, some wealthy powerholders [*müna'am ve ẓī-ḳudret kimesneler*] . . . had themselves appointed as ayans without community consent and unanimous agreement."[61] After clarifying the rules and principles in a phrase copied from earlier edicts, the new version declared that the communities and officeholders no longer needed to report the results of their elections. The condition that elected ayans were to be appointed only after the grand vizier's investigation and approval was revoked because of the delays and hassles it would cause. "As it is the old law," the edict continues, "when the ayan of a district dies, or if it is necessary to replace him owing to his mischief and misconduct, whomever the community of that district request as their ayan and elect [*ol belde ve ḳaża' ahālīsi 'ale'l-umūm her kimi a'yānlığa ṭāleb ve iḥtiyār ederler ise*] . . . will be appointed as ayan with the mediation of the court and unanimous agreement [*cümle ittifāḳıyla*]."

Under war conditions, the central administration preferred to with-
draw from close bureaucratic monitoring of provincial affairs and to increase the effectiveness of mobilizing provincial resources for the imperial
armies. Concurrently, however, the number of petitions from provincial
communities concerning the misconduct of the ayans increased dramatically. After the Treaty of Küçük Kaynarca (1774) between the Ottoman
and Russian empires, during the reigns of Abdulhamid I (r. 1774–89)
and Catherine II (r. 1762–96), there was a new spirit with regard to the
provincial question. In 1778, four years after the end of the Ottoman-
Russian war, the 1766 arrangement was reasserted and the grand vizier's
approval of ayan elections became necessary again.[62] The edict read:

[A]varicious individuals . . . have proclaimed ayanships without being elected
and chosen by [the] communities in [their] localities, contrary to the [former]
order and to my edicts. . . . There have been struggles for the ayan positions in
several districts. . . . From now on, as stipulated in my edicts of 1766 and 1767,
[the names of] individuals chosen by the communities of districts and settlements
will be submitted to the Exalted State with collective petitions and notes from
the kadis, the case will be reviewed by the grand vizier, and the ayans will be appointed only after his letters of appointment [are issued].[63]

During the interbellum years of 1774 to 1786, when another war
started between the Ottoman Empire and a Russian-Austrian coalition,
the central administration constantly strove to enforce the norm that
provincial communities elect their own ayans. In 1784, during the grand
vizierate of Halil Hamid Pasha (1782–85), under the reign of Abdulhamid I, the most detailed imperial decree was sent to the provinces.[64] In this
edict, the administration clarified what would happen if the community
could not reach an agreement on one person. "If the community [is] . . .
divided into two factions . . . it is up to the grand vizier to choose the ayan
from these two on the basis of his investigation for his good conduct, or
to appoint another suitable person from another community who has the
capacity to oversee the affairs of the district."[65]

The intensification of struggles among notables for ayanship encouraged factionalism in the districts. Repeating verbatim the previous decrees that specified the role of the ayan in the taxation and apportionment
process, the edict explained why military officeholders should not be involved in ayan appointments: "One cannot claim to be ayan by saying:
'I received a robe of honor from the governor, or I have his order, or the
community made me ayan and the community got me a certificate from
the kadi.' . . . Ayan appointment is solely related to the protection of the
subjects. Ayanship is not a military matter."[66] The text clearly differenti-
ates between military (*umūr-i 'askeriye*) and municipal (*umūr-i vilāyet*)
affairs. Ayanship pertained to civil matters related to the affairs of the
community, namely, dealing with public expenditures and apportionment

and overseeing public works and building. A critical arrangement related to apportionment was added: "The apportionment [*tevzī'*] registers will be copied from the court records and sent to the center, where they will be examined, and if there are unsubstantiated items contrary to the directions, the ayan of that district will immediately be punished."[67] Following this clarification, the last part of the decree addressed the ayans themselves: "Do not, aside from actual expenses, add expenses in the apportionment registers for your personal interest or for oppressors."

The ayans were given the capacity to report the troubles of governors and other imperial officeholders directly to the central administration without the mediation of the kadis: "If [the kadis] hesitate to send letters [about the situation] . . . [a] report [should be attached to the] collective petition from the muftis, ulema, notables, and ordinary members of the community."[68] Here, the intermediary role of the kadis between the ayan and the community came into question, and the ayans and the community were considered an integrated body able to act collectively. Rather than regarding the kadis as protecting community interests against the ayans, the authors of the edict evidently saw the communities and the ayans as a united bloc of local interests vis-à-vis imperial agents, namely, provincial governors and kadis.

Two principles of district management had been established by 1786. First, ayans were to be elected with the communities' unanimous consent and were appointed only after grand vizier's approval, following a review; in the event of factionalism, the grand vizier decided. Second, twice a year, before public expenditures were allocated to them, communities had to submit apportionment registers, kept by the ayans with their consent, to the central administration for auditing and approval. These precautions did not, however, stop complaints from the districts about those who claimed to be ayans without being elected or about misconduct in the apportionment registers. In 1786, under the grand vizier Koca Yusuf Pasha (1785–88), a radical solution was found. Yusuf Pasha abolished the institution of ayanship, replacing it with the older institution of town stewardship (*şehir kethüdālığı*).[69] An imperial decree issued in 1786 dismissed the current district ayans throughout the empire: "From now on, the title of ayan is entirely abolished in districts and towns. The communities can elect whomever they want as urban stewards to oversee taxation, apportionment, and district affairs."[70]

Stewardship (*kethüdālık*) was an institution traditionally associated with urban craft and merchant guilds (*eṣnāf*). In general, town stewards were supervisors elected by guild members and appointed by sultanic diploma.[71] They represented the voice of the *eṣnāf* in the city and the entire urban population in certain matters. In the eighteenth century, in some cities, we come across such urban stewards as the representatives and supervisors of public affairs in the cities, but not the entire district.[72] This change signifies a shift from the district level to the town level. The ayans were regional actors, overseeing the district economy, connecting the towns and villages in the hinterlands, whereas town *keṯẖüdā*s were depicted as weak and humble people, representing the *eṣnāf* and urban populace.[73] Through this institutional shift from ayanship to *keṯẖüdā*ship, the central authority intended to change the power structure by eliminating notable individuals and families entrenched in the district who monopolized ayan positions. The ayans were to be replaced by humbler urban actors who acquired their positions through less problematic and more procedural electoral practices, led by guilds.

We do not know how effective this change was. Documents illustrate that in some districts, the arrangement had only a nominal impact. Former ayans merely reestablished themselves as town stewards. In other districts, however, we see upstarts who took advantage of this institutional change, and were able to grasp the stewardships. In February 1786, the kadi of Nevrekop (today's Godse Delchev in Bulgaria) sent a note to Istanbul informing the imperial Divan that the edict about the abolition of the ayanship had reached the city, and that the community had reelected their ayan, Mehmed Agha, this time not as ayan but as town steward.[74] In addition to these nominal changes, we observe cases in which the abolition of ayanship triggered new competition between ayans and their challengers who captured stewardships with connections to guilds or urban crowds. In the summer of 1786, the kadi of Pravishta district (now in Macedonia) sent a note informing the imperial Divan that some individuals had complained of Halil Agha, who had allegedly proclaimed himself ayan. The community came to court and declared that they had elected another person as town steward to oversee public affairs after the edict was issued. The former ayan Halil Agha, head of the leading notable family of the district (*ḥānedān*), no longer had anything to do with district matters.[75]

In 1791, after the consolidation of the New Order in Istanbul under Selim III, the central administration revoked the 1786 edict and reinstituted ayanship. The 1791 edict stated that formerly a single ayan had been elected by the community from among its notable families (*kiṣizāde*s) to protect subjects and manage affairs in the districts. However, this institution had deteriorated owing to competition between local powerholders, whose struggles created disorder, threatening peace and security. As a response to corruption and struggle, the institution of ayan had been abolished and urban stewardship initiated. However, the edict declares, stewards had failed to protect the sultan's subjects and properly manage complex district matters and affairs of state during the Ottoman-Russian war of 1786–92. Henceforth, the ayanship was restored to its earlier role.[76] Istanbul was convinced that the ayans, who traditionally came from powerful wealthy families (*kişizādes*), were more capable of dealing with provincial affairs than the town stewards, who were associated with urban professional organizations. Following the 1791 edict, the principles of the ayan institution were reestablished. A note to Selim III summarized the principle: "According to the regulations, ayans should not be appointed by sultanic decree, or vizier's or governor's orders. As stated [in the recent edicts], ayans are to be elected unanimously by the entire [district] community. Only after a person demonstrates an approval of the people [*kabūl-i 'amme*] of the district to the court can he be appointed with a legal certificate."[77]

If "it was difficult for the entire district community to reach consensus on one person [*cümle ahālīnin ittifākını bir yere cem' etmek bir emr-i 'asīr olduğundan*]," someone could be appointed by the state. But as Selim III made it clear in his own note, in that case the term *ayan* was not used.[78] With the New Order, the ayanship, which was identified with collective elections, acceptance, and consent, was certainly reinstituted.

Electoral Practices and District Politics

From the 1760s on, the various reform agendas clearly aimed at creating an institutional basis for communities to elect their own ayans to handle district affairs and participate in the apportionment process. The reasoning was that both the handling of local communities' affairs with minimum friction and the efficient collection of the taxes and services due to the empire required district ayans who were the choice of their communities and had collective approval. Ayans who had the support of their constituencies would minimize complaints and unrest, optimizing the mobilization of resources.

How did the local communities respond to the district reform? Since the 1760s, communities in different parts of the empire had showered the Ottoman central administration with hundreds of collective petitions concerning their ayans. Some communities endorsed the ayan that they had elected in their petitions, while others protested that the person who claimed to be their ayan had in fact not been chosen by them. In yet other cases, the community was divided between two or more factions, with different candidates.

Here are some of the many examples found in collective petitions sent to Istanbul:

Mahmud Zâim acted with the vain conviction that the [community had] entrusted [the] ayanship to him. [A notification from the court of Pristina, today Kosovo, 1759][79]

After the imperial edict arrived in the district of Serres, it was opened and read aloud in the presence of the people in the court; accordingly we ask that Mehmed Salih, who is the protector of the poor through [his] loyalty and righteousness, be appointed as our ayan. [A notification from the court of Serres, 1763][80]

Since Mühürdarzade Hacı Abdurrahman, may God amplify his power, is caring and pious, he was elected and chosen as our representative [*vekīl*] . . . with unanimous agreement. [A notification from the court of Serres, 1765][81]

We are all happy and content with our ayan Ahmed Haseki, who became ayan with our deliberate opinion [*re'y-i tedbīr*]. [A notification from the court of Feres, western Thrace, 1786][82]

Our ayan, Seyyid Ebû Bekir Agha, minds his own business. He rebukes oppressors and helps the poor. All of us are pleased with him; thanks to his good conduct, he is our experienced elected [ayan]. [A notification concerning petitions from various communities near Tokat, central Anatolia, 1791][83]

The community expelled Hacı Hasan, the former ayan of Ruse, from [his] ayanship because of his ingratitude, corruption, and mischief. [A report from Ruse, 1797/78][84]

As in the past, overseeing and administering the ayanship's affairs was only possible with the unanimous votes of the community. [İsmail Agha of Ruse's petition concerning various districts in central and eastern Bulgaria, 1801/02][85]

Since we cannot tolerate the injustices of Ömer, who has been ayan of our *kaza* since 1803, we are asking for an order to verify the dismissal of Ömer and to replace him as ayan with Çandarlı Hayreddin Bey-zade Mustafa Bey, currently ayan of İznik, who is from a notable family [*kişizāde*], considerate to the [sultan's] subjects, tough on outlaws, [and] generous to the poor, . . . who is capable of maintaining order, expelling bandits, and supervising affairs of the state, and whose merits are obvious. . . . We are all pleased with his deeds, manners, and words. [A petition from some leading individuals of Yalova, western Anatolia, 1804][86]

Although the communities were empowered to choose their own ayans, the central authority did not dictate how exactly to choose them. As with apportionment, electoral practices were left to the internal dynamics, power structures, negotiations, and competition within the district communities. Under this procedural ambiguity, documents show that ayan appointments were much more than straightforward electoral practices. They were often fashioned by messy political contests, which occasionally included violence. Different subgroups in the communities, including urban craftsmen and merchants, villagers, and religiously bonded groups, established alliances or confronted powerful wealthy individuals and families who claimed the ayanship. Not only imperial actors, such as governors and military commanders, but local janissaries in the provinces were also involved in these contests. Kadis, who were meant to be impartial, could play partisan roles in the process. Often rival factions within the district sent contrasting narratives formulated in different petitions to the center. Some dispatched representatives or other local authorities to Istanbul to lobby for their case. The central administration responded to these contrasting declaration and petitions by sending inspectors to the localities to examine the controversial cases and report back on them. As a result, imperial inspectors constantly moved from one district to another, sending in one report after another about local conditions.

Rahova, 1784

In 1784, the deputy governor of the subprovince of Niğbolu (Nikopol) sent a detailed report to the imperial Divan about a controversy concerning two individuals who claimed to have been elected by the community and their partisan constituencies in Rahova (today Oryahovo), a small city on the Danube in northwestern Bulgaria.[87] Its community was heavily Orthodox Christian, with a small Muslim minority, and the district was part of the hinterland of Vidin, a major Danubian stronghold, with a janissary legion, on the Ottoman-Habsburg frontier. The provisioning of Vidin was partially provided by the Rahova community, and as a result the janissaries of Vidin often interfered in the district's affairs.[88] Moreover, since some villages in the Rahova district were held as private estates (*mālikāne*) by female members of the Ottoman dynasty, the ayan controversy there was also a matter of interest to members of the imperial elite in Istanbul.

According to the report, for some time, Ziştovili-zade Mehmed and Kozarko Hüseyin, two Rahova magnates, had been competing to be ayan of the district. Kozarko Hüseyin was connected to the janissaries of Vidin, giving him influence in the district. The competition between Mehmed and Hüseyin polarized the Rahova community. Different town and village dwellers clustered around Mehmed and Hüseyin, forming two parties. Both groups dispatched petitions to the imperial Divan, telling conflicting stories, and sent representatives to Istanbul to lobby for their ayanships.

Mehmed's supporters claimed that the prior ayan was corrupt and had added personal expenses into the apportionment account. As a result, the Rahova community had dismissed him and elected Mehmed as the new ayan. Mehmed's supporters accused the kadi of Rahova and the scribe of the court of not being impartial and of acting in alliance with the janissaries of Vidin to make Hüseyin the ayan of Rahova against the will of the community.

Hüseyin's supporters, for their part, accused Mehmed of conspiring to remove the earlier ayan with the help of the guardian (governor) of Vidin, who was apparently at odds with the city's janissaries. They claimed that Mehmed had sought to become ayan of Rahova by allying himself with the governor, and argued that the prior ayan had not been involved in corruption but simply lacked the financial skills to handle district affairs. The community had therefore dismissed him and elected Hüseyin. They asked the central authority to prevent Mehmed from intervening in the business of the district.

Confronted with these two conflicting stories, the center sent an inspector, Cafer Efendi, to Rahova to handle the case and discover the truth. Cafer met the kadi and representatives of the two parties in Rahova. "I authorized Hüseyin as ayan, and I would not give the certifying letter to another person," the kadi insisted. During the inspector's visit, a sizable group from the community came to him chanting, "We want Zistovili-zade Mehmed as our ayan." Hüseyin's supporters attacked them, killing one. Following this violence, supporters of Hüseyin in the villages of Rahova declared that if Mehmed became ayan, they would leave Rahova and settle in Wallachia, and some villagers in fact had already crossed the Danube and done so. Meanwhile, some supporters of Mehmed dispatched envoys to Istanbul to lobby on his behalf. They met with a military dignitary, Osman Agha, who was one of the chiefs of the imperial artillery corps and apparently had an estate in Rahova district. Although not terribly well informed about the situation in the district, the latter was persuaded to endorse Mehmed and submitted this opinion to the imperial Divan.

The Divan ordered that the 1784 edict that regulated ayan elections be read aloud in the court of the district in the presence of representatives of the Rahova community. The janissaries of Vidin were warned not to become involved in Rahova's affairs, and Cafer who had already been in the region as inspector, was asked to substantiate that the successful candidate had been elected by the community. If necessary, he was to visit neighborhoods, villages, and dwellings (*mekān mekān*) and determine the community's choice. The Muslim and Christian notables would then be assembled to petition the central authority collectively for the appointment of the ayan the district had chosen. No money was to be taken from the community during this inspection. "If we receive any information that somebody implicitly or explicitly forced the community to accept someone they did not consent to," the Divan declared, "these people will be severely punished [*marżīleri olmayan kimesneyi a'yānlığa kabūl edin deyü sırran ve 'alenen cebr olmamak*]."[89]

The Rahova case typifies contemporary Ottoman district politics: factions clustered around two competing notables, both seeking the post of ayan, and alliances with different actors, including janissaries from the neighboring town, the imperial governor, and absentee revenue holders in Istanbul. The factions, claiming to represent the entire district community, employed various strategies: petitioning, lobbying in Istanbul and other central towns, expressing the collective will through demonstrations in the town, threatening the authorities with emigrating to another region, and jeopardizing the district economy. Violence and armed conflict between the factions was often a component of the negotiations. If the district courts and the kadis failed to substantiate the will of the community, or there was a clear disagreement among community leaders concerning the collective will, the center might send an inspector to substantiate the truth of the case (*maddenin ṣaḥīḥi*). In the absence of a clear election procedure, voting mechanisms, and electoral records, the outcome was heavily based on impressions. Under these conditions, the inspector was also asked to discover the collective will, sometimes through extensive opinion surveys, sometimes by visiting each neighborhood or village and directly asking what the people's choice was.[90] Eventually, representatives of the community were invited to deliberate and declare their opinion and elect their ayan in a court assembly. As contentious and ambiguous as the process was, the conditions of "general agreement" (*cümlenin ittifāḳı*) or "public acceptance" (*ḳabūl-ı 'amme*) in decision-making signified collective participation as the underlying principle of district governance.[91]

COMMUNITIES AND IMMUNITIES

As with many early modern polities, the fiscal and administrative organization of the Ottoman landscape resembled a conglomerate patchwork. In addition to the hierarchical and interwoven divisions of provinces (*eyālet*), subprovinces (*sancaḳ/livā'*), and districts (*ḳażā'*), there were hundreds of large and small enclaves with immunities (*serbestiyet*) from administrative and fiscal intervention by officeholders and different fiscal and administrative regimes, separated from the jurisdiction of the larger provincial divisions in which they were physically located. The statuses of the immune enclaves varied. Some had *mālikāne* status. These were semi-private estates leased out or granted with life-term contracts to semi-private entrepreneurs, who were generally members of the imperial elite or provincial notables. Other enclaves remained under the administration of the imperial waqfs, which were supervised by trustees centered in Istanbul. And yet others were large estates (*ḥāṣṣ*) held by some imperial dignitaries, including male and female members of the Ottoman dynasty, viziers, and high-ranking military officers. It was common practice for the primary holders or supervisors of these enclaves to be absentees. Commonly, they outsourced their jurisdiction to local contractors in short- or long-term deals. In this variegated administrative and fiscal topology, the subcommunities in these enclaves within the districts were fiscally (and sometimes administratively) separated from the larger district community. The proliferation of these immune units, especially hundreds of *mālikāne* estates spread across the empire, deepened the variegated fiscal and administrative landscape of the empire, which caused various complications concerning administration and revenue collection, the status of the communities, and the jurisdiction of authorities in the eighteenth and early nineteenth centuries.[92]

Feres, 1786

Perhaps the best way to illustrate how the communities acted in this variegated fiscal and administrative landscape is to begin with an example. A 1786 controversy from the district of Feres (Firecik) in western Thrace is an illuminating case, in which multiple collective and individual actors with different fiscal statuses and claims interacted. The Feres district included a town (Feres) and numerous villages. Many of these villages were connected to an imperial waqf. This means that their revenues were collected for the waqf administration and the communities in these villages were under the protection of the waqf. The communities connected to the waqf were separated from the rest of the district community when it came to certain taxes, fees, and services they delivered. These village communities did not fully contribute to the district's apportionment. Instead, they delivered most of their taxes and fees directly to the waqf administration in Istanbul.

According to numerous petitions that the community of Feres sent the central authority, the scribe of the imperial waqf, who lived in Istanbul, had intervened in the business of governance in Feres and tried to manipulate the election of the district's ayan. According to the complaints, the scribe had organized a faction in the community with the help of local mercenaries to impeach the current ayan and install one of his men, a local mercenary, as the new ayan. The scribe, the petitioners argued, had even mobilized some women in the district and encouraged them to send grievances about the misconduct of the current ayan's bodyguards. Allegedly, his purpose was to collect more revenue for the waqf by manipulating the apportionment process, since the revenues of the waqf villages were also collected by the district ayan through the same settlements, but with a different matrix and separate rates, in the court of Feres.

Meanwhile, the waqf villagers were polarized. Some groups remained loyal to their patron, the scribe of the waqf, in Istanbul, and supported the candidate he wanted as ayan. Others, however, supported the current ayan and emphasized the cohesion of the district community, saying: "Since the old times, we have not separated from our neighbors."[93] Both groups hired local mercenaries against each other. Violence was unavoidable. Tribunals took place in Feres. Hundreds of community members convened with competing stories. Eventually, the case was submitted to the imperial Divan in Istanbul, which in this case functioned as a court of appeal. After the reports of kadis and the situation of the waqf scribe had been reviewed, the Divan ordered that the current district ayan keep his position. The Divan warned the scribe of the waqf and prevented him from having his man appointed as ayan through a long-distance operation.

This case illustrates not only possible tensions between different subgroups within the district community because of their different administrative and fiscal statuses but also the broader nexus of interests across local groups and absentee holders. Long-distance interference by absentee holders or waqf supervisors in Istanbul who had an interest in the district was commonplace. Such interference was also documented on various occasions, as in a note submitted to the Divan in September 1803:

Most of the grievances sent to Istanbul about the ayans, the overseers, and the deputy governors were not reliable. It is known that generally they were fabricated cases. It is required that the ayans who managed the districts should be elected and approved by the communities in their locality. The grievances and information, which were fabricated so that some people in Istanbul [i.e., absentee revenue holders] could intervene in the business of the district, and which were the source of disorder, should not be taken into consideration."[94]

This statement echoes the edicts on ayan elections previously analyzed. Keeping district management free from outside intervention was a basic principle of the Ottoman state in this reform era. Likewise, the primary agenda included the cohesion of district communities and minimization of tensions between various groups with different fiscal and administrative statuses. "Some communities of the immune units of the imperial domains or waqfs were treated favorably and others were treated as if they were not subjects of the Exalted State. Those subjects who were not protected through immunities were oppressed," an Ottoman bureaucrat complained, referring to the privileged statuses of some groups that received better protection from their powerful holders.[95]

In fact, some enclave communities were considered privileged since they remained under the jurisdiction of powerful individuals, including dignitaries of the empire or members of the dynasty. In these units the private interest of the holder and the public interest of the communities were seen as harmonized through the patron-client relationship between holder and community. This was especially the case in *mālikāne* contracts. It was believed that life-term guarantees and the full jurisdiction given to holders of these contracts synchronized the interests of the communities in the enclaves and the holder. The communities of the immune zones, which were under the authority of stronger holders, were considered favored, since they might receive better protection from their patrons. On several occasions, local communities petitioned the central administration to be integrated into an enclave of a holder whom the community preferred and who might offer better protection. In 1785, when the community of a minor locality in the Neşne district in Bosnia petitioned against their short-term tax collector, they asked that the unit be transformed into a *mālikāne*. "The purpose of this status change was to free the community from the oppression [of the short-term tax collectors]." The fiscal bureaucrats then recommended that the *mālikāne* should be granted to somebody the community approved of.[96]

Documents illustrate that these communities and the holders of the units were often in contact, even though the holders were most often absentees. The dozens of enclaves held by Esma Sultan (1778–1848), the daughter of Abdulhamid I (r. 1774–89), provide an example of such a patron, who established long-distance patronage relations with her communities. Esma Sultan regularly received petitions and reports from her *mālikāne* communities, sending inspectors to check on the conduct of the intendants she appointed.[97] But not only the leading dignitaries of the empire were keen to protect their communities. Sometimes petty holders in Istanbul had connections with their communities and had them protected. In 1792, for instance, Hüseyin Agha, a retired palace barber who lived in Istanbul and the holder of a minor *mālikāne* unit, the village of Yeni Köy near Skopje (Üsküb), submitted a petition to the Divan. He stated that, for some time, one Turfullu Mehmed Sipahi, who had assembled a force of several thousand Albanian mercenaries, had terrorized his *mālikāne*, the village of Yeni Köy, and neighboring villages. The communities of Yeni Köy had dispatched envoys to Hüseyin Agha and asked him to request that the Divan take action. "If the Exalted State expels the outlaws," Hüseyin Agha declared in his petition, "the Yeni Köy community and myself will be free of harm and damage."[98] The Istanbul administration appointed a local officer to check the case.

Cases involving an absentee *mālikāne* holder and the community, several local actors, and the central state, were fairly common.[99] However, the enclave communities were not always happy with their patrons. In 1805, when some representatives of the community of a *mālikāne* unit in Serres complained about Yusuf, the son of İsmail, the famous ayan of Serres, Yusuf seemed to panic and had a petition sent to the Divan, claiming that the petitioners did not have the necessary deeds documenting their eligibility to represent the entire community of the *mālikāne*. Yusuf accused the intendant of Drama, a neighboring district, who had allegedly conspired to provoke some of the members of the *mālikāne* community under his contract.[100] The *mālikāne* holders, faced with communal protest or complaints might be in trouble, since the possibility always existed of interference, or even the cancellation of a contract by the central state. In many *mālikāne* cases, the approval of the communities, while not required, mattered.

The *tīmār*s and *ze'āmet*s held by members of the traditional provincial cavalry did not fully disappear in the eighteenth century, although many of these old units were converted into *mālikāne*, and hundreds of them were outsourced to provincial magnates in toto. It was a common practice in the eighteenth century that *tīmār* or *ze'āmet* holders were also absentees, like *mālikāne* holders, and their administration was left to the district ayans or local contractors. Village communities under *tīmār* or *ze'āmet* jurisdiction also enjoyed different treatment, which was not necessarily favorable. Although the communities often participated in the apportionment process at the district level, they paid the traditional land taxes to the *tīmār* or *ze'āmet* holders. In the winter of 1789, the *tīmār* and *ze'āmet* communities of the Kystendil district (now in eastern Bulgaria) sent collective petitions against the ayan of the district, alleging that he forced members of the communities to work on his personal farms.[101]The absentee holder of these fiefs did not necessarily bother to take necessary steps to protect the peasants on them, since neither the jurisdictional capacity nor the revenues collected were as appealing to the proprietors as to *mālikāne* holders. The community collectively requested a change in the status of their lands from *tīmār* to *mālikāne*, which they believed provided them with more favorable protection.[102]

This discussion of communities under different jurisdictions in the same district offers a glimpse of the patchwork of Ottoman lands constituted by intermingled fiscal and administrative zones. In the complex interest nexus of different units, communities were often aware of their fiscal statuses, designed their own strategies to protect the collective interest, developed connections with absentee holders, and negotiated to participate in or isolate themselves from the broader district administration. In certain cases, to be a part of an immune unit was beneficial; in other cases it was not, depending on local conditions, the status and personality of the holder, and the unit. But overall the administration of these units was a complex process, since multiple actors, including the central administration, the provincial governor, the elected district ayans, the holders of *tīmār* and *mālikāne* divisions (absentee or not) in the district, the waqf administration, the subcontractors of absentee holders and waqfs, and possibly neighboring magnates, as well as various natural community leaders and factions, could be all part of the same equation.

In sum, ayanship became an essential institution of the Ottoman provincial order in the eighteenth and early nineteenth centuries. Ayans in many ways differed from other administrators. They were locally and

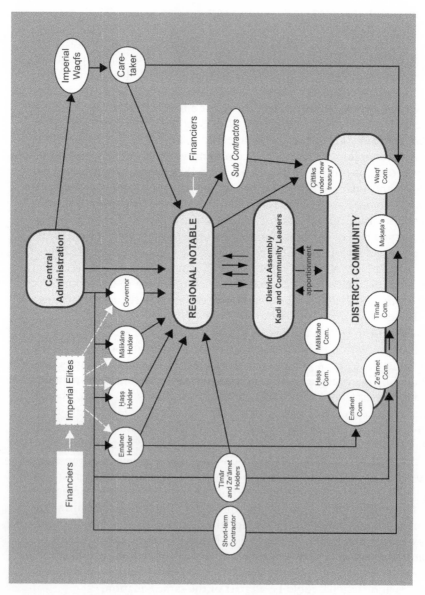

Figure 4. A scenario of provincial governance. The author and Deniz Coşkun.

communally elected, nominated, or approved to carry out public services. In this respect, they were like the elected mayors of modern times. But the ayans were at the same time entrepreneurs. As patron-creditors, they supplied communities with services and credit and collected commissions in exchange. In this regard, they were profit-seeking contractors performing a public service. In various cases, as we shall see in the next section, they were also protectors, often backed by armed forces. Some ayans were humble figures; others, like İsmail of Ruse or of Serres, became regional power-holders, as discussed in chapter 2. Still, as we have seen, ayans were not the only major actors operating at the district level. In districts predominantly populated by Christians, strongmen called *kocabaşıs*, empowered by local electoral politics, functioned like ayans. They were, so to speak, Christian ayans; sometimes they were termed representatives of the Christian community (*vekīl-i re'āyā*).[103] In districts entirely under the jurisdiction of imperial waqfs, estate intendants called *voyvoda*s, who were appointed by the waqf administration or the primary holders of the estates, or directly by the central administration, acted like ayans, albeit without the formal need for popular nomination. As already noted, some districts or even entire subprovinces, like the Çapanoğlus' Yozgat, were held by notable individuals and families with *mālikāne* contracts or similar deals, which provided autonomous rule in these large units. Still, we should not envision neat, precise divisions between various authorities, communities, revenue sources, or spatial units in this dizzying institutional agglomeration.

VIOLENCE, SECURITY, AND COLLECTIVE VOWS

Managing provincial units was not solely a fiscal and administrative operation. Since violence was generally a common component of provincial life, maintaining peace and order was as critical as administration. Four major wars in the years 1768–74, 1787–92, 1798–99, and 1806–12 disrupted the relative stability of several Ottoman regions, and numerous uprisings and banditry shook localities from Bosnia to Arabia. Abdi Pasha, one of the commanders of the Ottoman imperial army in the 1770s, complained of the spread of firearms among the communities: "Although it is their responsibility to obey the governors, if one goes to their locality, people meet the governor with . . . firearms. . . . [These] should be collected and conveyed to the imperial armory. Only then will it be clear who is a civilian [*re'āyā*] and who is military."[104]

In this insecure world, communities expected district ayans not only to supervise public finance and district affairs but also to maintain security. Ayans regularly hired mercenaries, adding the cost to the apportionment accounts. "From now on," an imperial edict warned notables in

the Balkan provinces in 1804, "ayans, voyvodas, and notable families
are not allowed to hire armed Albanians. The Albanians employed by
them will be sent to their hometowns. Instead, they [have] hired armed
bands from the local forces."[105] Albanian paramilitary groups spreading
in the Balkans after the turmoil in the Peloponnese in the 1770s were only
one example of how some regions produced a large market for freelance
troops looking for individual patrons or communities to hire them.[106]
When some district ayans became patrons of armed groups, the empire
regularly called on these in wartime. The communities responded by petitioning the central administration to absolve these notables from military
duties and from taking part in imperial campaigns.[107] As a result, the
martial capacity of some district ayans became part of their portfolios.

Perhaps more striking is the fact that some districts dismissed their
own ayans and invited in a strongman from outside as a new ayan to
protect the community. In 1786, the court at Gümülcine in northeastern
Greece (now Komotini) declared: "Our ayan, Mustafa Agha, is incapable
and old. He [has] resigned. . . . Meanwhile, Emin Agha from Hasköy
[Haskovo in today's southern Bulgaria], backed by a band of mercenaries, claimed to be ayan of our district and to protect the community
[*a'yānlık żabṭı ve rabṭ-ı memleket ve ḥimāyet ü siyānet-i ahālī ve rai'yyet
iddi'āsında*]. However, his men mostly come from gangs and riffraff." The
community accordingly invited in another protector, İsmail of Serres, a
leading powerholder in the region, saying: "Our well-being is only possible under the protection of İsmail Bey of Serres. We thus jointly choose
him and ask for his protection [*bi'l-ittifāḳ intiḫāb ve ṭālibkār olduğumuz*].
. . . if he does not accept [our offer], we shall perish."[108] The instability
of the political and social order in wartime and during internal uprisings
presented strongmen with military and economic power with new opportunities. With insecure communities looking for protection, some of
these men played the part of military and administrative entrepreneurs,
seeking communities to provide with security and administrative services
in return for wealth and power.

The initiatives taken by communities to elect, dismiss, or invite in
strongmen as their ayans to manage district affairs and provide protection were not the only collective actions. In addition to these initiatives,
there were several forms of collective vow, known as *nezīr*, a collective
oath by which members of a group promised to act in specified ways.
Members of the community signed a public pledge in which the conditions of the promise were stated in detail, with a list of signatories.
Most often, the contractors agreed to pay compensation if the promise was broken. The individual members of the group became guarantors (*kefīl*) liable for one another's actions. These collective vows were
regularly sworn by district communities, which were asked to promise

to pay necessary imperial dues. Such guarantees consolidated collective responsibilities. District communities became more responsible for their collective undertakings, while the central administration treated them as corporate bodies whose members were one another's guarantors.[109]

Communities were often asked by the state to pledge not to host outlaws or invite them in as ayans or mercenaries. In 1760, for example, the central authority asked several communities in Macedonia to pledge collectively not to accept Mahmud Zaim, an Albanian magnate who had been declared an outlaw, as their ayan.[110] These promises included the fee to be paid to the state if the community broke a collective promise. In December 1796, "the Muslim and non-Muslim subjects of Samako [in eastern Thrace] who were older than seven were bound to the collective surety [*küfelāya rabṭ*] that they will not ask for help from the outlaws or help them." The document was prepared under the supervision of the ayan, the kadi, and a special envoy of the governor. The register lists the individuals who became one another's guarantors.[111] These contracts were signed, not between the communities and the empire, but rather among members of communities. Individual members became one another's guarantors in a collective promise to the state. By listing individuals, these pledges differed from the collective and unanimous declarations at court assemblies. They were formulated in the format of the Islamic law of surety, which recognized people, rather than the community in the abstract, as a collective body.

In sum, neither bands of outlaws nor paramilitary teams were new in the late eighteenth and early nineteenth centuries. Thievery, plundering, rustling, smuggling, and extortion were common practices in the Ottoman provinces, as in any other premodern polity. Communities or cities had always looked for Seven Samurai–like figures to provide security services. What was new in the Ottoman provincial communities of the late eighteenth and early nineteenth centuries was their institutional framework, which allowed them to offer formal positions to leaders of armed men for protection and to manage their public affairs as their ayans. Such formal invitations were further consolidated with collective vows formulated as communal contracts.

CONCLUSION: THE ORDER OF COMMUNITIES

In the preceding pages, I have outlined some mechanisms through which communities participated in provincial governance; elected and dismissed their administrators, managers, patron-creditors, and protectors; and took collective action for protection and security in the Balkans and Anatolia in the late eighteenth and early nineteenth centuries. I have argued that during this period, collective practices became key to provincial order. In the beginning, these collective actions grew organically, without systematic intervention from the center. In the second half of the eighteenth century, however, the Ottoman administration took steps to recognize, formalize, standardize, and institutionalize these practices. Gradually, the collective voice of the district communities became an essential component of Ottoman provincial order.

By means of numerous edicts promulgated from the 1760s onward, the central administration gave communities the authority to nominate individuals who acted as district ayans. The communities unanimously approved or vetoed fiscal accounts kept by these notables, which included public expenses and how these were apportioned (*tevzi'*) among property owners. Ayans, who were generally wealthy, powerful individuals, were expected to be accountable to the communities. Although the state did not impose detailed procedures for how these electoral and auditing practices would be carried out, the central administration tried to monitor whether the unanimous will of the communities could be substantiated. Governors and other military and administrative officeholders appointed by the sultan from among the imperial hierarchies were not allowed to intervene in these collective practices. The kadis who supervised the assemblies where collective decisions took place were likewise supposed to be impartial.

These collective decisions were limited in that they required the center's final authorization. After approval in the local courts, the district accounts were to be reaudited and reapproved by the fiscal bureaucracy. Likewise, electoral practices were to be ratified (or vetoed) by the grand vizier on the basis of the appropriateness of individuals nominated by the communities. The state could, if necessary, change the status of the district administration, appoint someone from outside as administrator, and modify accounts without the consent of the community. The Ottoman government did not share its sovereignty with the communities or treat them as corporate entities with rights to negotiate collectively with the state. Although the state treated the community as an integrated unit, its collective pledges were not reciprocal contracts between the communities and the state. Rather, they were contracts between members of the community.

From the perspective of the imperial administration, the motivation in reforming district administration was twofold. First, it intended to consolidate, formalize, and standardize apportionment practices and electoral patterns in the central provinces. Apportionment and collective participation with local assemblies were thought to be more advantageous for both the state and communities, or public order in general, than top-down governance. In the absence of updated registers of local demographic and economic conditions, collective apportionment allowed the communities to bear the burden of public expenditures and taxes based on their real internal dynamics and local conditions, determined through deliberations. Likewise, the collectively elected ayans were to be more effective in the process. Unlike centrally appointed agents who had no local knowledge or limited ability to mobilize resources, the ayans were able to carry out administration and revenue collection with local knowledge and the consent of the communities, using less coercion.

The Ottoman agenda to reform the provincial order by empowering communities and district assemblies echoes the political and fiscal program of the physiocrats in ancien régime France. As in physiocratic theory, reform in an Ottoman district was based on the expectation that the participation of the community, first and foremost the property owners, in decision-making in revenue collection, apportionment, and electing their administrators "would create a precise nexus of interest and loyalty between the creators of wealth and the state itself."[112] These local assemblies did not share sovereignty with the sultan. In this respect they differed from feudal estates or republican assemblies. They were not designed to challenge or balance the power of the central state. On the contrary, they facilitated the administration and revenue collection of the state. With collective participation, the reformists believed, the Ottoman state would extract surplus value more peacefully and justly.

Second, by empowering communities in the accounting settlement and elections, the reformists intended to curtail the growing power of local elites, not only those acting as ayans but also regional magnates who monopolized governorships, deputy governorships, and other imperial offices. The bottom-up collective mechanisms were intended to protect the collective interests of the communities against the private interests of administrators and officeholders. These participatory mechanisms would also curtail the power of the provincial magnates who held governorships or fiscal, administrative, or military contracts and fostered mutual interest and a tacit alliance between the central state and provincial communities. This conformed to the old imperial theory that the interests of the empire and the communities should be harmonized (*enfā'*) at the expense of provincial governors and other powerholders, who had natural inclinations to commit injustice in jurisdictions under their control to maximize profits and power.[113] What was new in the late eighteenth and early nineteenth centuries was that the empire invited communities to be active participants in this contest. By empowering collectivities to elect administrators and approve their fiscal accounts, the empire shared the responsibility to maintain order and justice with the provincial people.

As we saw in chapter 1, district reform was one of the aims of the New Order movement, reflected in the number of reform proposals prepared by bureaucrats and intellectuals involved in its agenda. Although the main focus of these proposals was the military reorganization of the empire, the provincial question was an important element of the reform agenda. There was a visible trend, in particular among those who came from the fiscal bureaucracy, that emphasized the centrality of collective action in district administration and the role of the ayans. According to fiscal bureaucrats such as Mehmed Şerif, minister of fiscal affairs, and İbrahim Efendi, chief accountant in the reign of Selim III, the district, organized around the kadi court and ayan, would be the central unit in the provincial regime. The business of the state and the communities in the provinces should be managed exclusively by the ayans. Confusion owing to the proliferation of immune units should be removed. While the immune units should also be entrusted to the district ayans, the communities in these entities should be integrated into the rest of the district community.[114]

These reform agendas emphasized the central role in provincial governance of local communities and ayans, rather than imperial agents appointed by the center, and assumed that, given their economic capacity, local knowledge, and ability to mobilize local resources, local actors were much more capable of taking care of provincial affairs. Moreover, since they were from the local communities and since they were also to be elected by the communities and/or obtain collective consent, the communities would more easily comply with their decisions. Conflicts between the communities and the administrative class would be minimized through these electoral and consensual mechanisms. "The community will be at ease and the business of the state will be supervised nicely."[115] When word of the benefits of the new system spread, "other communities will also ask for this order through petitions."[116]

These neat ideas of reform hardly corresponded to the messy realities of the Ottoman provinces. It was not easy to prevent governors from interfering in district administration. The kadis or the proxy kadis were not impartial, since most of the time they were involved in factional politics. The hundreds of immune units spread out across the provinces could not be eliminated, since these units involved so many pressure groups and vested interests. The communities were given leverage to nominate or dismiss notables. However, no systematic procedure enabled them to use this authority. But it was obvious that the expansion of the apportionment system and electoral mechanisms invited new actors into the imperial state. With district reform, local actors, both notables and representatives of the communities, became active formal participants in governance.

Districts became lively political theaters, where the empire, communities, and notables actively performed in political mêlées. How should we see this provincial reform in the general framework of center-periphery relations? Should we understand it as an outcome of the decentralization of the Ottoman Empire? Or was it rather a process nurturing the forces of centralization and integration?

Several historians of Europe and Asia have challenged the conventional argument that bureaucratic centralization in the eighteenth and early nineteenth centuries automatically marginalized the local governance mechanism. On the contrary, in many cases, the forces of centralism established alliances with local forces and incorporated some local mechanisms into their designs. Likewise, local forces sought alliances with the central administration, and local institutions were reconfigured and integrated into centralizing projects. Regional estates were part of the centralization and integration process in northern Europe and France respectively, as Marie-Laure Legay has shown for Flanders and Julian Swann for Burgundy.[117] Philip Kuhn illustrates how fiscal reformists in the late Qing Empire designed electoral mechanisms through which villagers were to elect middlemen to manage local public affairs and the empire at the same time.[118] The Ottoman experience of reforming governance by empowering collective and individual local actors in the administration of public affairs, allowing greater space for participation and responsibility, and mobilizing resources through these local collective mechanisms did not signify a total process of decentralization. Rather, reform suggested a process of integration through decentralizing certain missions, responsibilities, and institutions.

"Although local governments were seen to be the site of many important changes and were, overall, vibrant places where new experiments with governance were being carried out, it was also repeatedly stressed that changes—whether for good or ill—were extremely vulnerable," Merilee S. Grindle writes of local experience in modern Latin America.[119] The experimental roots of nineteenth-century municipal democratic experience spread, too, in local politics, collective action, and leadership in Ottoman districts in the late eighteenth and early nineteenth centuries. Later, with the reforms between 1838 and 1870, electoral processes became more procedural and formal, based on ballot voting by property-owning males and majority rule (*ekseriyet-i ārā*) instead of unanimous agreement throughout the Ottoman lands. However, ayans would disappear as formally elected district administrators or managers. The earlier concept of ayans as natural leaders of the community was revived. While the voting practices of the communities expanded in municipal self-government and later at the imperial level, the central authority started to appoint bureaucrats, called *muhassıls*, to administer the fiscal affairs to every single municipal unit.[120] The Tanzimat period became a period of constant negotiations between communities, who acquired participatory habits in the late eighteenth and early nineteenth centuries, and the central Ottoman government, which was more and more interested in controlling social and political dynamics, recording resources, and transforming urban space. Immune statuses were abolished. Municipal assemblies were separated from kadi courts. Apportionment processes gradually disappeared. Massive tax surveys based on the property and incomes of the individual households eliminated lump-sum taxation, and a more complex income tax collection system was instituted.[121] Meanwhile the amorphous conception of a multiconfessional community gave way to the formalization of subcommunities organized around religious identities and confessional ties. From the mid nineteenth century on, not the amorphous district community, but formally defined Muslim, Christian, and Jewish communities, or *millets*, were key players in collective action in the Ottoman Empire.

CHAPTER 4

Crisis

Riots, Conspiracies, and Revolutions, 1806–1808

> It is as though everyone in Rumelia, Anatolia, and Istanbul
> combined [against the New Order].
>
> Mütercim Ahmed Asım

In August 1806, in the midst of political turmoil in the Balkans, a few
months after the apportionment episode in Ruse discussed at the start of
chapter 3, İsmail Agha was murdered on his farm. After İsmail's death,
notables of the community of Ruse assembled in the city court and announced that they had elected Bayraktar Mustafa Agha, the ayan of the
smaller and less strategic district of Razgrad (Hazergrad), south of Ruse,
as ayan of their district too, characterizing him as one of their late ayan's
loyal supporters in their petition asking that he be appointed. After meeting in court, the representatives of the Ruse community sent the following
letter to Istanbul:

This is the petition of your humble well-wisher to the Exalted State: The learned
and the virtuous and the imams and the preachers and the nobles and chiefs and
standard-bearers and the elders and the Muslim and the non-Muslim subjects
of the city of Ruse and its district, all together came to the court and declared:
Your servant Seyyid Tirsinikli İsmail Agha, who has been our ayan for eight to
ten years . . . passed away on August 12, 1806. During his time as our ayan,
we lived in peace and tranquility. [Bayraktar] Mustafa Agha, who was one of
İsmail's loyal followers and is currently ayan of Hazergrad, is our unanimously
elected and chosen one [*münteḫeb ve muḫtārı*]. His qualities are known. He
is one of the notables. He is caring. He shows a great zeal in carrying out and
executing the collection of necessary dues. If he becomes ayan of our district in
the place of the late İsmail, we shall live in peace and tranquility as before. In
this petition, we ask the Exalted State to issue a noble order to appoint Mustafa
as our ayan.[1]

Did Bayraktar become ayan through an election or did he, in fact, impose himself upon the community of Ruse? According to a report sent to Istanbul, Bayraktar was elected by the community with the involvement, perhaps persuasion, of İsmail's faction (*Tirsinikli ṭakımı*) in Ruse.[2] Before the petition reached Istanbul, the Divan had been informed of a letter from Manuk Bey, İsmail's Armenian financier, telling his partner in Istanbul that forty-one of the Ruse district's local leaders had assembled in the city and declared their obedience to Bayraktar. Meanwhile, Bayraktar sent messages to the Divan that if he were recognized as the ayan of Ruse, he would confiscate İsmail's substantial heritage and turn it over to the Treasury or spend it in the state's service.[3] After long deliberation, the Divan confirmed him in office.[4] In September, a letter was sent to him confirming his ayanship, with a note from Sultan Selim III: "The community of Ruse has elected you; you shall be the ayan of Ruse."[5]

Between the summer of 1806 and the winter of 1808, Mustafa Bayraktar became the key actor in a series of turbulent episodes that shook the entire empire. During these two years, three governments fell; as a result of popular riots or coups, two sultans were deposed, and thousands of people, including two deposed sultans and leading imperial elites, lost their lives. The crisis began in August 1806, when a group of provincial notables, acting in alliance with janissaries and local communities, blocked the New Army's exit to the Balkans in a clash in Edirne. This triggered a sequence of events in the Balkans and Anatolia, and eventually in Istanbul, that resulted in the fall of Selim III and his reformist party, the New Order, in a janissary-led popular rebellion in March 1807. Before long, developments in the Ottoman Empire became a major theme in European politics. In late 1806, the Ottoman Empire became an ally of Napoleon's France and found itself in a war against Russia. In the summer of 1808, Bayraktar and a group of New Orderists led a coup in Istanbul with support from several Balkan notables. Together, they suppressed janissary oligarchs in Istanbul and reinstated the New Order. But in November 1808, a janissary-led popular rebellion ended the restoration of the New Order. Mustafa Bayraktar was killed and the New Order was once again abrogated.

NARRATIVES OF THE CRISIS

Rather than a linear chain of events beginning with the New Order and ending with the restoration, these two years of turmoil represent a path of twists, turns, and dead ends. The crisis was provoked by violent changes that gave birth to unprecedented settlements, shifting coalitions, and pursuits to end the empire's predicaments in multiple political theaters, including Edirne, Istanbul, and Ruse. Several observers and historians have examined these years as a chain of connected episodes, during which radical transformations occurred and radical options appeared, but did not transpire.

In Ottoman historiography, various narratives titled the *Vaḳā'-i Cedīd* (Event of the New [Order]) or *Vaḳā'-i Selim III* (Event of Selim III), are devoted to aspects of these episodes. Other texts are dedicated to key figures, such as Kabakçı Mustafa, the leader of the first janissary-led popular revolt, Mustafa Bayraktar, and Selim III.[6] In addition to such focused histories, annals of wider scope, including the *Asım tarihi, Câbî tarihi*, and *Şanizade tarihi*, give special attention to these events in long entries.[7] In Ottoman political and popular culture, official and unofficial versions of the twists and turns from the New Order to the restoration of the old are contested territory. Writers take different approaches to the reform agenda, to anti-reform sentiments voiced by janissaries and other groups, and to the role of provincial notables in this struggle. While some have approved of or glorified the reform efforts of Selim III, depicting these changes as necessary for the empire, others have blamed the reforms for corrupting military culture with alien European ways, threatening vested interests, and fraudulently enriching the ruling elite. Some observers have portrayed Mustafa Bayraktar as a savior of the empire and protector of the poor against janissary oppression, while others depict him as a puppet magnate manipulated by the reformist or corrupted elite. In some narratives, janissary-led popular revolts are described as revolts of the general public against the New Order; others depict them as riots by mobs.

The narrative of the events of 1806–8 provided by the mid-nineteenth-century historian and jurist Ahmed Cevdet Pasha (1822–95) in his *Tarih-i Cevdet* (Cevdet's History; 1854–84) shaped later Ottoman Turkish accounts in the nineteenth and twentieth centuries.[8] In his long discussion of the causes of the events that resulted in the fall of the New Order, Cevdet argued that the real conflict was between the New Order party, led by Selim III, who aimed to reform the empire's military, and the outdated janissary corps, which indulged in its popular support. Over time, however, the New Orderists became corrupted by the power and wealth they acquired. Selim III had good intentions but he acted imprudently. Eventually, with the support of the populace, the janissaries were able to depose Selim and the reform party violently. Bayraktar, who established his control in the Danubian region, was dragged into the conflict to save the New Order. But Bayraktar had neither the preparation nor the capacity for such a mission.[9] "It was regretful that Alemdar [Bayraktar], who had good intentions and high zeal for his state and people, became such a victim," Cevdet wrote, and he added: "More regretful was the abolition of his trained army, the New Militia, which was recognized a second time. Alas, no attempt would work without God's permission."[10] The New Order was an effort to achieve necessary military reform, but it was poorly equipped and implemented. Despite the best intentions of its backers, the New Order failed again.

Despite their fascination with these dramatic events, Ottoman historians in the nineteenth century did not narrate these episodes as a single crisis or revolution. Rather, they depicted each event or crisis as one episode in a historical sequence, connected, but not necessarily part of a narrative of continuous change. The first historian to depict the events between 1806 and 1808 as one story constituted by connected episodes that triggered one another, culminating in a popular revolt and the fall of the New Order, was Antoine Juchereau de Saint-Denys (1778–1842),[11] a French émigré and military engineer employed by the Ottoman state as an expert in fortifications and artillery. His book *Révolutions de Constantinople* narrated the stormy events that he observed in the Ottoman capital in 1807 and 1808:

Three great revolutions shook up the Ottoman Empire in the years 1807 and 1808. In less than two years, two emperors were dethroned and strangled; five grand viziers were deposed, beheaded, or poisoned; several lower-ranking ministers were dismembered by the populace of Constantinople; new regular militias known as *nizam gedittes* (New Order) . . . were dissolved and partially exterminated. All these great events that followed one another at extraordinary speed have been seen in Europe as fearsome revolutions with disastrous consequences that would be felt for many years to come. The Turks, however, have seen in this only the happy result of ordinary resistance against an innovative government that wanted to change the civil and military laws of the empire.[12]

Since the seventeenth century, European writers had employed the French word *révolution* to define radical changes in the political order and violent falls of government, with or without popular rebellion. In the late eighteenth and early nineteenth centuries, the term gained new meaning. Keith Baker's analysis of changes in the concept of *révolution* illustrates the changing significance of the term in eighteenth-century France. While in the earlier period, *révolution* was generically used to define sudden, dramatic events in the political order, it gradually came to mean *a single* dramatic event that brought down the old order and built a new one. This moment was singularized as the definitive turning point for a new regime that came about through an expression of the will of the public or nation, and took on the significance of a world-historical event in the universal trajectory of history.[13]

Juchereau used *révolutions* to describe political and social turmoil, sudden and dramatic events, and radical and violent governmental changes. According to Juchereau, however, the revolutionary episode in the Ottoman Empire could not be isolated from the general context of other revolutions. The revolutions of Istanbul, or the Ottoman revolutions, belonged to many revolutions shaking Europe, which ended ancien régimes and triggered reform projects from the top and popular unrest from the bottom. The sequence of revolutions in the Ottoman capital did not produce *the* revolution. However, the historical context in which Juchereau situates Istanbul's revolutions explains why these episodes were not ephemeral and provisional, events that happened *de novo* as a result of conventional, recurrent struggles in the Ottoman capital. Rather, these connected episodes belonged to a larger battle that resonated beyond the boundaries of the Ottoman Empire in the eighteenth and early nineteenth centuries, a battle between the reform projects of an "enlightened" leader, Selim III, and resistance from groups that had vested interests in the corrupt old regime.[14]

Juchereau was not a revolutionary. He approved neither of Jacobinism in France nor of Napoleon's autocratic rule. Like Edmund Burke, Juchereau was a conservative who admired reform but detested popular violence, whether led by janissaries or sansculottes. Knowingly or unknowingly, many nineteenth-century European observers, diplomats, and historians followed Juchereau's interpretation of the 1806–8 events. After the Constitutional Revolution in 1908, Ottoman historians came up against this interpretation. In the revolutionary literature, both Selim and Bayraktar were presented as martyrs of progress, and the janissaries, who had been abolished in 1826 by Mahmud II, as reactionary.[15] This interpretation, based on the ongoing battle between progressive forces and the reactionary response, was entrenched in the ideology of the new regime of the Turkish Republic and continued throughout Turkish history.[16]

In this chapter, I propose an new interpretive narrative history of the 1806–8 crisis, from the Edirne incident to Mustafa Bayraktar's death, based on multiple Ottoman and European sources. The narrative revisits several themes of the age of revolutions. But understanding the broader context and some of the structural reasons behind the crisis, readers should keep in mind earlier chapters in this book and recall the larger context of war and diplomacy in Napoleonic Europe.

Both Ottoman and European historians have viewed events that occurred between 1806 and 1808 as a conflict between the old and the new.[17] The janissaries (and their allies) represented the old. The reform party, which flourished under the leadership of Selim III and Mustafa Baytarktar, reflected the new, epitomized in the name "New Order." While the new meant adopting Western ways and institutions, the old was a reaction to these adaptations. According to the dominant narrative on the events of 1806–8, the New (Order) failed because its advocates were not ready (*Şanizade*), were imprudent (*Cevdet*), became corrupt (*Asım* and

Cevdet), and were unpopular (Juchereau). This line of thinking in many ways continued to shape modern historiography in the twentieth century.

This chapter—and this book in general—revises this dualistic, linear depiction. First, as the narrative shows, the battle between the New Order and the janissaries was far more complex than simply a conflict between new and old, change and reaction, Western and Eastern. As discussed in chapter 1, opposition organized around the janissary banner had strong political and cultural roots in different segments of Ottoman society. In the seventeenth and eighteenth centuries, the number of individuals who were affiliated to the janissary corps expanded in both Istanbul and the provinces. Those janissary affiliates were incorporated into the urban and rural economies, and the boundaries between their civil and military identities gradually became porous. In the late eighteenth century, new groups—mainly new bachelor immigrants, who monopolized the lower segments of the urban economy, working as porters and rowers, for example—acquired janissary affiliations. Janissary opposition to reform did not, therefore, simply represent the corps, but also larger and more diverse segments of Ottoman society. Military reform came with an agenda, not only to recruit new soldiers and build a disciplined, well-drilled new army, but also to reshape urban society through new regulations and disciplinary measures, and various social segments were hostile to this.

The political skills of the janissaries proved equally important. In numerous protests and revolts over the course of the preceding two centuries, janissary affiliates had begun translating their claims into a representative, all-encompassing language for the general public. The janissaries claimed to represent not only corporate interests, but also order, laws, and vested rights and privileges. As a pillar of the Ottoman order, they cultivated a political culture to frame their protests with a public discourse. This capacity to integrate particular claims with the general assertions enabled the janissaries to mobilize the urban crowd in times of crisis. I argue that janissary opposition to the New Order was certainly conservative opposition, but it was also populist and popular. The janissaries presented themselves as protectors of rights against despotism or corruption.

My story also revises conventional arguments about the actors participating in these events. Most narratives depict the crisis as a battle between two parties, the New Order and the janissaries. But neither party was monolithic. Factions that established alliances with groups in other parties always existed within both. Moreover, other actors, foreign and Ottoman, religious and lay, participated in these episodes. In the age of revolutions and in a stormy political and diplomatic atmosphere, while alliances constantly shifted, the French, Russian, British, and Austrian diplomatic missions became part of Ottoman domestic politics. However, the whole episode unfolded, not as a dual, but as a triangular equation, inasmuch as provincial notables, who developed political awareness about their collective interests during the process, constituted the main group that we can consider a third party in the conflict, which began when a coalition of janissaries and provincial notables humiliated the New Order in Edirne in 1806–8, triggering its collapse in 1807. But after the fall of the New Order, the dynamics changed. The janissary–provincial notable coalition gave way to another coalition, this time between provincial notables and the New Order. It was this alliance, under the leadership of Mustafa Bayraktar, that carried out the coup against the janissary-led restoration government in August 1808 and drafted the Deed of Alliance. The Deed was to reconcile the impulses of the New Order and provincial powerholders. According to this reconciliation, provincial notables pledged to support military reform, and in return they secured guarantees for their statuses, offices, and wealth. More important, the Deed invited provincial dynasties to become active participants in the empire with full liability. This was to be a new empire.

AUGUST 1806–NOVEMBER 1808

The Edirne Incident in August 1806

The events that unfolded into the imperial crisis were instigated in Edirne, a provincial town in Thrace a hundred miles from Istanbul, when a coalition of provincial powerholders and communities blocked the New Army, preventing it from moving into the Balkans in August 1806. The New Army, consisting of soldiers recruited from among Anatolian peasants, under the command of Kadi Abdurrahman Pasha—one of the architects the New Order—assembled at the military base on the outskirts of Istanbul to move to Belgrade to suppress turmoil between janissaries and Serbian notables. But another military assemblage that included different forces collected and sent by various provincial magnates in the Balkans was gathering in Edirne. Dağdevirenoğlu Mehmed, the ayan of Edirne, acted as ad hoc commander of the Balkan forces.[18] According to reports by the British consul in Bucharest, however, 186 notables in the Balkans had united their forces and signed a formal pact to act together against the New Order, to dethrone Selim and enthrone his cousin Mustafa IV. While we cannot confirm the authenticity of this pact supposedly signed by several powerholders, we know that the assembled group included irregular forces, mercenaries sent by the main regional powers, and local janissaries. Ottoman and diplomatic observers across the region and in Istanbul noted that although the ayan of Edirne acted as commander of the assembled group, two prominent powerholders, İsmail of Ruse and İsmail of Serres, were behind him.[19] According to the court historian Mütercim

Ahmed Asım, İsmail of Ruse, who appeared to support the New Order, was in reality orchestrating opposition against Selim III and his associates in alliance with a clique in Istanbul.

In August, the New Army and the military assemblage of Balkan notables met outside Edirne. A regional war between the New Army and a coalition of provincial powerholders in the Balkans was imminent. Communities in Edirne and neighboring towns also participated in the encounter. Reports sent to Istanbul informed the center that there had been several skirmishes between provisioners of the army and various assemblages in Thrace.[20] A communication sent to Selim III noted, "the communities of Edirne assembled an alliance against Kadı Abdurrahman from all sides."[21] The administration worried that this alliance would also trigger protests against the New Order in Istanbul if the crisis reached the heart of the capital. Câbî Efendi, an amateur historian in Istanbul, heard news circulating in coffeehouses in the city. He reported that the communities of Thrace had collectively declared: "this matter is unacceptable. We do not have consent for the New Order in our region. If the state intends to build military barracks in Edirne for the New Army and asks for soldiers from us, we would not allow this."[22] Soon, the administration shut down dozens of coffeehouses to prevent information concerning the Edirne incident from circulating. Asım wrote that the Edirne incident showed that opposition to the New Order was not limited to Istanbul and the central janissaries. Rather, it was an empirewide phenomenon, which had the potential to trigger empirewide upheaval:

Those who established this [military] assemblage seemed to be from that region. However, in reality, most of the people in Rumelia, Bosnia, Albania, Istanbul, and Anatolia had suffered the oppression of the Exalted State [i.e., the New Order]. Therefore, they were fundamentally in alliance with the assemblage and approved their cause. As though everyone in Rumelia, Anatolia, and Istanbul acted in alliance.[23]

In mid August, when the crisis reached a climax, İsmail of Ruse, the alleged leader of the coalition of notables behind the scenes, was assassinated at his farm near Ruse by one of his closest associates.[24] İsmail was allied with the New Order and was one of its key provincial actors in the region, instrumental in providing security, collecting taxes, participating in campaigns against unruly powerholders, and performing all kinds of services. But, like his peers and several local communities in the region, he was adamantly opposed to the New Army's penetration of the Balkans. In his memo to the French foreign minister, Charles-Maurice de Talleyrand-Périgord, the French ambassador to Istanbul, Horace Sébastiani, who had recently been sent by Napoleon to try to invigorate relations between France and the Ottoman Empire against Russia and England, noted that

İsmail of Ruse had the capacity to raise an army of 80,000 soldiers from local notables in his region, and rumors swirled that he planned to initiate a coup against the New Order in Istanbul, in alliance with the janissaries and others.[25] The New Orderists joyfully received the news of İsmail's assassination, which was a blow to the anti–New Order coalition.

Despite the death of İsmail, Selim III ordered the retreat of the New Army back to camps in Istanbul. In Ottoman circles, officials publicly declared that Selim had generously withdrawn the army to prevent a civil war.[26] But in reality, the New Order had been humiliated in Edirne, and Kadı Abdurrahman and Selim III did not want to run the risk of major defeat by the Balkan notables.[27]

It was the other powerholder, İsmail of Serres, who mediated between the Edirne assemblage and the New Order commander to reach an agreement.[28] Meanwhile, the central government formally accused the community of Ruse of being part of the anti–New Order coalition and asked them to publicly sign a *nezīr* contract and promise not to be involved in such rebellious actions (*iḥtilāl*) again.[29] The New Army withdrew, and this incident helped Selim uncover possible collaborators with the anti–New Order faction in his administration. He dismissed Grand Vizier Hafız İsmail and Grand Mufti Ahmed Esad from their offices. The incident also showed the new regime and the army the scale of the opposition and its social bases. Selim III and his associates realized that opposition could easily spread from Istanbul to the provinces, through various networks, alliances, and connections, as well as information webs circulating in coffeehouses, public baths, and barbershops. It also illustrated that notables in the Balkans and Anatolia, two wings of the empire, held different positions vis-à-vis the New Order. The New Army, which was assembled largely by two major Anatolian families, the Çapanoğlus and the Karaosmanoğlus, consisted primarily of young Anatolian peasants. In a memorandum to Selim concerning the Edirne incident, an officer noted the enmity (*żiddiyet*) that existed between Rumelians and Anatolians.[30]

The Ottoman-Russian War and the Rise of Mustafa Bayraktar (Fall 1806)

The Edirne incident happened in the middle of a diplomatic crisis between the Ottoman and Russian empires, which would give rise to a six-year war on the Balkan frontier. At the core of the diplomatic crisis were the statuses of two Ottoman principalities, Wallachia and Moldavia (today Romania). Since 1711, Wallachia and Moldavia, which both enjoyed special administrative status, had been governed by *hospodar*s, or intendants, members of prominent Greek families appointed in Istanbul by the sultan. For the Ottoman Empire, the principalities not only served as a buffer zone against the Russian threat from the north, but also as grain hubs for the provisioning of Istanbul. This area was, however, a natural target of Russia's expansionist policy in the Ottoman Balkans. The Russian court had fostered connections with both the Phanariots, who monopolized governance of the principalities, and the native Romanian notables (boyars). After the Ottoman and Russian empires established an inevitable alliance against France following the French expedition to Egypt (1798), Selim III appointed the pro-Russian Greek Phanariots Constantinos Ipsilantis, and Alexander Mourouzis as intendants of Wallachia and Moldavia in 1802, with Russia's endorsement.[31] During the Edirne incident, in August 1806, Selim deposed Ipsilantis and Mourouzis. Ipsilanti was accused of collaborating with the insurgents in Edirne.[32] Indeed, it was no secret that Ipsilanti was a regional supporter of İsmail of Ruse, a city on the Danube in northern Bulgaria.[33] But the reasons for the dismissals went beyond the Edirne incident. For many Ottoman and diplomatic observers, it was France's *ambassadeur extraordinaire,* Sébastiani, who had arrived in Istanbul in August in the middle of the Edirne crisis as a special envoy of Napoleon to reinstitute the Ottoman-French alliance, who persuaded Selim to eliminate the pro-Russian party in his administration.[34] Since late 1805, Napoleon had tried to revive the Ottoman coalition against Russia and England,[35] sending letters to Selim "warning" him of the Russian party in the Ottoman administration.[36] For many observers, Sébastiani was behind Selim's decision to depose the intendants and other allegedly pro-Russian bureaucrats.[37]

The two crises—the Edirne incident, which shook the New Order in the Balkans, and the diplomatic wars in Istanbul over Wallachia and Moldavia—overlapped, and the Russian and British ambassadors in the capital protested the removal of the intendants of Wallachia and Moldavia. Ottoman administrators considered that war in the Balkans without the New Army, which had been halted by the coalition of Balkan notables in Edirne, would be hazardous. Moreover, Britain's firm response showed that its fleet in the Mediterranean could join with Russian forces in a possible war. This was too risky. Selim reacted to this threat by reappointing the two intendants. But it was too late. In October, the tsar ordered General Michelson, the commander of the Russian forces on the Dniester River, to occupy Bessarabia, Moldavia, and Wallachia. On October 19, around thirty thousand Russian troops crossed the Dniester. Ipsilantis joined the Russian forces, accompanying them to Bucharest. Meanwhile, Michelson sent agents with considerable funds to Belgrade.[38] Serbian notables took an oath "to fight for the Faith together with Russians, the Genuine Cross and the Orthodox Russian Grail."[39]

The rise of Mustafa Bayraktar occurred in domestic, regional, and international contexts. Bayraktar was born near Ruse in 1765 into a humble urban family. Like his father, he became a local janissary in Ruse at a young age.[40] He participated in the Ottoman-Russian War of 1787–92, during which the janissary corps granted him the title of Bayraktar/Alemdar (standard-bearer). By the late 1790s, Bayraktar had joined the retinue of İsmail of Ruse, a move that would change his life. His name was first heard in imperial circles in Istanbul in 1801, when Galib, an Ottoman diplomat and the future minister of foreign affairs (*re'īs efendi*), met Bayraktar in Ruse while en route to Paris. Galib presented Bayraktar to Istanbul as İsmail's closest associate and a disobedient, headstrong figure.[41] Ottoman administrators were eager to collect information on provincial upstarts who might serve as useful allies or be dangerous threats. As we shall soon see, the early encounter between Bayraktar and Galib was strategic, because Galib would later join the Friends of Ruse committee under Bayraktar's leadership that initiated the coup of September 1808 in Istanbul. In 1802 and 1803, Bayraktar fought against Pazvantoğlu as captain of İsmail's forces. He earned his reputation by delivering the severed head of Manav İbrahim, a celebrated brigand leader and close associate of Pazvantoğlu. In return for his services, Bayraktar was granted the imperial title of chief of the imperial gatemen (*kapıcıbaşı*), with a favorable reference from Constantinos Ipsilantis, who was then intendant of Wallachia.[42] Soon after, the community of Razgrad (Hazergrad), a town neighboring Ruse, elected him as their ayan with İsmail's endorsement.[43] Following the assassination of İsmail in mid-August 1806, the community of Ruse invited Bayraktar to the city, elected him as their ayan, and sent a collective petition to the center for confirmation of his appointment.[44]

Before the petition of the community of Ruse reached Istanbul, the Divan had already been informed of a memorandum sent by Manuk, the moneylender who had worked for the late İsmail, who told his partner in Istanbul that forty-one notables in the region had come to Ruse, declaring their obedience to Bayraktar, rather than to his competitor Pehlivan İbrahim Agha (the future Baba Pasha) another close associate of İsmail of Ruse. Meanwhile, Bayraktar sent envoys to Istanbul, assuring the administration that he would collaborate with the New Order and could confiscate and deliver İsmail's allegedly large inheritance to the state if his ayanship was recognized.[45] Many discussions about Bayraktar's appointment took place in the imperial Divan.[46] On the eve of a war with Russia, the Danubian city of Ruse was one of the strategic locations in the Ottoman Balkans. It would be highly advantageous for the New Orderists in Istanbul to have a strong, popular ayan in the region who was loyal to the administration and the New Order. "He is not like his late master but rather a rational, loyal man," one of the memoranda submitted to Selim stated.[47] Bayraktar's ayanship was perhaps the best possible scenario, since his authority rested on a strong public constituency. Dismissing him would create more problems in this shaky region, which was already tense because of the Edirne incident, İsmail's assassination, and the likelihood of an Ottoman-Russian conflict. Selim sent Bayraktar a letter and confirmed his ayanship,[48]

From August 1806 to March 1807, Bayraktar rose from ayan of Ruse to commander of the Danubian army and the most eminent magnate of the Ottoman Balkans. This rapid rise surprised many observers. A British diplomat wrote that Bayraktar, "a bold and enterprising man, had by his talents and courage, raised himself from one of the lowest ranks of life to the command of armies and had so signalized himself in the war against the Russians."[49] How did this happen? After his election as ayan of Ruse to replace İsmail, Bayraktar intended to expand his zone by having his men placed as ayans in neighboring districts. Soon he captured Silistra, another Danubian city, which was under Yılıkoğlu Süleyman, who had been İsmail's main regional competitor. Süleyman fled to regions under Russian control, and Bayraktar had one of his followers, Satıoğlu, elected ayan by the community of Silistra. He declared in a letter to the administration: "The community of Silistra does not want Yılıkoğlu. They have placed Satıoğlu in the ayanship of the district."[50] While Bayraktar expanded his zone of influence in northern Bulgaria by eliminating potential rivals and men elected by local communities, he needed more lucrative, revenue-generating fiefs. The district around the medieval town of Tarnovo in central Bulgaria was such a place. The populous town had rich agricultural hinterlands, and its inhabitants included large Bulgarian, Greek, and Jewish communities, whose poll taxes produced considerable funds. Acquiring Tarnovo would boost Bayraktar's fortunes.[51] However, the center would grant Tarnovo to Bayraktar only later, in return for his services in the war against the Russians.[52]

All of these initiatives required considerable financial capacity, and like other power entrepreneurs operating in the business of governance, Bayraktar tried to access financial markets for credit through financiers. As I briefly sketched in chapter 2, he established a close partnership with Manuk Mirzaian, İsmail of Ruse's Catholic Armenian financier.[53] Manuk had different business partnerships in Wallachia, Moldavia, and Istanbul, and he had connections in Russia. He was also a close associate of the Ipsilantis family. Constantinos Ipsilantis, the intendant of Wallachia, bestowed the courtesy title of bey on him so that he could become one of the boyars (Romanian notables) of Wallachia, despite his Armenian origins.[54] When İsmail of Ruse was killed, Manuk not only lobbied in Istanbul through his associates on behalf of Bayraktar, but also assisted in seizing İsmail's patrimony. With credit for the down payment provided by Manuk, Bayraktar was able to offer a large amount for the inheritance and acquire it.[55]

While Bayraktar was consolidating his power in Danubian Bulgaria, the Russian assault continued from the north. The sultan's New Army had returned to Anatolia in early September after the Edirne incident. The Danubian army in the region consisted primarily of janissaries and irregular forces supplied by leading notables in the Balkans. Combat coincided with a propaganda war. The Russians were well acquainted with the anti–New Order sentiments that flourished after the Edirne incident. Directing his propaganda at local janissaries and communities, General Michelson sought to link France with the New Order. He proclaimed that Russia's goal was to protect the Ottoman Empire from Napoleon and prevent the janissaries from being destroyed by the New Order. He also approached Bayraktar.[56]

Meanwhile, Pehlivan İbrahim Agha, who had lost the competition with Bayraktar to become ayan of Ruse, agreed, probably not very willingly, to accept Bayraktar's leadership. He moved to the strategic fortress at Izmail (now in southwestern Ukraine) to build a base against the Russian army with forces collected from the other local notables in the region. Michelson proposed an alliance, asserting the Russian emperor's "just motives" to Bayraktar and Pehlivan.[57] Like Ipsilantis and Yılıkoğlu, Bayraktar's switching sides to join the Russian army would change the dynamics of the conflict on the Danubian front. But in November, Pehlivan organized an assault on Russian forces in Giurgiu, on the Danube across from Ruse.[58] Pehlivan's victory against the Russian brigade enhanced his reputation, and he now became known as Pehlivan Baba Agha, Pehlivan the chief-father. This strengthened the hand of his patron, Bayraktar, in negotiations with the Ottoman central administration for financial support and military equipment. The crucial factor was that as the only viable powerholder in the region, Bayraktar had the capacity to mobilize forces in the region against the Russians.[59]

Bayraktar's rise, after taking the initiative and attacking the Russian brigade instead of accepting Michelson's offer and collaborating with him, changed power dynamics in the Balkans. In December, Bayraktar and his rival Osman Pazvanotoğlu, the Vidin strongman, who had just been pardoned by Selim III, agreed to an alliance and a joint front along the Danube, making waves in diplomatic circles.[60]A report sent to Paris stated that Pazvanotoğlu and Bayraktar had agreed to establish a "confederation" in the Ottoman Balkans.[61] The popular Leiden *Journal politique* announced the two magnates' alliance as follows:

The news of the Russian entry into Moldavia was received with indignation on all Turkey's borders. All [the Ottoman] commanders on the banks of the Danube focused on ways to stop the march of the Russians and to defend the Ottoman Empire. Mustafa Bayraktar, the ayan of Ruse, heir to the authority of Tirisiniklioğlu [İsmail of Ruse], and man of courage, moved troops to Bucharest to defend

Wallachia against the Russians, while [Osman] Pazvantoğlu, [the] pasha of Vidin, also had a corps of 12,000 men enter the principality; [this corps] was to join the troops of Mustafa Bayraktar and the two leaders, who had long disagreed, united to present a joint defense. . . . The pashas of the other provinces will join in this large-scale defensive strategy.[62]

The report in *Journal politique* illustrates how the politics of notables in the Ottoman Balkans became a major factor in the international crisis involving the Ottoman, Russian, French, and British empires. Upon hearing of the magnates' coalition to defend the empire, and perhaps with the encouragement of Sébastiani for a possible revival of an Ottoman-French pact, the imperial Divan declared a holy war against Russia in February 1807. The Ottoman public was informed that the enemy of their religion and state had attacked Ottoman lands, and that an opportunity had arisen to recapture Crimea from Russia.[63]

In late January 1807, Pazvantoğlu died in Vidin. Following controversy among Pazvantoğlu's followers, the Vidin notables nominated his treasurer, Molla İdris, to replace him, petitioning the Divan for his appointment as Vidin's guardian (*Vidin muḥāfızı*).[64] As with Bayraktar's ascent, the local community elected İdris, who sent envoys to Istanbul to lobby on his behalf, conveying the message that he would collaborate with the New Order. He also offered a million guruş for Pazvantoğlu's inheritance.[65] Since changing the dynamic of frontier politics while the war with Russia continued would have been imprudent, Selim III confirmed İdris's appointment. By early 1807, after the deaths of İsmail of Ruse and Osman Pazvantoğlu, their followers, Bayraktar and İdris, thus took over their regions through a similar process of communal nominations, seizing the patrimonies of their former patrons, and lobbying in Istanbul and diplomatic circles. The French government soon sent two special envoys, M. Mériage and M. Lamarre, to Vidin and Ruse respectively to establish direct communications with these two rising regional magnates on the Danube. The French even offered to send twenty-five thousand troops to Vidin and thirty thousand to Ruse in March to defend the Danubian frontier. Both Bayraktar and İdris refused the offer, however.[66]

War provided provincial magnates with new opportunities to negotiate for power and glory with the Ottoman administration led by the New Orderists. In February 1807, Behiç Efendi, a leading figure among the New Order elite who was originally from Ruse, was sent by the central administration to Bayraktar to persuade him to accept the governorship of Silistra, with the title of vizier and command of the Danubian front.[67] According to the historian Asım, "it was clearly a necessity to appoint a powerful vizier to the Danube. However, Mustafa Bayraktar would not accept a vizier imposed on him. Moreover, Selim appreciated Bayraktar's qualifications and power. Therefore, it was appropriate to grant this position to Bayraktar."[68] A memorandum submitted to the sultan stated that Bayraktar could only be convinced to accept the offer if Silistra was granted to him. In March 1807, while securing the acquisition of the Tarnovo district, Bayraktar accepted the deal, and was appointed commander of the Danube and governor of Silistra, with the title of vizier.[69] The letter of appointment was read to the community of Ruse at its court. Following this ceremony, copies of the letter were sent to the courts of other Danubian cities.[70] This was a major move in Bayraktar's career. When Selim learned that Bayraktar had accepted the offer, he wrote: "May God bless him and make him successful in his service to the state."[71] By May 1807, Bayraktar was able to consolidate his power as governor of Silistra and commander of the Danubian army.[72]

The British Incident and the Mobilization of Strongmen in the Balkans (January–April 1807)

An Ottoman-Russian war had the potential to reshuffle coalitions in Europe. Preserving the Ottoman Empire's neutrality was thus a major priority for Britain. War with Russia would push the Ottomans into an alliance with Napoleon. Furthermore, such a war would be a serious blow to British policy regarding Ottoman Egypt. After the defeat of French forces in Egypt by an Ottoman-British coalition in 1801, Muhammad Ali, an Albanian strongman from Kavala, came to Egypt to command Albanian irregulars in the Ottoman army to retake it after the French withdrawal. Rising to power amid civil strife in the city, he unexpectedly won the governorship in Cairo in 1805. Britain intended to maintain its favorable status in Egypt by establishing relations with the new governor. A war with the Ottoman Empire would not help British Egyptian policy.[73] The British prime minister, William Pitt the Younger, asked Charles Arbuthnot, the British ambassador to Istanbul, to do his best to prevent a war and an Ottoman-French pact. But the ambassador's demands that the Ottoman administration expel Sébastiani rankled the Ottomans, who saw these requests as undiplomatic.[74] Ebû Bekir Efendi, a contemporary observer, wrote of Arbuthnot: "this mulish English[man] was crazy [*mecnūn*] to insist [on such impossible demands]."[75] When it became clear in February 1807 that Arbuthnot would not be able to prevent a war by diplomacy, a British squadron under the command of Admiral Sir John Duckworth passed through the Dardanelles, anchored off the Princes' Islands, and trained its guns on Istanbul in a show of force.[76]

This incursion by a British fleet triggered ten days of agitation and panic in the city, whose residents called it "the English incident" (*vaḳ'a-i İngiliz*).[77] Bombardment was eminent and the city, with its weak fortifications and lack of effective land-based artillery to repel an attack from the sea, was vulnerable. After a meeting with the sultan,[78] Sébastiani declared that France was ready to mobilize all possible means, including French and Spanish military engineers, to assist in preparing Istanbul for the confrontation.[79] In a week, with the technical assistance of French and Spanish engineers, the inhabitants of the city, janissaries, artillerymen, and marines had shored up its defenses with extraordinary zeal.[80] Describing these stormy days, Antoine Juchereau de Saint-Denys, chief engineer of the fortifications, observed that "the popular ebullience changed the disposition of the [reluctant] ministers."[81] Meanwhile, the Ottoman authorities started negotiations with the British commander and ambassador. The Ottomans tried to gain more time to complete the fortifications. Ottoman representatives told Arbuthnot that if warships approached the city, the administration could not protect British subjects in Istanbul from popular unrest. Could Arbuthnot risk the lives of hundreds of British subjects in the city? Negotiations continued, and Duckworth did not order an attack.[82]

On March 1, the British squadron left Istanbul. Some argue that Duckworth did not catch a favorable wind for a quick attack and withdrawal. Duckworth was unlucky and perhaps too late. The Ottomans were successful in keeping the British busy with negotiations while strengthening the city's artillery defenses. However, it was not clear whether the British truly intended to bombard the city. In the end, the British government did not want a war with the Ottomans, especially during Napoleon's successful eastern campaign. Whatever the reasons, this was a failure for British military diplomacy. The British incident strengthened the Ottoman-French alliance and Sébastiani's position in Istanbul.[83] The major impact of the British incident was on the inhabitants of the Ottoman city. After chaos and panic, residents mobilized and prepared the city for war. Janissary affiliates and civilians were heavily armed.[84] Thousands of auxiliary troops, called *yamaks*, were brought in from the Black Sea provinces.[85] "I hear that the people of Istanbul are all armed. The public criers are stirring them up," Selim wrote to the Divan. "It may be hoped that the battle would be between two fleets with cannon. It would be wrong for the people not to go about their business and perambulate the city with firearms."[86] Selim was right to be concerned. Like the Edirne incident, the British incident politicized and armed the populace of Istanbul. For many, it was the New Order's hesitant and reluctant policy that had brought an eminent threat so close. In the city's coffeehouses, people mocked the New Order's incompetent administrators as the French ambassador's puppets. The mobilization, militarization, and politicization of the people of Istanbul were a prelude to the coming revolution.

After the British incident, it became clear that war with Russia was unavoidable. In March, the Ottoman administration started to assemble forces in the Balkans and Anatolia for deployment on the Danubian frontier. The imperial army, consisting of janissaries and other regular forces under the command of the grand vizier, Keçiboynuzu Hilmi İbrahim Pasha, and the janissary chief, Pehlivan Agha (not Pehlivan İbrahim Baba Agha), assembled in the military camps of Edirne. In late March, troops sent by two great families of Anatolia, the Çapanoğlus and the Karaosmanoğlus, joined it.[87] Provisioning was entrusted to İsmail of Serres and Ali Pasha of Ioannina.[88] Mustafa Bayraktar, then commander of Danubian forces and governor of Silistra, came from Ruse to Edirne to welcome the army.[89]

The core of the imperial army included mostly janissary units from Istanbul and some localities in the Balkans. The majority of troops positioned along the Danube, however, were under the control of six regional magnates of the Balkans and Anatolia: Mustafa Bayraktar and Pehlivan İbrahim Baba Agha, İdris of Vidin, İsmail of Serres, the Karaosmanoğlus, and the Çapanoğlus. Some divisions were the direct retinues of these men and families. Others were troops organized under the command of district ayans and intendants. Some Tatar troops were under the command of the Crimean Gerays, who had been settled in the Balkans since Russia's annexation of the Crimean khanate in 1782. Hüsrev Pasha, the governor of Bosnia, brought several units under the command of Bosnian notables, called *kapudan*s.[90]

This assemblage of forces did not include the reformed troops of the New Order. The New Army, which had been blocked in Edirne the previous year by a coalition of powerholders and janissaries, did not join the imperial army. The troops remained in their barracks in Levent and Üsküdar in Istanbul, a city that had just experienced the incursion by the British fleet. By May, the Ottoman-Russian war had begun. Istanbul was still agitated by the English incident a couple of months earlier. The war on the Danube and the British blockade left the city with very little wheat in its stores to supply its bakeries and very little meat for its butchers. The quality of the bread distributed to the poor declined dramatically, and there were shortages of coffee, olive oil, and rice.[91]

The Fall of the New Order (May–June 1807)

At the end of May 1807, a dramatic and in many ways unexpected event took place in the imperial capital. The New Order fell and Selim was deposed in a popular uprising, the Kabakçı revolt, named for Kabakçıoğlu Mustafa, one of its leaders. The revolt was instigated in the northern corner of the Bosporus by a group of *yamak*s. In just a week, the small uprising inflamed a massive urban mutiny, eliciting the participation of thousands of civilians and janissaries against the New Order.[92] The mutiny was first instigated when officers forced *yamak*s guarding the northern entrance of the Bosporus in Rumeli Feneri, a small village thirty miles from central Istanbul, to join the New Army. Most of these *yamak*s had recently been brought to Istanbul from the Black Sea coast during the British incident. But in short time, they joined the janissary corps as auxiliaries and mingled with janissary bullies in the city, who had openly criticized the New Army in public spaces they frequented after the Edirne incident. In early May, officers sent to Rumeli Feneri called on the *yamak*s to wear the blue and red uniforms of the New Army and to drill on a daily basis. Some considered this behavior as an open provocation or a foolish mistake, since the tensions between the janissary auxiliaries and the New Order had worsened since the British incident and the subsequent economic hard times in the city. When the *yamak*s refused the order, the dispute between the officers and the *yamak*s became a skirmish.

When the *yamak*s—perhaps by accident—killed the former Ottoman diplomat to London and minister of foreign affairs Mahmud Raif, a leading member of the New Order, outright conflict broke out between the New Order and the janissaries. This killing dismayed the government. The obvious response was to send in some New Army troops from Levend and Üsküdar. After several meetings, the Divan decided not to suppress the mutiny with the New Army, which, some thought, would stir up anti–New Order sentiment in the city. Rather, the Divan opted to contain the incident in Rumeli Feneri and quell anxieties.[93] Most Ottoman and European narratives agree that in this tense atmosphere, a clique inside the government, consisting of the deputy grand vizier, Köse Musa, Grand Mufti Ataullah, and members of Prince Mustafa's palace camarilla, secretly planned to depose Selim and remove the New Order party from the administration. According to the historian Mustafa Necib, the imperial army's move to Edirne, along with several members of the cabinet, created a power vacuum that provided Prince Mustafa's clique with a favorable environment. Observers such as Juchereau and Asım, and later the historian Cevdet, argue that this clique covertly provoked the *yamak*s.[94]

We cannot know for certain that the mutiny was a well-planned, coordinated conspiracy from the outset, but it gradually became an organized revolt. On May 26, the *yamak*s began a march to Istanbul along the shores of the Bosporus. They stopped in different spots along the way, inviting various communities, janissary affiliates, and civilians to join them and march with them. In Büyük Dere, the crowd held an assembly, discussed their aims, and formed a committee to lead them, electing Kabakcıoğlu Mustafa, a *yamak* sergeant in his thirties, as their spokesman. Kabakçıoğlu was originally from the Black Sea region, probably Kastamonu, but he had been in Istanbul for some years. A collective oath followed the election: the crowd swore to destroy the New Order, but not to harm the general public.[95]

The Büyük Dere assembly established leadership, stipulated the terms, and solidified the discourse of the revolt. When the march started up again, the crowd multiplied as various groups, such as boatmen, porters, and unemployed bachelors, joined in. This mutiny was no longer a revolt of the *yamak*s against the central authority. While the discourse of the revolt went beyond the corporate interests of the *yamak*s or the janissaries, the crowd developed a claim to be the voice the common people.[96]

On May 27, in the late afternoon, a crowd occupied Istanbul's Meat Square (Et Meydanı), an open space near the janissary barracks. For centuries, this had been the historical forum for janissary-led protests. Deliberations between *yamak*s and janissaries in the nearby Süleymaniye Mosque continued for a couple of days until an agreement was reached and the ancient ceremony of earlier janissary rebellions was launched. The moment the big kettles that were the ancient insignia of janissary revolts were brought and displayed in Meat Square, the *yamak* insurgency was transformed into a janissary demonstration that followed the scripted conventions of earlier revolts that had taken place since the seventeenth century.[97] When the crowd swelled to thousands, after new participants from the neighborhoods joined in, it was too late for the administration to subdue the revolt without violence in the center of the city. "In addition to the janissaries of Istanbul and the armorers, who had united with the *yamak*s," Mustafa Necib noted, "all those who claimed to be janissaries joined them in order to vent their ill will."[98] But Câbî stressed that the revolt's leadership was concerned about the discipline, reputation, and moral standing of the crowd. "Women and children, young and old, even prostitutes, were massed in Meat Square, but nobody dared to harass a single woman, not even with words."[99] The crowd's moral standing was further consolidated by guarantees by its leaders of the people's security of property, life, and honor. The leaders asked shopkeepers to stay open and carry on with business as usual. Câbî noted several dramatic episodes in which the leaders disciplined the revolt. In one episode, a *yamak* bought a bagel but only paid half the price to the seller. When the seller complained, the committee executed the culpable *yamak* on the spot to "demonstrate its justice to the people."[100]

After such incidents, the committee issued declarations barring executions without the assembly's consent.[101] Still, the revolt was in need of

legitimization from the learned hierarchy, or ulema, as the ultimate religious and legal authority. Through the grand mufti, Ataullah, who was
one of the alleged instigators of the conspiracy, the committee invited the
support of some members of the ulema, several of whom were at odds
with the New Order, while others acted as mediators between the government and the crowd. Learning of mass participation in the revolt, Selim
now saw that he was losing ground and declared that he would abolish
the New Army and the New Treasury.[102] Cheering, the crowd celebrated
Selim's message. But Selim's actions failed to put an end to the revolt.
With the backing of some ulema members, the crowd now demanded the
executions of key figures in the New Order party. The committee had
prepared a collective petition in which the names of eleven New Order
leaders appeared, including those of İbrahim Nesim; Ahmed Bey, director of the New Treasury; Selim's secretary, another Ahmed Bey; İbrahim
Efendi, chief of the Arsenal; the grain manager Memiş Efendi; and Ebû
Bekir Efendi, director of the Mint.[103]

While the revolt's objectives grew, Kabakçıoğlu targeted the New Order's grain management, which elicited grumbling over the rise in bread
prices and bread shortages in Istanbul. At this moment, Kabakçıoğlu gave
a historic speech to the crowd, showing two loaves of bread, one fresh
and soft, the other rotten and stale. He associated the fresh loaf with the
bread of the elites of the New Order, and the stale one with the bread
of the masses.[104] Kabakçıoğlu condemned the extravagant lifestyles of
members of the New Order, while the people experienced scarcity and
poverty. The revolt of the janissaries was now also the revolt of the poor.

Selim accepted the demands of the crowd, proclaiming the abolition of
the New Order. On the morning of May 29, however, the crowd began
chanting for Prince Mustafa. Since Osman II (1604–22), janissary-led
revolts had resulted in dramatic changes on the Ottoman throne. The
last janissary-led revolt had shaken Istanbul seventy-seven years earlier,
in 1730, when the crowd, under the leadership of an Albanian janissary,
Patrona Halil, had deposed Selim's grandfather, Ahmed III (r. 1703–30),
and enthroned Mahmud I (1730–54). As in Patrona Halil's rebellion,
Kabakçıoğlu led the crowd from Meat Square to Horse Square (At
Meydanı), the ancient Hippodrome, between the Aya Sofya (Hagia Sofia)
and Sultan Ahmed (Blue) Mosques. This move from Et Meydanı to At
Meydanı signified a shift in the crowd's expectations: now it wanted the
sultan to abdicate the throne. Ideas about how this decision was reached
are far from unanimous. Some mention the role of the palace faction clustered around Prince Mustafa, who lobbied for his accession. Others stress
the conviction among the rebels that even if the New Order were abolished, the leaders of the revolt could not trust Selim if he remained sultan.
Perhaps both versions are true. The committee, equipped with Ataullah's

generic fatwa (legal opinion) that legitimized the revolt and denounced the New Order, requested Selim's deposition. He is said to have accepted his fate calmly, while registering deep disappointment. There were two male heirs of the dynasty: Mustafa, aged twenty-eight, and Mahmud, aged nineteen. Both were sons of Abdulhamid I and cousins of Selim II. Mustafa received the grandees of the state and took the oath of allegiance in the inner yard of the Topkapı Palace. A rushed ceremony declared him the new sultan, and by noon, he had left the palace and appeared before the public at Friday prayers. May 29 was a Friday, and in the mosques of Istanbul, Friday sermons were delivered in the name of the new sultan.[105]

The Restoration of the Old Order in Istanbul and the Treaty of Tilsit (Summer 1807)

At a public ceremony on May 30, with the restoration government disarming and dispersing the New Army, the leaders of the revolt were rewarded with imperial titles and military appointments. Kabakçıoğlu was granted the title of "chief crane-keeper of the sultan" (*turnacıbaşı*) and appointed guardian of the Bosporus. Mustafa IV would give the janissaries and *yamak*s more than just these favors. On May 31, Münib Efendi, a leading senior member of the ulema hierarchy, prepared a legal document (*hüccet*) in the form of a contract (*sened* or *ta'ahhüdnāme*). According to the document, responsibility for the recent turmoil rested with the New Order's wicked innovations (*bi'dat*). These erroneous practices, which imitated conventions in Christian states, produced injustices and oppression (*zulm*) for the Muslim people. This oppression was also linked to the corruption and extravagant lifestyles of New Order elites. As a result, the New Order was abolished. Members of the janissary corps were to promise to be loyal to the sultanate, as before, and not to interfere in affairs of the state. In return, the new sultan declared: "With the beautiful name of almighty God, who created the universe from nonexistence and the illuminating spirit of our Prophet, Muhammad Mustafa, who is the ruler of two worlds, I promise (*ta'ahhüd*) that no one will be punished or considered responsible for the recent incident, neither on my side, holding the caliphate, nor by my grand viziers or thoughtful ministers and commanders of my everlasting state."[106] On June 2, the text was read aloud to participants in the revolt. Ataullah asked the crowd if it agreed with the conditions, and after declaring its agreement, it chanted long life to Sultan Mustafa IV.[107]

The document was a testament denouncing and abolishing the New Order and restoring the old. But it also signified an accord between Mustafa's regime and the main military-political corporate body of the empire, the janissary establishment. Mustafa IV intended to place janissary affiliates in his new government so that they would not challenge it; in return, the janissaries received assurances that they would not be punished later because of their role in the coup. The janissaries enjoyed a special status in their relations with the sultan. They were slave-soldiers of their benefactor, the sultan, who was presented as their "paternal" authority. Since the late sixteenth century, this paternal relationship had been challenged in numerous janissary revolts. In each revolt, relations between the sultanic authority and the janissaries were renegotiated.[108] However, such a contractual document after a revolt, which also included an amnesty, was unusual. Perhaps, for that reason, the court historian Mütercim Ahmed Asım calls the exchange of documents the most bizarre of bizarre events (*aġrebü'l-ġarā'ib*).[109]

We must still note that such contracts between collective bodies and the authorities were not unknown in the Ottoman Empire. In 1698, the central authority signed a contract with provincial militias (*sekbān*) organized under Ciridoğlu, a follower of Yeğen Osman Pasha, an unruly governor of late seventeenth-century Anatolia.[110] Throughout the eighteenth century, we see a growing practice of contractual agreements between communities and administrative authorities in Ottoman governance. As we have seen in chapter 3, *neẕīr* deeds, contracts signed between a community and the state, through which communities collectively agreed not to protect outlaws, became common in the eighteenth century.[111] The deed with the janissaries should not be viewed as outside this pattern of contractual practices between collective bodies and the ruling authorities. Such contractual documents gradually became more common in Ottoman imperial politics. As we shall see, when the Deed of Alliance was signed in fall 1808, it was between the sultan, the grandees of the state, and provincial powerholders.

By the time news of the revolt in Istanbul reached the Danubian front, the army had been drawn into internal strife. The former janissary chief Pehlivan, who had been dismissed by Selim III shortly before the revolution, attacked the camp of the grand vizier, Hilmi İbrahim Pasha, in Silistra. When Pehlivan seized control of the military camp in Silistra with the help of janissaries, the grand vizier and members of the imperial cabinet on the battlefield fled to Ruse, the neighboring town, seeking Mustafa Bayraktar's protection. This was a turning point in the aftermath of the revolt. By inviting the grand vizier and others, and providing the members of the New Order with safe haven in Ruse, Bayraktar now became the new patron of the party, while Selim III was caged in his chamber in Topkapı Palace without outside contact. Soon, key members of the party—Behic, Hasan Tahsin, Mustafa Refik, Galib, and Ramiz—who had fled the army or from Istanbul, arrived in Ruse, and joined Bayraktar.[112] Meanwhile, Mustafa IV appointed Çelebi Mustafa

Pasha, former governor of the Anatolian province, as grand vizier and commander in chief of the imperial army.[113] Although New Orderists were alleged to be gathering in Ruse under Bayraktar, Mustafa IV was not in a position to discharge him. Instead, he sent Bayraktar promises and gifts.[114] In a letter to the grand vizier, Mustafa IV wrote: "I have been informed of the services of Bayraktar, commander of the Danubian army and head of the janissary corps, to the religion and state, God bless them! . . . Those who have served you loyally will be considered to have served the religion and my state."[115] Bayraktar rushed to Silistra with five thousand men to welcome the new grand vizier. They held a meeting concerning the state of the army and developments in Istanbul. This was the first meeting between two figures who would have a turbulent relationship in the following months.

Bayraktar's Ruse was now a safe haven for the New Orderists, but the property of those who had been unable to flee and were executed during the revolution was confiscated and reallocated to key members of the new regime. Köse Musa seized such a considerable portion of this property that he earned the nickname *baş yağmacı* (chief of the plunderers).[116] The fall of the New Order and the elimination of its elite brought about a wealth transfer within the imperial elites. However, the new regime in Istanbul was far from stable. The revolution ended the New Order, but fell short of bringing about stability. The janissary-*yamak* leadership came to occupy critical positions and established themselves in the politics of the imperial city. It was not easy for Mustafa IV to assert his own authority against the new oligarchs. Since the New Army had been abolished and the imperial army was on the Danubian front, Mustafa had no military force on which to rely. Moreover, Selim was still alive in his chamber in the Topkapi Palace. Mustafa IV learned that Bayraktar now hosted a group of New Orderists in Ruse, which raised questions about his loyalty. In addition to political tensions, neither security nor economic stability could be ensured in Istanbul. Agitation by some janissaries and *yamak*s and the increasing prices of bread and meat, which were now even higher than during the New Order's rule, embittered the city's inhabitants, turning them against the restoration government.[117]

Given these conditions, perhaps the most unexpected development was the arrival of Tayyar Pasha of Canik in Istanbul. Tayyar had been a bitter opponent of the New Order in Anatolia since his defeat by the Çapanoğlu family, who were great supporters of it, and had fled to Crimea, which was under Russian control. As a political refugee in Russia, he met Emperor Alexander and established connections with the Russian court. Russia was a regular destination for many political refugees from the Ottoman Empire.[118] After the fall of the New Order in Istanbul, Tayyar dispatched messengers to the new government, stating that he wanted to return to Ottoman lands and work for the new sultan.[119] In August 1807, Mustafa IV pardoned him,[120] restoring to him his former provincial units, Trabzon and Canik; not long afterward, he invited Tayyar to Istanbul to be deputy grand vizier, replacing Köse Musa.[121] This was a radical move on the part of Mustafa IV. He intended to establish a new alliance with the notables of Anatolia who opposed the New Order. Tayyar was still a significant regional powerholder with strong connections to local notables in the Black Sea region. He might be able to establish authority over the *yamaks*, most of whom hailed from the same region. According to Oğulukyan, the *yamaks* met Tayyar with cheers when he arrived in Istanbul.[122] His connections with the Russian court would also help Mustafa IV in possible peace negotiations.[123] However, Tayyar was too controversial. His rise was not well received by the Çapanoğlu family. In fact, Çapanoğlu Süleyman sent letters to Mustafa IV expressing his discomfort with Tayyar.[124] Çelebi Mustafa, the grand vizier, also saw Tayyar as a challenge. Ataullah opposed Tayyar because of his organic relations with the *yamaks*, which would put Ataullah in a secondary position. The New Orderists in Rusçuk were against Tayyar, because whenever he was in this critical position, Selim's life was at risk. Sébastiani, who was still in Istanbul, was against him too, because he seemed too close to the Russians. Tayyar Pasha's tenure would not last; he was deposed on March 7, 1808.[125]

Mustafa IV's efforts to establish an alliance with a leading provincial magnate illustrates a recurring pattern of Ottoman politics in moments of crisis. Factions in the imperial establishment in Istanbul were constantly in need of forming such alliances with competing regional magnates, and vice versa. In fact, while Mustafa attempted to forge an alliance with Tayyar, the New Orderists developed a new political coalition with Bayraktar and other Balkan notables to save Selim's life.

While the May revolution was shaking the Ottoman Empire, in Europe, diplomatic currents were changing. Napoleon had defeated Russia and Prussia. The French had driven Russian troops from Poland and created the Duchy of Warsaw. On June 14, Napoleon defeated Tsar Alexander at Friedland, which enabled the French emperor to impose a peace treaty on the tsar on his own terms. The emperor and the tsar met in Tilsit in northern Germany on July 7, 1807, and signed the Treaty of Tilsit, which ended the war between Russia and France and launched an alliance between these two empires. France pledged to aid Russia in its war against the Ottoman Empire, while Russia agreed to join Napoleon's Continental System against Britain. With the initiative of the Prussians, a partition plan for Ottoman Europe was put on the table at Tilsit.[126]

On June 24, news of Selim III's fall reached Napoleon. Sébastiani, reporting to the emperor and describing the revolution, added that Mustafa IV did not seem to be as gracious to French interests as Selim III. The janissary revolt and regime change in Istanbul showed that the Ottoman Empire was not a stable partner, which was a disappointment for the French.[127] Napoleon was ready to negotiate the partition of Ottoman Europe with Russia and Prussia, but he would not do it openly. The emperor ordered Sébastiani to open good relations with Mustafa IV and the new government in Istanbul and to present France as the guarantor of Ottoman integrity.[128] He also persuaded the tsar to conclude an armistice with the Ottoman Empire. Russia would evacuate Wallachia and Moldavia (as well as the Ionian Islands), but the Ottoman army would not enter the provinces until the ratification of a peace treaty through French mediation. Napoleon decided to keep secret article 7 of the Treaty of Tilsit, to the effect that if the Ottoman sultan refused France's mediation, or if peace negotiations had no satisfactory result, Russia and France would occupy the Ottoman Balkan provinces and Istanbul.[129]

By imposing an armistice on Russia, Napoleon sent a message to Mustafa IV that France was still the guardian of Ottoman integrity. However, he kept the door open for the partition of Ottoman Europe with Russia.[130] Although the Tilsit Agreement was cautiously taken up in Istanbul, the Ottoman administration desperately needed an armistice. The leadership of the imperial army had recently changed, and unrest among the janissaries had culminated when the commander of the janissary corps was killed in an internecine dispute. Bayraktar, the key actor on the frontier zone, was nervous about these developments. Reports sent to Istanbul noted that the provisioning of the army, which was supervised by Bayraktar, had been halted for some time. Galib, the former foreign affairs minister (*re'is*), who was under Bayraktar's protection, was authorized as chief envoy in peace negotiations with Russia. In mid August, Galib; Alexander Soutzo, the Ottoman dragoman; and Guilleminot, a French colonel, met the Russian delegation. On August 24, an agreement for a cease-fire was signed in Slobozia, a city east of Bucharest.[131] Bayraktar organized the logistics of the meeting with his troops in Wallachia.[132] When the Russian army withdrew to the north, Sébastiani presented the cease-fire as a victory for Ottoman-French friendship.[133]

Instability continued. In September, the visit to Istanbul of a British delegation under Sir Arthur Paget to negotiate the post-Tilsit situation caused a diplomatic crisis between France and the Ottoman administration.[134] From the signing of the Slobozia armistice at the end of August 1807 to April 1808, which was the deadline established by the cease-fire, Ottoman diplomacy faced serious challenges. The peace treaty could not be signed. Negotiations stalled over the status of Wallachia and Moldavia. Meanwhile, Russia withdrew from the Adriatic, and French troops were deployed in the Ionian Islands in accordance with the Tilsit

Agreement. French intervention in the Ionians was strongly opposed by Ali Pasha of Ioannina, the magnate of Epirus, whose regional zone of influence extended to the Ottoman Adriatic.[135] This instability pushed Napoleon to reconsider the plans for partition. In March 1808, Russian and French officers began negotiating a new partition project, prepared by the Russian foreign minister, Nikolay Rumyantsev, in Saint Petersburg. In April, when Sébastiani left the Ottoman Empire for personal reasons, the Russian army had not evacuated the Romanian principalities and a peace treaty had not been signed.[136]

The Friends of Ruse and the Conspiracy
(Fall 1807–Summer 1808)

During these months, the foundation of a clandestine committee by leading members of the New Order, who gathered under the protection of Mustafa Bayraktar, changed the dynamics of Ottoman politics. According to most observers, the Friends of Ruse (Rusçuḳ yārānı) committee planned a coup in Istanbul to overthrow Mustafa IV and restore Selim III to the throne. The committee members intended then to eliminate leaders of the May revolution and restore the New Order. Ottoman historians depict this dramatic episode, from Rusçuḳ yārānı's foundation to the coup in July 1808, as a conspiracy (iḥtiyāl). According to Asım, the official chronicler of the time, the conspiracy was engineered by a group of high-ranking New Orderists, namely, Refik, Ramiz, Tahsin, Behiç, and Galib, who enjoyed Bayraktar's protection. Although their real aim was to enthrone Selim III, they secretly contacted Mustafa IV and his associates and gave Mustafa the impression that their goal was to free him from the janissary oligarchs in Istanbul. While engineering a plot, they persuaded their protector, Bayraktar, to take action to make the coup happen. Asım told this conspiracy story almost daily and in great detail, without sharing his sources with readers. The mid nineteenth-century Ottoman historian Ahmed Cevdet Pasha criticized Asım for placing too much stock in street rumors.[137] At Selim's funeral, Juchereau found dozens of storytellers in coffeehouses and nearby mosques telling different stories about the conspiracy and Selim's dramatic fate.[138] Asım might have collected these rumors. But he was close to palace circles. He may well have interviewed individuals who were involved in the conspiracy or were at least witnesses to the events.[139]

Asım's narrative, which depicts the episode as a great conspiracy by the New Orderists, shaped mainstream Ottoman history in the nineteenth and early twentieth centuries.[140] Despite his criticism, Cevdet, the Austrian orientalist Ottokar-Maria von Schlechta-Wsserhd, and others endorsed Asım's narratives.[141] İsmail Hakkı Uzunçarşılı, a prominent early republican Turkish historian who wrote a biography of Mustafa Bayraktar and a multivolume Ottoman history, followed this narrative and supported Asım's story with archival documents.[142] However, Asım's narrative was not the only one. Other observers argue that in fact Bayraktar was the plot's primary architect from the beginning.[143] Juchereau, Prévost, and Pierre Ruffin argue that it was Tayyar who met Bayraktar, after having been discharged from his office, and persuaded him to march on Istanbul and stage a coup against Mustafa IV.[144] In his monograph on Bayraktar, the Russian historian Anatolii Filippovich Miller argues that it was Bayraktar's Armenian banker Manuk who guided the conspiracy, along with other New Orderists.[145]

These many narratives, despite their nuances, signify an alliance between the New Order and Balkan provincial forces clustered around Bayraktar. Since the Edirne incident, when Balkan notables demonstrated their solidarity with the janissaries against Selim III and his New Army, the dynamics of the Ottoman politics had changed. A new alliance between the New Order and provincial notables against the janissary oligarchy and the old order in Istanbul was emerging. The foundation of the alliance must have been laid in February 1807, before the May revolution, when Behiç met Bayraktar in Ruse to persuade him to accept an imperial office.[146] According to Asım, it was Behiç who first acquainted him with the politics of Istanbul and the need for military reform.[147] After the May revolution, as Juchereau observed, Ruse became a refuge for enemies of the *yamak*s.[148]

The Friends of Ruse committee members had varied backgrounds. Ramiz came from a famous Crimean ulema family. His father was Feyzullah, once the chief kadı of Crimea. After the Russian annexation of Crimea, the family came to Istanbul. Feyzullah was appointed chief judge of the Balkan provinces. After a madrassa education, Ramiz pursued a military-administrative career. He became director of the military school founded by Selim, served in Egypt with Yusuf Ziya Pasha against the French, became inspector of the artillery, and was appointed chief accountant of the war cabinet when the Russian war began.[149] Another individual in the group who shared an ulema background was Tahsin. Behiç was originally from Ruse and was well acquainted with the situation in the Balkans. His family had longed served the empire. As a young man he embarked on the career path of the Ottoman fiscal bureaucracy. But he was more than just a bureaucrat. As discussed in chapter 1, he wrote a treatise on the reform, proposing new disciplinary measures to regulate the city of Istanbul and new entrepreneurial policies for state-sponsored industrialization.[150] He served in different ranks in the central bureaucracy. After the Edirne incident, he was appointed steward of the grand vizier, one of the most important positions, which had been occupied for nine years by the famous İbrahim Nesim, one of the architects of the New Order. Galib was a leading diplomat of his time. He served as ambassador to Paris and acted as chief minister responsible for foreign affairs. His experience in diplomacy made him indispensable to the state. He was the first person pardoned by Mustafa, because he was needed in negotiations with the Russians.[151] As we have seen, Manuk Mirzaian was İsmail of Ruse's moneylender and, after his death, Bayraktar's. In 1806, Manuk played an important diplomatic role in relations between the Ottoman Empire and Russia and in forging relations between Bayraktar and the Russians, particularly during the cease-fire. After starting his career as an Armenian merchant and financier, Manuk gradually became a crucial diplomatic figure.[152]

As in all other early modern polities, clandestine groups based on personal trust, confidence, and conspiracies were not unusual in Ottoman political culture. What was unusual in 1808 was the strong ideological orientation of the Friends of Ruse committee, which went much beyond the usual palace intrigues. The group was able to connect to various actors around the New Order's political agenda and developed the capacity to mobilize collective forces. Bayraktar patronized a group of provincial notables in the Ottoman Balkans. Ramiz had connections, not only with the dismissed officers of the New Order, but also with Crimean elites and the Gerays, the Khanate family that was spread across Ottoman Bulgaria and Thrace. Tahsin, Refik, and Behiç were attached to the bureaucratic establishment and fiscal administration in Istanbul. They were also members of the Naqshibandi-Mujaddidi order, a Sufi web organized throughout the empire and beyond that openly supported the reforms of Selim III.[153] The Friends of Ruse, therefore, signified not only an emerging coalition between provincial and central forces, but also the capacity to mobilize various groups and forces in a possible coup.

According to Asım, the Rusçuk yārānı's plan had two components. First, they intended somehow to persuade the grand vizier, Çelebi Mustafa, to introduce the imperial army into Istanbul to support the coup. This made the grand vizier a strategic figure. He was the only person who could control the thousands of janissaries in the imperial army, detach them from the *yamak*s and other janissaries in Istanbul, and prevent them from ruining the plot. Second, the committee planned to make Mustafa IV and his followers believe that the real motivation for the army occupying Istanbul was to rescue Mustafa IV's authority from the oligarchs of the *yamak*s, unruly janissaries, and the "riffraff" of the city, although the real aim was to enthrone Selim III.

A couple of months after the cease-fire between the Ottoman and Russian empires, Bayraktar succeeded in persuading Grand Vizier Çelebi Mustafa that the provisioning of the army on the Danubian frontier was difficult.[154] By late October, the imperial army had moved from Silistra back to Edirne. Meanwhile, Refik led the Istanbul branch of the conspiracy. In November, Refik arrived in the capital and contacted Deputy Treasurer Nezir Agha, Steward of the Treasury Ebe Selim, and the sultan's *çukadār* (lackey) Abdülfettah Agha, all of whom were close associates of Mustafa's. Refik informed them that Bayraktar was ready to act on behalf of Sultan Mustafa against the janissaries in Istanbul if the sultan invited Bayraktar to the city. This message was presented to the sultan, but he responded that the janissaries seemed to be complying, and that such an action against them was not needed at this stage.[155] Nevertheless, the sultan appointed Refik as a minister and sent him to the imperial army.[156]

In March, following the deposition of Tayyar, Mustafa IV pardoned other New Orderists in Ruse and appointed them to key positions. Galib became minister of foreign affairs, Refik steward of the grand vizier, and Tahsin chief of the imperial servants (*çavuşbaşı*). Seyyid Efendi, a relative of Bayraktar's, was appointed head butcher to the imperial army.[157] These appointments illustrated that Mustafa IV was gradually leaning toward an alliance with the Ruse party. He had failed to establish a coalition with Tayyar. Now Bayraktar, who sent warm messages, might be a promising option for the sultan. However, the sultan did not trust some members of the Ruse party. Many were New Orderists and connected to Selim III. But Selim was a hostage in the palace, and if Mustafa sensed a conspiracy, he could execute him. Moreover, Bayraktar and his two most important associates, Ahmed of Ruse and Manuk, were actively involved in negotiations with Russia. Mustafa IV needed the Ruse party for peace talks.[158]

But there was no guarantee that the Friends of Ruse would follow Istanbul's orders. In late March, as the deadline for the cease-fire approached, Bayraktar took the initiative. By early April, he proposed to Russian Field Marshal Alexander Prozorovsky that they start negotiations for a peace treaty without the mediation of the French.[159] He sent Bogos Sébastian, an associate of Manuk's, to Bucharest and expressed himself willing to meet the Russian delegation in person to discuss possible conditions for Ottoman-Russian peace talks. According to Miller, Bayraktar's proposal was even more ambitious. If Russia agreed to a peace treaty, he declared that he could support Russia against France with an army of three hundred thousand. In fact, Bayraktar not only negotiated for peace, but also proposed an alliance with Russia against Napoleon. The proposal was submitted to the tsar. On July 11, Bayraktar received a letter from Russian officers informing him that his coalition proposal was declined, but that the ceasefire would be extended.[160] Although Mustafa IV followed the talks and knew of Bayraktar's active involvement, he was not aware of the details of the proposal. This episode

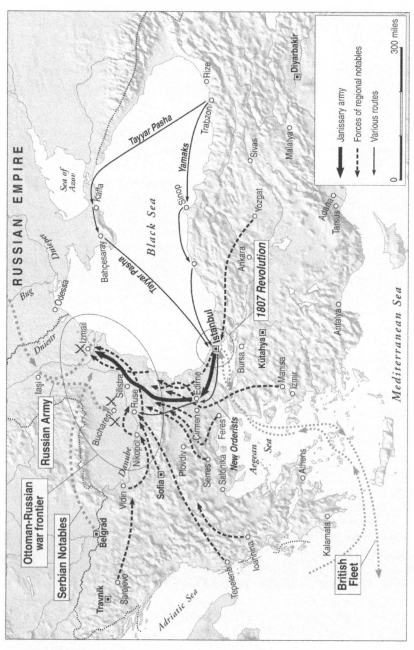

Map 4a. War and the 1807 revolution. The author and Philip Schwartzberg / Meridian Mapping.

shows that the Ruse party could bypass Istanbul to act independently in the diplomatic realm. By spring 1808, it was clear that the Ottoman Empire had two capitals, Ruse and Istanbul.

In May 1808, Behiç went to Istanbul to meet Mustafa IV's associates to discuss the conditions for allowing Bayraktar into Istanbul for a military intervention against the janissaries. When associates of Mustafa's expressed an interest in Selim's execution, Behiç convinced them that it was not the right time for this, because Napoleon would object. As a result, Mustafa's associates agreed to support the coup by Bayraktar clandestinely, but not to harm Selim. Mustafa IV appointed Behiç as financial director of the imperial army and sent him back to Edirne.[161] The second leg of the conspiracy was in Edirne. The plan was to persuade the grand vizier to lead the imperial army to Istanbul. In early July, Bayraktar, with his close associate Ahmed of Ruse, unexpectedly came to Edirne with five or six thousand cavalrymen to visit the imperial army.[162] On the way, several other provincial notables, such as the intendant of Skopje, the ayan of Hasköy, the intendant of Drama, the intendant of Plovdiv, the ayan of Pazarcık, the ayan of Shumen, and the *çorbacı* (Bulgarian notable) of Pravişte, joined Bayraktar's forces. Tayyar, who had been dismissed from his office of deputy grand vizier, met Bayraktar on his way, but he did not join him.[163] In mid July, Bayraktar arrived in Edirne with considerable forces, which were not expected by the grand vizier.[164] This visit was also a demonstration of force to the grand vizier, who had invited the rival notables of Bayraktar to Silistra for a possible alliance. It was not clear whether Bayraktar disclosed the real plan to the grand vizier. According to Asım, he did not. Bayraktar, Behiç, and Refik persuaded the grand vizier to take the army back to Istanbul. According to the protocol of the meeting, Bayraktar gave a long speech and complained of high prices in Edirne, which made provisioning difficult.[165] The best option was to move the army to Istanbul. Bayraktar added that he would join them so that he could kiss the sultan's feet.[166]

The Friends of Ruse's Coup (July 1808)

A couple of days before the imperial army moved on Istanbul, Bayraktar asked Ketencioğlu Ali, ayan of Pınar Hisar, a small town in eastern Thrace, to go to the citadel in the village of Rumeli Feneri and kill Kabakçıoğlu Mustafa, the leader of the May revolution, so as to nip any resistance to the planned coup in the bud. On July 15, before the *yamaks* and janissaries in Istanbul heard about the assassination of Kabakçıoğlu, the imperial army started to move, arriving four days later at Davud Pasha, the military camp in front of the walls of Istanbul. According to Arif Efendi, Mustafa IV's privy secretary (*sırr-kātibi*), no one in the palace expected this move: "His Majesty, the grandees and the ulema, the notables and the commoners, everybody asked the same question, 'What is going on, what might be the reasons behind the coming of the army?' Misleading news was circulating. Everybody was surprised and asked, 'What is going on, and what is going to happen?'"[167] It seems that Sultan Mustafa did not reveal his familiarity with the plan to his privy secretary.

After the imperial army and Bayraktar's forces set up their tents on the Davud Pasha plain, the imperial ceremony took place. Sultan Mustafa received the grand vizier and Bayraktar close to the camp, where the imperial standard, symbolizing the sovereign, was delivered to the sultan. This was the first face-to-face encounter between Bayraktar and Sultan Mustafa. On July 21, Bayraktar, with his couple of thousand men, entered the city. It was the first time that the magnate of Ruse had been in the imperial capital. Bayraktar and the grand vizier held a conference, whose immediate result was the deposition of Grand Mufti Ataullah, one of the actors in the May revolution. According to Asım, between July 21 and July 27, there were serious disagreements between Bayraktar's party and the grand vizier over a number of issues. Asım noted that the grand vizier might have even informed the sultan of the real plan of Bayraktar and his associates. He proposed collaborating with the janissaries and subduing Bayraktar's forces. But the sultan did not accept this offer. This meeting, which must have taken place on July 27, was recorded in different sources.[168]

At dawn on July 28, Bayraktar began to occupy Istanbul, with around ten thousand troops, under the command of several Balkan notables. There was no serious resistance reported from the yamaks and other janissaries. Some of the forces took control of strategic locations. The main body of the army moved toward the Topkapı Palace. Meanwhile, Kalyoncu Ali, the ayan of Bilecik in western Anatolia, who had just arrived in Üsküdar on the Asian side of the Bosporus, crossed over with two thousand of his men to join Bayraktar. When Bayraktar arrived at the residence of the grand vizier, which was a mile from the Topkapı Palace, Refik and Tahsin accompanied him. His men broke into the grand vizier's palace, used force to take the imperial seal, arrested the grand vizier, and sent him out of the city. Some sources note that Bayraktar accused the grand vizier of betraying their cause by disclosing their secret plans to Sultan Mustafa.[169] Soon thereafter, the group moved to the Topkapı Palace. "The ulema, the grandees of the eternal state, the notables of Rumelia, and the dynasties of Anatolia all demand [ṭāleb] the reenthronement of Sultan Selim," Bayraktar exclaimed when they entered the first yard and arrived at the gate of the central palace. "They have all gathered here."[170]

In so saying, Bayraktar, now the coup's spokesman, made it clear that the central and provincial elites had combined to bring it about. The janissaries, who had initiated major changes in the Ottoman regime since the early seventeenth century, were excluded from the alliance. This was not only a new kind of coalition but also an expression of the shift from the traditional script of popular janissary-led movements and factions within the administration to a movement by a larger coalition of elites from the inner and outer segments of the empire, clustered around the ideological premises of the New Order.

Upon Bayraktar's declaration, the gates of the palace were closed. The Topkapı community was in a panic. After a short consultation, Sultan Mustafa ordered the executions of Selim III and Prince Mahmud, which would make him the only male in the Ottoman dynasty. About twenty palace guards entered Selim III's private chambers. After scuffles with Selim's servants, Mustafa's men strangled Selim. But at the last minute, some harem retainers rescued Prince Mahmud. The guards took Selim's body from his chamber to the palace gates. Bayraktar was prepared to smash down the gates, but Selim's corpse was found lying at the entrance of the inner yard of the palace. It was reported that upon seeing it, Bayraktar expressed his sorrow that he had not been able to save him. Following this dramatic encounter, Prince Mahmud was found in the harem. In a couple of hours, in a swift ceremony, Mahmud II was declared the new sultan. Bayraktar and the new grand mufti, Arabzade Efendi, presented their allegiance first, before members of the palace's inner circle, which was customary. Bayraktar was soon appointed grand vizier. In Asım's narrative, members of the Divan openly declared that they wished to see Bayraktar as grand vizier. Bayraktar expressed this collective will to the sultan, and Mahmud appointed him to the office.[171] When the cannon fire started, the people of Istanbul understood that Mustafa IV had been deposed, but they did not know who had become sultan, whether it was Selim or Prince Mahmud. The next day, a Friday, Selim's funeral took place. Mahmud II's first Friday prayer followed in quick succession. He left the Topkapı Palace as the new sultan and appeared before the public.[172]

Backed by a few reformist bureaucrats, a petty ayan in the small Balkan city of Hazergrad had launched a coup, deposed the sultan, and enthroned a new one, in short order becoming grand vizier with extraordinary powers. The provincial power of Ruse, in alliance with the New Order party, now ruled the empire. Bayraktar represented the new social and political authority growing in the Ottoman provinces, from the Balkans to the Arab lands, throughout the eighteenth century. He openly told Mahmud, after making him sultan, that he represented more than just his own power. Most of the notables of Rumelia were with him.[173] Bayraktar and his followers were, however, unfamiliar with the ways of the imperial elite. When he and his men entered the Privy Chamber with their guns, Prince Mahmud told them to behave properly and leave their guns outside.[174] The historian Şanizade recorded this minor incident to illustrate that the provincial magnates, of whom he was not terribly fond, had not yet learned the manners of high Ottoman culture.

The Restoration of the New Order (August–November 1808)

After the coup came the executions. From early August, leading *yamak*-janissary oligarchs and Mustafa IV's associates, who were considered responsible for the execution of Selim, were put to death. Their heads were presented to the public in Istanbul, with warrants announcing their crime.[175] Mustafa IV was locked in his chambers. Mahmud II would execute his older brother a couple of months later. Tayyar, who had met Bayraktar on his way to Edirne before the coup, was executed in Varna. The elimination of this controversial figure not only strengthened Bayraktar's hand but was also a gesture to the Çapanoğlu family, Tayyar's main rivals in Anatolia, whose support was necessary for the new regime.[176] A majority of the *yamak*s who had come to Istanbul from Black Sea Anatolia the previous year were arrested and sent back to their homelands.[177] The forces of Bayraktar and other Balkan notables—collectively named *kırcalı* soldiers by Istanbulites, echoing memories of the Balkan militia stopping the New Army in Edirne—occupied the city. The invasion of the capital by the Balkan notables and their militias made a deep impression on public memory. One observer, Galatalı Hüseyin, depicted the popular feeling among the people of Istanbul:

Raiders of Istanbul, the mountaineer youngsters,
Alemdar [Bayraktar] Pasha's wrestlers
With their couches set up for executions
Will never leave again, the *kırcalı* soldiers
In short jackets with long sleeves and knickers . . .[178]

The New Army's tight blue and red uniforms had disgusted the janissaries. But now the streets of Istanbul were occupied by Balkan militiamen wearing their peculiar outfits and provincial styles. Galatalı Hüseyin, probably a janissary bard, was captivated. The Friends of Ruse meanwhile established themselves as the leading cadres of the new regime. Ramiz became grand admiral. A new Ministry of Holy War was established, and Behiç was appointed its minister.[179] Tahsin, Galib, and Refik kept their key positions in the Divan. The first action of the new administration was to abolish the monopolies for the provisioning of the city, which reduced the prices of bread and meat, and to freeze the salaries (*esâme*) of the janissaries. This gesture to the public was aimed at preventing the janissaries from stirring up the Istanbul street against the new government.

Meanwhile, Ottoman scribes prepared an imperial proclamation informing provincial communities of the enthronement of Mahmud II, copies of which were sent to the provinces, from Bosnia to Egypt. In it, Mahmud II himself, speaking in the first person, informed his subjects of his enthronement. The proclamation then immediately goes on to say that the former commander of the Danubian army, Mustafa Pasha, had been appointed grand vizier. He could use this authority, the proclamation declared, "with absolute freedom and authority [*istiklāl-i ṭam ve ruḥṣat-ı kāmile*]" as sultan's representative.[180]

By late August, there was noticeable anxiety in Istanbul. Several magnates from the Balkans and Anatolia, with large entourages and armed forces, arrived on the outskirts of the city. The Austrian ambassador, Baron von Stürmer, informed Vienna that an extraordinary gathering had taken place outside the city walls. According to public opinion, he noted, Bayraktar was prepared to take radical action against the janissaries, possibly abolishing the corps. Probably to this end, a number of battalions under the control of several "provincial vassals and ayans from Anatolia and Rumelia" were "mysteriously" gathering in the vicinity of Istanbul.[181] Later it became clear that Bayraktar had invited provincial powerholders to Istanbul for an imperial assembly to negotiate the empire's affairs and put an end to the crisis. Unfortunately, we do not know all the details of when and how this invitation took place. Şanizade states that the magnates were summoned by an imperial order from Mahmud II.[182] However, it was likely that some were called before the coup. According to Câbî, Bayraktar decided, during his meeting with the grand vizier in mid July, to summon many provincial notables to Edirne.[183] This might be correct, since some notables joined him during that meeting on his way to Istanbul. İsmail of Serres arrived at Istanbul in mid August with a couple of thousand men. Çapanoğlu Süleyman and Karaosmanoğlu Ömer, leaders of the two prominent dynasties of central and western Anatolia, arrived in late August. Ahmed Agha of Şile, Seyyid İbrahim of Bolu, and Mustafa of Çirmen followed.[184] Ali Pasha of Ioannina sent his grandson to the city with a full retinue, while Muhammad Ali of Egypt sent his brother, who was ayan of Praviște, a small town near Kavala, and later his son İbrahim, by ship from Alexandria.[185] Kadı Abdurrahman Pasha, one of the architects of the military reforms, arrived with some forces from Karaman from the dispersed New Army.[186] In early September, Manuk, who was in Ruse during the coup, arrived with his small Armenian militia.[187]

Such an assembly was unprecedented in Ottoman history. Moreover, some notables, such as Nasuhoğlu of Uşak, did not attend, although invited, since they did not wish to leave their regions for an extended period.[188] Some Anatolian notables who were in the Çapanoğlus' zone of

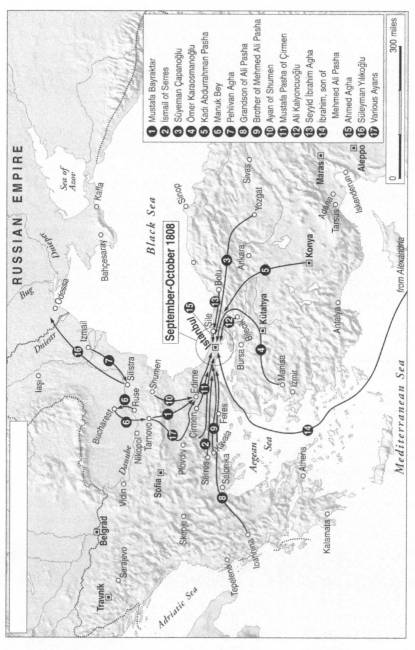

Map 4b. The 1808 imperial Assembly of Notables. The author and Philip Schwartzberg / Meridian Mapping.

influence were invited, but Süleyman Çapanoğlu asked them to stay home to prevent a power vacuum in their localities.[189] Nevertheless, many sent their representatives. The invitation did not include every single notable individual or family. No Bosnian notable, no one from northern Albania, eastern Anatolia, Syria, or Iraq came to the meeting. The assembly was more or less limited to the most prominent powerholders of the central provinces of Rumelia and Anatolia, who could reach the capital relatively quickly. Bayraktar's competitors Molla İdris of Vidin and Yılıkoğlu Süleyman of Dobruca were not present either. No representatives from the Canikli family attended the meeting. The Austrian diplomat Franz Freiherr von Ottenfels, who wrote a detailed report of the coup, remarks that with this move, the whole power of the Ottoman government came to reside in Bayraktar's person (*Die Ganze Macht der Regierung in seine Person einschließenden Bairaktar Mustafa Pascha*).[190]

The assembly was a formal meeting. With their forces deployed outside Istanbul, many notables stayed in the mansions of the city's imperial grandees. The inner and outer circles of the empire were getting to know each other. The meeting became an opportunity for provincial notables to settle old feuds and disputes in their regions. As arbiter of several disputes, Bayraktar mediated settlements.[191] In late September 1808, a conference took place at Saadabat Palace in Kağıthane on the Golden Horn. For the first time, a sultan, imperial elites, and provincial notables from different regions came together at the same meeting, saw and became acquainted with one another. Before the assembly, delegates were received by Mahmud II and declared their loyalty. According to the scribe of the Privy Chamber, Mahmud II expressed his sympathy to provincial notables.[192] However, this first-person encounter between high imperial circles and provincial leaders had various awkward moments. Câbî records some that circulated as rumors outside the palace, noting that before meeting Mahmud, İsmail of Serres preemptively stated that he would refuse any imperial office, including a governorship, even if Mahmud II insisted on offering it. İsmail also said he would not stay in the chamber reserved for him in the palace, but in the camp with his men. He refused to be part of the imperial elite and adopt their ways. Even if he accepted a title, he said, he would refuse to grow a beard and wear a turban—marks of the Ottoman elite.[193] Clearly, the provincial magnates did not see the assembly as an occasion for the Ottoman center to co-opt them in the service of the state. They came to Istanbul expecting to deliberate mutual interests after years of turmoil in the empire. The historian Şanizade recorded Bayraktar's opening speech at the imperial assembly:

We were originally affiliated with the [janissary] corps. So our fidelity to the corps is well known. However, the late Sultan Selim . . . decided to set up an army of trained soldiers. We condemned this, which [I now realize] was a mistake. But his efforts brought about his death. When I was honored with the title of vizier and became a commander, I saw the reasons for the enemy's success. I understood that the enemy was successful because its soldiers were well trained and orderly, its officers were proficient in military science, and the troops were united. I realized that our way was not right and our knowledge was not correct. I understood that the good deed of the late sultan was only to strengthen religion and state. When I shared my ideas with some men of reason whom I trust, I saw that they were even more upset. Later, when the sultanate was changed [in May 1807] and things turned back to their old ways, the military became even more disorderly, and the people of Islam became ten thousand times weaker than before. All of you know about the situation in Istanbul in these days. We realized that if things continued this way, the enemy would even invade the capital. I deliberated with some individuals who held important offices, and we mutually agreed to act to return the throne to Sultan Selim and to [re]establish the order of his time. If Mustafa IV continued to rule, everyone saw that this would cause the collapse of the Sublime State. However, our primary intention was not realized [we could not give the throne back to Selim]. But by the grace and mercy of God, His Majesty—the divinely chosen padişah and caliph of the world [Sultan Mahmud II]—is well qualified with learning, virtue, and intelligence. We all testify that because of his natural qualities and education, he is well aware of the problems that we witness. He is a zealous, courageous man with lofty aims. His ultimate goal is to protect the empire from enemy attack. . . . This was only possible with unity between the ministers of state, viziers, commanders, and men of law. All the provincial notables and the great families have thus been invited here by imperial order. They have come and they declare their alliance to strengthen the constitution [*bünyān*] of the state, which has been ruined. Now, let us discuss the situation and think about what should be done . . .[194]

After deliberating, the participants in the assembly agreed on a document known as the Deed of Alliance, with seven clauses concerning matters of state in the center and in the provinces (discussed in chapter 5). Toward the end of the assembly, Mahmud II visited the palace to meet the members of the assembly. The Deed was then submitted to the sultan, and Mahmud II confirmed the agreement with his own words written at the top of the document.

The Deed allied the central state and provincial powerholders for the survival of the Ottoman Empire. Regarding the notion of collective interest, provincial powerholders pledged loyalty to the sultanate and the state and pledged to participate in military reforms; in return, members of the central government promised to recognize the established authority of the provincial notables in the provinces and serve as guarantors of their lives, status, and property. While the signatories each stood mutual surety for one another, the sultan undertook the role of high guarantor for the application of the Deed, which redefined the basis of the Ottoman Empire. The boundaries between imperial and provincial, inner and outer domains, center and periphery, even ruler and ruled, were redrawn. The central establishment recognized the provincial powerholders' participation on their own terms, as legitimate in the imperial order.

By the end of September, the provincial magnates started to leave Istanbul for their regions.[195] Bayraktar sent letters to other provincial powerholders who did not attend the meeting, informing them of the alliance of the central and provincial elites, and asking them to sign the Deed. As he had done in his inaugural speech at the conference, Bayraktar conceded in his letter to Muhammad Ali of Egypt that, like others, he had resisted Selim's military reforms. But now he realized that these changes were inevitable and necessary. "All the old Anatolian dynasties, such as Çapanoğlus and Karaosmanoğlus, and the Balkan dynasties, such as that of İsmail of Serres, intendant of Drama, and others arrived in the capital and agreed to draft soldiers against the enemy," he noted. Bayraktar asked Muhammad Ali to cooperate with the new regime to fight the empire's internal and external enemies on other side of the Mediterranean; together "they would carve honor and glory in the universe for eternity."[196] Behind these bold words, there was a tacit threat to other provincial magnates who might not join the alliance. News and letters about Bayraktar's coup and the Deed circulated through the empire, and various notable families in the provinces, such as the al-Umari of Mosul, followed the unfolding developments from a distance with concern.[197]

Bayraktar also sent letters to the communities of Rumelia, informing them of his appointment as grand vizier and requesting their collaboration.[198] However, the Deed was not publicly announced to the communities. Both the public and diplomatic circles learned of the contents of the document from informants connected to the palace or Bayraktar and from rumors.[199] Between September and November, the Bayraktar regime implemented its reform agenda. Recruitment for the New Army, now renamed the New Militia (Sekbān-ı Cedīd), had already begun. The regional origin of recruits was perhaps the main difference between Bayraktar's New Militia and Selim III's New Order. The Sekbān-ı Cedīd consisted of soldiers drafted, not only from Anatolia, as with the New Army, but also from Istanbul and the Balkans. Sultan Mahmud II and Bayraktar issued declarations inviting the young men of Istanbul to join the New Militia. Kadı Abdurrahman Pasha was appointed its minister. At the same time, a regiment composed of Armenian privates was established.[200] The New Militia was not the New Army, with its disciplined, drilled, strongly hierarchic and uniformed structure. It was a diverse militia, gathered from the regional armies of the provincial notables. Christian militias under different Balkan notables were also included. However, the New Militia was established on the basis of the New Army experience. Many officers of the New Army became part of the New

Militia. It was an experiment to create a disciplined, well-drilled army out of various experienced teams of different military cultures, styles, and even languages and religions of various regions of the Balkans and Anatolia.[201]

The New Militia obviously disturbed the janissaries. Although after the coup, the leaders of the May revolution were executed or sent into exile, Bayraktar did not touch the janissary corps. The imperial army was now deployed outside Istanbul, and a number of janissaries in the army returned to their barracks. According an account by Yayla İmamı, Bayraktar signed a deed with elders of the janissary corps and solicited promises from them that they would not oppose the New Militia.[202] He visited the barracks of the 42nd unit, with which he had been connected in his youth, and conversed with elders.[203] However, Bayraktar intended to reorganize the daily salaries of janissary affiliates and to discharge thousands of them. The new government prohibited the selling or renting of janissary salaries and statuses. Mahmud II opposed this initiative.[204]

Meanwhile, the new government began reconfiguring Ottoman diplomacy. Manuk Bey, Bayraktar's financier, became the new chief dragoman, or interpreter, who acted as secretary under the director of foreign affairs. The Greek Phanariot families of Istanbul had monopolized this key post throughout the eighteenth century. Now an Armenian businessman from Wallachia became one of the main actors in Ottoman diplomacy. Peace talks with Russia continued between Manuk and Pozorwksky, the chief Russian diplomat. Mustafa Bayraktar offered various deals to the Russians through Manuk, clearly conveying that he had reintegrated the empire after the turmoil, and that the provincial notables backed him. Through Manuk, Bayraktar informed the Russians that France was in trouble in Spain. He had even offered to mount an anti-French campaign from Algeria. An Ottoman-Russian alliance would be mutually beneficial.[205] Soon a Russian delegation arrived in Istanbul to pursue the possibility of negotiating peace with the Ottoman Empire. Its head, Aleksandr Grigor'evich Krasnokutskii, noted in his diary that Bayraktar was still behind the proposal that he had made to Alexander I to start peace talks without French involvement. This time there was a strong government in Istanbul. However, he added, it was not clear whether Bayraktar had really subdued the opposition of the janissaries and controlled the general public.[206]

The Fall of Bayraktar and the Rise of Mahmud II
(November 1808)

The new regime tried to avoid the stormy days of previous revolutions. Security on the streets was bolstered. The prices of bread and meat were reduced. The administration developed policies to prevent the mob from intervening in politics. The month of Ramadan arrived, and while Bayraktar took action to ban "political conversations" (*devlet sohbeti*) in public spaces such as coffee- and bathhouses, he encouraged the people of Istanbul to make use of the promenades in the city and on the Bosporus, listen to storytellers and watch shadow theater, liberate themselves from worry, and enjoy the holy month.[207] Despite such measures to divert the public's attention from janissary politics to entertainment and amusement, Krasnokutskii was right to be concerned. In late October, observers recorded several minor episodes of unrest in the city. Early signs of a rebellion against Bayraktar appeared in mid October. A crowd jeered Ubeydullâh Kuşmânî, a popular preacher and a strong supporter of the New Order, who had mercilessly ridiculed the janissaries in his *Letters* and sermons (see chapter 1). Soon afterward, a massive janissary gathering around the Fatih Mosque protested against Kuşmânî, and the government expelled him from the city to calm the protesters.[208]

Bayraktar's attempts to stop the daily salaries paid to some janissary affiliates and to draft soldiers for the New Militia generated serious tensions. Mahmud II was said to have secretly backed the janissaries against the grand vizier in this conflict.[209] Grand Admiral Ramiz's decision to repeal the fees collected from foreign vessels at the docks by the marinas created discord between the mariners, rowers, and porters of Galata harbor and the new regime. Most of these harbor workers had janissary affiliations. Tensions only amplified after the New Militia stormed dockside coffeehouses and the sailors' leader, Kahvecioğlu Mustafa Agha, was executed on Bayraktar's orders.[210]

Conflict between the new regime and janissary affiliates was just one problem that the New Orderists faced. Support from palace circles was also shaky. The deposed Sultan Mustafa IV remained alive, ensconced in his chamber, and his supporters, particularly his sister Esma Sultan, who was a generous benefactor of the janissaries, lobbied among the elders of the corps on his behalf. According to a historian, at one moment, some janissaries spoke of Esma Sultan as a possible candidate for the Ottoman throne.[211] Although the credibility of this report is unsure, the possibility of a pro–Mustafa IV revolt with her support was not totally to be discounted. Perhaps the most important development that left Bayraktar's regime vulnerable was the fact that he had already sent most of his troops to the Danubian front in October. By early November, Bayraktar did not have enough of a military presence in Istanbul to protect his regime. Reporting to Vienna, an Austrian diplomat summarized the situation in Istanbul:

After the troops of Mustafa Pasha and the armies of other pashas who had been invited to the capital city [for the assembly] left the city for their regions, the janissaries raised their heads and picked up their courage again. For a couple of weeks, rumors and murmurs, which had been suppressed, started to circulate among the people once again. But these were not taken into consideration, because such chatter had long been common ever since the arming of the general public after the arrival of the British fleet in February 1807. New songs and expressions mocking the New Militia emerged. People ridiculed the soldiers' hats. According to one rumor, the keys of the twenty-four gates of the city, which had been held by the janissaries, would be taken from them and given to the New Militia. This was the state of the people on the night of November 14.[212]

At a dinner party organized by Manuk at his mansion in honor of the Russian delegation, Signora Pizzani, the wife of an Italian consultant to several embassies in Istanbul, told Krasnokutskii that people were angry at Bayraktar because of his treatment of the janissaries. She said that another revolt soon would not be unexpected.[213] As Signora Pizzani anticipated, the next day, November 15, the storm began. Bayraktar visited the chief mufti's residence for the ceremony of Night of Destiny, a holy day in Ramadan. On his way back to his palace with his entourage, he encountered protests. Observers mention notes attached to the walls predicting that blood would soon be shed on the streets of Istanbul. Before long, various groups were heard to have mobilized in different parts of the city. These began marching on Bayraktar's residence, which was not well guarded, and around midnight, a large number of janissaries attacked it.

Rather imprudently, Bayraktar had sent his closest associate and bodyguard, Boşnak Agha, to Ruse, following news from the region that Molla İdris, the magnate of Vidin, was preparing to harass Ruse in Bayraktar's absence. According to Câbî, Boşnak's other mission was to find a way somehow to eliminate Pehlivan İbrahim Baba Agha, a war hero ever since his success in the defense of Giurgiu against the Russians.[214] Baba Agha, some believed, had never forgotten his political defeat in Ruse, when Bayraktar was elected the ayan of the district with the support of Manuk and others. However, Boşnak Agha failed to carry out this mission. Baba Agha would soon become Vizier Baba Pasha when Sultan Mahmud offered him a military command.

Back in Istanbul on November 15, the janissaries besieged Bayraktar's mansion. Noting that he himself was a janissary, connected to the 42nd unit, Bayraktar protested that he had even had a fountain built at their barracks, so how could he be against the janissary cause? He asked the crowd to let women and servants leave the mansion. Following skirmishes with a handful of his guards, an explosion then occurred in the building when ammunition exploded in a storage area. The building collapsed, and dozens of janissaries were killed. It was not clear whether Bayraktar was dead or whether he had escaped through a tunnel from his mansion. People would later believe that he had committed suicide.

Soon groups attacked the mansions of other members of the ruling elite, slaughtered many of them, and plundered their property, while others attacked the New Militia's remaining troops. Many soldiers of the New Militia came from the Balkans, were not familiar with the streets of the city, and in many cases, found themselves trapped by the janissaries on dead-end streets. These scuffles continued for several days in different neighborhoods of Istanbul, in Galata, and in Üsküdar. This mutiny was not nearly as well organized as the May revolution, and in many ways not typical of janissary revolts. This episode was more violent, uncontrolled, and widespread. On several occasions, janissary elders and some members of the ulema tried to hold back the crowd. In fact, to limit the struggle to overthrow Bayraktar, they prevented janissaries from attacking mansions in which provincial notables were being hosted. It remained possible that the notables who had left and those who had stayed in Istanbul would unite, as provided for in the Deed of Alliance, and that they would attack the janissaries to save Bayraktar and the New Order. But this did not happen.

The real turning point came when Ramiz Pasha ordered his ships to bombard the janissary barracks from the Golden Horn. According to many observers, the bombardment shifted public opinion. The explosions triggered a massive fire. In a short time, the janissaries were able to garner support from thousands of people who were trapped between the new regime and the janissaries. When Bayraktar's body was pulled from under the rubble of his mansion, put on display, and publicly humiliated, groups that did not belong to the initial insurgency took to the streets and attacked the New Militia. As a result, the janissaries secured a victory. According to a Russian diplomat, fifteen thousand people lost their lives and seven thousand houses burned down.[215] The fire continued to burn in different parts of the city for several days. Some observers argued that Mahmud secretly supported the janissaries by doing nothing during the revolt. A couple of days later, Mahmud issued an order, declaring that the New Order had once again been done away with.[216]

Fears lingered that supporters of the New Order in the Balkans and Anatolia who had signed the Deed of Alliance would strike back.[217] But by the time supporters received news of the revolution, it was already too late. "The New Order has been entirely abolished," Sultan Mahmud decreed. "It was clearly cursed [*la'net*]. . . . The provincial dynasties should free themselves from this passion."[218] Ramiz, Kadı Abdurrahman, Manuk, Behiç and Bayraktar's treasurer, Köse Ahmed fled to the Balkans and Anatolia. Later, Ramiz, Köse Ahmed, Behiç, and Manuk would take refuge in Russia.[219] Mahmud wrote to the new grand vizier: "They bombarded Istanbul. . . . Think of what should be done under Sharia and Kanun to those who caused all that damage!"[220] Memiş Pasha was appointed grand vizier in Bayraktar's place.[221] The peace negotiations collapsed, and war with Russia started up again.

CONCLUSION

The Austrian diplomat Franz Freiherr von Ottenfels, who closely followed the episode in Istanbul, wrote in a memorandum:

After these events, one of the bloody and horrifying revolutions tarnishing the Ottoman crown came to an end. In the past fourteen months, two sultans were deposed. But the earlier revolutions were not as bloody. This time, the monarch was not deposed. However, the elimination of the grand vizier caused a stream of blood. The streets became filled with dead bodies, and the majority of the city was engulfed in fire. Due to extraordinary luck, a probable catastrophe was prevented. But all these events indicate only one thing about the future. Although in previous revolutions, the [janissary] party had been suppressed, it was able to survive. But now the [New Order] party has been suppressed and uprooted for good. Now no one believes that the reforms, which were embedded in the spirit [*Geist*] of the New Order, will be revived again. We see the janissary army as the seed of the Ottoman nation [*nazion*]. Twice the *nazion* became furious, rejecting new institutions. The victory of the *nazional militz* [janissaries] made people change their minds about the necessity for reform. Now we see that the struggle between the janissaries and the New Army was not just over the differences between their military headgear. It is a struggle for the Ottoman *nazion*'s characteristic nationality [*Eigenthümliche nazionalität*]. Now it is clear that the destruction of the janissaries, who are embedded in the military and religious constitution [*Verfassung*] of the Ottoman Empire, would destroy the Ottoman sultanate.[222]

Ottenfels, a graduate of the Austrian Oriental Academy, was closely acquainted with the Ottoman world. Like Juchereau, he interpreted the whole episode as a battle between the New Order, which had tried to change the constitution of the empire, and the Ottoman people, which the janissaries claimed to represent. The failure of the New Orderists under both Selim III and Bayraktar was not only because of a lack of prudence and rigorousness, but also due to their inability to persuade the Ottoman public. Eventually, it was the Ottoman public—or, more accurately, the people of Istanbul—who had decided the empire's fate in the latest incident. The janissaries proved that they were not only more successful at popular mobilization but also more integrated into the public. Observers like Juchereau and Ottenfels inherently disagreed with conventional depictions of the empire in Enlightenment Europe, typified by the French political philosopher Montesquieu, who described the Ottoman Empire as an Oriental despotism, where all power was in the hands of the sultan. On the contrary, according to Ottenfels, the Ottoman regime was like a republic; public opinion mattered, and the janissaries were its partisans. In seeking to bring about reform, the New Order had established a despotic—albeit enlightened—regime, but the empire could only reform itself under an autocracy supported by the people. "We will allow ourselves to attribute to the party of the janissaries a stronger tendency toward the republican constitution, whereas the principles of the New Order party lean more toward unlimited despotism" Ottenfels wrote.[223]

Although neither the supporters nor the opponents of the New Order used the terms "republicanism" or "despotism," their interpretation did not differ much from those of Ottoman intellectuals. As we saw in chapter 1, an author (or authors) called Koca Sekban Başı wrote a treatise a few years before the 1806–8 events rejecting "[the opinion of] the populace [*redd ül-a'vām*]," criticizing the janissaries, and arguing that the Ottoman Empire could only survive through military reforms creating a new, disciplined, well-drilled army. Koca Sekban Başı wrote not just to counter popular opinion circulating on the streets but also to persuade the public. This attempt at persuasion was exactly what Juchereau thought necessary, even though it was unsuccessful. The janissaries and the general public were so enmeshed that the New Order was unable to separate them.

The intervention of provincial powerholders from the Balkans and Anatolia under Bayraktar's leadership on behalf of the New Order was not enough to save the new regime. From the Edirne incident to the Friends of Ruse and Bayraktar's coup, many provincial powerholders shifted their positions from the janissary bloc to become supporters of the New Order. In September 1808, for the first time, many provincial strongmen and strong families from different part of the empire, acted collectively, changing the dynamics of Ottoman politics. A new alliance of the provincial elite and the imperial elite gave birth to an imperial assembly and its Deed of Alliance, which radically reoriented the Ottoman order and made provincial elites partners in the empire. But the political infrastructure was not prepared for such a coalition. The janissaries were neither integrated into the new coalition nor eliminated. A new "new army" was nascent. Mahmud II, the Palace, and many reformists were not entirely persuaded by the new program. And the population of Istanbul, while giving credit to Bayraktar, soon grew disenchanted with the new regime. As Şanizade put it, "the age of Bayraktar [*devr-i 'Alemdāriyye*]" brought various uncustomary things that were destined to fail.[224] The age of Bayraktar was one episode in the age of revolutions. Like some others, it was a turning point in which history did not turn.

The elites of the New Order on the Bosporus and in the city fled their mansions and were stripped of their wealth or killed during the turmoil. Lamenting the lost elite of the New Order, the twentieth-century writer Ahmet Hamdi Tanpınar observes in his book *Beş Şehir* (Five Cities): "The revolt in 1807 did not end the new life on the Bosporus, but perhaps changed its owners. The elites of the new period were not as polite and elegant. The two revolts, one after the other, changed the elites of Istanbul. One would have to wait a very long time to see the blossoming of the taste again."[225] After Bayraktar's death, Mahmud II proclaimed renewed confidence in the janissaries, declaring in an imperial decree that "the janissary corps that I inherited from my noble ancestors are soldiers of my imperial domain. History records how they rendered great service to my ancestors. They are [the source of] my esteem. God willing, with my imperial power I order them to render great services in holy wars and make me a holy warrior [*ġāzī*]."[226]

At that moment, no one could have prophesied that eighteen years later, Mahmud II would abolish the janissaries in a bloody massacre carried out by his new army with the enthusiastic participation of the people of Istanbul.

CHAPTER 5

Settlement

The Deed of Alliance and the Empire of Trust (1808)

Trust is only possible with mutual surety and liability in unity and alliance.

The Deed of Alliance, Article 5

The Deed of Alliance (Sened-i İttifāḳ) was drafted and signed in late September 1808 in a consultative assembly in Istanbul, ending a crisis that had shaken the empire for two years. As discussed in the previous chapter, Istanbul and the provinces experienced a series of crises that threatened the integrity and order of the empire, beginning with the Edirne incident in August 1806, when provincial notables and communities in western Thrace blocked the New Army and humiliated the New Order. The outbreak of the Ottoman-Russian war and the British fleet's assault on Istanbul in late 1806 were followed by a janissary-led popular revolt in the capital and the fall of Selim III and the New Order in March 1807. Mustafa Bayraktar, the commander of the Danubian army and a leading provincial magnate in Danubian Bulgaria, led a coup d'état in alliance with members of the reform party in the Ottoman bureaucracy. The group dethroned Mustafa IV and enthroned Mahmud II. Mustafa Bayraktar became grand vizier and restored the New Order.

Bayraktar sent letters to a number of leading provincial notable families, inviting them to Istanbul for an unprecedented consultative assembly to deliberate how to bring an end to the political crisis. By September 1808, some leaders or representatives of families from the Balkans and Anatolia arrived in Istanbul. The assembly took place over several days at the Sa'adabat Kiosk in Kağıthane on the stream that runs into the Golden Horn. As a result of several meetings at the assembly, participants drafted and signed the so-called Deed of Alliance. The document's twenty-five signatories included the grand vizier, Mustafa Bayraktar, members of the Divan, the chief judges of Rumelian and Anatolian provinces, chiefs of the janissary and cavalry corps, and the heads of four major notable families from the provinces. By way of the Deed, signatories loyally pledged to protect the sultan and sultanate and to recruit men for the reformed state army. In return, the Deed guaranteed life and status to provincial notables and their dynasties. Alongside these mutual guarantees among elites, the Deed introduced profound changes on maintaining the empire's integrity and order and defining rights and obligations. At one stage in the deliberations, Mahmud II visited the assembly and met delegates, honoring them with his presence. Most likely during his visit, the sultan signed on to the Deed and became one of its contractors.

The state did not announce the Deed to the public with the usual imperial edicts. According to observers, the assembly was held in closed sessions.[1] Nevertheless, according to the Ottoman chronicler Şanizade Ataullah, who wrote ten years after the event, the confirmation of the sultan appeased possible opposition in the public opinion (*re'y-i cumhūr*) against the new regime.[2] Although the Deed was not publicly announced, many among the imperial elite had copies of it transcribed for their personal records.[3] Order in Istanbul was still shaky after the coup. The Deed's authors' intention to refurbish the reform agenda had the potential to trigger a variety of reactions. Within three months of signing the Deed, Mustafa Bayraktar, the architect of the episode that gave birth to it, and several other members of the alliance, died in a janissary revolt. The process initiated by the Deed was now cut short. Although not officially revoked, for all practical purposes, the Deed became void. After this event, neither the sultan nor the signatories who remained alive would refer to the Deed. Many learned the details of the document much later in 1819, when Şanizade provided the text in his *History*.

Was the Deed an anticlimax? It depends on how we understand history. If we consider the short lifetime of the political coalition that produced the Deed, and the fact that it was not implemented, we can see it as a failure. However, if we consider the long-term patterns that shaped Ottoman political culture throughout the nineteenth and early twentieth centuries, we can well argue that the Deed and the political dynamics producing it were in fact a test, a precursor of future developments. In fact, the final section of this chapter shows that some of the principles of the Deed would directly continue to shape the political and constitutional culture of the Ottoman Empire in the nineteenth century that laid the groundwork for the Tanzimat edict of 1839 and the later constitutional codifications.

The Deed of Alliance consists of an introduction, seven articles, a conclusion or epilogue, the signatories' names and seals, and the writ of the sultan at the top of the document.[4] This chapter provides a translation of the Deed alongside close textual analysis. It examines the meaning of the Deed and its place in the Ottoman and global contexts of the age of revolutions. I argue that the Deed signified a radical possibility in Ottoman history with the potential to change political and institutional dynamics profoundly. I also contend that when compared with other major documents of the global age of revolutions, the Deed was especially important. Examining the Deed enriches and expands our assumptions about the textual forms, legal instruments, and philosophical premises of constitutional documents in the late eighteenth and early nineteenth centuries.

THE DEED OF ALLIANCE

Introduction

Praise be to God, who strengthened Islam by means of men who acted with accord and in harmony.[5] Peace be upon our Master Muhammad, who removed discord and dissension from his community, his family and companions, who struggled for his cause.

Now to our subject: The reason for writing this auspicious document is that the Exalted Ottoman State, which is the benefactor of all, is a Muhammadan sultanate, and it is a self-evident fact that the conquests, victories, glory, and might that it has enjoyed since its foundation have been accomplished through union, unity, and the removal of selfishness and dissent; recently, however, as a result of the passage of time, this order has severely deteriorated; selfishness and dissent have become apparent among ministers of the state and the provincial dynasties for various reasons; consequently the power of the imperial sultanate disintegrated; and its inner and outer influence has been disturbed. This situation brings about weakness and disorder for rich and poor, high and low, in sum, for the entire Muslim community. Young and old acknowledge that this situation has taken on a loathsome form, and because of these known unjust and shameful acts it has reached a point at which the very foundation of the sultanate is in utter ruins. In the name of God, the most merciful, the most compassionate, all of us comprehend and understand that for the sake of the blessed intention of turning this disorder into unity and exerting efforts toward securing and manifesting the Exalted State's full power, a warning must be taken from previous affairs, the pillars of the order of state and religion must be maintained, and the highest word of God be exalted in compliance with the illustrious verse of the Qur'an "So take warning, O you with eyes" [59:2]. This is incumbent upon piety and an obligation of loyalty. Hence numerous meetings were held, and we exerted effort for the reinvigoration of religion and the state, as a single body and in union and alliance. We discussed [the ways to] proliferate essential power and various administrative issues; consulted on agreeable directions; and recorded the articles of alliance in the deed below.

In the introduction to the Deed, which offers guidance for understanding the rest of the document, the emphasis is on unity (*ittiḥād*) and alliance (*ittifāḳ*). Only with unity and alliance can the state (*devlet*) and sultanate (*salṭanat*), and therefore religion and the whole Muslim community, be saved and their power reinstituted. The emphasis on integration, unity, and alliance drew support from the Arabic invocation at the beginning of the text, which underlined the concepts of accord (*waḥīd*), alliance (*ittifāḳ*), concord (*vifāḳ*), and the removal of discord (*nifāḳ*) and dissent (*şiḳāḳ*). But from whom did the Deed's authors expect unity and alliance? The Deed maintains that both in the inner sphere (*dāḥil*), among grandees of the central state, and in the outer sphere (*ḥāric*), among provincial dynasties (*ḥānedān*), dissent and cleavages exist. Unity and alliance were to be reached within the inner and outer spheres. The Deed suggests a demarcation between the inner and outer circles of the empire, that is, between the center and the provinces. Throughout the text, juxtapositions appear between the inner and outer spheres, or *devlet-i ʿāliyye* (central state) and *taşra* (province), or grandees of the central state and provincial dynasties or notables (*ḥānedān* and *vücūh*). However, the discord and dissent were not necessarily between the center and provinces. They were also within the center and within the provinces.

In the introduction, the emphasis on "known shameful incidents" refers to events in the center and the provinces, such as the 1806 Edirne incident and the coup by Mustafa Bayraktar. The Deed's signatories clarify that several meetings were held in a single body, in unity and alliance, to discuss and consult on how to reinvigorate religion and the state (*dīn ü devlet*), or the Ottoman existence, and how to perfect the essential power (*ḳuvvet-i ẕātiyye*), referring the power of the sultanate and the sultan, and the empire's administration.

How does the Deed conceptualize the state? In the introduction, the first sentence following the invocation begins with a definition: the Exalted Ottoman State is a Muhammadan sultanate. The Deed clarifies the two main characteristics of the "state." The Exalted Ottoman State is a sultanate and is Islamic. The sultanate refers to absolute sovereignty, which was represented and executed by the sultan, who came from the Ottoman dynasty. The term "Muhammadan" refers to the state's Islamic character. The Deed establishes a relationship between the power of the state and the interests of the Muslim community. Islam is an overarching concept, connecting the state to the people. The authors of the Deed thus envisioned Islam and its law as a point of reference that, transcending state and sultanate, connected the community and polity.

Article 1

Since our glorious, generous, majestic, and powerful sultan, who is our and the entire world's benefactor, is the most eminent person in the Eternal State, all of us are contractors and liable for both the [protection of] his exalted sovereign person and the strengthening of his imperial sultanate, in accordance with God the Almighty's grace and benevolence and the divine guidance of the Prophet Muhammad. If at some time either ministers, ulema, high officials, [provincial] dynasties, or janissary corps commit a betrayal or actions against his edict[s] and wishes, by word or deed, secretly or overtly, after judicial investigation [if this person's fault is substantiated], let us all, in the capital and provinces, act in alliance to punish the individual who dared to commit such an act and use this punishment as a warning to others. In this matter, let serious efforts also be made in alliance to punish anyone who manifests tolerance [of such actions] and to make him an example to others. And if someone does not join this circle of alliance, let all of us take action against him and force him to obey [this] article of the agreement by words and deeds. In short, let all of us, personally and with our resources, undertake and [be] liable to [protect] his imperial personality, maintain the state and power of the imperial sultanate, and ensure [the implementation of] his edicts and wishes, and his being free from betrayals and conspiracies. As long as we live, let us guarantee this, and afterward let our sons and dynasties do so. In this way the goodwill of His Majesty the Sultan toward all of us becomes apparent and consequently allows us to give necessary thanks and continuously to serve and increase our merit.

Article 1 operates as a collective promise by grandees of the central state and notables of the provinces to protect the sultan. Signatories promised and guaranteed the protection of his person (*zāt*) and sultanate (*salṭanat*). Article 1 stipulates that the sultan, the most eminent person in the state, who is also the benefactor of the people, including the Deed's signatories, represents two identities: his imperial person (*zāt-i hümāyūn*) and his sultanate (*salṭanat*). These two bodies of the sultan refer to the personal existence (*zāt*) of the current sultan and the institutional existence of Ottoman dynastic sovereignty (*salṭanat*). This distinction between the sultan's *zāt* and the sultan's *salṭanat* appears in several places in the text. In the sultan's writ (*ḥaṭṭ-ı hümāyūn*), Mahmud II declares "I, my imperial person [*zāt-i hümāyūnum*], undertake the execution and implementation of the letter of promises and recognized conditions written in this deed of agreement." Here, the sultan, as a person, becomes a signatory to the Deed. In Article 1, the Deed's signatories undertake and guarantee the protection of *his* person and the strengthening of the structure of *his* imperial sultanate. This distinction between *zāt* and *salṭanat* made it possible for the sultan to act as a person with rights and duties, undertaking the execution of the Deed, as we shall see in his writ.

Two concepts emerge in Article 1 of the Deed: the *müte'ahhid* (from *'ahd*, to undertake and being a contractor) and *żamīn* (from *żamn*, being a surety or guarantor). These two concepts, *'ahd* and *żamn*, to promise as a contractor and to be a guarantor or liable, gave the deed its character as a mutual promise and surety of members of the inner and outer, central and provincial zones of the state. Dignitaries of the center, as individuals, and notables of the provinces, as individuals and provincial magnates and as representatives of their households, promised, not only to protect the life of the sultan and his sultanate, but also to punish offenders collectively. Magnates promised to adhere to the Deed, not only in their names, but also in the names of their descendants. Thus they forced other signatories (including fellow provincial notables) implicitly to accept the perpetuity of their dynasties. The document qualified the notion of offense. Actions against sultanic edicts, wishes, and consent (*hilāf-ı emr ü rıżā*), broadly understood, were reinforced by the notion of betrayal or treason (*ihānet*). Signatories promised to take action against offenders who betrayed the sultan in deed or in word. The threat of betrayal obligated signatories to enforce stipulations of the Deed against wrongdoers, or those who did not accept the Deed, who were to be integrated in the circle of alliance. However, the Deed was also intended to limit arbitrary action by stipulating that enforcement was only possible after a judicial investigation (*ba'de't-tahkīk*). The concept of judicial investigation will be revisited in my discussion of Article 5 below.

Article 2

Since the maintenance of the Exalted State and the proliferation of its power and glory are [also] the basis of the survival for us and our dynasties, as a result of deliberation among us, we all agreed that soldiers and privates to be drafted from the imperial domains for the strengthening of the power of the sultanate should be drafted and recruited as state soldiers in accordance with the order decided at the deliberative councils; and all of us should strive and exert efforts toward the perfection and maintenance [of this order]. Let all grandees and servants [of the state] and the provincial dynasties in the center and the provinces strive for the regulation and aligning [of this order]. Since this issue of [drafting] soldiers for the sake of the fulfillment of religion and state was decided through unanimous vote, if anyone permits its modification by stirring up conspirators and mischief-makers by claiming that this order has been voided because of the changing times or something else, or if the janissary corps disapprove or oppose this, then let all of us take action in alliance and consider anyone, even those uttering such ideas, let alone those who dare to disapprove or terminate or alter it, to be a traitor, and strive and exert efforts toward his punishment, suppression, and removal; let not a single person among us differ on this issue. And since exerting efforts toward the prevention and repression of any enemy act regardless of its origin and moving against the enemy in the quickest way are principal rules, let no action against this tenet be taken at any time.

In Article 2, the provincial dynasties pledged to draft soldiers from their regions and mobilize them for the service of the empire. As discussed in earlier chapters, some notables were already actively involved in the recruitment process for the New Order during the reign of Selim III. Article 2 standardized this practice. While provincial dynasties became essential partners of the military apparatus of the empire in the provinces, as formulated at the beginning of the Deed, their lives and the perpetuation (*beḳā'*) of their dynasties were seen as dependent on the state and sultanate. This mutual dependence was enhanced by an arrangement that armies drafted by notables were to be named state soldiers. Article 2 also enforced the collectivity of signatories as guardians of the new military order. Signatories pledged not to tolerate dissent against the new arrangement by the state, the janissaries, or the people.

The term "state soldier" signifies an alternative to the janissaries and the semi-private armies of provincial powerholders or governors. In another document, issued just after the Deed, we see details that explain how the new army would be drafted.[6] According to the new arrangement, each district (*ḳażā'*) in the central provinces was expected to provide and maintain a number of soldiers according to their capacity. These solders were organized under chiefs (*baş buğ*), who were appointed by regional powerholders. Each soldier would be paid ten *ġuruş* monthly. The names of chiefs and soldiers would be recorded and the registers would be sent to the central administration. Every six months, powerholders reported on the troops. These men were deployed to military camps. Powerholders carried out regular inspections in the camps. Each district community financed a division deployed in its district. The details concerning the district's capacity to maintain a military division and matters concerning the financing of troops were to be decided through negotiations between provincial notables (ayans) and community leaders. Troop expenditures, added to the apportionment registers of the districts,[7] were collected from the community as taxes every six months, with cooperation from regional magnates and district notables.

Using this method, the political authority envisioned the creation of a standing army, which would be financed by district communities as a result of their obligations to the empire, and would be deployed in military camps in the provinces in peacetime. Provincial magnates and other subordinate notables under their authority were to supervise recruitment, organization, and mobilization. These were the major duties of leaders of the provincial dynasties who signed the document. They were expected to supervise the empire's most strategic institution, the New Army, as provincial leaders.

Article 3

Enhancing the glory of the sultanate is our primary aim, and we undertake to work on this matter in alliance. Thus, just as we endeavor to increase the number of troops in order to enhance the power [of the state], so too do we undertake the maintenance of the Public Treasury of Muslims and the revenues of the Exalted State. We pledge and guarantee to carry out, in alliance, the fair collection of revenues from the localities; to protect [these localities] from damage and harassment; and to execute and implement the orders and decrees of the sultan and punish anyone who opposes [their] implementation and shows disloyalty; and let this rule be perpetually obeyed.

While Article 2 laid down the new military order, Article 3 regulated revenue collection. Like building the New Army, duties surrounding revenue collection were also entrusted to provincial elite. The Public Treasury of Muslims (*Beytü'l-māl-ı Müslimīn*) and revenues of the Exalted State (*vāridāt-ı Devlet-i 'Āliyye*) referred to different fiscal aspects of the Ottoman polity. The emphasis on the public treasury of Muslims underlined that the Ottoman state was a state of Muslims. These two treasuries also implied different tax sources, namely revenues collected as religious levies, which were in theory collected in the Public Treasury of Muslims, and revenues collected as administrative levies, which were collected as revenues of the administration. Article 3 did not describe complex revenue-collection mechanisms in detail, but rather emphasized principles, such as fair collection, protection of local communities, and implementation of imperial edicts. Like the other articles, Article 3 stressed the Deed's overarching principle, namely, that individuals opposed to regulations accepted in the assembly, to the Deed, and to imperial decrees were to be collectively punished by the signatories. In addition to carrying out the Deed's principles, the duty to punish those who dissented heightened the signatories' collective responsibility.

Article 4

Since early times, the order and the law of the Exalted State and the entire [corpus of] sultanic orders and prohibitions have been dispensed to all grandees and ministers, in the center or provinces, through the absolute deputy [i.e., the grand vizier]. Thus, henceforth let everyone know his superior and not set himself up to interfere with matters other than his duties. And let the orders and prohibitions [of the grand vizier] be considered orders and prohibitions of the sultan, and let nobody dare to disobey them. And we will act together against anyone who interferes with affairs that are not his own or that fall under the jurisdiction of others, and by saying "although this matter is the duty of others, such an individual interferes in such a way," we all undertake to dismiss that individual. We all undertake to submit all matters to the grand vizier and to ask for his authorization and [act] in accordance with his orders and decisions. In addition, if the grand vizier commits unlawful and corrupt acts against mutual agreement, causing immediate harm to the provinces and the Exalted State's internal situation, let all of us act to prevent him. And we unanimously promise that if a grand vizier acts spitefully and slanders someone by saying, "Others asked me to suppress this person," we shall prevent the former and protect the latter, thus let these [rules] be perpetually abided [by].

Article 4 clarifies the status of the grand vizier: he is the absolute deputy, *plenitudo potestatis*, of the sultan. Although it goes unmentioned in the Deed, the grand vizier was appointed and dismissed by the sultan. All imperial edicts were dispensed through him. The grand vizier was the head of the state and the voice of the sultan.[8] The Deed's signatories pledged to obey the orders and decisions (*re'y*) of the grand vizier as their superior. As in the case of the other articles, signatories promised to act collectively against individuals disobeying the grand vizier's decisions, as well as against those interfering with the jurisdiction of others. While the document stressed the boundaries of jurisdictions and duties of officeholders and dynasties, the grand vizier was presented as the key figure to whom all individuals were to report actions against others. The grand vizier was not only the highest authority in the empire under the sovereign sultan, but also the imperial coordinator of acts by members of the alliance.

But the deed also introduced a condition: if the grand vizier committed unlawful actions, the signatories, again collectively, had the right to act against him. In other words, the authority of the grand vizier was limited by the collective will of the circle of alliance. Spiteful behavior (*nefsāniyet*) and slander (*müfteriyāt*) were mentioned as acts the grand vizier was to avoid. Here, not only mutual agreement and procedures, but also trust became key components of the contract. Although the Deed failed to clarify how to substantiate spiteful behavior and slander, unlike "judicial process" (*taḥḳīḳ*) for other wrongdoing, this condition diminished the distance separating the grand vizier from other signatories. Article 4 suggests that in the minds of the Deed's signatories, the grand vizier became a kind of *primus inter pares* among other signatories, despite the fact that, formally, he was appointed by the sultan to represent him.

Article 5

As we all guarantee and undertake to protect the imperial person [the sultan], the power of the sultanate, and the order of the state, it is a major imperative that the dynasties and notables of the provinces should trust the Exalted State, and that the grandees and dignitaries of the state in the capital should trust one another; it is certain that trust and confidence are possible with [mutual] surety and liability in unity and alliance; therefore, let both the dynasties and notables [of the provinces] and the ministers, grandees, and dignitaries [of the center] who participate in this circle of alliance similarly guarantee and undertake to ensure one another's personal safety and that of their dynasties. In this manner, even if there has been no act violating the conditions of the agreement, if an assault or act of treachery or a conspiracy is perpetrated by the Exalted State or viziers in the provinces against one of the dynasties, or if such acts are carried out by one dynasty against another, then let all of us in alliance work toward punishment and preventing it, regardless of distance. And since all ministers will guarantee and undertake the perpetuity and maintenance of the leaders of the notable houses as long as they are alive, and afterward of their families, let those dynasties likewise provide pledges and guarantees for those notables under their jurisdiction. And let nobody be permitted to plot against the lives of those notables out of greed or anything else. If the guilt or treachery of one of them in violating his guarantees and agreement becomes apparent, then let the dynasties in charge work toward his dismissal, punishment, and replacement with someone else, after carrying out judicial investigation and submitting information to the grand vizier. And let nobody force his way or transgress into any area that is even a span outside the region entrusted to him. Let all take action, regardless of distance, if somebody carries out such an assault, and prevent him [from doing so]. And if he does not take warning, let us work unanimously toward prevention and punishment of the person responsible for the strife. And let all provincial dynasties, and notables of the provinces unanimously strengthen their work toward suppressing revolts and strife. And let us also unanimously work toward punishment and correction of anyone who mistreats and oppresses the poor or opposes the implementation of the sacred Sharia. And since all the dynasties and notables in the provinces guarantee and undertake to work toward preventing any treachery or plot arising out of provocation or conspiracy against ministers, ulema, high officials, and servants of the state at any time, and to prevent any punishment unless somebody's guilt has become apparent in the eyes of all, just as in the case of the guarantee given to all dynasties and notables, let nobody act against this. And if somebody openly committed a fault, as a result of human nature, upon manifestation of this guilt to all, let the person be punished by the grand vizier's office according to the degree of his offense.

Article 5 established bonds of trust (*emniyet*) between signatories of the deed in the center and the provinces. Emphasizing trust as imperative to the continuity of order, Article 5 stipulated that to establish bonds of trust, members of the circle of alliance should pledge to be surety and liable (*kefālet* or *żimāmet*) for the protection of the sultan, sultanate, and the state, as well as one another's security. Bonds of trust established through mutual surety did not only include the personal safety of signatories, but also the safety and perpetuity (*bekā'*) of provincial dynasties. By collectively guaranteeing the perpetuity of provincial dynasties, this condition challenged the old convention of sultanic authority to revoke statuses, offices, and contracts and order confiscations and executions. Article 5 further enhanced this condition, by stipulating that dynasties also guaranteed one another's safety and would not interfere with one another's jurisdiction. The Deed was thus intended to cement the de facto situation by establishing bonds of trust through mutual surety, in which provincial dynasties could not be removed from the lands entrusted to them (*muḥavvel*). But perhaps the most striking condition was that members of the circle of alliance were obligated to act against perpetrators if the state or imperial officeholders committed an assault, act of treachery, or conspiracy against provincial dynasties. Here, the Deed explicitly limited the power of the central authority vis-à-vis the prominent families of the provinces who signed—or would sign—it.

Article 5 also stipulates that the dynasties became guarantors to notables (*a'yān ve vücūh*) under their administration. As noted in chapter 3, in the second half of the eighteenth century, a district management system was established. According to this system, district ayans nominated and/ or elected by district communities or who acquired public consent from the community managed public affairs and finances in the district. In the late eighteenth century, this system, based on the collective participation of the communities, was gradually institutionalized in the central provinces. As chapter 2 illustrated, the consolidation of regional powerholders also occurred in the eighteenth century. Several magnates rose to establish power at the regional level and build regional zones of influence through various mechanisms, deals, and statuses within the state and local communities. In these regional zones, where several other notables, Muslim ayans or Christian *kocabaşı*s, operated either as deputies or district administrators/managers, some local notables were under the patronage of regional powerholders, while others collaborated with regional powerholders as partners or entered into conflict with them.

Article 5 of the Deed was intended to transform this complex provincial order. The new arrangement took the right to elect ayans from the communities and granted to regional dynasties. The document framed the dynasties as the principal authority in provincial order, establishing a hierarchical system, with the powerholding dynasties at the top. How the Deed understood these hierarchies becomes evident in a decree Mahmud II sent to İsmail of Serres, one of the Deed's signatories, following its promulgation. According to this decree, İsmail had authority to appoint and dismiss district ayans:

If the notables [*a'yān ve vücūh*] oppose you, the right to punish and admonish of such individuals is entrusted to your free will because of your independent responsibility. . . . Accordingly, [the right] to elect, uphold, punish, or favor the ayans of the districts is granted to you. . . . Without your consent, they do not have the right to collect [taxes] from the community. If the ayans of the districts have business in Istanbul, there will be no approval without your letter of confirmation.[9]

To prevent arbitrary power on the part of provincial magnates and their dynasties, other bonds of trust were created between them and subordinate local notables through mutual surety. Through the bonds of mutual surety, the Deed established an empirewide web of trust, from the center to regional dynasties, and from regional dynasties to subordinate local notables.

As the Deed stressed in several places, Article 5 stated the condition that fault, treason, or conspiracy called for collective punishment by members of the bonds of trust and the circle of justice. Methods of punishment were further detailed in Article 5, which forbade punishment "unless someone's guilt has become apparent in the eyes of all," and if a judicial investigation (*ba'de't-taḥḳīḳ*) substantiated blame. Furthermore, the Deed implied that human beings made mistakes; therefore, punishments should reflect the severity of the crimes and should not exceed what wrongdoers deserved. In addition to guarantees given for the perpetuity of the dynasties, this condition, which outlawed arbitrary punishment, confirmed the Deed's agenda, namely, to put an end to volatility, minimize risk, and establish an order of stability and trust in which members of the empire, in both the center and the provinces, received mutual guarantees of security.

Article 6

If any treacherous act or conspiracy led by the janissary corps or another group in the imperial capital should occur, all provincial dynasties will hasten to reach Istanbul and those individuals and janissaries who dared [to act in this way] will be removed or abolished. That is to say, those persons or military groups that caused such a treacherous act and conspiracy should be judicially investigated, and in the case of a group, they should be subdued and punished and their revenues and muster rolls should be annulled, as in the case of the guards of the Bosporus Castle who engaged in conspiracies; in the case of individuals, they should be executed upon judicial investigation regardless of their rank. All dynasties and notables in the provinces undertake this, and they all guarantee the security and order of the imperial capital. Thus let us unanimously and continuously work and exert efforts toward acquiring the means necessary to establish such a strong bond.

Article 6 sent a message to the janissary corps and groups affiliated with it, such as the *yamak*s of the Bosporus Castle who initiated the revolution of 1807, that an insurgence or conspiracy would evoke an immediate counteraction from the provincial dynasties. The Deed presented the provincial dynasties as protectors and guarantors of the state. This protection and guarantorship was particularly aimed at the internal threat of the janissaries. Punishment would be capital: execution after judicial investigation.

As discussed in previous chapters, the janissary corps was more than an army. It was a military-civil corporate group with more than one hundred thousand empirewide affiliates of different ranks and statuses. The janissary corps also led political opposition and mobilized the public. Janissaries were engaged in coalitions with other groups, including factions of ulema and financiers that had achieved considerable autonomy from the central bureaucracy and imperial household. Sultan Selim's alternative New Army was dismantled after the revolution of 1807. The Deed revitalized the project of an alternative military establishment. The document presents the janissaries as a separate or autonomous group, as a collectivity (*sınıf*) against which all signatories, those connected both to the central state and to dynasties in the provinces, promise to take action in the case of rebellion or conspiracy. As stated in Article 2, a new army, called the state army, would be drafted in the provinces, and if the janissary corps disapproved or opposed the draft, members of the circle of alliance would act against them.

The status of the janissaries and their connection to the sultan and state establishment was problematic. While the Deed does not refer to the corps as an integral part of the state, in another text, it figures as part of the state. The document signed between Mustafa IV and the janissaries in 1807 presented the chiefs and soldiers of the janissary corps as "zealous [servants] of the Exalted State since the old days."[10] Later, in 1809, Mahmud II, in a letter to the janissaries, declared that the janissary army was the army of his imperial person.[11] The Deed envisioned the janissary corps as an autonomous unit connected to the Exalted State, but not under the direct and unconditional control of the central administration. Neither the grand vizier nor any other officeholder had direct command and control over the corps. For that reason, Article 6 obligated signatories of the Deed to act against the janissaries if an act of rebellion or conspiracy occurred. The Deed assumed de facto but also, implicitly, de jure autonomy of the janissary corps.

Article 7

Since protection and support of the poor and subjects are essential, it is necessary that the dynasties and notables in the provinces pay attention to providing order and being moderate in levying taxes on the poor and subjects in the district[s] under their administration. Thus, let everyone give serious attention to establishing and continuously implementing any decision to be taken by ministers and provincial dynasties after deliberation in regard to preventing oppression and adjusting taxes, and let everyone give serious attention to preventing oppression and transgression from taking place in convention of these decisions. And let provincial dynasties scrutinize each other and inform the Exalted State if one such provincial dynasty commits oppression and transgression in violation of orders and the sacred Sharia, and let all provincial dynasties unanimously work toward preventing such actions.

Only Article 7 mentions the well-being of tax-paying subjects. The poor and the subjects (*fuḳarā' ve re'āyā*), a generic term for the urban and rural unprivileged masses subject to provincial notables, were to be protected and supported by provincial dynasties. The meaning of the term "under their administration" (*zīr-i idāre*) was also open. As we have seen in previous chapters, the administrative structure of the Ottoman provinces was complex, including overlapping jurisdictions, zones of influence, and revenue-collection licenses. Provincial notables acquired offices, contracts, and deals pertaining to management, administration, or revenue collection in various provincial units. The Deed did not detail the nature of the administration of provincial dynasties. Instead, employing a generic tone, it instructed provincial magnates to be just and fair.

However, a more concrete condition appeared in the document, declaring that provincial dynasties should follow the decisions, taken in deliberative consultations, between members of the circle of alliance. The emphasis on deliberations (*müẕākere*) stressed the negotiational nature of the process. Decision-making, according to the Deed, was to be carried out through negotiation, deliberation, and agreement. But this negotiation process did not include provincial communities. The Deed did not mention bottom-up collective action or electoral mechanisms, both growing practices in the Ottoman provinces throughout the eighteenth century, as chapter 3 examines in great detail. Instead, according to the Deed, decision-making took place within a circle of alliance and bonds of trust, which included central and provincial elites, in a horizontal manner, through constant negotiations and deliberations. Yet the Deed did not go into detail as to the mechanisms and the place for these negotiations and deliberations. There was no mention of a standing assembly or procedural details on how to summon the deliberative assembly. The Deed implied that negotiations would take place ad hoc and in a continuous manner.

Article 7 concludes with a condition that members of the circle of alliance should constantly keep an eye on one another and report oppressors and transgressors to the Exalted State. According to the Deed, the circle of alliance was also a circle of checking. As other articles explained, in such transgressions, the transgressor was to be suppressed by the collective action of the alliance.

Conclusion

Since the said seven articles have been decided upon through deliberation, and an oath in the name of God and Prophet has been taken not to act against it, the present deed is written and copied for the sake of preserving these solemn promises. "Then whoever alters the bequest after he has heard it—the sin is only upon those who have altered it. Allah is indeed All-Hearing and All-Knowing

[Qur'an 2/181]." Written in the middle ten days of the honored month of Shaban in the one thousand two hundred and twenty-second year of the noble and glorious Hijra [October 1808].

The conclusion of the deed emphasized that decisions were taken through deliberation (*müzākere*) and accepted after signatories had sworn to observe the conditions in the name of God and the Prophet. Mutual oaths made the Deed a valid (*mu'teber*) contract. The contractual nature of the Deed was supported by the qur'anic verse 2/181, which stresses the sin of altering a decision already made.

Appendix

The articles in this legal document are fundamental principles in strengthening and reinvigorating the religion and the Exalted State with the help of God. Thus its perpetual implementation as a guiding principle is a duty. In order to prevent it from being altered because of changing times and persons, those who henceforth hold the posts of the grand vizierate and the office of the grand mufti, before they are appointed and occupy their posts, will read and sign this deed, and work for its execution to the letter. During replacement, in order to avoid any delay in the comprehension of the deed, the director of the imperial Divan should immediately take the original deed from the scribal bureau, inform the steward of the grand vizier and the minister of foreign affairs, and bring it to the person who holds the posts of the grand vizierate or grand muftiship. Let this practice be recorded in the office of the imperial Divan and regarded as a guiding principle. And since copies of this deed will be given to the necessary people, let a copy of it be kept by His Majesty the Sultan, and let our imperial majesty personally supervise its continuous and perpetual implementation.

The appendix stipulated a procedural detail about how to maintain the validity of the Deed over time. Dignitaries of the state and provincial dynasties were always required to follow the Deed, despite changes over time and generations. Before a new grand vizier or grand mufti was appointed, he was obligated to read, comprehend, and sign the original Deed, a master copy of which was kept in the scribal bureau (*kalemiye*).[12] Taking out the Deed and bringing it to new appointees so that they could read and sign it were to be part of the appointment procedure for these two offices, which were responsible for administrative affairs and the implementation of Sharia. After the officer of the Scribal Bureau brought the original document to be signed by the new grand vizier and grand mufti, other copies were to be prepared and sent to other members of the alliance for fresh signatures.

This procedure perpetuated the Deed, regardless of changes in time and personnel. But only when the grand vizier and grand mufti were appointed was this procedure followed. Only these two officeholders, as heads of state and religious affairs, were required to sign when appointed.

When other officeholders and heads of dynasties changed, new signatures were not needed. The epilogue concludes with an obligation granted to the sultan. This process and the Deed's implementation were to be overseen (*nezāret*) by His Majesty. Accordingly, the sultan kept a copy of the deed for himself to consult if necessary. The Deed did not ask new sultans to sign the document. However, Mahmud II signed the deed and became one of its contractors.

The Sultan's Writ

Copy of the imperial writ: I took refuge in God. "If you had spent all that is in the earth, you could not have brought their hearts together; but God brought them together [Qur'an 8/63]." According to the tenor of this illustrious verse of the Qur'an, it is manifest that the reinvigoration of religion, the Exalted State, and the whole Muslim community depends upon the cardinal unity of and alliance among the dignitaries and ministers, and it is evident that the accomplishment of this goal, with the help of God, is contingent upon the continuous implementation of these auspicious promises and compacts. Therefore, with the grace of God, I, my imperial person, undertake the execution and implementation of the letter of the promises and recognized conditions written in this deed of alliance, and thus let my grand vizier, my grand mufti, the viziers, the learned, the ministers of my state, and the dynasties of my imperial dominions, too—I seek refuge in God—exert their power and resources for the execution and implementation of the aforementioned promises to the letter for love of God, in compliance with the sacred order "to fulfill the contracts you have made [Qur'an 2/177]" and by applying them as a guiding principle in the capital and provinces. If anyone commits the smallest infraction, or, God forbid, dares to avoid the contract, let him be the object of God's curse and suffer serious consequences and punishment in this world and the next.

Mahmud II put his writ on top of the document as a contractor (*müte'ahhid*) to the Deed. In his writ, the sultan stressed that realizing the driving idea of the document, the reinvigoration of the religion, state, and the Muslim community, was only possible with the sincere unity and alliance of dignitaries. Mahmud, in accordance with the spirit of the document, mentioned religion, state, and the Muslim community as the three constituencies of the Ottoman order. The Deed, in this respect, was necessary to provide the unity of the order. This was the reason, Mahmud wrote, why his imperial person (*zāt*) undertook the execution and implementation of the deed. In accordance with Islamic law of contract, only real persons could sign the Deed. Therefore, as we see in Article 1, the sultan's person was distinguished from his sultanate, and Mahmud signed the document as a real person, rather than the personification of the state.

Mahmud was one of the contractors to oversee the implementation of the Deed. But he was not one of the guarantors or sureties, as signatories were. He was not part of the circle of alliance whose members served as mutual guarantors and gave surety to one another to implement the Deed. The sultan, as a pillar (*kuṭb*) of the state, undertook the implementation of the Deed, as an overseer and the highest authority. Nevertheless, since he legally promised its implementation, he was not above the Deed either. With his writ, Mahmud tied himself to the Deed as a guiding principle of unity and order. Quranic quotations emphasized the contractual nature of the deed. Since the Deed had been understood and signed by its contractors, to break it was a sin. Mahmud, as the overseer of the contract and supreme contractor, called on God to curse those who broke it.

Signatories

Contractor of its contents, Mustafa [Bayraktar], grand vizier

Contractor of the execution of its contents, Mehmed Salihzade Ahmed Esad (May they be forgiven)

Contractor of the execution of its contents, Esseyyid Abdullah Ramiz, grand admiral

Contractor of the contents, Abdurahman, vizier, governor of Anatolia

Contractor of what is written in it, Mehmed Derviş, chief military judge of Rumelia

Contractor of the execution of its contents, Dürrizade Esseyyid Abdullah, warden of the descendants of the Prophet

I have looked at the content and found them to be correct, and I am contractor of its content. Signed by Emin Paşazade Mehmed Emin, the servant who prays for the Exalted State, holder of the rank of military judge of Rumelia

Contractor of what is written in it, Hafız Ahmed Kamili, military judge of Anatolia

Contractor of what is written in it, Mehmed Tahir, kadı of Istanbul

And one of the contractors, Mustafa Refik, steward of the grand vizier

And one of the contractors, Mustafa Agha, chief of the janissaries at the sultan's court

And one of the contractors, Mehmed Emin Behiç, minister of finance

And one of the contractors, Seyyid Mehmed Said Galip, minister of foreign affairs

And one of the contractors, Mustafa Reşid, former steward of one of the sultan's equerries

And one of the contractors, Seyyid Ali, minister of the navy

And one of the contractors, Seyyid Mehmed Tahsin, chief of the sergeants of the imperial Divan[13]

And one of the contractors, Mehmed Emin, senior officer in charge of the daybook of receipts and expenditures

And one of the contractors, Süleyman Cabbarzade [Çapanoğlu]

And one of the contractors, İsmail of Serres

And one of the contractors, El-hac Ömer Karaosmanzade [Karaosmanoğlu]

And one of the contractors, Ahmed, who is the senior accountant

And one of the contractors, Mehmed, Agha [chief] of the cavalry troops at the sultan's court

And one of the contractors, Mehmed İzzet, director of the imperial Divan, the transcriber of this [document]

And one of the contractors, Hüseyin Hüsnü, director of the office in charge of correspondence between the imperial palace and the grand vizier's office

And one of the contractors, Mustafa, governor of Çirmen

Twenty-five individuals signed the deed as contractors (*müte'ahhid*). Twenty-two held office in the military, bureaucratic, or learned hierarchies of the Ottoman administration. Three signatories were leaders of three provincial dynasties in the Balkans and Anatolia. The core group of the New Order party that initiated the coup in August–September 1808 under the leadership of Mustafa Bayraktar were among signatories. They occupied key bureaucratic and military positions. Mustafa Bayraktar, as leader of the coup and now grand vizier, was the Deed's first signer. Grand Admiral Ramiz and the governor of the Anatolian provinces, Kadı Abdurrahman, were the two major members of the New Order party who occupied significant military-administrative positions.[14] The governor of Anatolia signed the deed, but the governor of Rumelia, Hurşit Ahmet Pasha, who was in charge in Sofia, was not present at the assembly, like other provincial governors, who were either with their units or charged with military missions.[15] However, the governor of Çirmen in western Thrace, Mustafa Pasha, who had come to Istanbul with Bayraktar during the coup, signed the Deed.

Salihzade Ahmed Esad, who had just been appointed grand mufti, was the second signatory after the grand vizier.[16] The judge of Istanbul; the chief military judges of the Balkan and Anatolian provinces; who were responsible for appointments of judges in their provinces, the warden of the descendants of the Prophet (a prestigious position in the learned hierarchy); and a member of the learned hierarchy, who held the sinecure of chief military judge of Rumeli followed the grand mufti.[17] Commanders of the janissaries and the cavalry unit of the imperial palace represented the central military corps. Although the janissaries were the main targets of the Deed, the chief of the corps, who was appointed after the coup of the friends of Ruse, was asked to be part of the contract, so that the janissaries were also bound to the deed through their commander. Several members of the central bureaucracy and fiscal bureaus were also part of the contract. The Deed was drafted and compiled by one of these bureaucrats, Mehmed İzzet (d. 1809), director of the Divan office.[18]

There were two kinds of statuses for signatories in the Deed: appointive and hereditary. Most signatories held office in the central administration by appointment and signed in that capacity. Should they be dismissed, their replacements were required to endorse the deed in turn. However, Çapanoğlu Süleyman, Karaosmanoğlu Ömer, and İsmail of Serres signed as the leaders of their respective provincial dynasties. Upon their deaths, their heirs had to endorse the Deed and remained bound by it. The signatories of the Deed were thus not only partners in a contract but founders of a new order, which would continue after they were dismissed or died.

It is striking that only three leaders of provincial dynasties signed the Deed. As we saw in chapter 4, dozens of provincial notables came to Istanbul, following Mustafa Bayraktar. Other notables who traveled to Istanbul with Bayraktar or other leaders were not among the signatories, since they were considered subordinate notables. As indicated in Article 5, leaders of the provincial dynasties were also guarantors to and liable for their subordinates in their zones of administration. Although they did not sign the agreement, the latter thus unilaterally became part of the surety bond. Other major dynasties of the empire either did not choose to or could not, however, attend the assembly. Some could not attend because the assembly was held at short notice. Others chose not to be present because they did not trust Bayraktar and preferred to observe developments from afar. After the Deed was signed, Bayraktar sent copies of the documents to be endorsed by some major families and officeholders. The grandson of Ali Pasha of Ioannina, who attended the assembly with his tutors, brought the deed to his grandfather with a note from Ali's associate in Istanbul, who advised him to sign this binding document.[19] In his letter to Muhammad Ali of Egypt, which was later made public and recorded by observers, Bayraktar, informed the governor of Egypt of the assembly, saying: "The old dynasties of Anatolia, like [the] Cabbarzade [Çapanoğlus] and Karaosmanzade, as well as İsmail Bey of Serres and the intendants of Drama, among the Rumelian dynasties, among others, were present in Istanbul and proceeded on issues concerning the recruitment of soldiers against enemies. Meanwhile, you were in Egypt."[20]

However, despite the fact that notables in various provinces were informed of the process, the Deed was drafted and signed by a closed group without public announcement. Even some individuals who were invited to the assembly were not acquainted with the details of the Deed. One

participant in the assembly, Feyzibey-zade Mehmed Efendi, a member of
a learned hierarchy, derisively expressed his frustration years later that he
had not been included in the circle that drafted the Deed, even though he
had been invited to the assembly:

We were invited with our Çelebi Efendi. At three o'clock, we took our boat and
reached Kağıthane [where the assembly took place]. A guide met and accompanied us to one of the tents. We had breakfast. Then Çelebi Efendi and I engaged
in a long conversation until evening. Then dinner came. We ate and drank. At
night, the assembly was adjourned. We took our boat back to our homes. We did
not have any idea what happened [in the assembly] . . . [and] I was confused. If
we did not grasp the secret [of the assembly], why were we invited? Then I came
across someone who knew about the secrecy of the assembly. I asked him what
was our task in Kağıthane. He said that "all the dignitaries would meet the sultan.
However, most of them were young, with black beards. They thought it would be
nice to have some with white beards. [The attendance of the elders] would befit
the fame of our state in the eyes of foreign states." So they thought and invited
Çelebi Efendi and myself. My lord, we attended that banquet for the sake of our
beards! . . . The assembly in Kağıthane was only among a few and somehow it
was decided to draft state soldiers ['asker-i ḥāḳāniye]. God knows best.[21]

Unlike the message of the Deed, which was inclusively binding, the
meeting was not an all-inclusive assembly. Rather, it was a meeting of a
political party, clustered around Mustafa Bayraktar and his affiliates and
important provincial dynasties, whose support was guaranteed. Thus the
signatories were, if not an ad hoc group, then members of the political
coalition that initiated the coup and other leading figures in the center
and provinces who accepted a special invitation from this coalition.

Mehmed İzzet, who was trained in the imperial chancellery, drafted
the Deed. We do not know the details of the deliberations in the meeting
and how these deliberations were transcribed into a draft by Mehmed
İzzet. However, from the text, we can conclude that many individuals
made their points. These points were transformed into the legal language
of a contract and presented for endorsement by the attendees. The Deed
underscored that signatories had decided on drafting soldiers with a
unanimous vote (ittifāḳ-ı ārā). How did they reach unanimity? Ahmed
Vasıf Efendi, a historian of the late eighteenth century, provides us with
a depiction of the assemblies held under the supervision of a grand vizier.
"This is the opinion (re'y) of the dignitaries," said the grand vizier and
added, "however, this opinion is not the final decision. The final opinion is to be reached in this assembly. We shall see what the unanimous
opinion will be." During the deliberations, participants voiced several
ideas. If a decision was being shaped, the grand vizier formulated the
decision into a formal one and asked the members of the assembly: "Do
you consent?" (Rāżılar mısız?) Each participant was expected to say, "we

consent" (*Rāżılarız*) out loud. After all the participants had voiced consent, the grand vizier asked the entire group for reconfirmation: "Speak righteously. Do not change your mind later. We have agreed unanimously all together. No word is to be said after that. This is the word." If there was no opposition, one of the scribes formulated the decision in written form. The final text was read again to the assembly. If there was no opposition, the participants offered words of their agreement (*müte'ahhid*) to be added to the text.[22]

THE MEANING OF THE DEED OF ALLIANCE

The Deed of Alliance was transcribed in an assembly during a political crisis, which had shaken the empire since the summer of 1806. Those who prepared the Deed intended to end the crisis through a general accord of leading political actors in the center and provinces. The authors of the Deed did not openly claim to introduce radical changes. On the contrary, the declared aim of the Deed was to restore (*iḥyā*) the glorious days of religion, sultanate, and the state. This reference to restoration implied that the Deed was not an unlawful innovation (*bi'dat*). Despite this reference, the Deed profoundly reconfigured rights and obligations, the logic of integrity, and the mechanisms to maintain order.

According to the document, the invigoration of the power of the Ottoman state was only possible with alliance (*ittifāḳ*), unity (*ittiḥād*), and trust (*emniyet*), as well as the rejection of discord (*nifāḳ*), dissent (*şiḳāḳ*), and enmity (*nefsāniyet*) among dignitaries of the central state and the provincial dynasties. To achieve this aim, signatories became contractors (*müte'ahhid*) to the implementation of the Deed; they became guarantors (*kefīl*) to one another's person and claim; and liable (*żāmin*) for one another's actions. Signatories also pledged to guarantee the protection of the sultan and sultanate. In return, the sultan promised to oversee the Deed's implementation. Furthermore, provincial dynasties became guarantors to and liable for subordinate notables in their regions. In this sequential system, *ta'ahhüd*, *kafāla*, and *żamān/ḍamān*, or promise and commitment, surety and liability—and their derivatives *müte'ahhid*, *kefīl* and *żāmin/ḍāmin*—were the essence of the Deed.[23] It was a mutual promise, or contract, but at the same time a bond of surety .

Islamic law manuals included independent chapters on *kafāla/ḍamān* that spelled out the conditions of guaranty and suretyship in contractual or donative commitments between individuals.[24] In its conventional definition in Hanafi jurisprudence, which was accepted by the Ottoman imperial elite as an authoritative school of law, "a guarantee [*kafāla*] consists of the addition of an obligation to an obligation in respect to a demand for a particular thing." "It consists of one person joining himself to another person, and binding himself also to meet the obligation that accrues to that other person."[25] Conventionally, jurists distinguished between a personal guarantee (*kafāla bi-n-nafs*) and a guarantee for property or debt (*kafāla bi-l-māl* or *damān*). Guarantee of a person is a guarantor's commitment to bring (*izhār*) the guaranteed person to a court in the event of a summons due to alleged crime or debt. But guarantee of property or debt refers to the obligation to make good the loss suffered. Accordingly, the guarantor is obligated to assume responsibility for the due amount or debt of the guaranteed person. According to the Hanafi school "a person may validly be a guarantor of a guarantor," and "there may also be more than one guarantor."[26]

The Deed of Alliance adapted this legal instrument, which was used for transactions between private individuals, and made it a permanent and overarching constitutional principle. In the Deed, all the signatories, appointed or hereditary, mutually bind themselves to one another as co-sureties. All the contracting parties would be liable to prevent a fault, compensate a failure, and ensure the appearance of the wrongdoer. Likewise, the right of each contractor applied to all the contractors collectively; therefore, an act against one would be considered an act against all. Hence, signatories were obligated to act together to prevent such an act or compensate it. Furthermore, signatories unilaterally became guarantors for the sultan, his person, and his status. Any act against him would be considered an act against all. Analogous collective surety bonds through which individuals mutually became guarantors to one another and liable for one another's actions were common in the eighteenth century. As we saw in chapter 3, the central authority asked members of the provincial communities, and certain groups in the imperial capital with greater frequency, to mutually bind themselves to meet pecuniary or other obligations to the state or to be liable for one another's actions.[27] The Deed of Alliance simulated these bonds at the imperial level. The Deed as surety bond established a fictive empirewide web of trust, though which dignitaries of the central state and leaders of dynasties in the provinces were horizontally knotted to one another as an organic unity. The parties united their responsibilities and claims and promised to act together as partners.

Although the Deed was between multiple parties, rather than two, these parties were concentrated in the inner (*dāhil*) or outer (*hāric*) realms of the empire. The inner realm referred to the central government, constituted by appointed officeholders hierarchically organized under the supervision of the grand vizier as the absolute deputy of the sultan. But the outer realm referred to the provinces, which were under the authority (*zīr-i idāre*) of provincial dynasties, whose authority became hereditary with the Deed. This reciprocity was also reflected in the voice of the Deed. The Deed was sometimes transcribed as the single voice of all signatories, sometimes as a dialogue between the central and provincial elites. In this twofold scheme, the Deed created reciprocity: provincial dynasties promised to protect the sultanate and committed to military recruitment. In return, they acquired a guarantee of their perpetuity from dignitaries of the state. The Deed limited the sultan's prerogative, as the sovereign authority, to order confiscations and executions and provided provincial dynasties with security of life, hereditary status, and property.

While the Deed was transcribed to establish unity among the elites of the center and provinces, it was first and foremost aimed at the janissaries and groups allied with them. The Deed was to guarantee collective mobilization of elites against janissary-led resistance, revolt, or conspiracies against the central authority. But the signatories would also punish other wrongdoers in a collective manner in accordance with the surety they committed themselves to. Signatories both in the center and provinces would take action collectively against wrongdoers who broke the circle of alliance and the conditions of the Deed. All signatories undertook to participate in collective action to prevent wrongdoing. However, any fault, whoever committed it, would be recognized only after judicial investigation (*tahkīk*), and had to be proved in the eyes of the general public (*cümle 'indinde ta'ayyun*).[28] If the grand vizier or other dignitaries broke the Deed, or if an individual was punished without proper juridical investigation, the Deed gave provincial dynasties the right to dissent, to act against the central state, and to stop the transgressor.

The Deed was binding, not only on current signatories, but also on future officeholders and members of the dynasties. It thus stipulated that both the current leaders of dynasties and their heirs were granted the same security. Leaders of provincial dynasties who participated in the circle of alliance, secured their power, status, and wealth; in return for this security, leaders were obligated to provide security to subordinate notables. Regional dynasties could not punish or remove subordinate notables without judicial investigation. This stipulation extended the web of alliance, security, and trust to local notables who operated in the zone of regional dynasties. Furthermore, as the Deed stipulated, dynasties that had not signed the Deed would be included in the circle of alliance, by force, if necessary. In the Deed of Alliance, the death or dismissal of signatories did not revoke the bond. The passage of time and changes in personnel would not justify altering the conditions of the Deed. The Deed was both a perpetual and a common document. It was to be valid everywhere, for everyone, and forever.

The Deed did not end the supreme role of the sultan, but it profoundly redefined it. It altered sultanic authority from an omnipotent power, without formal limitations, into that of a supreme contractor who formally undertook to oversee the implementation of the Deed. In return, the sultan secured a guarantee and surety from provincial dynasties for loyalty and protection of his person and his sultanate. This reciprocity created a fictive order. It was not a top-down system, in which authority descended hierarchically from the sultan to officeholders; rather, it was based on a horizontal web of alliance, trust, surety, and liability, in which members of the inner and outer realms became part of the alliance and partners of the empire under the oversight of the sultan.

Despite its collective, overarching character, the Deed was a surety contract among central and provincial elites rather than a political contract between the people and the state or a social contract among citizens. The "people" were mentioned on many occasions in the Deed as the Muslim community (*millet-i Beyżā-yı Muḥammediyye*) or the poor and tax-paying subjects (*fuḳarā' ve re'āyā*). The document implied that the state's ultimate aim was the prosperity of the Muslim sultanate and Muslim people; officeholders and provincial dynasties should be just and self-restrained in levying taxes on taxpayers. Taxes were decided through deliberations between the inner and outer elites, not between the state and communities. The "people" as a corporate entity did not actively participate in the Deed, and neither did signatories claim to represent the people vis-à-vis the state. Nevertheless, the Deed, by asserting that the Ottoman state was a Muhammadan sultanate, claimed that the empire was ultimately the sultanate of the Muslim community, which included non-Muslims (*ẕimmīs/dhimmī*) who accepted Muslim rule.

The deed was a constituting document that established the logic of order, how to maintain it, and the rights and obligations of actors. It amounted to a constitution in Carl Schmitt's sense of an act that "constitutes the form and type of the political unity, the existence of which is presupposed."[29] It did not give detailed procedures, but rather stipulated overarching principles (*dustūr*). Everyone was obligated to observe these principles in actions and thought. To achieve this goal, the Deed did not divide power, but united it, through mutual trust, pledge, surety, and liability among elites in the center and provinces. In terms of its legal framework, the Deed was formulated in the framework of a surety bond in the Islamic law of contract. Trust, pledge, surety, and liability, the key concepts of the Deed, were legal instruments for commercial, financial, or agricultural contracts between creditors and debtors or between partners. The Deed of Alliance adapted a contract based on the Islamic law of obligations between real individuals at the constitutional level and reconfigured the political order accordingly.

THE AFTERMATH OF THE SIGNING OF THE DEED

The Deed was signed in September 1808. After the dissolution of the assembly, the notable heads of dynasties returned to their regions. As we saw in chapter 4, Mustafa Bayraktar—now grand vizier—and his associates in the cabinet launched another military reform project. The armed forces that had come with Bayraktar from the Balkans were drafted as state soldiers, as Sekbān-ı Cedīd, the New Militia. While peace talks with the Russians continued, the newly drafted forces were deployed to the Danubian region. Military reforms were followed by administrative arrangements to increase state revenues. Officials took tough measures to establish order and security in the capital. But in November, as a response to these tough measures and as a result of the decreasing popularity of Mustafa Bayraktar, a janissary revolt shattered Istanbul anew. Mistakes made by members of the cabinet in suppressing the revolt led the people of Istanbul to support the janissaries. After a week of violence that killed thousands of people and fires that destroyed many neighborhoods of Istanbul, the nascent Bayraktar regime collapsed. Allegedly Mahmud II, the sultan put on the throne by Bayraktar in August, did not try to prevent the revolt. On the contrary, according to some observers, he tacitly backed it, since he wanted Bayraktar, who had imposed himself as a dictator in the capital, to be eliminated. Many signatories to the Deed were executed or became fugitives. Some crossed the Danube, fleeing to Russian-controlled lands.[30]

The chiefs of provincial dynasties who had returned to their regions did not have the opportunity to come to Bayraktar's aid. The revolt unfolded too quickly. Provincial notables could not fulfill their promises. Mahmud soon honored the janissaries. The New Order was eliminated. Mahmud sent decrees to the provincial dynasties asking them to forsake their desire for military reform. The three dynasties who had signed the deed—the Çapanoğlus, Karaosmanoğlus, and Serezlis—and notables under their patronage did not rebel against Mahmud. On the contrary, as promised in the Deed, they declared their loyalty to him through their representatives in Istanbul. It would not be wrong to argue that the Deed of Alliance was stillborn. Nevertheless, with the Deed, the insecure new sultan, Mahmud II, was able to secure the loyalty of leading provincial dynasties, whom he had personally met in the assembly. The Deed was a "vanishing mediator," to use Slavoj Žižek's term.[31] It appeared, served to end a political crisis, and vanished. Nevertheless, several historians tried to make sense of this unprecedented document, beginning with Şanizade Atullah, the official chronicler of the reign of Mahmud II, who published it eleven years later.[32]

Şanizade found the Deed troublesome. According to him, the term "dynasty" (*ḥānedān*), referring to notable families of the provinces, was inconsistent with the sultanic order. The term *ḥānedān* could be used for those who enjoyed exclusive rights over their lands and whose wealth was not acquired as a result of their service to the sultanate. These families did not need to fear executions or confiscations (*katl ve müşadere*). They were to enjoy freedom and security (*azādegī ve emniyet*) in accordance with Islamic law. Şanizade argued that the chiefs of provincial dynasties who signed the Deed were usurpers, since their wealth and status came from their service to the sultanate. They did not have the right to establish permanent control over the lands they enjoyed. Calling these notable families "dynasties," he argued, signified that these families had appropriated and partitioned imperial lands that legally belonged to the state, thus making it appear as if they were making themselves partners (*teşrīk*) of the sultanate. Therefore, Şanizade implied, the Deed of Alliance did not conform to the order of the Ottoman Empire.[33]

Later, Ahmed Cevdet Pasha followed Şanizade in arguing that Mahmud II had accepted the Deed solely for strategic reasons, to secure the loyalty of unruly provincial families. Mahmud had signed the Deed after consulting with his advisors and had simply then waited for the right moment to revoke it, which came when the janissaries killed Bayraktar a couple of months later.[34] Both Şanizade and Cevdet recognized the radical innovations that the Deed of Alliance conveyed. It not only gave provincial dynasties rights to and security for their statuses and wealth but also made them partners in ruling the empire.[35]

After 1812, the Ottoman Empire embarked on a new path of bureaucratic and administrative reform. In the 1810s and 1820s, Mahmud II was able to suppress many provincial notable families.[36] In so doing, he made use of, among others, another local magnate, İsmail of Ruse's intimate—and Bayraktar's rival—Pehlivan İbrahim Baba Agha, to whom the sultan proposed a special mission, with a vizierate as the reward. Accordingly, Pehlivan collected an army from the Balkans, mainly from among İsmail's men in northern Bulgaria, and ranged across Anatolia and then the Balkans to curb the provincial powerholders. Challenging the established powerholding families as he moved from one province to another, Baba Pasha became known throughout the empire as one of Mahmud's intimate viziers in his project of political centralization. His transition from Baba Agha to Baba Pasha, from regional magnate to vizier, and from a provincial figure to a central one illustrated that a military career in the Ottoman central establishment was still an option, and that one could be a hero and an intimate servant of the sultan at the same time. A Halveti sheikh, Gazzizade Abdullatif Efendi, who wrote Baba Pasha's biography, described how he received the order from the Divan to suppress the Kösepaşas:

After the consultation in the Exalted State [on how to suppress Köse Pasha], the dignitaries asked: "What is the remedy?" The wise men of the state prudently maintained: "Köse Pasha's location is pretty steep. Plus, it is difficult to fight [his] Kurdish [forces]. Only Baba Pasha could handle this." This motion was presented to the sultan and the sultan ordered the execution of Köse Pasha and appointed Baba Pasha to this service. An imperial decree was prepared and sent to Sivas where Baba Pasha resided as governor.[37]

Baba Pasha suppressed Köse Pasha and some others. In the late 1810s, political centralization continued with the help of Baba Pasha and other imperial governors, who suppressed or pacified some of the regional powerholders in central Anatolia. However, most of the established families continued to exist, albeit with less power, fewer offices and contracts, and smaller zones. In 1819, Halet Efendi, a leading bureaucrat and diplomat in Mahmud's reign prepared a regulation for the intendants of Wallachia and Moldavia approving four Greek Phanariaot "dynasties" to control the Romanian principalities in rotation.[38] The liquidation of Ali Pasha of Ioannina and his sons in 1822—Baba Pasha was involved in the initial stages of this, but died in Ioannina—epitomizes Mahmud's war against provincial powerholders. But not all were eliminated. While Mahmud eradicated Ali Pasha in Greece, Muhammad Ali of Egypt expanded his control, building his dynasty in the southern shore of the Mediterranean. As a hereditary dynasty recognized by the sultan, in many ways as provided for by the Deed of Agreement, Muhammad Ali and his family would be the biggest exception to the overall trend.

The real turning point came in 1826, when the janissary corps was abolished, following a massacre in which thousands of janissaries were slain by Mahmud's new militia, which would turn into another New Army.[39] Mahmud's reforms curtailed the power of the provincial dynasties that had culminated in the Deed of Alliance. Instead, under his reign, provincial reform consolidated municipal elections and the participation of communities in local governance.[40] In 1827, after the janissary corps was abolished, Mahmud convened a large assembly, to which he invited the provincial notables, this time not as dynasties (*ḫānedān*) or partners of the empire, but rather as notables (*a'yān ve vücūh*) or representative leaders of provincial communities.[41]

In 1839 and 1856, Sultan Abdülmecid (r. 1839–61) issued the famous Tanzimat edicts, promising (*'ahd ü misāḳ*) security of life, property, and honor to Ottoman officeholders and subjects, Muslim or non-Muslim. In the Criminal Code of 1840, confiscations and executions without judicial investigation were abolished for good.[42] The Tanzimat reforms foreshadowed demands for constitutional government by Ottoman intellectuals. The Young Ottomans in the second half of the nineteenth century, who intended to further limit sultanic authority, might be thought to have seen the Deed of Alliance as a reference point for their constitutional struggles, but that was not the case. In the years following the proclamation of

Figure 5. The tomb of Bayraktar Mustafa Pasha in the Zeyneb Sultan Mosque cemetery, Istanbul, Turkey. Author's photograph.

> Until twenty years after his death
> It was not possible to pay him due respect.
> Now God helped this perfected vizier.
> He took his revenge on that crowd
> By putting them to the sword.
> He made this martyr's tomb visible
> And his name eternal.

the first Ottoman constitution (Ḳānūn-ı Esāsī) and parliament in 1876, would-be reformers suggested the importance of the tradition of consultative assemblies in Islamic and Ottoman history for the new constitutional order that they intended to establish, but did not mention the consultative assembly in Kağıthane as a historical point of reference. Rather, they argued that the janissaries and the ulema were to be considered constitutional forces limiting the sultan's power in Ottoman political culture.

The leading dissenter and constitutionalist intellectual Namık Kemal wrote in one of his journal articles in 1868: "the Ottoman Empire was governed by the will of the community in a sort of constitutionalism until the destruction of the janissaries. People assumed the right to administer [the state], which they would delegate to parliament, themselves. . . . The janissaries were the armed consultative assemble of the people."[43] With the abolition of the janissary corps, Namık Kemal argued, the checks and balances restricting sultanic despotism vanished.[44] He saw the struggle between the janissaries and the New Order of Selim and later Mahmud II as a struggle between the people and despotism. In his historical spectrum of Ottoman constitutional struggles, provincial notables did not play a central role. Perhaps the reason that he discounted provincial families in Ottoman constitutionalism was that provincial notables who had lost their leverage but retained social prestige in the provinces in the late nineteenth century, such as the Çapanoğlus and Karaosmanoğlus, were allies of the Palace of Sultan Abdülaziz (r. 1861–76) and later Abdulhamid II (r. 1876–1908) against the constitutionalists.

In the years leading up to the 1908 Young Turk Revolution, fascination arose with Mustafa Bayraktar, remembered as a hero with an ordinary background who had attempted to change the political order a hundred years earlier. In 1911, Bayraktar's bones were exhumed from a graveyard on the outskirts of Istanbul and conveyed by a well-attended procession to be reinterred, along with those of his associates, in a central location across from the city's Gülhane Park. It was not long before a historian published Bayraktar's biography in the first academic history journal to appear in Turkish.[45]

After World War I, the Ottoman Empire collapsed. In Turkey, an Ankara-centered provincial assembly mounted resistance against the Ottoman government in Istanbul and the occupying forces of Great Britain, France, and Greece, and celebrated victory. The subsequent assembly claiming to represent the Turkish nation abolished the sultanate and declared a republic. The National Assembly was in fact a coalition of bureaucratic and military elites and provincial notables, somewhat similar to the coalition of 1808.[46] But not all notable families participated in the resistance. The Çapanoğlus, for instance, refused to collaborate with the Ankara government. After the war, they were demonized by the new regime, together with other provincial dynasties.[47] During one-party rule (1923–46), while radical republican reforms profoundly changed social and cultural life in Turkey, the regime's relationship with provincial notables and their history was ambivalent.

The republican regime did not change the social structure through land reform, as the Bolsheviks did in Russia. Most notable families, particularly those who participated in the resistance, kept their leverage in their localities and claimed their lands under the new land regime. However, some ideologues of the new regime were inclined to present provincial notables as *mütegallibe*, feudal usurpers.[48] In the republican version of Ottoman history, the period was presented as a war between reactionary forces, namely, the janissaries, provincial notables, and the ulema, and the reform-minded forces of the bureaucratic and military elite, who were graduates of modern military and medical schools. The reform-minded Ottomans, according to this narrative, were able to suppress reactionary forces, but were defeated by national awakenings in the Balkans and in the Arab world. Responding to events, however, local historians in many regions wrote alternative histories that negotiated the official republican narrative, presenting notable families in the provinces as cofounders of the republic.[49]

Meanwhile, in the post-Ottoman Balkans and in Arab lands, new states depicted the Ottoman past as a dark age under the Turkish yoke. The late eighteenth and early nineteenth centuries were seen as periods of Ottoman decline, but also of national revival. In this framework, the notables of the late eighteenth and early nineteenth centuries were seen as centrifugal forces that were instrumental in national awakenings. Ali Pasha of Ioannina was depicted as an important figure in the Greek War of Independence and the later Albanian national awakening,[50] and Osman Pazvantoğlu as an unruly Muslim notable who helped Christians (Greeks and Bulgarians) in their national movements.[51] In the Arab world, however, some of the provincial dynasties of the late Ottoman era were among the founders of new regimes.[52] In Egyptian historiography, Muhammad Ali was seen as the architect of modern Egypt; scholars ignored his Ottoman and Balkan roots.[53] Many figures from the Ottoman age of revolutions were remembered in the age of nationalism. Mustafa Bayraktar's Armenian moneyman Manuk Bey, one of the architects of the 1808 coup, is an interesting example. In the late nineteenth and early twentieth centuries, Manuk was venerated by Armenian historians in the Balkans, who wrote biographies of him that verge on hagiographies.[54]

Beginning in the 1950s, discussion around the Deed of Alliance was ignited at Turkish universities. Alongside political debates about constitutional reform in Turkey, several historians and scholars of constitutional law viewed the Deed of Alliance as the beginning of modern constitutional history on a continuous spectrum from the late Ottoman

Empire to the Republic of Turkey. In this respect, some historians saw continuity between the Deed of 1808, the Tanzimat edicts of 1838 and 1856, and the empire's first modern constitution, the 1876 Ḳānūn-ı Esāsī. Some scholars compared the Deed to England's Magna Carta (1215) as a constitutional document that limited the power of the sovereign in favor of provincial elites with guarantees of life and property through judicial due process. In this linear constitutional narrative, the Deed of Alliance was considered a *late* Magna Carta.[55] This perspective, inspired by British constitutional history, assumed that the Ottoman Empire reached the stage of constitutional limitations at a very late date, as a result of political and economic underdevelopment.[56] This line of thinking resonated in Western academia. For Bernard Lewis, the Deed's constitutional significance lay in its character as a negotiated contract, an agreement between the sultan and groups of his servants and subjects, in which the latter appear as independent contracting parties, receiving and conceding certain rights and privileges.[57] The Deed, Norman Itzkowitz writes, "was an opening gun of the constitutional struggle that would grip the Ottoman Empire in the nineteenth century and that would not be resolved until its destruction by Atatürk and the birth of the Turkish Republic."[58]

Many historians, however, have approached this linear constitutionalist narrative with suspicion. In a seminal article comparing the Deed of Alliance to the Tanzimat edict of 1839, Halil İnalcık argues that the Deed was the practical result of political crisis and was not intended specifically to reform state and society. Eventually, the Deed was obliterated. Its survival would have resulted in the early disintegration of the empire under Muslim dynasties, rather than a constitutional transformation.[59] Marxist historians, who followed İnalcık's interpretation, suggested that the Deed was an attempt to legalize the responsibilities and mutual demands of the estates of the realm. Nevertheless, it was not systematic and it did not contain practical procedures that could be considered a constitutional step. Moreover, it was not inclusive. The Deed excluded the majority of notables, as well as commoners and non-Muslims. The magnates did not represent the people or legalize seigniorial rights.[60]

The third modern interpretation associates the Deed with centralization, rather than decentralization. According to Avdo Sućeska, although the Deed gave many guarantees to the provincial dynasties, in fact it was to link them to the Ottoman state.[61] According to Şerif Mardin, reformist bureaucrats who "aimed at curbing the powers of the local dynasties," designed the Deed. Therefore "the Deed of Alliance, far from being a Magna Carta, was one of the first steps toward the transformation of the Ottoman Empire into a modern state."[62] This perspective, which placed the Deed, not in a linear constitutional narrative, but in an account of political centralization and integration, was further enriched by Ariel Salzmann and Karen Barkey, who suggested that the Deed was meant to strengthen economic and fiscal ties between the center and provinces. Thus, it had more of a centralizing than decentralizing effect.[63] Accordingly, the Deed was intended to incorporate provincial magnates into the imperial network.

THE DEED AND THE AGE OF REVOLUTIONS

Was the Deed a primary document of the constitutional history of the late Ottoman Empire? Or was it a radical text that would have triggered a new crisis and the early disintegration of the empire if the episode that produced the document had continued? Or, did the Deed serve political centralization and the integration of the empire? The Deed was the first constitutional document to limit sultanic authority for political executions and confiscations without formal legal process. In this respect it foreshadowed later Ottoman constitutional documents. The condition of formal legal investigation before punishment later continued to be one of the fundamental ideas in the Tanzimat edict of 1839, the first criminal code in 1840, and the first Ottoman constitution of 1876.[64] However, as Halil İnalcık argued, this does not mean that the clauses of the Deed, unlike the later edicts and constitution 1876, covered every (male) individual in the empire. Although the deed claimed to be inclusive, it was limited to the elite. In this respect, the Deed left the empire to the initiatives of central and provincial elites and established an empirewide oligarchy, which claimed to run the empire as a collective project under the sultan, the supreme contractor who oversaw it all.

This oligarchic character of the Deed was fundamentally different from the egalitarian and inclusive feature of the later Ottoman edicts and constitution. In spite of this oligarchic and limited aspect, however, the Deed could also be seen as promoting integration of the empire. It was drawn up as a result of the collective initiative of the elites of the center and provinces, embodied in an integrative assembly. The Deed not only integrated the empire's provincial elites but called for soldiers drafted in the provinces to constitute the army of the state. This signified a monopoly of violence by the state. In sum, I argue that while the Deed of Alliance can be seen in the context of the general constitutional narrative of the late Ottoman Empire, and some of its clauses fostered political centralization and integration, it differed from later constitutional documents by reason of its explicitly oligarchic character. But what made the Deed of Alliance a radical and perhaps unique document, both in the Ottoman political culture and in other polities of the age of revolutions, was its mechanism. The Deed was a joint project of elites in the center and provinces, who both claimed to be part of the state and pledged to protect the sultan, the sultanate, and one another in a collective manner.

In terms of procedure and legal form, the Deed was not only unprecedented in Ottoman political culture, but also exceptional among the constitutional documents of the age of revolutions. The Deed differed from edicts granted from rulers to notables or subjects in a top-down fashion, such as we see in imperial texts from the Ottoman Empire and elsewhere in the eighteenth and nineteenth centuries. In the Ottoman Empire, the old convention of sultans' proclaiming judicial edicts (*'adālet-nāme*) to their subjects continued to be the essential element of Ottoman imperial politics.[65] In the nineteenth century, this established practice was transformed into a new type of edict, in which sultans granted rights and guarantees to their subjects and pledged to obey their own promises. The amnesty that Mustafa IV granted to the janissaries in 1807 and the Tanzimat edicts of 1839 and 1856, in which sultans guaranteed life, property, and religious freedom, are examples of this new type. We see similar edicts granted by rulers to notables or the people in general in several countries in the age of revolutions. Catherine II's Charter of the Nobility of 1785 in Russia, the Swedish Act of Union and Security in 1789, the Prussian General Code of 1791, and the Canada Act proclaimed by Britain in 1791 are some examples of edicts by which sovereigns bestowed rights and privileges, ranked orders, and at the same time bound themselves with their own pledges.[66]

The Deed of Alliance also differed from the constitutional documents legislated by individuals and groups claiming to represent the land or the people, either in estates and diets or in national assemblies in a bottom-up fashion. In Ottoman political culture, although the consultative assemblies (*meşveret meclisi*) were an essential component of decision-making processes,[67] there was no empirewide tradition of estates such as we see in medieval and early modern polities in Europe and Russia.[68] In the late eighteenth century, the republican revolutions in America and France altered the estate tradition and gave birth to new republican constitutions legislated by assemblies claiming to represent the people or the nation. These assemblies deliberated and agreed on documents that regulated the political order—rights, obligations of citizens, and national sovereignty— and accepted it as a social contract.[69]

The assembly that gathered in Kağıthane in September 1808 was neither a diet nor a national assembly, but rather an unprecedented meeting of leading office- and powerholders in the center and provinces who agreed to act together in alliance. Their Deed of Alliance assumed a new idea of state, which was maintained through their collective action and liability. At the same time, the state, as a collective enterprise, guaranteed their safety and perpetuity. Therefore, in contrast with top-down or bottom-up constitutional documents of the time, the Deed of Alliance envisioned a horizontal partnership of elites, whose safety was mutually guaranteed, with full liability.

Despite its horizontal procedural character, the Deed of Alliance had much in common with contemporary political documents in various countries that experienced different forms of constitutional and republican order. The Deed established certain mechanisms to limit the power of the sovereign, juridical processes, and the right to oppose. It retracted the sultan's power to confiscate and execute without judicial process. Moreover, it also had participatory elements, as we see in republicanism, since it constituted the political order as a common and participatory enterprise by participants in the circle of alliance. It guaranteed its continuity through mutual obligations, sureties, and liabilities. Taxes were to be decided through deliberations. Local families would draft soldiers collectively. Despite these limiting and participatory elements, however, the Deed did not produce an electoral or representative system. Powerholders were either appointed by the sultan or inherited their posts from their families in the provinces. They were not elected to represent communities from the bottom up. In this respect, the Deed did not include the growing electoral and participatory practices institutionalized throughout the eighteenth century. As discussed in chapter 3, in various provinces, communities came to elect managers and patron-creditors (ayans) who were responsible for public administration and finance. These bottom-up electoral mechanisms were formalized and institutionalized by the central authority later in the eighteenth century. While the Deed did not integrate these participatory practices into its system, subordinate notables were entrusted to the patronage of regional dynasties through unilateral surety mechanisms.

In this respect, the similarities and contrasts between the Ottoman and Polish cases in the eighteenth century are striking. In Poland, strong aristocratic traditions dating back to the sixteenth century gave the provincial nobility the right to elect the king and veto his decisions (*liberum veto*) in diets.[70] While these rights were seen as guarantees of liberty, the regime became the epitome of robust anti-monarchism. In the eighteenth century, kings who tried to abolish these limitations and build an enlightened absolutism clashed with the provincial nobility. This conflict dragged Poland into a constitutional crisis and eventually led to its partition among Prussia, Russia, and Austria between 1772 and 1795.[71] In the Ottoman Empire, the centralized reforms of Mehmed the Conqueror (r. 1451–81) and Süleyman the Magnificent (r. 1520–66) generated a resilient anti-aristocratic convention. The sultan's prerogative to execute officeholders and confiscate their property for the sake of order constituted a volatile system for those who served the state, with high risk but also high gain. In the seventeenth and eighteenth centuries, recurring janissary revolts, which engendered a tradition of popular revolutions, and provincial notables, who established dynasties in several provinces, profoundly challenged supreme sultanic authority. But volatility and insecurity continued to be essential components of the order of empire until the nineteenth century. Neither the janissary-led revolts nor the provincial notables pushed the center into a formal settlement for a stable order.

In 1808, as a result of political crisis, the possibility of profoundly altering this order emerged. In 1807, the New Order, which had carried out a military and administrative reorganization program since 1789, failed against popular opposition mobilized under the leadership of the janissaries. The restoration government ended the New Order. In 1808, members of the reform party were able to establish a coalition with provincial notables against the janissaries. The coalition initiated a coup in 1808 and suppressed the restoration government. The Deed of Alliance was the product of this coalition. While symbolizing this new coalition, it also signified a new regime. The new regime would replace the insecurity and volatility of the old imperial order with security and trust. While the new regime was to be maintained by mutual guarantees from elites, the provinces were entrusted to the provincial dynasties, which had been operating under the constant menace of executions and confiscations under the old regime. The Deed did not introduce a division of power between the state and provincial notables, as in Poland, but a unification of power. The new empire would be a participatory and oligarchic polity, in which each actor pledged to act for all and all actors pledged to protect one another.

In conclusion, then, the dramatic events of 1806 and 1808 gave birth to the Deed of Alliance, a dramatic document that had the potential to radically alter the Ottoman order, but did not do so. Like many other countries shattered by similar dramatic events in this revolutionary period, the Ottoman Empire experienced change in fits and starts, with many dead ends. The Deed vanished and was remembered, if at all, as one of the "odd" documents of the age of revolutions. Perhaps Mustafa Bayraktar's imprudence was responsible for its failure. He could have prevented the janissary revolt, but did not. Or perhaps Mahmud II consigned the Deed to oblivion with his tacit, temporary coalition with the janissaries. Or perhaps the Deed was always destined to vanish, since its conditions were utopian and far from feasible. Or perhaps it was anachronistic. It belonged to eighteenth-century political culture, in which the empire was a theater for various actors who engaged in limited violence and competition. Since it established a partnership, rather than a centralized, hierarchical state, it could not survive in the nineteenth-century world of bureaucratic and military centralization. Alternatively, perhaps it was premature, since neither the central Ottoman state nor the provincial powerholders were ready for a solution based on partnership, which might have evolved into a kind of federal settlement between regions of the empire (think a dozen or more Muhammad Ali Pashas running the empire collectively). Many of the elements problematized in the Deed, such as security of life and property, trust, and the concepts of a state army and due process, continued to be major concerns in Ottoman constitutional history. In the final analysis, however, the Deed offered the political actors in the Ottoman center and provinces the experience of negotiating a coalition, settling disputes, ending a crisis, and building a new polity. As such, it may be seen as a kind of road test.

Conclusion

No notable of the Ramazanoğlus has been troubled like him since
Mamluk and Seljuk times. . . . The family has only one MP in
parliament.

Yaşar Kemal, *İnce Memed* (*Memed, My Hawk*)

Throughout this book I examine various aspects of the Ottoman Empire's transformation and crisis in the late eighteenth and early nineteenth centuries.[1] Like other countries, the empire responded to challenges and crises during this unstable period by trying various reform options. Examining this chapter in Ottoman history, we see competing discourses of the old order and the new, the rise and fall of collective and individual actors, and shifting coalitions and alliances among diverse individuals and groups. New institutional configurations appeared and disappeared, while constitutional texts were codified and annulled. The Ottoman transformation in the age of revolutions was not a linear transition from the old order to the new, from a decentralized to a centralized state, from Eastern to Western institutions, and from premodern to modern society. Rather, it involved both intersecting paths and dead ends, offering a rich repertoire of possibilities to be followed, reinterpreted, or forgotten.

In chapter 1, I focused on the major characteristics of the Ottoman order in the eighteenth century and explained how some members of the Ottoman elite came up with the New Order, a military, fiscal, and social reform agenda that challenged the vested rights, socioeconomic benefits, and conventions of some segments of Ottoman society. The janissaries, a colossal socio-military group that was profoundly integrated into urban society, voiced opposition to the New Order. And different advocates of the New Order responded to the opposition. In chapters 2 and 3, I then examined two structural trends as facets of Ottoman transformation throughout the eighteenth and early nineteenth centuries. Chapter 2 scrutinizes the consolidation of provincial powerholders in the Ottoman provinces. I analyzed how these great magnates acted as administrative and military entrepreneurs in a highly volatile and competitive imperial sector, without securing guarantees for their wealth, status, or even their lives. I discussed how and why some of these notables joined the New Order coalition and others participated in the opposition. Chapter 3 analyzes provincial communities and discusses how various collective and participatory processes developed organically, gradually becoming integrated into the reform program.

I argue that these eighteenth-century realities can be understood as three competing orders, which I call "the new order of empire," "the order of notables," and "the order of communities." The new order of empire was a reform program to transform the empire to a centralized bureaucratic polity, in which the central state kept its monopoly on violence and established military discipline, social order, and full jurisdiction over resources in provincial units through its agents. The order of notables was a system in which provincial notables established power bases in their regions through local connections and deals with the center and engaged in contractual and negotiational relations with the state. The order of communities was a set of institutional mechanisms through which communities administered public finance through their leaders, who were collectively elected (or claimed to be). In the late eighteenth and early nineteenth centuries, all three orders offered possibilities for an Ottoman transformation to modernity. The empire tested different configurations and combinations of these: centralized and bureaucratic, decentralized and contractual, participatory and democratic. We might also say: top-down, horizontal, and bottom-up.

In the eighteenth century, in many corners of the world, wars and fiscal reform set the political agenda. States competed for stronger and more disciplined armies and to adopt new military technologies. To achieve these goals, they engaged in fiscal reform to extract greater resources from their people (or colonies). These fiscal and military reforms often triggered new programs for social regulation and for reordering and disciplining society in general. Responses to military-fiscal-social reform agendas came from a variety of groups, including urban crowds, provincial elites, religious circles, merchants, and guilds. New coalitions and alliances emerged. At times, these coalitions and alliances united reformists and other groups who found it advantageous to act with the reformers. In other cases, these coalitions and alliances counted themselves among the opposition to reform.

Regimes suppressed or co-opted opposition in a variety of ways. Britain perhaps most successfully dealt with the challenges of military reform, which it did through the parliamentary politics of taxation and new instruments for internal borrowing.[2] But what succeeded in Britain proved a failure in America. The American Revolution flared as a part of empire-wide opposition to the British monarchy's reform program.[3]

In some cases, opposition to reform and mismanagement by the central government resulted in the collapse of entire regimes. This was the case in Iran, when Safavid rulership (and Nadir Shah's short-lived reign) collapsed in the early eighteenth century as a result of rising tribal opposition to state centralization and Afghan invasion.[4] France in 1789 provides another dramatic example of regime collapse, with which everybody is more familiar. To this list we can add Poland, where the conflict between the monarchy and aristocracy on the nature of reform could not be resolved, resulting in the country's partition and disappearance as a polity. In Russia, Peter the Great's earlier consolidation and success in co-opting and integrating the Russian aristocracy into the central establishment enabled Russian emperors to continue to rule without facing a major upheaval, if we do not count the Cossack rebellion led by Yemelyan Pugachev in the 1770s.[5]

We should examine the Ottoman experience of the New Order and its collapse in this general global framework. The Ottoman Empire's military failures pushed the central establishment to launch a reform that included fiscal and social components. A variety of groups clustered around the janissaries opposed the reform agenda. In response, reformists negotiated with others, mainly provincial powerholders. As we see in chapter 4, the Ottoman Empire experienced a major constitutional crisis between 1806 and 1808. The New Order collapsed after a janissary revolt but was restored in a modified form by an alliance between reformists and provincial powerholders. As we see in chapter 5, the deal between the New Order and provincial notables was transformed into a new partnership based on shared resources, collective responsibility, security, and trust. But the New Order then collapsed again after another popular janissary revolt.

If we extend our story into the nineteenth century, we see that despite this crisis, the empire neither disintegrated nor underwent total regime change. The janissary movement was unable to maintain (or to be part of) a larger coalition and offer a feasible program for alternative reform in which it took the initiative. Mahmud II supported its members for strategic reasons. Guilds and merchants gradually detached from the janissaries as a result of new market regulations.[6] The ulema were increasingly committed to reform.[7] Like the provincial communities, ordinary people in Istanbul who did not receive janissary stipends also became alienated from janissary claims. Under these circumstances, it took Mahmud II eighteen years to complete what the New Order had intended to achieve. In 1826, the janissary corps was abolished and, with the participation of the people of Istanbul, thousands of janissary affiliates were massacred by Mahmud II's militias.[8]

The option of creating an order of notables through partnership with provincial notables, which culminated in the Deed of Alliance, did not survive either. Beginning in 1809, Mahmud II took measures to eliminate, suppress, or pacify powerful provincial dynasties. Sometimes the sultan used governors from the imperial establishment, such as Hüsrev Pasha, who had a Caucasian slave background and did not have connections to a locality.[9] In other cases, provincial notables were willing to abandon their local claims and join the growing bureaucratic establishment. One such was Baba Pasha, who, after a career as a local ayan in Danubian Bulgaria, accepted Mahmud II's offer of a vizierate and roved across the empire pacifying provincial dynasties.[10]

Mahmud II wrote once to the Divan: "Since these men [referring to the provincial magnates] have not seen a governor in their provinces for a long time, they could not tolerate the rule of the viziers."[11] In fact, Mahmud's deliberate policy of pacifying the magnates with the help of viziers, who were given extraordinary authority and resources, was successful in some cases, unsuccessful in others. Families in the Ottoman provinces that had formerly held important offices and contracts with substantial military power had different options after 1808. Those who were convinced to abandon their contracts, statuses, and military power became active in municipal politics as natural leaders of the community. Others integrated into the growing bureaucratic state. Some families, like the Çapanoğlus, opted for both. This omnipotent dynasty, whose members had controlled half of Anatolia in the eighteenth century, lost that territory. But in the nineteenth century, the family was able to maintain two branches, one in Yozgat and the other in Istanbul. The Yozgat branch of the family played an active role in local politics throughout the nineteenth and early twentieth centuries, when municipal councils became a major component of Ottoman political modernization. The Istanbul branch became a bureaucratic dynasty that for generations provided the Ottoman bureaucracy with administrators and diplomats.[12]

But some powerholders vigorously resisted pacification. Between the 1810s and 1850s, we see resistance of provincial magnates in various provinces to the central administration. Three well-known examples from different parts of the empire are seen in the resistance to military and administrative centralization (or rebellion, from the perspective of the Ottoman center) of Ali Pasha of Ioannina in Greece and Albania, of Hüseyin Kapudan Gradaščević in Bosnia (in alliance with Bosnian janissaries who rejected the abolition of their corps in 1826), and of Bedirhan Bey in Kurdistan.[13] While these magnates developed various forms of resistance to centralization, they also employed agendas of regional autonomy under their leaderships, referring to the deals they had made since the late eighteenth century. Some of these figures would later be depicted as heroes of national revivals against the Ottoman Empire. However, the boundaries between being Ottoman, regional, or national were always negotiable during this period. Even descendants of provincial magnates who had been put to death were able to find places in Ottoman municipal politics and the bureaucracy. Thus, for example, İsmail Rahmi, a grandson of Ali Pasha of Ioannina (d. 1822), had a career, not as a member of a provincial dynasty in Epirus, but as governor of various Ottoman provinces, including Crete. (He is depicted, together with his brother, on the cover of this book.)[14]

After the age of revolutions began in the late eighteenth century, revolutions and reforms seemed endless. Starting with the Tanzimat edict of 1839, reform programs did what the earlier Deed of Alliance had failed to do, namely, abolish the practice of sultanic confiscations and executions without trial. The Tanzimat edict's promise to abolish tax-farming and the outsourcing of revenue collection to local entrepreneurs was not, however, fulfilled. Top-down sultanic edicts and codifications that gave and guaranteed rights continued to be promulgated throughout the nineteenth century. Land reforms from 1858 on affected different regions of the Ottoman Empire in various ways. In some regions, such as in central Anatolia, small peasant households consolidated at the expense of great families.[15] In other regions, notably southern Anatolia, Kurdistan, and Syria, provincial grandees took over large areas and transformed them into private estates, becoming landlords with official titles. Bulgaria, Macedonia, and Bosnia all witnessed enduring tensions between Christian peasants (and Christian notables) and Muslim powerholders, inasmuch as both claimed land in their different capacities.[16]

Commercial agriculture and international trade grew throughout the nineteenth century, especially after the 1838 Anglo-Ottoman trade treaty, and offered opportunities to strongmen with land and financial means. In various regions, but especially in Macedonia, western Anatolia, and Lebanon, commercial farming continued to expand in the nineteenth century to different degrees. In this transition from the order of notables to an order of market, some old provincial notables (but not all) and many new ones became agricultural capitalists and joined global commercial networks in different capacities. Revived global trade networks consisting of foreign merchants and their local partners perhaps truly ran the mid-nineteenth-century cotton boom.[17]

The most successful magnate of this generation was, of course, Muhammad Ali of Egypt, who did not sign the Deed of Alliance and was able to institutionalize his family's rule in Egypt after the Ottoman sultan had recognized his dynasty as the legitimate permanent authority there. His family alone acquired security and guarantees from the central administration as stipulated in the Deed. Muhammad Ali not only established a state within the empire, with a full-fledged bureaucracy and a disciplined, well-drilled army, but also initiated an elaborate agricultural administration and a monopoly system for cotton production, becoming one of the world's most important exporters of it. He is considered the founder of modern Egypt. It is noteworthy that his descendants and the Ottoman imperial elite in Istanbul maintained close ties during the nineteenth and twentieth centuries.[18]

In the nineteenth century, in addition to the janissaries, provincial notables, district communities, and religious authorities, a new actor appeared in the political spectrum: the imagined ethno-religious collective community, or nation. The nineteenth century was an age of nations and nationalisms, as well as of empires and imperialism. In the early nineteenth century, as we know, greater numbers of people acquired a sense of belonging to a large group "that conceived of itself as a political actor with a common language and destiny."[19] These imagined collective bodies developed new mechanisms of representation and became critical actors within empires or against them and challenged the monopoly of imperial and provincial elites in politics and governance. The nineteenth and twentieth centuries witnessed a long process of consolidation of, and claims to authority by, these collective bodies in different forms, as a result of what David Armitage calls the contagion of the notion of national sovereignty.[20]

In this book, I do not elaborate on ethno-religious communities and collective activisms based on ethno-religious identities, which evolved into forms of nationalism through the nineteenth century, or, in the spirit of my discussion, "the order of nations." In the early nineteenth century, Serbian, Greek, and Wahhabi movements that flourished in Belgrade, the Peloponnese, and the Arabian Peninsula eventually transformed into massive separatist/nationalist programs. The Pazvantoğlus' alliance with the janissaries of Belgrade against the Serbian notables, Ali Pasha of Ioannina's involvement against the Greek fighters for independence, and Muhammad Ali's actions against the Wahhabi insurgency suggest that the Ottoman politics of notables and the emergence of nationalist movements were not separate phenomena.[21]

Peter Brown writes: "What we are tempted to describe as the 'decline and fall' of an entire civilization is never quite the end of the world. It may be no more than the result of a regional shift in the patterns of 'intensification.'"[22] Nationalisms in the Ottoman Empire eventually brought about its end. Beginning in the 1820s with the Greek war of independence, former "Ottoman nations" became major players on the global stage. When the Ottoman regime under Mahmud II eliminated Ali Pasha of Ioannina to establish firmer control in Greece and Albania, it could not prevent the Greek national movement from replacing Ali's regime with a full-fledged agenda of national independence. While a nation was replacing the order of an Ottoman notable in Greece, Muhammad Ali transformed his order in Egypt into a nation-building project within the Ottoman Empire. Between 1830 and 1831, when he was dissatisfied with Ottoman offers in return for his help in suppressing the Greek rebellion, Muhammad Ali's new Egypt occupied Ottoman Syria and half of Anatolia. These episodes illustrate, not only the range of possibilities for radical changes, but also how the order of notables and order of communities (now nations) were interwoven in the nineteenth-century Ottoman world. By the 1850s, the Ottoman regime came to recognize Christian and Jewish communities as "nations" (*millet*) of the empire that constituted structural bodies in local politics. From the 1870s on, with the rise and fall of the constitutional monarchy and parliamentary experience, national identities became consolidated at the imperial level. With the Ottoman Empire becoming an empire of nations, Jews and citizens of various Christian ethnicities came to imagine empirewide communities stretching beyond their immediate localities. International agreements between the Ottoman Empire and the great powers pushed the central state to give collective rights to Christian communities/nations with foreign protection under the multinational umbrella of the imperial Ottoman state. Starting in the late nineteenth century, Muslim nations, Arabs, Albanians, Kurds, and eventually Turks, too, came to cultivate their national identities, languages, and histories.[23]

In the process of national identity formation, the order of communities and the order of notables, which flourished in the late eighteenth and early nineteenth centuries, provided the necessary institutional background and leadership pool. Eighteenth-century electoral processes became formalized and more elaborate. District assemblies and forms of collective participation flourished in the eighteenth century, as we saw in chapter 3, and were transformed in the nineteenth century into new forms of municipal governance. The politicized provincial communities, divided by ethno-religious motivations, transformed the local assemblies into loci of provincial politics. Some of the Muslim and Christian notables who rose in these arenas would became the founding fathers of their nation-states after the collapse of the Ottoman Empire.[24]

Meanwhile, the Ottoman state adopted an aggressive approach to building a new disciplined, well-drilled army, drawing heavily on Muslim citizens through mass conscription. After the New Order was restored for good, a disciplined army sought to discipline the entire society. Measures to regulate urban life and property relations, reduce poverty, and boost education coincided with constant efforts to codify administrative and legal reforms. Emigration from and immigration to the Ottoman lands—and the proliferation of interimperial networks of trade, education, technology, and religion—made the Ottoman Empire a highly mobile, open place. The loss of both Egypt in 1882, and the Balkans, beginning in 1878, coincided with the emergence of the so-called Eastern Question, namely, various agendas and ideas about what would happen after the Ottoman Empire's disintegration. Opposition to Sultan Abdulhamid's despotism triggered the consolidation of an empirewide mass politics, in which not only Ottoman state elites but Muslims, Christians, and Jews participated, and this gave birth to the 1908 constitutional revolution. The Ottoman marriage between national bodies and the empire did not survive. Atrocities committed by the new Ottoman state and ethnic and religious intercommunal violence in Macedonia and eastern Anatolia following the Balkan Wars endorsed the notion that the Ottoman Empire had forever lost its capacity to contain nations and nationalisms in the imperial body.[25]

The empire disintegrated after World War I. Post-Ottoman nation-states, whether independent or under mandate, had their own epic stories of national independence, in which different actors, some old and others new, played transformative roles. Not all were happy, however, with the empire's collapse. Transregional merchants lost their larger imperial market. Muslim notables of Albania were among the architects of Albanian independence, but complained of lost connections to their peers in the empire.[26] Many nations referred to the Ottoman age of revolutions in their founding myths and ideals. Some of the notable Greek families in the Peloponnese who were the key actors in Ottoman provincial governance in the late eighteenth and early nineteenth centuries were among the founding fathers of modern Greece, and Ali Pasha of Ioannina also willy-nilly entered into the Philhellenic pantheon.[27] Later, Ali Pasha was also declared one of the champions of Albanian claims to modern Albania, much the way Muhammad Ali (who was also Albanian) was seen as the founder of modern Egypt.[28]

In Anatolia, between 1918 and 1925, the *kuvvā-yı milliye*, or national powers, alliance gave birth to a Turkish national regime. Regional congresses, the national assembly in Ankara—which fought against the partition of Anatolia by European powers—and the Ottoman regime in Istanbul were in fact alliances between Muslim military-bureaucratic elites (many of Balkan origin) and Anatolian Muslim provincial powerholders, much like the 1808 coalition. Yet some major players, like the Çapanoğlus, now preferred to remain outside the coalition, and were eliminated by a Circassian warlord, Ethem, who accepted Mustafa Kemal's offer to suppress the unruly notables of Anatolia with his militia, much as Baba Pasha had done in the 1810s. The National Assembly of the 1920s was able to maintain a new coalition, which promulgated a document, the National Oath (Misāḳ-ı Millī), that reconfigured the elite partnership of the Deed of Alliance of 1808 into a national and territorial framework.[29]

However, this coalition excluded Armenians, who were victims of state-sponsored violence in 1915, and Greeks, since the government in Athens was allied with Britain and France. In the beginning, Islam persisted as an overarching framework, but the idea of the Ottoman New Order was replaced with Turkish nationalism in a republican nation-state. After 1925, the republican regime annulled this coalition through attempts to establish a firmly centralized republic, perhaps something like Mahmud II had done in 1808. Secularism and other reforms were initiated to discipline society and create new meaning for republican Turkey. Neither the order of communities nor the order of notables disappeared, however. In the 1930s, the newly formulated official history of the young Turkish republic belittled the role of the provincial notables in the war of independence and the new state-building process, sometimes denigrating them as usurpers, *mütegallibe* (much as Şanizade did in the 1820s and Turkish Marxists would do in the 1960s). In response, provincial notables subtly defended themselves against the official narrative with local family histories, which assigned a crucial role to themselves as partners of the republic's founding fathers. The enhancement of electoral practices and the multiparty system that developed in the 1940s provided new possibilities for collective political action by provincial communities and for the revival of the old and emergence of a new provincial elite in Turkish politics. But that is a subject of another book.

Select Bibliography

ABBREVIATIONS

Books

Asım tarihi: Ahmed Asım, *Āṣım tārīḫi*, 2 vols. (İstanbul: Ceride-i Havadis Matbaası, 1284 [1868])

Câbî tarihi: Câbî Ömer Efendi, *Câbî tārīḫi: Tarih-i Sultan Selim-i Salis ve Mahmud-i Sani: Tahlil ve tenkidli metin*, ed. Mehmet Ali Beyhan (Ankara: Türk Tarih Kurumu Basımevi, 2003)

Mustafa Necib Efendi tarihi: Mustafa Necip, *Muṣṭafa Necīb Efendi tārīḫi* (Derasitane: Matbaa-yi Ceride-yi Havadis, 1280 [1863 or 1864])

Şanizade tarihi: Şanizade Mehmed Ataullah Efendi, *Şânîzâde târîhî: 1223–1237 / 1808–1821*, 2 vols., ed. Ziya Yılmazer (İstanbul: Çamlıca, 2008)

SO: Mehmed Süreyya Bey, *Sicill-i Osmanî: Yahud tezkire-i meşahir-i Osmaniye* ([İstanbul] Matbaa-i Âmire, 1308–1311 [1890–1893]; new ed. by Nuri Akbayar and Seyit Ali Kahraman, İstanbul: Kültür Bakanlığı ile Türkiye Ekonomik ve Toplumsal Tarih Vakfı, 1996)

Tarih-i Cevdet: Ahmed Cevdet Paşa, *Tārīḫ-i Cevdet: Tertīb-i cedīt*, 12 vols. (İstanbul: Matbaa-i Osmaniye, 1309 [1893])

Uzunçarşılı, *Alemdar Mustapha Paşa*: Uzunçarşılı, İsmail Hakkı, *Meşhur Rumeli âyanlarından Tirsiniklı İsmail, Yılıkoğlu Süleyman Ağalar ve Alemdar Mustafa Paşa*. İstanbul: Maarif Matbassaı, 1942.

Vekâyi'-i Baba Paşa: Gazzizade Abdullatif Efendi, *Vekâyi'-i Baba Paşa fî't-tarih*, ed. Salih Erol (Ankara: Türk Tarih Kurumu Basımevi, 2013)

Journals and Reference Works

Actes	*Actes du Premier congrès international des études balkaniques et sud-est européennes*
B	*Belleten* (Ankara)
Bel	*Belgeler* (Ankara)
DİA	*Türkiye Diyanet Vakfı İslam ansiklopedisi* (İstanbul: Türkiye Diyanet Vakfı (İstanbul, 1988–2013)
EB	*Études balkaniques* (Sofia)
EH	*Études historiques* (Sofia)

EI2   *Encyclopaedia of Islam*, 2nd ed., ed. P. Bearman et al. (Leiden: Brill, 1954–2009)

EI3   *Encyclopaedia of Islam*, 3rd ed., ed. Kate Fleet et al. (Leiden: Brill, 2007–

İA   *İslam ansiklopedisi: İslâm âlemi coğrafya, etnografya ve biyografya lûgati* (Istanbul: Milli Eğitim Bakanlığı,1950–88)

IJMES   *International Journal of Middle East Studies*

IJTS   *International Journal of Turkish Studies*

JOS   *Journal of Ottoman Studies*

JTS   *Journal of Turkish Studies*

OTAM   *Ankara Üniversitesi Osmanlı Tarihi Araştırma ve Uygulama Merkezi Dergisi*

SI   *Studia Islamica*

TAD   *Tarih araştırmaları dergisi* (Ankara)

TD   *Tarih dergisi* (İstanbul Üniversitesi Fen Edebiyat Fakültesi) (Istanbul)

TED   *Tarih Enstitüsü dergisi*

TM   *Türkiyat mecmuası*

TOEM   *Tarih-i Osmanı encümeni mecmuası*

TT   *Tarih ve toplum*

TV   *Tarih vesikaları*

VD   *Vakıflar dergisi*

Archives

1. Austria

HHStA: Haus-, Hof- und Staatsarchiv, Austrian Diplomatic Archives, Vienna.

2. Bulgaria

KM: Orientalski Otdel kim Narodnata Biblioteka "Kiril i Metodii," Sofia.

3. France

   i. AMAE: Archives du Ministère des affaires étrangères, Paris

   ii. AN: Archives nationales, Paris

4. Great Britain

PRO: National Archives, Public Record Office, London

5. Turkey

   i. BOA: Başbakanlık Osmanlı Arşivi [Prime Ministry Ottoman Archives], Istanbul

   Müh: Mühimme defterleri

   HAT: Hatt-ı Humayun tasnifi

   C: Cevdet Tasnifi: Adliye (ADL), Askeriyi (A), Belediye (B), Dahiliye (D), Hariciye (H), Maliye (ML), Saray (S), Zaptiye (ZB)

   KK: Kamil Kepeci

MAD: Maliyeden Müdevver
A.DVN: Divan (Beylikçi) Kalemi Defterleri
A.AMD: Bab-ı Asafi Amedi Kalemi
ii. TSA: Topkapı Palace Archives, Istanbul
iii. MK ŞS: Turkish National Library (Milli Kütüphane) Court Record (Şeriye Sicilleri) Collection, Ankara
iv. SK: Süleymaniye Library (Süleymaniye Kütüphanesi), Istanbul

REFERENCE AND PRIMARY SOURCES

Ahmed Asım [Mütercim]. *Āṣım tārīḫi.* 2 vols. Istanbul: Ceride-i Havadis Matbaası, 1284 [1868].
Ahmed Cevdet Paşa. *Mecelle-yi aḥkam-ı 'adliye.* Istanbul: Matbaa-yı Osmaniye, 1300 [1883].
———. *Tārīḫ-i Cevdet: Tertīb-i cedīt.* 12 vols. Istanbul: Matbaa-yi Osmaniye, 1309 [1893].
Ahmed Osmanzade Taib. *Hadīḳā ül-vüzerā.* Supplemented by Bağdadi Abdülfettah Şefkati Efendi. Istanbul, 1271 [1854].
Ahmed Vasıf Efendi, *Mehâsinü'l-âsâr ve hakâikü'l-ahbâr.* Edited by Mücteba İlgürel. Istanbul: Istanbul University Press, 1978.
Akyıldız, Ali. "Sened-i İttifak'ın ilk tam metni." *İslam araştırmaları dergisi* 2 (1998): 209–22.
Akyıldız, Ali, and Şükrü Hanioğlu. "Negotiating the Power of the Sultan: The Ottoman Sened-i İttifak (Deed of Agreement), 1808." In *The Modern Middle East: A Sourcebook for History,* ed. C. M. Amin, B. C. Fortna, and E. B. Frierson, 22–30. Oxford: Oxford University Press, 2006.
Andreasyan, Hrand D. "III. Selim ve IV. Mustafa devirlerine ait Georg Oğulukyan'ın Ruznamesi." *TD* 12, no. 16 (1962): 63–70.
Arapyan, Kalost. *Rusçuk âyânı Mustafa paşa'nın hayatı ve kahramanlıkları.* Translated by Esat Uras. Ankara: Türk Tarih Kurumu Basımevi, 1943.
Arbuthnot, Charles. *The Correspondence of Charles Arbuthnot.* London: Royal Historical Society, 1941.
Archeio Ali Pasa: Syllogēs I. Chōtzē. 4 vols. Edited by V. Panagiotopoulos, D. Dimitropoulos, P. Mikhailaris, et al. Athens: National Hellenic Research Foundation, 2007–9.
Arslan, Mehmet, ed. *Osmanlı sadrazamları hadîkatü'l-vüzerâ ve zeylleri.* Istanbul: Kitabevi, 2013.
Avlonyalı Ekrem Bey. *Osmanlı Arnavutluk'undan anılar (1885–1912).* Istanbul: İletişim, 2006.
Bardakçı, Murat. *Üçüncü Selim devrine ait bir bostancıbaşı defteri.* Istanbul: Pan, 2013.
Başar, Fahammedin. *Osmanlı eyalet tevcihatı, 1717–1730.* Ankara: Türk Tarih Kurumu Basımevi, 1997.
Baykal, Bekir Sıtkı. "A'yânlık müessesesinin düzeni hakkında belgeler." *Bel* 1, no. 2 (1931): 221–25.

Beaujour, Louis-Auguste Félix. *Tableau du commerce de la Grèce formé d'après une année moyenne, depuis 1787 jusqu'en 1797.* Paris: Ant.-Aug. Renouard, 1800.

Behiç, Es-Seyyid Mehmed Emin. "Sevânihü'l-levâyih." Edited by Ali Osman Çınar. MA thesis, Marmara University, Istanbul, 1992.

Berker, Aziz. "Mora ihtilali tarihçesi veya Penah Efendi mecmuası, 1769." *TV* 2, no. 7 (1942): 63–80; no. 8 (1942): 153–60; no. 9 (1942): 228–40; no. 10 (1942): 309–20; no. 11 (1943): 385–400; no. 12 (1943): 473–80.

Beydilli, Kemal. *Osmanlı döneminde imamlar ve bir imamın günlüğü.* Istanbul: Tarih ve Tabiat Vakfı, 2001.

Beydilli, Kemal, and İlhan Şahin, eds. *Mahmud Râif Efendi ve Nizâm-i Cedîd'e dâir eseri.* Ankara: Türk Tarih Kurumu Basımevi, 2001.

Beyhan, Mehmer Ali, ed. *Saray günlüğü (25 aralık 1802–24 ocak 1809).* Istanbul: Doğu Kütüphanesi, 2007.

Bianchi, Thomas-Xavier, and Jean-Daniel Kieffer. *Dictionnaire turc-français à l'usage des agents diplomatiques et consulaires, des commerçants, des navigateurs, et autres voyageurs dans le Levant.* 2nd ed. Paris: Dondey-Dupré, 1850.

Câbî Ömer Efendi. *Câbî tarihi: Tarih-i Sultan Selim-i Salis ve Mahmud-i Sani: Tahlil ve tenkidli metin.* Edited by Mehmet Ali Beyhan. Ankara: Türk Tarih Kurumu Basımevi, 2003.

Canning, Stratford. "Account of the Three Last Insurrections at Constantinople and the Present State of the Turkish Empire." March 25, 1809. PRO: FO 78/63: 182–96.

Cerfberr, Samson [pseud. Ibrahim-Manzour-efendi]. *Mémoires sur la Grèce et l'Albanie pendant le gouvernement d'Ali-Pacha; par Ibrahim-Manzour-efendi, commandant du génie au service de ce visir, ouvrage pouvant servir de complément à celui de M. de Pouqueville.* Paris: P. Ledoux, 1826. 2nd ed., 1827.

Chénier, Louis de. "Révolutions de l'empire Ottoman." In *Contribution à l'histoire du commerce de la Turquie et la Bulgarie,* ed. Nikola V. Michoff, 3: 42–57. Svishtov, Bulgaria: Akademia, 1950.

Çağman, Ergin. *III. Selim'e sunulan ıslahat lâyihaları.* Istanbul: Kitabevi, 2010.

Çeçen, Kazım, and A. M. Celal Şengör. *Selim III, Sultan of Turks, 1761–1808: Mühendishane-i Berri-i Humayun'un 1210/1795 tarihli kanunnamesi.* Istanbul: İ.T.Ü. Bilim ve Teknoloji Tarihi Araştırma Merkezi, 1988.

Cousinéry, Esprit Marie. *Voyage dans la Macédoine, contenant des recherches sur l'histoire, la géographie et les antiquités de ce pays.* Paris: Imprimerie royale, 1831.

Danacı Yıldız, Aysel, ed. *Âsiler ve gâziler: Kabakçı Mustafa risalesi.* Istanbul: Kitap Yayınevi, 2007.

Defter–i ḳażā ve livā. Süleymaniye Kütüphanesi, Ayasofya, MS no. 3774.

Dehérain, Henri. *Orientalistes et antiquaires.* Vol. 1, pt. 2: *La vie de Pierre Ruffin, orientaliste et diplomate, 1742–1824.* Paris: P. Geuthner, 1930.

Derin, Fahri. "Kabakçı Mustafa ayaklanmasına dair bir tarihçe." *TD* 27 (1973): 99–110.

———. "Yayla İmamı risalesi." *TED* 3 (1973): 213–72.

———. "Tüfengçi-başı Arif Efendi Tarihçesi." *B* 38 (1974): 399–443.

Dimitrov, Strashimir A. "Les timars et le 'Nizam-i cedid' selon le defter matricule des affermages de fiefs en 1804 et 1805." In *Sur l'état du système des timars des*

XVIIe–XVIIIe ss., ed. Vera P. Mutafčieva and Strashimir A. Dimitrov, 33–56. Sofia: Éditions de l'Académie bulgare des sciences, 1968.

Driault, Édouard, ed. *Mohamed Aly et Napoléon (1807–1814): Correspondance des consuls de France en Égypte recueillie et publiée par Édouard Driault.* Cairo: Imprimerie de l'Institut français d'archéologie orientale pour la Société royale de géographie d'Egypte, 1925.

Dupré, Louis. *Voyage à Athènes et à Constantinople, ou Collection de portraits, de vues et de costumes grecs et ottomans peints sur les lieux, d'après nature, lithographiés et coloriés.* Paris: Dondey-Dupré, 1825.

Ebû Bekir Efendi. *Vaka-i cedid.* Istanbul: Tıb ve Fen Kitaphanesi, 1332 [1916]. Critical edition by Aysel Danacı Yıldız, *Asiler ve gaziler: Kabakçı Mustafa risalesi* (Istanbul: Kitap Yayınevi, 2007).

Gazzizâde Abdullatif Efendi. *Vekâyi'-i Baba Paşa fî't-tarih.* Edited by Salih Erol. Ankara: Türk Tarih Kurumu Basımevi, 2013.

Guboglu, Mihail. *Catalogul documentelor turceşti.* Bucharest: Direcţia Generală a Arhivelor Statului din Republica Populară Romînă, 1960.

Hasan İzzet Efendi. *Ziyânâme: Sadrazam Yusuf Paşa'nın Napolyon'a karşı Mısır seferi (1798–1802).* Edited by M. İlkin Erkutun. Istanbul: Kitabevi, 2009.

Hitzel, Frédéric, et al., eds. *Hatice Sultan ile Melling Kalfa: Mektuplar.* Istanbul: Tarih Vakfı Yurt Yayınları, 2001.

Hobhouse, John Cam [1st Baron Broughton]. *Travels in Albania and Other Provinces of Turkey in 1809 & 1810.* London: J. Murray, 1855.

Hovnanean, Ghewond. *Mirzayean Manuk Pēyin varuts' patmut'iwnĕ.* Vienna: Pashtpan S. Astuatsatsni Vank'ĕ, 1852.

Hughes, Thomas Smart. *Travels in Sicily, Greece & Albania.* London: J. Mawman, 1820.

Hurmuzaki, Eudoxiu de, ed. *Documente privitoare la istoria românilor.* 19 vols. Bucharest: C. Göbl, 1887–1938.

İbrahim Efendi. "Muhasebe-i evvel el-Hac İbrahim Efendi layihası." In *III. Selim'e sunulan islahat layihaları*, ed. Ergin Çağman, 31–45, 100–109. Istanbul: Kitabevi, 2010.

Inventory of Ottoman Turkish Documents about waqf Preserved in the Oriental Department at the St. St. Cyril and Methodius National Library. Edited by Evgeni Radushev, Svetlana Ivanova, and Rumen Kovachev. Sofia: Narodna biblioteka "Sv. sv. Kiril i Metodiǐ," 2003.

James, William. *The Naval History of Great Britain, from the Declaration of War by France in 1793 to the Accession of George IV.* London: R. Bentley, 1837.

Jelavic, Vjekoslav. "Pazvan-Oglu od Vidina (Izvjesce francuskog pukovnika Mériage)." *Glasnik Zemaljskog Muzeja u Sarajevu* 17 (1905): 173–216.

Juchereau de Saint-Denys, Antoine. *Révolutions de Constantinople en 1807 et 1808. Précédées d'observations générales sur l'état actuel de l'Empire ottoman.* Paris: Brissot-Thivars, 1819.

Kadić, Muhammed Enver. "Tārīḫ-i Anvārī." Gazi Hüsrev Beg Library / Gazi Husrev–begova biblioteka, Sarajevo, MS no. R 7317.

Karahasanoğlu, Selim. *Politics and Governance in the Ottoman Empire: The Rebellion of 1730: An Account of the Revolution That Took Place in Constantinople in the Year 1143 of the Hegira/Vâki'a Takrîri Bińyüzukirküç'de Terkîb*

Olunmuşdur. Cambridge, MA: Department of Near Eastern Languages and Civilizations, Harvard University, 2009.

Karal, Enver Ziya. "Nizam-ı Cedid'e dair layihalar." *TV* 8 (1942): 104–11; 11 (1943): 342–51; 12 (1943): 424–32.

———. *Selim III'ün hatt-ı hümayunları*. Ankara: Türk Tarih Kurumu Basımevi, 1942.

———. *Selim III'ün hatt-ı hümayunları: Nizam-ı Cedid, 1789–1807*. Ankara: Türk Tarih Kurumu Basımevi, 1946.

Kavanin-i Yeniçeriyan—Yeniçeri Kanunları. Edited by Tayfun Toroser. Istanbul: Türkiye İş Bankası Kültür Yayınları, 2011.

Kethüda Said Efendi. "Tarih." Edited by Ahmet Özcan. MA thesis, Kırıkkale University, Turkey, 1999.

Kinneir, John Macdonald. *Journey Through Asia Minor, Armenia, and Koordistan in the Years 1813 and 1814; with Remarks on the Marches of Alexander and Retreat of the Ten Thousand*. London: J. Murray, 1818.

Koca Sekbanbaşı. *Hulasât ül-kelâm fî redd il-a'vâm: Koca Sekban başı'nin idare-i devlet hakkında yazdığı layihadir*. Ca. 1805. Istanbul: Hilal Matbaası, 1332 [1916].

———. *Koca Sekbanbaşı Risâlesi*. Edited by Abdullah Uçman. Istanbul: Kervan Kitapçılık, 1974.

Krasnokutskii, Aleksandr Grigor'evich. *Dnevnye zapiski poezdki v Konstantinopol' v 1808 godu, samim im pisannye*. Moscow: S. Selivanovskogo, 1815.

Kurz, Marlene. *Das Sicill aus Skopje. Kritische Edition und Kommentierung des einzigen vollständig erhaltenen Kadiamtsregisterbandes (Sicill) aus Üsküb (Skopje)*. Wiesbaden: Harrassowitz, 2003.

Kuşmânî, Dihkânîzâde Ubeydullâh. *Nizâm-ı Cedîd'e dair bir risâle: Zebîre-i Kuşmânî fî ta'rîf-i nizâm-ı İlhâmî*. Edited by Ömer İşbilir. Ankara: Atatürk Kültür, Dil ve Tarih Yüksek Kurumu, Türk Tarih Kurumu Yayınları, 2006.

Leake, William Martin. *Travels in Northern Greece*. 4 vols. London: J. Rodwell, 1835.

Macmichael, William. *Journey from Moscow to Constantinople, in the years 1817, 1818*. London: J. Murray, 1819.

Mahmud Raif Efendi. *Tableau des nouveaux règlements de l'Empire ottoman*. Constantinople: Nouvelle imprimerie du Génie, 1798.

Mehmed, Mustafa A. *Documente turceşti privind istoria Romaniei*. Bucharest: Editura Academiei Republicii Socialiste România, 1986.

Mehmed Paşa, Sarı. *Zübde-i vekayi'at*. Edited by Abdülkadir Özcan. Ankara: Türk Tarih Kurumu Basımevi, 1995.

Menemencioğlu Ahmed Bey. *Menemencioğlu tarihi*. Edited by Yılmaz Kurt. Ankara: Akçağ, 1997.

Mikhailovskii-Danilevskii, Aleksandr Ivanovich. *Russo-Turkish War of 1806–1812*. Translated and edited by Alexander Mikaberidze. West Chester, OH: Nafziger Collection, 2002.

Miović, Vesna. *Dubrovačka Republika u Spisima Namjesnika Bosanskog Ejaleta i Hercegovačkog Sandžaka*. Dubrovnik: Državni Archiv u Dubrovniku, 2008.

Molla Mustafa. *XVIII. yüzyıl günlük hayatına dair Saraybosnalı Molla Mustafa'nın mecmuası*. Edited by Kerima Fidan. Sarajevo: Connectum, 2011.

Mustafa Necip. *Muṣṭafa Necīb Efendi tāriḫi.* Derasitane: Matbaa-yi Ceride-yi Havadis, 1280 [1863 or 1864].

Napoleon I. *Correspondance de Napoléon Ier; publiée par ordre de l'empereur Napoléon III.* 32 vols. Paris: Imprimerie impériale, 1858–69.

Nenadović, Mateja. *The Memoirs of Prota Matija Nenadović.* Translated from the Serbian and edited by Lovett F. Edwards. Oxford: Clarendon Press, 1969.

Nizâm-ı Cedîd kanunları (1791–1800). Edited by Yunus Koç and Fatih Yeşil. Ankara: Türk Tarih Kurumu, 2012.

Oğulukian, Georg. *Georg Oğulukyan'ın ruznamesi; 1806–1810 isyanları, III. Selim, IV. Mustafa, II. Mahmud ve Alemdar Mustafa Paşa.* Translated and edited by Hrand D. Andreasyan. Istanbul: Edebiyat Fakültesi, 1972.

Ohsson, Ignace Mouradja d'. *Tableau général de l'Empire othoman, divisé en deux parties dont l'une comprend la législation mahométane, l'autre, l'histoire de l'empire othoman.* 3 vols. Paris: Firmin Didot, 1787–20.

Okumuş, Sait. "Benlizâde İzzet Mehmed Bey'in Sâkînâmesi." *Turkish Studies* 4, no. 2 (2009): 900–910.

Olivier, Guillaume Antoine. *Travels in the Ottoman Empire, Egypt and Persia Undertaken by Order of the Government of France, During the First Six Years of the Republic.* London: Longman & Rees, 1801.

Orhonlu, Cengiz. "Osmanlı teşkilatına aid küçük bir risale 'Risale-i terceme.'" *Bel* 4, nos. 7–8 (1967): 39–48.

Oruç, Arif. *Alemdar Mustafa Paşa.* Vol. 1. Istanbul: [Tecelli Matbaası], 1932.

Osman Nuri Ergin. *Mecelle-yi umur-ı belediye.* 5 vols. Istanbul: Arşak Garoyan Matbaası, 1914.

Öz, Tahsin. "Fransa Kralı Louis XVI'nin Selim III'e namesi." *TV* 3 (1941): 198–202.

Özdemir, Zafer. "Sivas'ın iki yılı (6 numaralı Sivas şeri'yye sicil defteri H.1214–1215 / M.1799–1800) transkripsyon ve değerlendirme." MA thesis, Erciyes University, Kayseri, Turkey, 2010.

Özkaya, Yücel. "Canikli Ali Paşa'nın risalesi 'Tedâbirü'l-gazavât.'" *Tarih araştırmaları dergisi* 7, nos. 12–13 (1969): 119–91.

———. "XVIII. yüzyılın ikinci yarısına ait sosyal yaşantıyı ortaya koyan bir belge." *OTAM* 2 (1991): 303–34.

Öztelli, Cahit, ed. *Uyan padişahım.* Istanbul: Milliyet Yayınları, 1976.

Pakalın, Mehmet Zeki. *Osmanlı tarih deyimleri ve terimleri sözlüğü.* 3rd ed. Istanbul: Millî Eğitim Basımevi, 1983.

Panaitescu, P. *Corespondența lui Constantin Ypsilanti cu guvernul rusesc, 1806–1810: Pregătirea eteriei și a renașterii politice romanești.* Bucharest: Cartea românească, 1933.

Papademetriou, Tom. *Render unto the Sultan: Power, Authority, and the Greek Orthodox Church in the Early Ottoman Centuries.* Oxford: Oxford University Press, 2015.

Patmagirkʻ Eozkati ew shrjakaytsʻ (Gamirkʻ) Hayotsʻ. Edited by Armēn Darean and Andranik Erkanean. Beirut: Hratarakutʻiwn Eozkati ew Shjakaytsʻ (Gamirkʻ) Hayrenaktsʻakan Miutʻean, 1988.

Pouqueville, François-Charles-Hugues-Laurent. *Travels in Greece and Turkey,*

Comprehending a Particular Account of the Morea, Albania, etc. [1806] 2nd ed. London: Henry Colburn, 1820.

Précis historique des révolutions de Constantinople, en 1807, 1808 et 1826. Translated from the Turkish by Mathieu Puscich. Marseille: Olive, 1830.

Prévost, Baron. "Constantinople en 1806 et 1807" and "Constantinople en 1808." *Revue contemporaine* 14 (1854): 5–24, 161–86, 321–41, 481–505.

Redhouse, James W. *A Turkish and English Lexicon.* Istanbul: A. H. Boyacijan, 1890.

Relazione della catastrofe di Selim III. ed elevazione al trono di Constantinopoli di Mustafa IV. Venice: Fenzo, 1808.

"Revolution in Konstantinopel am 28sten Mai 1807." *Europäische Annalen* 3 (1808): 197–216.

Russia. Foreign Ministry. *Vneshniaia politika Rossii XIX i nachala XX veka: Dokumenty Rossiĭskogo ministerstva inostrannykh del.* Moscow: Nauka, 1960.

Sak, İzzet. *47 numaralı Konya şer'iyye sicili 1128–1129 / 1716–1717: Transkripsiyon ve dizin.* Konya: Tablet Kitabevi, 2006.

Şanizade Mehmed Ataullah Efendi. *Şânîzâde târîhî: 1223–1237 / 1808–1821.* Edited by Ziya Yılmazer. 2 vols. Istanbul: Çamlıca, 2008.

Sened– İttifâk. Süleymaniye Kütüphanesi, Hüsrev Paşa, MS no. 863.

Scudamore, Frank Ives. *France in the East; a Contribution Towards the Consideration of the Eastern Question.* London: W. H. Allen, 1882.

III. Selim'e sunulan ıslahat lâyihaları. Edited by Ergin Çağman. Istanbul: Kitabevi, 2010.

Şemseddin Sami. *Kamusü'l- a'lam: tarih ve coğrafya lugati ve tabir-i asahhıyle kaffe-i esma-yi hassayı camidir.* Istanbul: Mihran Matbaası, 1306 [1898].

Sertoğlu, Mithat. "III. Selim'in öldürülüşüne ve Alemdar Mustafa Paşa olayına ait bilinmeyen bir vekayîname." *Hayat Tarih Mecmuası* 2, no. 8 (1973): 48–57; no. 11 (1973): 31–38.

Seyyid Mustafa. *Diatribe de l'ingénieur Séid Moustapha sur l'état actuel de l'art militaire, du génie et des sciences, à Constantinople.* Scutari, 1803. Reprint. Paris: J.-B. Sajou, 1810.

———. *İstanbul'da askerlik sanatı, yeteneklerin ve bilimlerin durumu üzerine risale.* Edited by Hüsrev Hatemi and Kemal Beydilli. Istanbul: TÜYAP, 1986.

Steingass, Francis Joseph, and Francis Johnson. *A Comprehensive Persian-English Dictionary.* New York: Routledge, 1988.

"Sultan Selīm-i S̲ālis'in ḥāl'ine dāir risale." Millet Kütüphanesi, Istanbul, Ali Emiri collection, MS no. 33.

Süreyya Bey, Mehmed. *Sicill-i Osmanî: Yahud tezkire-i meşahir-i Osmaniye.* Istanbul: Matbaa-i Âmire, 1308–1311 [1890–1893]. New edition by Nuri Akbayar and Seyit Ali Kahraman. Istanbul: Kültür Bakanlığı ile Türkiye Ekonomik ve Toplumsal Tarih Vakfı, 1996.

"Takrir-i Mütesellim-i Cezzâr Ahmed Paşa." TSA: E. 4029.

Tatistcheff, Serge. *Alexandre Ier et Napoléon d'après leur correspondance inédite, 1801–1812.* Paris: Porrin, 1891.

Tatarcık Abdullah Ağa. "Sulṭān Selīm-i S̲ālis devrinde nizām-ı devlet ḥakkında müṭalaʿāt." *TOEM* 3 (1916): 257–84, 321–56; 4 (1917–18): 15–34.

Tott, François de. *Mémoires du baron de Tott sur les Turcs et les Tartares.* Amsterdam: n.p., 1785.

Tugay, Emine Foat. *Three Centuries: Family Chronicles of Turkey and Egypt.* New York: Oxford University Press, 1963.

Ursinus, Michael. *Grievance Administration (şikayet) in an Ottoman Province: The Kaymakam of Rumelia's 'Record Book of Complaints' of 1781–1783.* London: Routledge, 2005.

Uzunçarşılı, İsmail Hakkı. "Selim III'ün veliaht iken Fransa kralı Louis XVI ile muhabereleri." *B* 2, nos. 5–6 (1938): 191–246.

———. "Kabakçı Mustafa isyanına dair yazılmış bir tarihçe." *B* 6 (1942): 253–61.

Vaka-ı Cedid—Yayla İmamı tarihi ve yeni olaylar. Edited by Yavuz Senemoğlu. Istanbul: Tercüman, 1975.

Vaudoncourt, Frédéric François Guillaume. *Memoirs on the Ionian Islands, considered in a commercial, political, and military, point of view . . . including the life and character of Ali Pacha, the present ruler of Greece.* London: Baldwin, Cradock, & Joy, 1816.

Voyage pittoresque de Constantinople et des rives du Bosphore, d'après les dessins de M. [Anton-Ignace] *Melling, dessinateur et architecte de Hadidgé-Sultane, sœur de l'empereur.* Paris: Pierre Didot l'aîné, 1803.

Vraçalı Sofroni. *Osmanlı'da bir papaz: Günahkâr Sofroni'nin çileli hayat hikâyesi, 1739–1813.* Translated by Aziz Nazmi Şakir-Taş. Istanbul: Kitap Yayınevi, 2003.

Wilkinson, William. *An Account of the Principalities of Wallachia and Moldavia: With Various Political Observations Relating to Them.* London: Longman, Hurst, Rees, Orme, & Brown, 1820.

Yazar, İlyas, ed. *Kânî dîvânı: Tenkidli metin ve tahlîli.* Istanbul: Libra, 2010.

Yılmaz, Kâşif. *III. Selim (İlhamî): Hayatı, Edebî Kişiliği ve Divanının Tenkitli Metni.* Edirne, Turkey: Trakya Üniversitesi Yayınları, 2001.

SECONDARY SOURCES

Abadan, Yavuz, and Bahri Savcı. *Türkiye'de anayasa gelişmelerine bir bakış.* Ankara: Ankara Üniversitesi Siyasal Bilgiler Fakültesi Yayınları, 1959.

Abdullah, Thabit. *Merchants, Mamluks, and Murder: The Political Economy of Trade in Eighteenth-Century Basra.* Albany: State University of New York Press, 2001.

Abou El Fadl, Khaled. *Rebellion and Violence in Islamic Law.* New York: Cambridge University Press, 2001.

Abou-El-Haj, Rifa'at Ali. "The Ottoman Vezir and Paşa Households, 1683–1703: A Preliminary Report." *Journal of the American Oriental Society* 94, no. 4 (1974): 438–47.

———. *The 1703 Rebellion and the Structure of Ottoman Politics.* Leiden: Nederlands Historisch-Archaeologisch Instituut te Istanbul, 1984.

———. *Formation of the Modern State: The Ottoman Empire, Sixteenth to Eighteenth Centuries.* 1991. 2nd ed. Syracuse, NY: Syracuse University Press, 2005.

Abu-Manneh, Butrus. "The Naqshbandiyyah-Mujaddidiyyah in the Ottoman Lands in the Early 19th Century." *Die Welt des Islams* 22 (1982): 1–36.

Acemoglu, Daron, and James A. Robinson. *Why Nations Fail: The Origins of Power, Prosperity and Poverty*. New York: Crown, 2012.

Açıkgözoğlu, Ahmet Sacit. "Zeyneb Sultan Külliyesi." *DİA* 44 (2013): 362.

Acun, Hakkı. *Bozok Sancağı (Yozgat İli)'nda Türk mimarisi*. Ankara: Türk Tarih Kurumu, 2005.

———. *Çapanoğulları ve eserleri*. Ankara: Başbakanlık Devlet İstatistik Enstitüsü, 2005.

Adanır, Fikret. "The Ottoman Peasantries, c. 1360–c. 1860." In *The Peasantries of Europe from the Fourteenth to the Eighteenth Centuries*, ed. Tom Scott, 269–310. New York: Longman, 1998.

———. "Semi-autonomous Forces in the Balkans and Anatolia." In *The Cambridge History of Turkey: The Later Ottoman Empire, 1603–1839*, ed. Suraiya N. Faroqhi, 157–84. New York: Cambridge University Press, 2006.

Adanır, Fikret, and Suraiya N. Faroqhi, eds. *The Ottomans and the Balkans: A Discussion of Historiography*. Leiden: Brill, 2002.

Ağır, Seven. "Grain Redistribution in a Principal-Agent Framework: Practice of '*Mubayaa*' in Ottoman Macedonia, 1774–1838." Paper presented at Yale University, January 2012.

———. "The Evolution of Grain Policy Beyond Europe: Ottoman Grain Administration in the Late Eighteenth Century." *Journal of Interdisciplinary History* 43, no. 4 (Spring 2013): 571–98.

Ágoston, Gábor. "Military Transformation in the Ottoman Empire and Russia, 1500–1800." *Kritika: Explorations in Russian and Eurasian History* 12, no. 2 (2011): 281–319.

———. "Firearms and Military Adaptation: The Ottomans and the European Military Revolution, 1450–1800." *Journal of World History* 25, no. 1 (2014): 85–124.

Aharoni, Re'uven. *The Pasha's Bedouin: Tribes and State in the Egypt of Mehemet Ali, 1805–1848*. London: Routledge, 2007.

Akarlı, Engin D. "Provincial Power Magnates in Ottoman Bilad al-Sham and Egypt, 1740–1840." In *La vie sociale dans les provinces arabes à l'époque ottomane*, ed. Abdeljelil Temimi, 3: 41–56. Zaghouan, Tunisia: Centre d'études et de recherches ottomanes, morisques, de documentation et d'information, 1988.

———. "Economic Policy and Budgets in Ottoman Turkey, 1876–1909." *Middle Eastern Studies* 28 (1992): 443–76.

———. "*Gedik*: A Bundle of Rights and Obligations for Istanbul Artisans and Traders, 1750–1840." In *Law, Anthropology and the Constitution of the Social: Making Persons and Things*, ed. Alain Pottage and Martha Mundy, 166–200. Cambridge: Cambridge Univeristy Press, 2004.

———. "Law in the Marketplace, 1730–1840." In *Dispensing Justice in Islam: Qadis and Their Judgements*, ed. M. Khalid Masud, Rudolph Peters, and Davis S. Powers, 245–70. Leiden: Brill, 2006.

———. "*Maslaha*: From 'Common Good' to 'Raison d'état' in the Experience of Istanbul Artisans, 1730–1840." In *Hoca, 'Allame, Puits de Science: Essays in Honor of Kemal Karpat*, ed. Kaan Durukan, Robert Zens, and A. Zorlu-Durukan, 63–79. Istanbul: Isis, 2010.

Akbayrak, Hasan. *Osmanlı'dan Cumhuriyete tarih yazımı (Milletin tarihinden ulusun tarihine).* Istanbul: Kitabevi, 2012.

Akçura, Yusuf. *Osmanlı devletinin dağılma devri: XVIII. ve XIX. asırlarda.* 3rd ed. Ankara: Türk Tarih Kurumu Basımevi, 1988.

Akdağ, Mustafa. *Celâlî isyanları (1550–1603).* Ankara: Ankara Üniversitesi Basımevi, 1963.

———. "Osmanlı tarihinde âyânlık düzeni devri, 1730–1839." *TAD* 8–12 (1970): 14–23.

———. *Türkiye'nin iktisadî ve içtimaî tarihi.* Vol. 2. Ankara: Türk Tarih Kurumu Basimevi, 1971.

Akın, Banu Ayten. "Existing Performances in the Ottoman Empire at [*sic*] the Islamic Framework: Meddah, Karagöz and Orta Oyunu." *Zeitschrift für die Welt der Türken* 5, no. 2 (2013): 33–42.

Akın, İlhan. *Kamu hukuku.* 1966. 2nd ed. Istanbul: Üçdal Nesriyat, 1979.

Aksan, Virginia. "Ottoman Political Writing, 1768–1808." *IJMES* 25, no. 1 (1993): 53–69.

———. *An Ottoman Statesman in War and Peace: Ahmed Resmi Efendi, 1700–1783.* Leiden: Brill, 1995.

———. "Breaking the Spell of the Baron de Tott: Reframing the Question of Military Reform in the Ottoman Empire, 1760–1830." *International History Review* 24, no. 2 (2002): 253–77.

———. "War and Peace." In *The Cambridge History of Turkey*, vol. 3: *The Later Ottoman Empire, 1603–1839*, ed. Suraiya Faroqhi, 81–116. Cambridge: Cambridge University Press, 2006.

———. *Ottoman Wars 1700–1870: An Empire Besieged.* Harlow, Eng.: Longman, 2007.

Akşin, Sina. "Sened-i İttifak ile Magna Carta'nın karşılaştırılması." *Ankara Üniversitesi Dil Tarih Coğrafya Fakültesi dergisi* 16, no. 26 (1994): 115–23.

Aksu, Fehmi. "Yılanlı Oğulları hakkında vesikalar." *Ün dergisi* 4, no. 48 (1938): 685–89.

Aktepe, Münir. "Tuzcuoğulları isyanı." *TD* 5–6 (1953): 21–52.

———. *Patrona isyanı (1730).* Istanbul: Edebiyat Fakültesi Basimevi, 1958.

———. "Manisa ayanlarından Karaosmanoğlu Mustafa Ağa ve üç vakifyesi hakkında bir araştırma." *VD* 9 (1971): 367–83.

Aktuğ, İlknur. *Nevşehir Damat İbrahim Paşa Külliyesi.* (Ankara: Kültür Bakanlığı, 1992.

Aktüre, Sevgi. "19. yüzyılda Muğla." In *Tarih içinde Muğla*, ed. İlhan Tekeli, 34–113. Ankara: ODTÜ Mimarlık Fakültesi Yayını, 1993.

Akyıldız, Ali, "Osmanlı'da idari sorumluluğun paylaşımı ve meşrutiyet zemini olarak Meclis-i Meşveret." In Ali Akyıldız, *Osmanlı bürokrasisi ve modernleşme*, 31–44. Istanbul: İletişim, 2004.

Aldıkaçtı, Orhan. *Anayasa hukukumuzun gelişmesi ve 1961 anayasası.* Istanbul: Özdemir Basımevi, 1968–72.

Alexander, John Christos. *Brigandage and Public Order in the Morea, 1685–1806.* Athens: n.p., 1985.

Alexandrescu-Dersca-Bulgaru, Marie Mathilde. "Contribution à l'étude des relations de Seid Abdullah Ramiz Pacha avec les Principautés roumaines." *Studia et acta orientalia* (Bucharest) 7 (1968): 77–94.

Algar, Hamid. "Political Aspects of Naqshbandî History." In *Naqshbandîs: Cheminements et situation actuelle d'un ordre mystique musulman*, ed. Marc Gaborieau, Alexandre Popovic, and Thierry Zarcone, 123–52. Istanbul: Isis, 1990.

Allardyce, Gilbert. "The Rise and Fall of the Western Civilization Course." *American Historical Review* 87, no. 3 (June 1982): 695–725.

Altınay, Ahmed Refik. "Sultan Selim-i Salisde Halk ve Millet Muhabbeti." *Yeni mecmua* 23–24 (1917): 449–69.

Anastasopoulos, Antonis. "Lighting the Flame of Disorder: Ayan Infighting and State Intervention in Ottoman Karaferye, 1758–79." *International Journal of Turkish Studies* 8 (2002): 73–88.

———. "The Mixed Elite of a Balkan Town: Karaferye in the Second Half of the Eighteenth Century." In *Provincial Elites in the Ottoman Empire*, ed. id., 259–68. Rethymnon, Greece: Crete University Press, 2005.

———. "Albanians in the Eighteenth-Century Ottoman Balkans." In *The Ottoman Empire, the Balkans, the Greek Lands: Toward a Social and Economic History. Studies in Honor of John C. Alexander*, ed. Elias Kolovos, Phokion Kotzageorgis, Sophia Laiou, and Marinos Sariyannis, 37–47. Istanbul: Isis, 2007.

———. "Political Participation, Public Order, and Monetary Pledges (Nezir) in Ottoman Crete." In *Popular Protest and Political Participation in the Ottoman Empire: Studies in Honor of Suraiya Faroqhi*, ed. Eleni Gara, M. Erde, Kabadayi, and Christoph K. Neumann, 127–42. Istanbul: İstanbul Bilgi Üniversitesi Yayınları, 2011.

———, ed. *Provincial Elites in the Ottoman Empire: Halcyon Days in Crete, V: A Symposium held in Rethymno, 10–12 January 2003*. Rethymnon, Greece: Crete University Press, 2005.

Anderson, Matthew Smith. *The Eastern Question 1774–1923: A Study in International Relations*. London: Macmillan, 1966.

Anıl, Şahin. *Osmanlı'da kadılık*. Istanbul: İletişim Yayınları, 1993.

Anscombe, Frederick F. *State, Faith, and Nation in Ottoman and Post-Ottoman Lands*. New York: Cambridge University Press, 2014.

Aravantinos, P. *Historia Ali Pasha*. Athens: Pyrros, 1895.

Arel, Ayda. "Aydın bölgesinde ayan dönemi yapıları." In *Ege'de mimarlık sempozyumu*, ed. M. Başakman, 148–64. Izmir: Dokuz Eylül Üniversitesi, 1986.

———. "Cincin köyünde Cihanoğullarına ait yapılar." In *IV Araştırma sonuçları toplantısı: Ankara, 26–30 Mayıs 1986*, 43–75. Ankara: Başbakanlık Basımevi, 1987.

———. "Aydın ve yöresinde bir ayan ailesi ve mimarlık: Cihanoğulları." In *Osmanlı'dan Cumhuriyet'e: Problemler, araştırmalar, tartışmalar, I. Uluslararası Tarih Kongresi bildirileri*, 184–221. Ankara: Tarih Vakfı Yurt Yayınları, 1993.

———. "Gothic Towers and Baroque Mihrabs: The Post-classical Architecture of Aegean Anatolia in the Eighteenth and Nineteenth Centuries." *Muqarnas* 10 (1993): 212–18.

Armitage, David. *The Declaration of Independence: A Global History*. Cambridge, MA: Harvard University Press, 2007.

———. *Foundations of Modern International Thought*. Cambridge: Cambridge University Press, 2013.

Armitage, David, and Sanjay Subrahmanyam, eds. *The Age of Revolutions in Global Context, c. 1760–1840*. New York: Palgrave Macmillan, 2010.

———. "Introduction: The Age of Revolutions, c. 1760–1840—Global Causation, Connection, and Comparison." In *The Age of Revolutions in Global Context, c. 1760–1840*, ed. id. and Sanjay Subrahmanyam, xii–xxxii. New York: Palgrave Macmillan, 2010.

Artan, Tülay. "A Composite Universe: Arts and Society in Istanbul at the End of the Eighteenth Century." In *Ottoman Empire and European Theatre*, vol. 1: *The Age of Mozart and Selim III (1756–1808)*, ed. Michael Hüttler and Hans Ernst Weidinger, 751–94. Vienna: Hollitzer Wissenschaftsverlag, 2013.

Aslanian, Sebouh David. *From the Indian Ocean to the Mediterranean: The Global Trade Networks of Armenian Merchants from New Julfa*. Berkeley: University of California Press, 2011.

Atalay, Ayten. "Tahmiscioğlu isyanı, 1832–1833." Seminar essay no. 565, Department of History, Istanbul University, 1956.

Atanasov, Khristiian. *V Osmanskata periferiia: Obshtestvo i ikonomika vŭv Vidin i okolnostta*. Sofia: IK Sineva, 2008.

Avrich, Paul. *Russian Rebels, 1600–1800*. New York: Schocken Books, 1992.

Aymes, Marc. *Un grand progrés—sur le papier: Histoire provinciale des réformes ottomans à Chypre au XIXᵉ siécle*. Paris: Peters, 2010.

———. *A Provincial History of the Ottoman Empire: Cyprus and the Eastern Mediterranean in the Nineteenth Century*. London: Routledge, 2014.

Bajraktarević, Fehim. "Paswan-Oghlu." In *EI2*, http://referenceworks.brillonline.com/entries/encyclopaedia-of-islam-2/paswan-oghlu-SIM_6096 (accessed June 30, 2015).

Bakardjieva, Teodora. "Between Anarchy and Creativity: the Story of a Peripheral Town at the end of the 18th and the beginning of the 19th century." In *The Great Ottoman-Turkish Civilization*, vol. 2: *Economy and Society*, ed. Kemal Çiçek, 765–73. Ankara: Yeni Türkiye, 2000.

———. "Güçlü Rumeli ayanlarından Terseniklizade İsamil Ağa (1795–1806)'nın siyasi portresine yeni bir katkı." Unpublished paper.

Bakardjieva, Teodora, and Stoân Yordanov, *Ruse: Prostranstvo i Istoriya*. Ruse: n.p., 2001.

Baker, Keith Michael. "Fixing the French Constitution." In id., *Inventing the French Revolution: Essays on French Political Culture in the Eighteenth Century*, 252–305. Cambridge: Cambridge University Press, 1990.

———. *Inventing the French Revolution: Essays on French Political Culture in the Eighteenth Century*. Cambridge: Cambridge University Press, 1990.

———. "Political Language of the French Revolution." In *The Cambridge History of Eighteenth-Century Political Thought*, ed. Mark Goldie and Robert Wokler, 636–59. Cambridge: Cambridge University Press, 2006.

———. "Revolution 1.0." *Journal of Modern European History* 11, no. 2 (2013): 187–220.

Baltacı, Cahit. "Arpalık." *DİA*, 3 (1991): 392–393.
Barbir, Karl. "From Pasha to Efendi: The Assimilation of Ottoman into Damascene Society, 1516–1783." *IJTS* 1, no. 1 (1979–80): 68–83.
———. *Ottoman Rule in Damascus, 1708–1759*. Princeton, NJ: Princeton University Press, 1980.
———. "One Marker of Ottomanism: Confiscation of Ottoman Officials' Estates." In *Identity and Identity Formation in the Ottoman World: A Volume of Essays in Honor of Norman Itzkowitz*, ed. Baki Tezcan and Karl Barbir, 135–146. Wisconsin: University of Wisconsin Press, 2007.
Barkan, Ömer Lutfi. "Çiftlik." *İA*, 3 (1945): 392–97.
———. "Timar." *İA*, 12, no. 1 (1974): 286–333.
———. "Türk toprak hukuku tarihi tarihinde Tanzimat ve 1274 (1858) tarihli Arazi Kanunnamesi." In id., *Türkiye'de Toprak Meselesi: Toplu eserler*, 1: 291–375. Istanbul: Gözlem Yayınları, 1980.
Barkey, Karen. *Bandits and Bureaucrats: The Peculiar Route of Ottoman State Centralization*. Ithaca, NY: Cornell University Press, 1994.
———. *Empire of Difference: The Ottomans in Comparative Perspective*. Cambridge: Cambridge University Press, 2008.
Başaran, Betül. *Selim III: Social Control and Policing in Istanbul at the End of the Eighteenth Century*. Leiden: Brill, 2014.
Başarır, Özlem. "XVIII. yüzyılda Diyarbekir voyvodalığı'nın mekânsal örgütlenmesi." *Uluslararası sosyal araştırmaları dergisi* 4, no. 18 (2011): 196–229.
Bayly, Christopher Alan. *The Birth of the Modern World, 1780–1914: Global Connections and Comparisons*. Malden, MA: Blackwell, 2004.
———. "The Age of Revolutions in Global Context: An Afterword." In *The Age of Revolutions in Global Context, c. 1760–1840*, ed. David Armitage and Sanjay Subrahmanyam, 209–17. New York: Palgrave Macmillan, 2010.
Bayrak-Ferlibaş, Meral. "Alemdar Mustafa Paşa'nın muhallefatı." *Türk kültürü incelemeleri dergisi* 21 (2009): 63–120.
Baysun, Cavid. "Ali Paşa, Tepedelenli." *İA*, 1 (1940): 343–48.
———. "Musâdere." *İA*, 8 (1960): 669–73.
———. "Mustafa Paşa, İşkodralı, Buşatlı, Şerifi." *İA*, 8 (1960): 727–32.
Beales, Derek Edward Dawson. *Enlightenment and Reform in Eighteenth-Century Europe*. London: I. B. Tauris, 2005.
Berkes, Niyazi. *The Development of Secularisms in Turkey*. Montreal: McGill University Press, 1964.
———. *Türkiye'de çağdaşlaşma*. Istanbul: Doğu-Batı Yayınları, 1978.
Berktay, Halil. "The Feudalism Debate: The Turkish End—Is 'Tax vs. Rent' Necessarily the Product and Sign of Model Difference?" *Journal of Peasant Studies* 14 (1986–87): 291–333.
———. "The Search for the Peasant in Western and Turkish History/Historiography." In *New Approaches to State and Peasant in Ottoman History*, ed. Halil Berktay and Suraiya Faroqhi, 109–82. London: Frank Cass, 1992.
Beyatlı, Osman. *Bergama'da yakın tarih olayları, XVIII–XIX yüzyıl*. Izmir: Teknik Kitap ve Mecmua Basımevi, 1957.
Beydilli, Kemal. "Ignatius Mouradgea d'Ohsson (Mouradcan Tosunyan)." *TD* 34 (1984): 247–314.

————. *Türk bilim ve matbaacılık tarihinde Mühendishâne, Mühendishâne Matbaası ve Kütüphânesi, 1776–1826.* Istanbul: Eren, 1995.

————. "Halil Hamid Paşa." *DİA*, 15 (1997): 316–18.

————. "Halil Hamid Paşa." *Yaşamları ve yapıtlarıyla Osmanlılar ansiklopedisi*, 1: 516. Istanbul: Yapı Kredi Yayınları, 1999.

————. "Küçük Kaynarca'dan Tanzimat'a islahat düşünceleri." *İlmî araştırmalar* 8 (1999): 25–64.

————. "Evreka, Evreka veya Errare Humanum Est." *İlmî Araştırmalar* 9 (2000): 45–66.

————. "İshak Bey." *DİA*, 22 (2000): 527.

————. "Kabakçı isyanı akabinde hazırlanan Hüccet-i Şer'iyye." *Türk kültürü incelemeleri dergisi*, no. 4 (2001): 33–48.

————. *Osmanlı döneminde imamlar ve bir imamın günlüğü.* Istanbul: Tarih ve Tabiat Vakfı, 2001.

————. "Pehlivan İbrâhim Paşa." *DİA*, 34 (2007): 222–23.

————. *Yeniçeriler ve bir yeniçerinin hatıratı.* Istanbul: Yitik Hazine Yayınları, 2013.

Bianchi, Thomas Xavier. *Notice historique sur M. Ruffin.* Paris: Dondey-Dupré, 1825.

Bilgin, Mehmet. *Doğu Karadeniz'de bir derebeyi ailesi: Sarıâlizadeler [Sarallar].* Trabzon, Turkey: Serander Yayınları, 2006.

Bingöl, Yüksel. *İshak Paşa Sarayı.* Ankara: Türkiye İş Bankası Kültür Yayınları, 2000.

Birge, John Kingsley. *The Bektashi Order of Dervishes.* London: Luzac, 1965.

Birinci, Ali. "Koca Sekbanbaşı Risalesinin müellifi Tokatlı Mustafa Ağa (1131–1219)." In *Prof. Dr. İsmail Aka armağanı*, 105–20. İzmir: n.p., 1999.

Birken, Andreas. *Die Provinzen des Osmanischen Reiches.* Wiesbaden: Reichert, 1976.

Blumi, Isa. *Reinstating the Ottomans: Alternative Balkan Modernities, 1800–1912.* New York: Palgrave, 2011.

Bolsover, G. H. "Nicholas I and the Partition of Turkey." *Slavonic and East European Review* 27, no. 68 (1948): 115–45.

Bonney, Richard. *Economic Systems and State Finance.* Oxford: Clarendon Press, 1995.

Boppe, Auguste. *L'Albanie et Napoléon (1797–1814).* Paris: Hachette, 1914.

Börekci, Mehmet Çetin. "Saruhan mütesellimi Hacı Hüseyin Ağa ve Yılanoğulları." Seminar essay no. 653, Department of History, Istanbul University, 1963.

————. *Osmanlı İmparatorluğu'nda Sırp meselesi.* Istanbul: Kutup Yıldızı Yayınları, 2001.

Bosher, John F. *French Finances, 1770–1795: From Business to Bureaucracy.* Cambridge: Cambridge University Press, 1970.

Boyar, Ebru, and Kate Fleet. *A Social History of Ottoman Istanbul.* New York: Cambridge University Press, 2010.

Bradisteanu, Stancu. *Die Beziehungen Russlands und Frankreichs zur Türkei in den Jahren 1806 und 1807.* Berlin: E. Ebering, 1912.

Brenner, Neil. *New State Spaces: Urban Governance and the Rescaling of Statehood.* Oxford: Oxford University Press, 2004.

Brewer, John. *The Sinews of Power: War, Money, and the English State, 1688–1783.* Cambridge, MA: Harvard University Press, 1990.

Brown, Peter. *The Rise of Western Christendom: Triumph and Diversity, A.D. 200–1000.* 2nd ed. Malden, MA: Blackwell, 2003.

Brunner, Otto. *Land and Lordship: Structures of Governance in Medieval Austria.* Philadelphia, PA: University of Pennsylvania Press, 1984.

Bryer, Antony. "The Last Laz Risings and the Downfall of the Pontic Derebes, 1812–1840." *Bedi Kartlisa: Revue de Kartvélologie* 26 (1969): 191–210.

Butcher, John, and Howard Dick, eds. *The Rise and Fall of Revenue Farming: Business Elites and the Emergence of the Modern State in Southeast Asia.* New York: St. Martin's Press, 1993.

Butterfield, Herbert. *The Peace Tactics of Napoleon, 1806–1808.* Cambridge: University Press, 1929.

Çadırcı, Musa. "Türkiye'de muhtarlık teşkilatının kurulması üzerine bir inceleme." *B* 83, no. 192 (1970): 409–20.

———. "Ankara sancağında Nizâm-ı Cedîd ortasının teşkili ve Nizâm-ı Cedîd askerî kanunnamesi." *B* 36, no. 141 (1972): 1–13.

———. "17–19. yüzyıllarda sanayi ve ticaret merkezi olarak Tokat." In *Türk Tarihinde ve Kültüründe Tokat Sempozyumu,* 145–70. Tokat, Turkey: Tokat Valiliği Şeyhülislâm İbn Kemal Araştırma Merkezi, 1987.

———. *Tanzimat döneminde Anadolu kentleri'nin sosyal ve ekonomik yapıları.* Ankara: Türk Tarih Kurumu Basımevi, 1991.

Çakır, Baki. *Osmanlı mukata'a sistemi (XVI–XVIII Yüzyıl).* Istanbul: Kitabevi, 2003.

———. "Geleneksel dönem (Tanzimat öncesi) Osmanlı bütçe gelirleri." In *Osmanlı maliyesi: Kurumlar ve bütçeler,* ed. Mehmet Genç and Erol Özvar, 167–96. Istanbul: Osmanlı Bankası Arşiv ve Araştırma Merkezi, 2006.

Campos, Michelle U. *Ottoman Brothers: Muslims, Christians, and Jews in Early Twentieth-Century Palestine.* Stanford, CA: Stanford University Press, 2011.

Canbakal, Hülya. "On the 'Nobility' of Provincial Notables" In *Provincial Elites in the Ottoman Empire,* ed. Antonis Anastasopoulos, 39–50. Rethymnon, Greece: Crete University Press, 2005.

———. *Society and Politics in an Ottoman Town: 'Ayntab in the 17th century.* Leiden: Brill, 2007.

———. "Reflections on the Distribution of Wealth in Ottoman Ayntab" *Oriens* 37 (2009): 237–52

———. "Vows as Contract in Ottoman Public Life (17th–18th Centuries)." *Islamic Law and Society* 18, no. 1 (2011): 85–115.

Çelik, Yüksel. *Şeyhü'l-Vüzerâ Koca Hüsrev Paşa: II. Mahmud devrinin perde arkası.* Ankara: Türk Tarih Kurumu Yayınları, 2013.

Çelikel, Ali, and Abdurrahman Sağırlı. "Tokat şeri'ye sicillerine göre salyane defterleri." *TD* 41 (2005): 95–145.

Cengiz, Ahmet. *Karaman tarihi (XVIII. yüzyıl).* Konya: Çizgi, 2014.

Cernovodeanu, Paul. "Mobility and Traditionalism: The Evolution of the Boyar Class in the Romenian Principalities in the 18th Century." *Revue des études sud-est européennes* 24, no. 3 (1967): 447–60.

Cezar, Mustafa. *Osmanlı tarihinde levendler.* Istanbul: Çelikcilt Matbaasi, 1965.

Cezar, Yavuz. "Bir ayanın muhallefatı: Havza ve köprü kazaları ayanı Kör İsmail-Oğlu Hüseyin (müsadere olayı ve terekenin incelenmesi)." *B* 41, no. 161 (1977): 41–71.

———. "Osmanlı mali tarihinde 'eshâm' uygulamasının ilk dönemlerine ilişkin bazı önemli örnek ve belgeler," *Toplum ve bilim* 12 (1980): 124–43.

———. "Osmanlı maliyesinde XVII. yüzyılın ikinci yarısında 'İmdadiye' uygulaması." *İstanbul Üniversitesi Siyasal Bilgiler Fakültesi dergisi* 2 (1983): 69–102.

———. *Osmanlı maliyesinde bunalım ve değişim dönemi (XVIII. yüzyıldan Tanzimat'a malî tarih)*. Istanbul: Alan, 1986.

———. "Osmanlı aydını Süleyman Penah Efendi'nin sosyal ve malî konulardaki görüş ve önerileri." *Toplum ve bilim* 42 (1988): 111–32.

———. "Osmanlı devletinin merkez malî bürokrasisine giriş: XIII. yüzyılda Bab-ı Defterî." *Toplum ve bilim* 4 (1993): 129–60.

———. "Comments on the Financial History of the Ottoman Provinces in the 18th Century: A Macroanalysis." In *Essays on Ottoman Civilization: Proceedings of the XIIth Congress of the Comité international d'études pré-Ottomanes et Ottomanes = Archiv Orientální: Supplementa* 8 (1996): 85–92.

———. "18. ve 19. yüzyıllarda Osmanlı taşrasında oluşan yeni mali sektörün mahiyeti ve büyüklüğü üzerine." *Tarih ve toplum* 9 (1996): 89–43.

———. "The Role of the *sarraf*s in Ottoman Finance and Economy in the Eighteenth and Nineteenth Centuries." In *Frontiers of Ottoman Studies: State, Province, and the West*, ed. Colin Imber and Keiko Kiyotaki, 61–76. New York: I. B. Tauris, 2005.

Çızakça, Murat. *A Comparative Evolution of Business Partnerships: The Islamic World and Europe, with Specific Reference to the Ottoman Archives*. Leiden: Brill, 1996.

Clayer, Nathalie. *Mystiques, état et société: Les Halvetis dans l'aire balkanique de la fin du XVe siècle à nos jours*. Leiden: Brill, 1994.

———. "The Myth of Ali Pasha and the Bektashis. The Construction of an Albanian Bektashi National History." In *Albanian Identities: Myth and History*, ed. Stephanie Schwandner-Sievers and Bernd J. Fischer, 127–33. Bloomington: Indiana University Press, 2002.

———. *Aux origines du nationalisme albanais: La naissance d'une nation majoritairement musulmane en Europe*. Paris: Karthala, 2007.

———. "Ali Paşa Tepedelenli." *EI3*, http://referenceworks.brillonline.com/entries/encyclopaedia-of-islam-3/ali-pasa-tepedelenli-COM_23950 (accessed June 30, 2015).

Clogg, Richard. *A Concise History of Greece*. 3rd ed. Cambridge: Cambridge University Press, 2013.

Cohen, Amnon. *Palestine in the 18th Century: Patterns of Government and Administration*. Jerusalem: Magnes Press, Hebrew University, 1973.

Coller, Ian. "East of Enlightenment: Regulating Cosmopolitanism Between Istanbul and Paris in the Eighteenth Century." *Journal of World History* 21, no. 3 (2010): 447–70.

Coquelle, P. "L'ambassade du maréchal Brune à Constantinople (1803–1805)." *Revue d'histoire diplomatique* 18 (1904): 50–59.

Corfus, Ilie. "Cronica meşteşugarului Ioan Dobrescu, 1802–1830." *Studii şi articole de istorie* 8 (1966): 309–403.

Coşgel, Metin, and Boğaç Ergene. " Inequality of Wealth in the Ottoman Empire: War, Weather, and Long-term Trends in Eighteenth-Century Kastamonu." *Journal of Economic History* 72, no. 2 (2012): 308–31.

Craswell, John. "From the Tulip to the Rose." In *Studies in Eighteenth Century Islamic History*, ed. Thomas Naff and Roger Owen, 328–55. Carbondale: Southern Illinois University Press, 1977.

Crecelius, Daniel. *The Roots of Modern Egypt: A Study of the Regimes of Ali Bey al-Kebir and Muhammad Abu al-Dhahab, 1760–1775*. Minneapolis: Bibliotheca Islamica, 1981.

Cvetkova, Bistra A. "L'évolution du régime féodal turc de la fin du XVe jusqu'au milieu du XVIIIe siècle." *EH* 1 (1960): 71–206

———. "Otkupnata sistema (iltizam) v Osmanskata imperija prez XVI–XVIII v. s ogled na Balgarskite zemi." *Izvestija na Instituta za Pravni Nauki* 11, no. 2 (1960).

———. *Les institutions ottomanes en Europe*. Wiesbaden: Steiner, 1978.

Danişmend, İsmail Hami. *İzahlı Osmanlı tarihi kronolojisi*. 4 vols. Istanbul: Türkiye Yayınevi, 1947–55.

Darling, Linda. *Revenue-Raising and Legitimacy: Tax Collection and Finance Administration in the Ottoman Empire, 1560–1660*. Leiden: Brill, 1996.

———. "Public Finances: The Role of the Ottoman Centre." In *The Cambridge History of Turkey*, vol. 3: *The Later Ottoman Empire, 1603–1839*, ed. Suraiya Faroqhi, 118–31. Cambridge: Cambridge University Press, 2006.

Davies, Norman. *God's Playground: A History of Poland in Two Volumes*. Oxford: Clarendon Press, 2005.

Davison, Roderic H. *Essays in Ottoman and Turkish History, 1774–1923: The Impact of the West*. Austin: University of Texas Press, 1990.

Davison, Roderic H. *Reform in the Ottoman Empire, 1856–1876*. Princeton, NJ: Princeton University Press, 1963.

———. "The Advent of the Principle of Representation in the Government of the Ottoman Empire." In *Beginnings of Modernization in the Middle East*, ed. William R. Polk and Richard L. Chambers, 93–108. Chicago: University of Chicago Press, 1968.

Desan, Suzanne, Lynn Hunt, and William M. Nelson, eds. *The French Revolution in Global Perspective*. Ithaca, NY: Cornell University Press, 2013.

Devereux, Robert. *The First Ottoman Constitutional Period: A Study of the Midhat Constitution and Parliament*. Baltimore: Johns Hopkins University Press, 1963.

DeWeese, Devin. "Fusing Islam and Chinggisid Charisma: Muhammad Shibanî Khan's Religious Program in 16th-Century Central Asia." Workshop paper, Stanford University, 2012.

Di-Capua, Yoav. *Gatekeepers of the Arab Past: Historians and History Writing in Twentieth-Century Egypt*. Berkeley: University of California Press, 2009.

Dichter, Bernhard, Zalman Baumwoll, and Alex Carmel. *Akka: Sites from the Turkish Period*. Haifa: Gottlieb Schumacher Institute, University of Haifa, 2000.

Dickson, Peter George Muir. *Finance and Government under Maria Theresia, 1740–1780.* Vol. 1: *Society and Government*; vol. 2: *Finance and Credit.* Oxford: Clarendon Press, 1987.

Dilçin, Cem. "Şeyh Galib'in şiirlerinde III. Selim ve Nizam-ı Cedid." *Türkoloji dergisi* 11, no. 1 (1993): 207–19.

Djuvara, Neagu M. *Le pays roumain entre Orient et Occident: Les principautés danubiennes au début du XIXe siècle.* Cergy-Pontoise: Publications orientalistes de France, 1989.

Doğru, Halime. *Bir kadı defterinin ışığında Rumeli'de yaşam.* Istanbul: Kitap, 2007.

Donzel, E. van. "Mudjaddid." *EI2*, http://referenceworks.brillonline.com/entries/encyclopaedia-of-islam-2/mudjaddid-COM_0773 (accessed June 30, 2015).

Doumani, Beshara. *Rediscovering Palestine: Merchants and Peasants in Jabal Nablus, 1700–1900.* Berkeley: University of California Press, 1995.

———. "Endowing Family: Waqf, Property Devolution and Gender in Greater Syria, 1800–1860." *Comparative Studies in Society and History* 40, no. 1 (1998): 3–41.

Doumani, Beshara, ed. *Family History in the Middle East: Household, Property, and Gender.* Albany: State University of New York Press, 2003.

Driault, Édouard. *Études napoléoniennes: La politique orientale de Napoléon: Sébastiani et Gardane, 1806–1808.* Paris: F. Alcan, 1904.

———. *Napoléon et l'Europe; Tilsitt, France et Russie sous le premier empire: La question de Pologne (1806–1809).* Paris: F. Alcan, 1917.

Duben, Alan. "Turkish Families and Households in Historical Perspective." *Journal of Family History* 10 (1985): 75–96.

Dukič, T. "Izvestaji o bojevima Crno-goraca s Mahmud pašom Bušatliom." *Istoriski Zapisi* 8 (1951): 480–87.

DuRivage, Justin. *Revolution Against Empire: Taxes, Politics, and the Origins of Independence.* New Haven, CT: Yale University Press, forthcoming [2017].

Duru, Mehmed. "Yozgat Çapanoğlu Camii ve vakfiyeleri." *VD* 13 (1981): 71–89.

Duygu, Süleyman. *Yozgat tarihi ve Çapanoğulları.* Istanbul: Sayar Basımevi, 1953.

Efdaleddin [Mehmed Tekiner]. "Alemdar Mustafa Paşa." *TOEM* 3, no. 18 (1328/1912): 1109; 4, no. 19 (1329/1913): 1161–76; 4, no. 20 (1329/1913): 1232–45; 4, no. 21 (1329/1913): 1304–27.

Eclisiarul, Dionisie. "Cronograful Tarii Romanesti de la 1764 pana la 1815." In *Tesaur de monumente istorice pentru Romania*, 11: 159–236. Bucharest, n.p., 1863.

Eldem, Edhem. *French Trade in Istanbul in the Eighteeth Century.* Leiden: Brill, 1999.

Emecen, Feridun. "Kayacık kazasi avariz defteri." *TED* 12 (1982): 159–70.

———. "Osmanlı hanedanlığına alternatif arayışlar üzerine bazı örnekler ve mülahazalar." *İslam Araştırmaları dergisi* 6 (2002): 63–76.

Erdoğan, Meryem Kaçan, Meral Bayrak Ferlibaş, and Kamil Çolak. *Rusçuk ayanı: Tirsiniklizâde İsmail Ağa ve dönemi (1796–1806).* Istanbul: Yeditepe, 2009.

Erdoğlu, Nuran. "Ali Molla'nın isyanı, 1811–1814." Seminar essay no. 573, Department of History, Istanbul University, 1956.

Erefe, İklil. "Bread and Provisioning in the Ottoman Empire, 1750–1860." MA thesis, Bilkent University, 1997.

Eren, Ahmet Cevat. *Selim III'ün Biyografisi*. Istanbul: Nurgök matbaasi, 1964.

———. *Mahmud II. zamanında Bosna-Hersek*. Istanbul: Nurgök Matbaası, 1965.

Ergenç, Özer. "Osmanlı şehirlerinde yönetim kurumlarının niteliği üzerine bazı düşünceler." In *VIII. Türk Tarih Kongresi bildirileri* 8, no. 2 (1981): 1265–74.

———. "Osmanlı şehrindeki mahallenin işlev ve nitelikleri üzerine." *JOS* 6 (1984): 69–78.

———. "XVIII. yüzyılda Osmanlı taşra yönetiminin mali nitelikleri." *JTS* 10 (1986): 87–96.

———. "Some Notes on the Administration Units of the Ottoman Cities." In *Urbanism in Islam: The Proceedings of the International Conference on Urbanism in Islam (ICUIT)*, Oct. 22–28, 1989, 1: 425–41. Tokyo: Daisan-Shokan, 1989.

———. "Osmanlı klasik dönemindeki eşrâf ve ayân üzerine bazı bilgiler." *JOS* 3 (1992): 110–11.

———. *Osmanlı klasik dönemi kent tarihçiliğine katkı: XVI. yüzyılda Ankara ve Konya*. Ankara: Ankara Enstitüsü Vakfı Yayınları, 1995.

———. "Osmanlı klasik düzeni ve özellikleri üzerine bazı açıklamalar." *Osmanlı* 4 (1999): 32–39.

———. "The Sphere of *muqata'a*: A Particular Dimension of Ottoman Spatial Organization and Control." Paper presented at Conference in Honor of Professor Halil İnalcık: Methods and Sources in Ottoman Studies, Harvard University, Cambridge, MA, April 29–May 2, 2004.

———. *XVI. yüzyılın sonlarında Bursa: Yerleşimi, yönetimi, ekonomik ve sosyal durumu üzerine bir araştırma*. Ankara: Türk Tarih Kurumu Yayınları, 2006.

———. "'Ayân ve eşrâf' diye anılan seçkinler grubunun XVIII. yüzyılda Osmanlı toplumundaki rolü üzerine." In *Şehir, toplum, devlet: Osmanlı tarihi yazıları*, ed. id., 396–416. Istanbul: Tarih Vakfı Yurt Yayınları, 2012.

———. "Osmanlı'da enfa' vkuralının devlet ve re'âyâ arasındaki mâlî ilişkiler açısından anlamı." In *Şehir, toplum, devlet: Osmanlı tarihi yazıları*, ed. id., 429–41. Istanbul: Tarih Vakfı Yurt Yayınları, 2012.

———. "Toplumsal düşünce açıklama kanalı olarak: Cem'-i Gafir ve Cem'-i Kesir." In *XVI. Türk Tarih Kongresi: 20–24 Eylül 2010*, 4, pt. 2: 1063–72. Ankara: Türk Tarih Kurumu, 2015.

Ergene, Boğaç A. *Local Court, Provincial Society, and Justice in the Ottoman Empire: Legal Practice and Dispute Resolution in Çankırı and Kastamonu (1652–1744)*. Leiden: Brill, 2003.

Ergene, Boğaç, Atabey Kaygun, and Metin Coşgel. "A Temporal Analysis of Wealth in Eighteenth-Century Kastamonu." *Continuity and Change* 28, no. 1 (2013): 1–26.

Erken, Adil. "Osmanlı Devleti'nde bir danışma organı olarak Meclis-i Meşveret, 1774–1838." MA thesis, Afyon Kocatepe University, Afyonkarahisar, Turkey, 2006.

Ermiş, Farih. *A History of Ottoman Economic Thought: Developments Before the Ninteenth Century*. London: Routledge, 2014.

Ertman, Thomas. *Birth of the Leviathan: Building States and Regimes in Medieval and Early Modern Europe.* Cambridge: Cambridge University Press, 1997.

Esen, Hüseyin. "İslam hukuku açısından müsadere." *DEÜ İlahiyat Fakültesi Dergisi* 15 (2002): 192–225.

Esmer, Tolga U. "A Culture of Rebellion: Networks of Violence and Competing Discourses of Justice in the Ottoman Empire, 1790–1808." PhD diss., University of Chicago, 2009.

———. "Economies of Violence, Banditry and Governance in the Ottoman Empire Around 1800." *Past & Present* 224, no. 1 (2014): 163–99.

Fahmy, Khaled. *All the Pasha's Men: Mehmed Ali, His Army, and the Making of Modern Egypt.* Cairo: American University in Cairo Press, 2002.

Farge, Arlette. *Subversive Words: Public Opinion in Eighteenth-Century France.* Cambridge: Polity Press, 1994.

———. "Rumor." In *Encyclopedia of the Enlightenment*, ed. Michel Delon, 2: 1164–67. London: Fitzroy Dearborn, 2001.

Faroqhi, Suraiya. *Towns and Townsmen of Ottoman Anatolia: Trade, Crafts, and Food Production in an Urban Setting, 1520–1650.* New York: Cambridge University Press, 1984.

———. "Räuber, Rebellen und Obrigkeit im osmanischen Anatolien." *Periplus* 3 (1993): 31–42.

———. "Crisis and Change, 1590–1699." In *An Economic and Social History of the Ottoman Empire*, vol. 2: *1600–1914*, ed. Halil İnalcık, Donald Quataert, and Suraiya Faroqhi, 411–636. 2nd ed. Cambridge: Cambridge University Press, 1997.

———. "Exporting Grain from the Anatolian South-West: The Power and Wealth of Tekelioğlu Mehmed Ağa and His Magnate Household." In *Provincial Elites in the Ottoman Empire*, ed. Antonis Anastasopoulos, 295–320. Rethymnon, Greece: Crete University Press, 2005.

———. "Newshehir." In *EI2*, http://referenceworks.brillonline.com/entries/encyclopaedia-of-islam-2/newshehir-SIM_5896 (accessed July 5, 2015).

Feuerwerker, Albert. *State and Society in Eighteenth-Century China: The Ch'ing Empire in Its Glory.* Ann Arbor: Center for Chinese Studies, University of Michigan, 1976.

Filipczak-Kocur, Anna. "Poland-Lithuania Before Partition." In *The Rise of the Fiscal State in Europe, ca. 1200–1815*, ed. Richard Bonney, 443–79. Oxford: Oxford University Press, 1999.

Findley, Carter V. *Bureaucratic Reform in the Ottoman Empire: The Sublime Porte, 1789–1922.* Princeton, NJ: Princeton University Press, 1980.

———. "Writer and Subject, Self and Other: Mouradgea d'Ohsson and His *Tableau général de l'Empire othoman.*" In *The Torch of the Empire: Ignatius Mouradgea d'Ohsson and the Tableau général of the Ottoman Empire in the Eighteenth Century*, ed. Sture Theolin, 23–57. Istanbul: Yapı Kredi Kültür Sanat Yayıncılık, 2002.

———. *Turkey, Islam, Nationalism, and Modernity: A History, 1789–2007.* New Haven, CT: Yale University Press, 2010.

———. "Madjlis al-Shūrā." In *EI2*, http://referenceworks.brillonline.com/entries/encyclopaedia-of-islam-2/madjlis-al-shura-SIM_4745 (accessed July 5, 2015).

Fischer-Galaţi, S. "Revolutionary Activity in the Balkans from Lepanto to Kuchuk Kainardji." *Südost-Forschungen* 21 (1962): 194–213.

——. "Revolutionary Activity in the Balkans in the Eighteenth Century." *Actes* 4 (1969): 327–37.

Fleischer, Cornell H. *Bureaucrat and Intellectual in the Ottoman Empire: The Historian Mustafa Âli (1541–1600)*. Princeton, NJ: Princeton University Press, 1986.

Fleming, Katherine Elizabeth. *The Muslim Bonaparte: Diplomacy and Orientalism in Ali Pasha's Greece*. Princeton, NJ: Princeton University Press, 1999.

Foucault, Michel. *Discipline and Punish: The Birth of the Prison*. 2nd ed. New York: Vintage Books, 1995.

Frangakis-Syrett, Elena. "The Trade of Cotton and Cloth in İzmir: From the Second Half of the Eighteenth Century to the Early Nineteenth Century." In *Landholding and Commercial Agriculture in the Middle East*, ed. Çağlar Keyder and Faruk Tabak, 97–111. Albany: State University of New York Press, 1991.

——. *The Commerce of Smyrna in the Eighteenth Century: 1700–1820*. Athens: Centre for Asia Minor Studies, 1992.

Frey, Frederick W. *The Turkish Political Elite*. Cambridge, MA: MIT Press, 1965.

Frost, Robert I. "The Nobility of Poland-Lithuania, 1596–1795." In *The European Nobilities in the Seventeenth and Eighteenth Centuries*, ed. H. M. Scott, vol. 2: *Eastern Europe*, 183–222. New York: Palgrave Macmillan, 1995.

Fukuyama, Francis. *The Origins of Political Order: From Prehuman Times to the French Revolution*. New York: Farrar, Straus & Giroux, 2011.

Furet, François. *Revolutionary France, 1770–1880*. Oxford: Blackwell, 1988.

Gandev, Hristo. "L'apparition des rapports capitalistes dans l'économie rurale de la Bulgarie du nord-ouest au cours du XVIII s." *EH* 1 (1960): 207–20.

Gara, Eleni. "In Search of Communities in Seventeenth Century Ottoman Sources: The Case of the Kara Ferye District." *Turcica* 30 (1998): 135–61.

——. "Moneylenders and Landowners: In Search of Urban Muslim Elites in the Early Modern Balkans." In *Provincial Elites in the Ottoman Empire*, ed. Antonis Anastasopoulos, 135–47. Rethymnon, Greece: Crete University Press, 2005.

Gara, Eleni M., Erdem Kabadayı, and Christoph K. Neumann, eds. *Popular Protest and Political Participation in the Ottoman Empire: Studies in Honor of Suraiya Faroqhi*. Istanbul: Bilgi İletişim Grubu Yayıncılık, 2011.

Gelvin, James L. *Divided Loyalties: Nationalism and Mass Politics in Syria at the Close of Empire*. Berkeley: University of California Press, 1998.

——. "The 'Politics of Notables' Forty Years After." *Middle East Studies Association Bulletin* 40, no. 1 (June 2006): 19–29.

Genç, Mehmet. "Osmanlı maliyesinde mâlikâne sistemi." In *İktisat tarihi semineri*, ed. Osman Okyar and Ünal Nalbantoğlu, 231–96. Ankara: Meteksan, 1975.

——. "A Comparative Study of the Life Term Tax Farming and the Volume of Commercial and Industrial Activities in the Ottoman Empire During the Second Half of the 18th Century." In *La révolution industrielle dans le sud-est européen: XIXe siècle*, ed. Nikolai Todorov, 243–80. Sofia: Institut d'études balkaniques, 1979.

——. "XVIII. yüzyılda Osmanlı ekonomisi ve savaş." *Yapıt: Toplumsal araştırmalar dergisi* 49, no. 4 (1984): 51–61.

———. "17–19. yüzyıllarda sanayi ve ticaret merkezi olarak Tokat." In *Türk tarihinde ve kültüründe Tokat Sempozyumu*, 145–70. Tokat: Tokat Valiliği Şeyhülislâm İbn Kemal Araştırma Merkezi, 1987.

———. "Osmanlı iktisadî dünya görüşünün ilkeri." *Sosyoloji dergisi* 3, no. 1 (1989): 175–85.

———. "XVIII. yüzyılda Osmanlı sanayii." *Toplum ve ekonomi* 2 (1991): 99–124.

———. "L'économie ottomane et la guerre au XVIIIe siècle." *Turcica* 27 (1995): 177–96.

———. "Eshâm: İç Borçlanma." In id., *Osmanlı İmparatorluğunda Devlet ve Ekonomi*, 186–95. Istanbul: Ötüken, 2000.

———. "İltizâm." *DİA*, 22 (2000): 154–58.

———. "A Study of the Feasibility of Using Eighteenth-Century Ottoman Financial Records as an Indicator of Economic Activity." In *The Ottoman Empire and the World-Economy*, ed. Huri İslamoğlu-İnan, 345–59. 1987. Reprint. Cambridge: Cambridge University Press; Paris: Maison des sciences de l'homme, 2004.

Georgescu, V. "The Romanian Boyars in the Eighteenth Century: Their Political Ideology." *East European Quarterly* 7, no. 1 (1973): 31–40.

Georgieva, Gergana. "Administrative Structure and Government of Rumelia." In *Ottoman Rule and the Balkans, 1760–1850: Conflict, Transformation and Adaptation*, ed. Antonis Anastasopoulos and Elias Kolovos, 3–19. Rethymnon, Greece: Crete University Press, 2007.

Gerber, Haim. "Sharia, *kanun*, and Custom in the Ottoman Law: The Court Records of 17th century Bursa." *IJTS* 2 (1981): 131–47.

———. *The Social Origins of the Middle East*. Boulder, CO: L. Rienner, 1987.

———. *Economy and Society in an Ottoman City: Bursa, 1600–1700*. Jerusalem: Institute of Asian and African Studies, Hebrew University of Jerusalem, 1988.

———. "Anthropology and Family History: The Ottoman and Turkish Families." *Journal of Family History* 14, no. 4 (December 1989): 409–21.

———. *State, Society and Law in Islam: Ottoman Law in Comparative Perspective*. Albany: State University of New York Press, 1994.

Ghobrial, John-Paul A. *The Whispers of Cities: Information Flows in Istanbul, London, and Paris in the Age of William Trumbull*. Oxford: Oxford University Press, 2013.

Gillis, John R. "Aristocracy and Bureaucracy in Nineteenth-Century Prussia." *Past & Present* 41 (December 1968): 105–29.

Giz, Adnan. "İki padişahın otuz günü, III Selim ve II. Mahmud." *Belgelerle Türk Tarih dergisi* 4 (1968): 50–53; 5 (1968): 49–50.

Göçek, Fatma Müge. *Rise of the Bourgeoise, Demise of Empire: Ottoman Westernization and Social Change*. New York: Oxford University Press, 1996.

———. "Muṣādara—3. In the Ottoman Empire." In *EI2*, http://referenceworks .brillonline.com/entries/encyclopaedia-of-islam-2/musadara-COM_0804 (accessed 30 August 2014).

Goffman, Daniel. "The Jews of Safed and the *Maktuʿ* System in the Sixteenth Century: A Study of Two Documents from the Ottoman Archives." *JOS* 3 (1982): 81–90.

Gökbel, Asaf, and Hikmet Şölen. *Aydın ili tarihi: Eski zamandan Yunan işgaline kadar.* 2 vols. Aydın, Turkey: Ahmed İhsan Basımevi, 1936.

Gökbilgin, Tayyip. "Arpalık." *İA* 1 (1940): 592–95.

Gökçe, Cemal. "Edirne ayanı Dağdevirenoğlu Mehmed Ağa." *TD* 17, no. 22 (1967): 97–110.

Gökhan, İlyas, and E. Kasım Bal. *Osmanlı dönemi Maraş'ın idari tarihinde Dulkadirli ve Beyazidli idareciler (1700–1850).* Kahramanmaraş, Turkey: Ukde Kitaplığı, 2013.

Gölpınarlı, Abdülbâki. *Mevlânâ'dan sonra Mevlevilik.* 2nd ed. rev. Istanbul: İnkilâp ve Aka Kitabevleri, 1983.

Gommans, Jos J. L. *The Rise of the Indo-Afghan Empire, c. 1710–1780.* Leiden: Brill, 1995.

Gorceix, Septime. *Bonneval Pacha, pacha à trois queues: Une vie d'aventures au XVIII. siècle.* Paris: Plon, 1953.

Gorvine, Albert. *An Outline of Turkish Provincial and Local Government.* Ankara: Yeni Matbaa, 1956.

Gould, A. G. "Lords or Bandits: The derebeys of Cilicia." *IJMES* 7 (1976): 491–505.

Göyünç, Nejat. "Kapudan-ı Deryâ Küçük Hüseyin Paşa." *TD* 3, nos. 3–4 (1952): 35–50.

———. "Osmanlı devleti'nde taşra teşkilatı (Tanzimat'a kadar)." In *Osmanlı,* vol. 6: *Teşkilat,* ed. Güler Eren, 77–88. Ankara: Yeni Türkiye, 1999.

Gradeva, Rossitsa. "War and Peace along the Danube: Vidin at the End of the 17th Century." In *The Ottomans and the Sea,* ed. Kate Fleet = *Oriente moderno,* n.s., 20 (81), no. 1 (2001): 149–75.

———. "Osman Pazvantoglu of Vidin: Between Old and New." In *The Ottoman Balkans, 1750–1830,* ed. Frederick F. Anscombe, 115–61. Princeton, NJ: Markus Wiener, 2006.

Greene, Molly. "An Islamic Experiment? Ottoman Land Policy on Crete." *Mediterranean Historical Review* 11 (1996): 60–78.

———. "The Ottomans in the Mediterranean." In *The Early Modern Ottomans: Remapping the Empire,* ed. Virginia Aksan and Daniel Goffman, 104–16. Cambridge: Cambridge University Press, 2007.

———. *Catholic Pirates and Greek Merchants: A Maritime History of the Mediterranean.* Princeton, NJ: Princeton University Press, 2010.

Grehan, James. *Everyday Life & Consumer Culture in 18th-century Damascus.* Seattle: University of Washington Press, 2007.

Grindle, Merilee S. *Going Local: Decentralization, Democratization, and the Promise of Good Governance.* Princeton, NJ: Princeton University Press, 2007.

Grosul, G. S., and R. V. Danilenko. "K voprosu ob učastii volonterov iz Dunajskich knjažestv v russko-tureckoj vojne 1806–1812 gg." *Izvestija Moldavskogo filiala Akademija nauk* 2, no. 80 (1961): 3–25.

Grześkowiak-Krawawics, Anna. "Anti-Monarchism in Polish Republicanism in the Seventeenth and Eighteenth Centuries." In *Republicanism: A Shared European Heritage,* ed. Martin van Gelderen and Quentin Skinner, 1: 43–59. Cambridge: Cambridge University Press, 2002.

Güçer, Lütfi. *XV–XVII asırlarda Osmanlı İmparatorluğunda hububat meselesi.* Istanbul: İstanbul Üniversitesi, İktisat Fakültesi, 1964.

Güler, Mustafa. *Cezzar Ahmed Paşa ve Akka savunması.* Istanbul: Çamlıca, 2013.

Günay, Vehbi. "Yerel kayıtlar ışığında XVIII. yüzyıl sonlarında İzmir." *Tarih İncelemeleri dergisi* 25, no. 1 (July 2010): 253–68.

Güner, Selda. *Osmanlı Arabistanı'nda kıyam ve tenkil: Vehhâbî-Suûdîler (1744–1819).* Istanbul: Tarih Vakfı Yurt Yayınları, 2013.

Güthenke, Constanze. *Placing Modern Greece: The Dynamics of Romantic Hellenism, 1770–1840.* Oxford: Oxford University Press, 2008.

Habermas, Jürgen. *The Structural Transformation of the Public Sphere: An Inquiry into a Category of Bourgeois Society.* Translated by Thomas Burger with the assistance of Frederick Lawrence. Cambridge, MA: Harvard University Press, 1989.

Hacısalihoğlu, Mehmet. *Trabzon'da ayanlık mücadelesi: Hacısalihzâde Hasan Ağa, Ömer Ağa ve Büyük Ali Ağa (1737–1844).* Trabzon, Turkey: Serander Yayınevi, 2014.

Hadjikyriacou, Antonis. "Society and Economy on an Ottoman Island: Cyprus in the Eighteenth Century." PhD diss., School of Oriental and African Studies, University of London, 2011.

Halaçoğlu, Yusuf. *XIV–XVII. yüzyıllarda Osmanlılarda devlet teşkilatı ve sosyal yapı.* Ankara: Türk Tarih Kurumu Basımevi, 1991.

———. *Osmanlılarda ulaşım ve haberleşme, menziller.* Ankara: PTT Genel Müdürlüğü, 2002.

Hallaq, Wael B. *Sharī'a: Theory, Practice and Transformations.* Cambridge: Cambridge University Press, 2009.

Halm, Heinz. "Dawr." In *EI2,* http://referenceworks.brillonline.com/entries/encyclopaedia-of-islam-2/dawr-SIM_8466 (accessed July 5, 2015).

Hamadeh, Shirine. *The City's Pleasures: Istanbul in the Eighteenth Century.* Seattle: University of Washington Press, 2008.

Hanioğlu, M. Şükrü. *A Brief History of the Late Ottoman Empire.* Princeton, NJ: Princeton University Press, 2008.

Hathaway, Jane. *The Politics of Households in Ottoman Egypt: The Rise of the Qazdağlıs.* Cambridge: Cambridge University Press, 1997.

———. *A Tale of Two Factions: Myth, Memory, and Identity in Ottoman Egypt and Yemen.* Albany, NY: State University of New York Press, 2003.

Haynes, Michael, and Jim Wolfreys, eds. *History and Revolution: Refuting Revisionism.* London: Verso, 2007.

Heppner, Harald. "Pazvandoğlu—ein Prüfstein der habsburgischen Südosteuropapolitik im Jahre 1802." *Mitteilungen des Österreichichen Staatsarchivs* 38 (1985): 347–55.

Heyd, Uriel. "The Ottoman ulema and Westernization in the Time of Selim III and Mahmud II." In *Studies in Islamic History and Civilization,* ed. Uriel Heyd, 63–96. Scripta Hierosolymitana 9. Jerusalem: Hebrew University of Jerusalem Press, 1961.

Heywood, Colin J. "The Ottoman *Menzilhane* and *Ulak* System in Rumeli in the Eighteenth Century." In *Social and Economic History of Turkey (1071–1920):*

Papers presented to the First International Congress on the Social and Economic History of Turkey, ed. Osman Okyar and Halil İnalcık, 179–86. Ankara: Meteksan, 1980.

———. "Ḳarā Maḥmūd Pasha." In *EI2*, http://referenceworks.brillonline.com/entries/encyclopaedia-of-islam-2/kara-mahmud-pasha-SIM_3893 (accessed July 5, 2015).

Hickok, Michael Robert. *Ottoman Military Administration in Eighteenth-Century Bosnia*. Leiden: Brill, 1997.

Hitchins, Keith. *The Romanians, 1774–1866*. Oxford: Clarendon Press, 1996.

Hitzel, Frédéric. "Les écoles de mathématiques turques et l'aide française (1775–1798)." In *Collection Turcica*, vol. 8, Histoire économique et sociale de l'Empire ottoman et de la Turque (1361–1960). Paris: Peeters, 1995: 813–825.

Hobsbawm, Eric J. *The Age of Revolution: Europe, 1789–1848*. London: Weidenfeld & Nicolson, 1975.

Hochstrasser, Timothy. "Physiocracy and the Politics of Laissez-faire." In *The Cambridge History of Eighteenth-Century Political Thought*, ed. Mark Goldie and Robert Wokler, 419–42. Cambridge University Press: Cambridge, 2006.

Hovannisian, Richard G., and David N. Myers, eds. *Enlightenment and Diaspora: The Armenian and Jewish Cases*. Atlanta: Scholars Press, 1999.

Hovnanean, Ghewond. *Mirzayean Manuk Pēyin varuts' patmut'iwnĕ*. Vienna: Pashtpan S. Astuatsatsni Vank'ĕ, 1852.

Howard, Douglas A. "The Ottoman *timar* System and Its Transformation, 1563–1656." Ph.D. diss., Indiana University, 1987.

———. "Ottoman Historiography and the Literature of 'Decline' of the Sixteenth and Seventeenth Centuries." *Journal of Asian History* 22, no. 1 (1988): 52–77.

Hourani, Albert. "Ottoman Reform and the Politics of Notables." In *Beginnings of Modernization in the Middle East*, ed. William R. Polk and Richard L. Chambers, 41–68. Chicago: University of Chicago Press, 1968.

Hunt, Lynn. "The French Revolution in Global Context." In *The Age of Revolutions in Global Context c. 1760–1840*, ed. David Armitage and Sanjay Subrahmanyam, 20–36. New York: Palgrave Macmillan, 2010.

Hunter, F. Robert. *Egypt under the Khedives, 1805–1879: From Household Government to Modern Bureaucracy*. Pittsburgh: University of Pittsburgh Press, 1984.

İbnülemin, Mahmud Kemal. "Arpalık." *Türk Tarihi encümeni mecmuası* 17, no. 94 (1926): 276–83.

İlgürel, Mücteba. "Balıkesir'de âyânlık mücadeleleri." *TED* 3 (1972): 63–73.

İnalcık, Halil. *Tanzimat ve Bulgar meselesi*. Ankara: Türk Tarih Kurumu Basimevi, 1943.

———. "Yeni vesikalara göre Kırım Hanlığının Osmanlı tabiliğine girmesi ve ahidname meselesi." *B*, no. 30 (1944): 185–229.

———. "Arnavutluk'ta Osmanlı Hakimiyetinin Yerleşmesi ve İskender Bey İsyanının Menşei." *Fatih ve İstanbul* (Istanbul: Fetih Derneği) 1, no. 2 (1953): 153–75.

———. "Ottoman Methods of Conquest." *SI* 2 (1954): 103–29.

———. "Osmanlılarda raiyyet rüsumu." *B* 23 (1959): 575–610.

———. "The Nature of Traditional Society: Turkey." In *Political Modernization in Japan and Turkey*, ed. Robert E. Ward and Dankwart A. Rustow, 42–63. Princeton, NJ: Princeton University Press, 1964.

———. "Sened-i İttifak ve Gülhane Hatt-ı Hümâyûnu." *B* 28 (1964): 603–22.

———. "Adaletnameler." *B* 2, nos. 3–4 (1965): 49–145.

———. "Capital Formation in the Ottoman Empire." *Journal of Economic History* 29, no. 92 (1969): 97–140.

———. "Application of Tanzimat and Its Social Effects." *Archivum Ottomanicum* 5 (1973): 97–128.

———. "Centralization and Decentralization in Ottoman Administration." In *Studies in Eighteenth Century Islamic History*, ed. Thomas Naff and Roger Owen, 27–52. Carbondale: Southern Illinois University Press, 1977.

———. "Servile Labor in the Ottoman Empire." In *The Mutual Effects of the Islamic and Judeo-Christian Worlds: The East European Pattern*, ed. Abraham Ascher, Tibor Halasi-Kun, and Béla K. Kiraly, 25–52. New York: Brooklyn College Press, 1979.

———. "Military and Fiscal Transformation in the Ottoman Empire, 1600–1700." *Archivum Ottomanicum* 6 (1980): 283–337.

———. "Rice Cultivation and the Çeltükci-Reaya System in the Ottoman Empire." *Turcica* 14 (1982): 69–141.

———. "The Emergence of Big Farms, Çiftliks: State, Landlords, and Tenants." In *Contributions à l'histoire économique et sociale de l'Empire ottoman*, ed. Jean-Louis Bacqué-Grammont and Paul Dumont, 105–26. Louvain: Peeters, 1983.

———. "Power Relationships Between Russia, the Crimea and the Ottoman Empire as Reflected in Titulature." In *Passé turco-tatar, présent soviétique: Études offertes à Alexandre Bennigsen*, ed. Ch. Lemercier-Quelquejay, G. Veinstein, and S. E. Wimbush, 370–411. Louvain: Peeters; Paris: École des hautes études en sciences sociales, 1986.

———. "The Appointment Procedure of a Guild Warden (*kethuda*)." *Wiener Zeitschrift für die Kunde des Morgenlandes, Festschrift Andreas Tietze* 76 (1986): 135–42.

———. "Şikayet hakkı: arz-ı hal ve arz-ı mahzarlar." *JOS* 7–8 (1988): 33–54.

———. "Comments on 'Sultanism': Max Weber's Typification of the Ottoman Polity." *Princeton Papers in Near Eastern Studies* 1 (1992): 49–72.

———. "Köy, köylü ve imparatorluk." In *Osmanlı İmparatorluğu* ed. id., 2nd ed., 1–14. Istanbul: Eren Yayıncılık, 1993.

———. "Stefan Duşan'dan Osmanlı İmparatorluğu'na: XV. asırda Rumeli'de Hıristiyan sipahiler ve menşeleri." In *Osmanlı İmparatorluğu: Toplum ve Ekonomi*, ed. id., 67–108. 2nd ed. Istanbul: Eren Yayıncılık, 1993.

———. *The Ottoman Empire: The Classical Age, 1300–1600*. 1973. Reprint. London: Phoenix, 1994.

———. "Political Modernization in Turkey." In id., *From Empire to Republic: Essays on Ottoman and Turkish Social History*, 123–41. Istanbul: Isis, 1995.

İnalcık, Halil (ed.) *An Economic and Social History of the Ottoman Empire*, vol. 1: 1300–1600, ed. id. with Donal Quartaert. 2nd ed. Cambridge: Cambridge University Press, 1997.

———. "Autonomous Enclaves in Islamic States: *Temlîks, Soyurghals, Yurdluḳ-Ocaḳlıḳs, Mâlikâne-Muḳâṭa'as* and *Awqâf*." In *History and Historiography of*

Post-Mongol Central Asia and the Middle East: Studies in Honor of John E. Wood, ed. Judith Pfeiffer and Sholeh A. Quinn, 112–34. Wiesbaden: Harrassowitz, 2006.

———. "İskender Beg." In *EI2*, http://referenceworks.brillonline.com/entries/encyclopaedia-of-islam-2/iskender-beg-SIM_3637 (accessed August 21, 2015).

İnkaya, Güzide. "Tekelioğlu İbrahim Bey'in isyanı, 1812–1814." Seminar essay no. 312, Department of History, Istanbul University, 1942.

Ionescu, Stefano. *Manuc Bei: Zaraf şi diplomat la începutul secolului al XIX-lea*. Cluj-Napoca, Romania: Dacia, 1976.

Iorga [Jorga], Nicolae. *Geschichte des Osmanischen Reiches*. 5 vols. Gotha: F. A. Perthes, 1908–13.

İpşirli, Mehmet. "Esad Efendi, Salihzâde." *DİA*, 11 (1995): 345–46.

İşbilir, Ömer. "Dihkānîzâde Ubeydullah Kuşmânî." *DİA* 9 (1994): 290–91.

İslamoğlu, Huri. "Property as a Contested Domain: A Reevaluation of the Ottoman Land Code of 1858." In *New Perspectives on Property and Land in the Middle East*, ed. Roger Owen, 3–61. Cambridge, MA: Harvard Center for Middle Eastern Studies, 2000.

Itzkowitz, Norman. "Eighteenth-Century Ottoman Realities." *SI* 16 (1962): 73–94.

———. "Men and Ideas in the Eighteenth-Century Ottoman Empire." In *Studies in Eighteenth Century Islamic History*, ed. Thomas Naff and Roger Owen, 15–26. Carbondale: Southern Illinois University Press, 1977.

Ivanova, Svetlana. "*Varoş*: The Elites of the *Reaya* in the Towns of Rumeli, Seventeenth-Eighteenth Centuries." In *Provincial Elites in the Ottoman Empire*, ed. Antonis Anastasopoulos, 201–46. Rethymnon, Greece: Crete University Press, 2005.

———. "Widin." In *EI2*, http://referenceworks.brillonline.com/entries/encyclopaedia-of-islam-2/widin-SIM_7913 (accessed July 6, 2015).

Jamgocyan, Onnik. *Les banquiers des sultans: Juifs, Francs, Grecs et Arméniens de la haute finance: Constantinople, 1650–1850*. Paris: Bosphore, 2013.

Jasanoff, Maya. "Revolutionary Exiles: The American Loyalist and French Émigré Diaspora." In *The Age of Revolutions in Global Context, c. 1760–1840*, ed. David Armitage and Sanjay Subrahmanyam, 37–58. New York: Palgrave Macmillan, 2010.

Jennings, Ronald C. "Kadi, Court, and Legal Procedure in 17th Century Ottoman Kayseri: The Kadi and the Legal System." *SI* 48 (1978): 133–72.

Joudah, Ahmad Hasan. *Revolt in Palestine in the Eighteenth Century: The Era of Shaykh Zahir al-'Umar*. Princeton, NJ: Kingston Press, 1987.

Kadı, İsmail Hakkı. *Ottoman and Dutch Merchants in the Eighteenth Century: Competition and Cooperation in Ankara, Izmir, and Amsterdam*. Leiden: Brill, 2012.

Kafadar, Cemal. "Yeniçeri-esnaf Relations: Solidarity and Conflict." MA thesis, McGill University, 1981.

———. "On the Purity and Corruption of the Janissaries." *Turkish Studies Association Bulletin* 15 (1991): 179–90.

———. "The Myth of the Golden Age: Ottoman Historical Consciousness in the

Post-Süleymanic Era." In *Süleymân the Second and His Time*, ed. Halil İnalcık and Cemal Kafadar, 47–58. Istanbul: Isis, 1993.

———. "Yeniçeriler." In *Dünden bugüne İstanbul ansiklopedisi*, 7: 472–76. Istanbul: Tarih Vakfı, 1993–95.

———. *Between Two Worlds: The Construction of the Ottoman State*. Berkeley: University of California Press, 1995.

———. "Osmanlı siyasal düşüncesinin kaynakları üzerine gözlemler." In *Modern Türkiye'de siyasî düşünce*, vol. 1: *Tanzimat ve Meşrutiyet'in birikimi*, ed. Mehmet Alkan, 23–37. Istanbul: İletişim, 2001.

———. "Janissaries and Other Riffraff of Ottoman Istanbul: Rebels Without a Cause?" In *Identity and Identity Formation in the Ottoman World: A Volume of Essays in Honor of Norman Itzkowitz*, ed. Baki Tezcan and Karl K. Barbir, 114–33. Madison: University of Wisconsin Press, 2007.

Kafadar, Cemal, and Hakan T. Karateke. "Late Ottoman and Early Republican Turkish Historical Writing." In *The Oxford History of Historical Writing*, ed. Stuart Macintyre, Juan Maiguashca, and Attila Pók, 4: 559–77. Oxford: Oxford University Press, 2012.

Kamberović, Husnija. *Husein-kapetan Gradaščević (1802–1834): Biografija: uz Dvjestotu Godišnjicu Rođenja*. Gradačac, Bosnia and Herzegovina: BZK Preporod, 2002.

Kaminsky, Howard. "Estate, Nobility, and the Exhibition of Estate in the Later Middle Ages." *Speculum* 68, no. 3 (July 1993): 638–709.

Karaca, Ali. *Anadolu ıslahatı ve Ahmet Şakir Paşa (1838–1899)*. Istanbul: Eren, 1993.

Karagöz, Mehmet. *XVII. ve XVIII. asırlarda Malatya*. Malatya, Turkey: Karizma Yayınları, 2003.

Karagöz, Rıza. *Canikli Ali Paşa*. Ankara: Türk Tarih Kurumu Basımevi, 2003.

———. *Karadeniz'de bir Hanedan Kurucusu: Haznedarzade Süleyman Paşa*. Samsun, Turkey: Etüt Yayınları, 2009.

Karakaya-Stump, Ayfer. "Subjects of the Sultan, Discipline of the Shah: The Formation and Transformation of the Kizilbash/Alevi Communities in Ottoman Anatolia." Ph.D. diss., Harvard University, 2008.

Karal, Enver Ziya. *Fransa-Mısır ve Osmanlı İmparatorluğu, 1797–1802*. Istanbul, 1938.

———. *Halet Efendi'nin Paris büyük elçiliği, 1802–1806*. Istanbul: Maarif Basımevi, 1940.

———. "Osmanlı tarihine dair vesikalar." *B* 4 (1940): 14–15.

———. "Tanzimat'tan evvel garplılaşma hareketleri, 1718–1839." *Tanzimat* 1 (1940): 13–30.

———. "Ragıb Efendi'nin islahat layihası." *TV* 1, no. 5 (1941): 356–68.

———. *Osmanlı tarihi*, vol. 5: *Nizam-ı Cedid ve Tanzimat devirleri, 1789–1856*. Ankara: Türk Tarih Kurumu Basımevi, 1947.

Karaman, K. Kivanç, and Şevket Pamuk. "Ottoman State Finances in European Perspective, 1500–1914." *Journal of Economic History* 70, no. 3 (2010): 593–629.

Karataş, Mehmed. "18–19. Yüzyıllarda Osmanlı Devleti'nde Bazı Müsadere Uygulamaları." *OTAM* 19 (2006): 219–38.

Karataş, Yakup. *Bayezid sancağı ve idarecileri (1700–1914)*. Istanbul: Kitabevi, 2014.

Kardam, Ahmet. *Cizre-Bohtan beyi Bedirhan: direniş ve isyan yılları*. Ankara: Dipnot 2011.

Karışman, Selma. *Erzurumlu İbrahim Hakkı ve Adam Smith: 'marifet' ile 'zenginlik' arasında iki düşünce, iki dünya*. Istanbul: Ötüken, 2010.

Karkalos, Eleutherios. *Historia tēs polēs tōn Iōanninōn*. Athens: Dodone, 2005.

Karpat, Kemal H. "Land Regime, Social Structure, and Modernization in the Ottoman Empire." In *Beginnings of Modernization in the Middle East: The Nineteenth Century*, ed. William R. Polk and Richard L. Chambers, 69–90. Chicago: University of Chicago Press, 1968.

———. "Transformation of the Ottoman State, 1789–1908." *IJMES* 3 (1972): 243–81.

———. "Some Historical and Methodological Considerations Concerning Social Stratification in the Middle East." In *Commoners, Climbers and Notables*, ed. C. A. O. van Nieuwenhuijze, 83–101. Leiden: Brill, 1977.

———. *The Politicization of Islam: Reconstructing Identity, State, Faith, and Community in the Late Ottoman State*. Oxford: Oxford University Press, 2001.

Kasaba, Reşat. *The Ottoman Empire and the World Economy: The Nineteenth Century*. Albany: State University of New York Press, 1988.

Katardžiev, Ivan. *Serskata oblast (1780–1879): Ekonomski, politički, i kulturen pregled*. Skopje, Republic of Macedonia: Institut za natsionalna istorija, 1961.

Kayalı, Hasan. *Arabs and Young Turks: Ottomanism, Arabism, and Islamism in the Ottoman Empire, 1908–1918*. Berkeley: University of California Press, 1997.

Kayhan, Leyla. "Negotiating Matrimony: Marriage, Divorce, and Property Allocation Practices in Istanbul (1750–1840)." Ph.D. diss., Harvard University 2013.

Kaynar, Reşat. *Mustafa Reşit Paşa ve Tanzimat*. Ankara: Türk Tarih Kurumu, 1954.

Kazıcı, Ziya. *Osmanlı vergi sistemi*. Istanbul: Bilge, 2005.

Keenan, Brigid. *Damascus: Hidden Treasures of the Old City*. New York: Thames & Hudson, 2000.

Kendirici, Hasan. *Meclis-i Mebusan'dan Türkiye Büyük Millet Meclisi'ne: Kopuş ve Süreklilikler*. Istanbul: Kitap Yayınevi, 2009.

Khoury, Dina Rizk. "The Introduction of Commercial Agriculture in the Province of Mosul and Its Effects on the Peasantry 1750–1850." In *Landholding and Commercial Agriculture in the Middle East*, ed. Çağlar Keyder and Faruk Tabak, 155–71. Albany: State University of New York Press, 1991.

———. *State and Provincial Society in the Ottoman Empire: Mosul, 1540–1834*. Cambridge: Cambridge University Press, 1997.

———. "The Ottoman Centre Versus Provincial Power-Holders: An Analysis of the Historiography." In *The Cambridge History of Turkey*, vol. 3: *The Later Ottoman Empire, 1603–1838*, ed. Suraiya Faroqhi, 135–56. Cambridge: Cambridge University Press, 2006.

Khoury, Philip S. *Urban Notables and Arab Nationalism: The Politics of Damascus, 1860–1920*. Cambridge: Cambridge University Press, 1983.

————. "The Urban Notables Paradigm Revisited." *Revue du monde musulman et de la Méditerranée* 55–56, no. 1 (1990): 215–28.

Kiel, Machiel. "Little-known Ottoman Gravestones from Some Provincial Centres in the Balkans, Eğriboz/Chalkis, Niğbolu/Nikopol and Rusçuk/Russe." In *Cimetières et traditions funéraires dans le monde islamique*, ed. Jean-Louis Bacqué-Grammont and Aksel Tibet, 319–32. Ankara: Türk Tarih Kurumu Yayınları, 1996.

Kili, Suna, and A. Şeref Gözübüyük. *Türk Anayasa metinleri: tanzimattan bügüne kadar*. Ankara: Ajans-Türk Matbaası, 1957.

Kılıç, Orhan. *18. yüzyılın ilk yarısında Osmanlı devletinin idari taksimatı-eyalet ve sancak tevcihatı*. Elazığ, Turkey: Şark Pazarlama, 1997.

————. "XVII yüzyılın ilk yarısında Osmanlı devleti'nin eyalet ve sancak teşkilatlanması." In *Osmanlı*, ed. Güler Eren and Kemal Çiçek, Cem Oğuz, vol. 6: Teşkilât, 89–110. Ankara: Yeni Türkiye Yayınları, 1999.

Kılıç, Rüya. *Osmanlıda Seyyidler ve Şerifler*. Istanbul: Kitap, 2005.

Kırımlı, Hakan, and Nicole Kançal-Ferrari. *Kırım'daki Kırım Tatar (Türk-İslam) mimari eserleri*. Istanbul: T. C. Başbakanlık, Yurtdışı Türkler ve Akraba Topluluklar Başkanlığı, 2015.

Kırımlı, Hakan, and Ali Yaycıoğlu. "An Heir of Chinghis Khan in the Age of Revolutions." Work in progress.

Kitromilides, Paschalis. "The Enlightenment East and West: A Comparative Perspective on the Ideological Origins of the Balkan Political Traditions." *Canadian Review of Studies in Nationalism* 10, no. 1 (1983): 51–70.

————. *The Enlightenment as Social Criticism: Iosipos Moisiodax and Greek Culture in the Eighteenth Century*. Princeton, NJ: Princeton University Press, 1992.

————. *Enlightenment and Revolution: The Making of Modern Greece*. Cambridge, MA: Harvard University Press, 2013.

Klooster, Wim. *Revolutions in the Atlantic World: A Comparative History*. New York: New York University Press, 2009.

Koçu, Reşat Ekrem. *Türk giyim, kuşam ve süslenme sözlüğü*. Ankara: Başnur, 1967.

————. *Kabakçı Mustafa: bir serserinin romanlaştırılmış hayatı*. 1968. 2nd ed. Istanbul: Doğan, 2001.

Köker, H. Sıdkı. "Osmanlı İmparatorluğu'nda âyân teşkilatı." *Ülkü* 4, no. 42 (1950): 19–24.

Koller, Markus. *Bosnien an der Schwelle zur Neuzeit: Eine Kulturgeschichte der Gewalt (1747–1798)*. Munich: Oldenbourg, 2004.

Kolodziejczyk, Dariusz. "Khan, Caliph, Tsar and Emperor: The Multiple Identities of the Ottoman Sultan." In *Universal Empire: A Comparative Approach to Imperial Culture and Representation in Eurasian History*, ed. Peter Filiber Band and Dariusz Kolodziejczyk, 175–82. Cambridge: Cambridge University Press, 2012.

Konrad, Felix. "Coping with 'the Riff-Raff and Mob': Representations of Order and Disorder in the Patrona Halil Rebellion (1730)." *Die Welt des Islam* 54, nos. 3–4 (2014): 363–98.

Konstantios, Dimitris N. *The Kastro of Ioannina*. Athens: Ministry of Culture, Archaeological Receipts Fund, 1997. 2nd ed., 2000.

Kontogiorgis, Giorgios. *Oi ellinikes koinotites tis tourkokratias.* Athens: A. A. Libani, 1982.

Köprülü, M. Fuad. "Asım." *İA* 1 (1940): 665–73.

Kornrumpf, Hans Jürgen. "Zur Rolle des Osmanischen Meclis im Reformzeitalter." *Südost-Forschungen* 34 (1975): 241–46.

Köse, Osman. *1774 Küçük Kaynarca anlaşması: Oluşumu, tahlili, tatbiki.* Ankara: Türk Tarih Kurumu, 2006.

Koselleck, Reinhart. *Kritik und Krise: Eine Studie zur Pathogenese der bürgerlichen Welt.* Frankfurt am Main: Suhrkamp, 1989. Translated as *Critique and Crisis: Enlightenment and the Pathogenesis of Modern Society* (Cambridge, MA: MIT Press, 1988).

Kostantaras, Dean J. "Christian Elites of the Peloponnese and the Ottoman State, 1715–1821." *European History Quarterly* 43, no. 4 (October 2013): 628–56.

Koyuncu, Nuran. "Osmanlı devleti'nde tarrafların mültezimlere kefilliği." *İnönü Üniversitesi Hukuk Fakültesi dergisi* 5, no. 1 (2014): 295–326.

Kreševjaković, Hamidja. *Kapetanije u Bosni i Hercegovini.* Sarajevo: Narodna Štamparija, 1954.

Kubalı, Hüseyin Nail. *Türk esas teşkilat hukuku dersleri.* Istanbul: Siralar Matbaasi, 1960.

Kuban, Doğan. *Osmanlı Barok mimarisi hakkında bir deneme.* Istanbul: İstanbul Teknik Üniversitesi, 1954.

———. "Osmanlı mimarisinde Barok ve Rokoko." In *Türk ve İslam sanati üzerine denemeler,* 115–22. Istanbul: Arkeoloji ve Sanat, 1982.

———. "Tarih-i Cami-i şerif-i Nur-u Osmanî ve onsekizinci yüzyıl Osmanlı yapı tekniği üzerine gözlemler." In *Türk ve İslam sanati üzerine denemeler,* 123–40. Istanbul: Arkeoloji ve Sanat, 1982.

Küçük, Harun. "The Case for the Ottoman Enlightenment: Natural Philosophy and Cosmopolitanism in Eighteenth Century Istanbul." *Perspectives on Europe* 42, no. 2 (2012): 108–10.

———. "Natural Philosophy and Politics in the Eighteenth Century: Esad of Ioannina and Greek Aristotelianism at the Ottoman Court." *JOS* 41 (2013): 125–59.

Küçükömer, İdris. *Düzenin yabancılaşması.* Istanbul: Bağlam, 1969.

Kuhn, Philip A. *Rebellion and Its Enemies in Late Imperial China: Militarization and Social Structure, 1796–1864.* Cambridge, MA: Harvard University Press, 1980.

———. *Origins of the Modern Chinese State.* Stanford, CA: Stanford University Press, 2002.

Kunčević, Lovro, and Gábor Kármán, eds. *The European Tributary States of the Ottoman Empire in the Sixteenth and Seventeenth Centuries.* Leiden: Brill, 2013.

Kuneralp, Sinan. *Son dönem Osmanlı erkân ve ricali, 1839–1922: Prosopoprafik rehber.* 1999. 2nd ed. Istanbul: Isis, 2003.

Kunt, Metin. *Sancaktan eyalete, 1550–1650 arasında Osmanlı ümerası ve il idaresi.* Istanbul: Boğaziçi Üniversitesi Matbaası, 1978.

———. *The Sultan's Servants: The Transformation of Ottoman Provincial Government, 1550–1650.* New York: Columbia University Press, 1983.

―――. "Royal and Other Households." In *The Ottoman World*, ed. Christine Woodhead, 103–15. London: Routledge, 2012.

Kuran, Timur. *The Long Divergence: How Islamic Law Held Back the Middle East*. Princeton, NJ: Princeton University Press, 2011.

Kütükoğlu, Bekir. "Sultan II. Mahmud Devri Osmanlı Tarihçiliği." In *Sultan II. Mahmud ve reformları semineri, 28–30 haziran 1989, bildiriler*. Istanbul: İstanbul Üniversitesi Edebiyat Fakültesi, 1990.

Kütükoğlu, Mübahat. *İzmir tarihinden kesitler*. İzmir: İzmir Büyükşehir Belediyesi Kültür Yayını, 2000.

Kuyulu, İnci. *Kara Osman-oğlu ailesine ait mimari eserler*. Ankara: Kültür Bakanlığı, 1992.

Lambton, Ann K. S. "Persia: The Breakdown of Society." In *The Cambridge History of Islam*, vol. 1A, ed. P. M. Holt, Ann K. S. Lambton, and Bernard Lewis, 430–67. Cambridge: Cambridge University Press, 1970.

Legay, Marie-Laure. *Les états provinciaux dans la construction de l'état moderne aux XVIIe et XVIIIe siècles*. Geneva: Droz, 2001.

Levy, Avigdor. "The Ottoman Ulema and the Military Reforms of Sultan Mahmud II." *Asian and African Studies* 7 (1971): 13–39.

Lewis, Bernard. "The Impact of the French Revolution on Turkey: Some Notes on the Transmission of Ideas." *Cahiers d'histoire mondiale* 1 (1953): 105–25.

―――. "Some Reflections on the Decline of the Ottoman Empire." *SI* 9 (1958): 111–27.

―――. *The Emergence of Modern Turkey*. Oxford: Oxford University Press, 1961.

―――. *Istanbul and the Civilization of the Ottoman Empire*. Norman: University of Oklahoma Press, 1963.

―――. "Djānīkli Ḥādjdji ʿAlī Pasha." In *EI2*, http://referenceworks.brillonline.com/entries/encyclopaedia-of-islam-2/djanikli-hadjdji-ali-pasha-SIM_1994 (accessed July 6, 2015).

―――. "Mashwara." In *EI2*, http://referenceworks.brillonline.com/entries/encyclopaedia-of-islam-2/mashwara-SIM_5010 (accessed July 6, 2015).

Lewis, Bernard, et al. "Dustur." In *EI2*, http://referenceworks.brillonline.com/entries/encyclopaedia-of-islam-2/dustur-COM_0199 (accessed July 6, 2015).

Lieberman, Victor. "Transcending East-West Dichotomies: State and Culture Formation in Six Ostensibly Disparate Areas." *Modern Asian Studies*, special issue: *The Eurasian Context of the Early Modern History of Mainland South East Asia, 1400–1800* 31, no. 3 (July 1997): 463–546.

Lier, Thomas. *Haushalte und Haushaltspolitik in Bagdad, 1704–1831*. Würzburg: Ergon, 2004.

Longrigg, Stephen Hemsley. "Bābān." *EI2*, http://referenceworks.brillonline.com /entries/encyclopaedia-of-islam-2/baban-SIM_0981 (accessed on 16 August 2015).

Lurie, Yehoshua. *Acre, the Walled City: Jews Among the Arabs, Arabs Among the Jews*. Tel Aviv: Yaron Golan, 2000. In Hebrew.

Madariaga, Isabel de. "The Russian Nobility in the Seventeenth and Eighteenth Centuries." In *The European Nobilities in the Seventeenth and Eighteenth Cen-*

turies, vol. 2: *Eastern Europe*, ed. H. M. Scott, 223–73. New York: Palgrave Macmillan, 1995.

Maden, Fahri. *XVIII. yüzyılın sonlarında Kastamonu*. Istanbul: Roza Yayınevi, 2012.

Maier, Charles S. *Among Empires: American Ascendancy and Its Predecessors*. Cambridge, MA: Harvard University Press, 2006.

Mantran, Robert. *Histoire de l'Empire ottoman*. Paris: Fayard, 1989.

———. "Arpalık." In *EI2*, http://referenceworks.brillonline.com/entries/encyclo paedia-of-islam-2/arpalik-SIM_0731 (accessed July 6, 2015).

Marcus, Abraham. *The Middle East on the Eve of Modernity: Aleppo in the Eighteenth Century*. New York: Columbia University Press, 1989.

Mardin, Şerif. *The Genesis of Young Ottoman Thought: A Study in the Modernization of Turkish Political Ideas*. Princeton, NJ: Princeton University Press, 1962.

———. "Freedom in the Ottoman Perspective." In *State, Democracy, and the Military: Turkey in the 1980s*, ed. Metin Heper and Ahmet Evin, 23–35. New York: W. de Gruyter, 1988.

Marino, Brigitte. "Les constructions d'Isma'il Pacha al-'Azm à Damas (1137–1143 / 1725–1730)." In *Syria and Bilad al-Sham under Ottoman Rule: Essays in Honour of Abdul Karim Rafeq*, ed. Peter Sluglett and Stefan Weber, 241–68. Leiden: Brill, 2010.

Masters, Bruce. "Semi-autonomous forces in the Arab provinces." In *The Cambridge History of Turkey*: vol. 3, *The Later Ottoman Empire, 1603–1839*, ed. Suraiya Faroqhi, 186–206. Cambridge: Cambridge University Press, 2006.

Mathews, Annie-Christine Daskalakis. "A Room of 'Splendor and Generosity' from Ottoman Damascus." *Metropolitan Museum Journal* 32 (1997): 111–39.

Matuz, Joseph E. "Contributions to the Ottoman Institution of *iltizam*." *JOS* 11 (1991): 237–49.

McGowan, Bruce. *Economic Life in Ottoman Europe: Taxation, Trade, and the Struggle for Land, 1600–1800*. Cambridge: Cambridge University Press, 1981.

———. "Osmanlı avarız-nüzül teşekkülü." In *VIII Türk tarih kongresi*, 2: 1327–31. Ankara: Türk Tarih Kurumu Basımevi, 1981.

———. "The Study of Land and Agriculture in the Ottoman Provinces Within the Context of an Expanding World Economy in the 17th and 18th Centuries." *IJTS* 2, no. 1 (1981): 57–63.

———. "The Age of the *Ayans*." In *An Economic and Social History of the Ottoman Empire*, vol. 1, ed. Halil İnalcık and Donald Quataert, 658–72. Cambridge: Cambridge University Press, 1994.

McGrew, William W. *Land and Revolution in Modern Greece, 1800–1881: The Transition in the Tenure and Exploitation of Land from Ottoman Rule to Independence*. Kent, OH: Kent State University Press, 1985.

Meehan-Waters, Brenda. *Autocracy & Aristocracy: The Russian Service Elite of 1730*. New Brunswick, NJ: Rutgers University Press, 1982.

Meeker, Michael E. *A Nation of Empire: The Ottoman Legacy of Turkish Modernity*. Berkeley: University of California Press, 2002.

Meriwether, Margaret. "Urban Notables and Rural Resources in Aleppo, 1770–1830." *IJTS* 4 (1987): 55–73.

———. *The Kin Who Count: Family and Society in Ottoman Aleppo, 1770–1840.* Austin: University of Texas Press, 1999.

Mert, Özcan. *XVIII. ve XIX. yüzyıllarda Çapanoğulları.* Ankara: Kültür Bakanlığı, 1980.

———. "Âyân." *DİA* 4 (1991): 195–98.

———. "XVIII. ve XIX. yüzyıllarda Osmanlı İmparatorluğu'nda kocabaşı deyimi, seçimleri ve kocabaşılık iddiaları." In *Prof. Hakkı Dursun Yıldız armağanı,* 402–20. Ankara: Türk Tarih Kurumu Basımevi, 1995.

Midhad, Kemal. *Ayanlar devrinde Bolu.* Bolu, Turkey, 1334 [1915].

Mikhail, Alan. *Nature and Empire in Ottoman Egypt.* Cambridge: Cambridge University Press, 2011.

Mile, Logor. "Sur la caractère du pouvoir d'Ali Pacha de Tépélène." *Actes* 4 (1969): 145–99.

Miller, Anatolii Filippovich. "Abdullah Ramiz Pacha en exil." *Revue des études sud-est-européennes* (Bucharest) 2, nos. 3–4 (1946): 423–32.

———. *Mustapha Pacha Bairaktar.* Bucharest: Association internationale d'études du Sud-Est européen, 1975.

Minoglou, Ionna Pepelasis. "Ethnic Minority Groups in International Banking: Greek Diaspora Bankers of Constantinople and Ottoman State Finances, c. 1840–1881." *Financial History Review* 9 (2002): 125–46.

Minorsky, Vladimir. "Sulaymāniyya." In *EI2,* http://referenceworks.brillonline.com/entries/encyclopaedia-of-islam-2/sulaymaniyya-COM_1113 (accessed August 16, 2015).

Mitchell, Timothy. *Colonising Egypt.* Cambridge: Cambridge University Press, 1988.

Moalla, Asma. *The Regency of Tunis and the Ottoman Porte, 1777–1814: Army and Government of a North-African Ottoman Eyâlet at the End of the Eighteenth Century.* London: Routledge, 2004.

Moaz, Moshe. *Ottoman Reform in Syria and Palestine, 1840–1861.* Oxford: Oxford University Press, 1968.

Mordtmann, Johannes Heinrich, and Bernard Lewis. "Derebey." In *EI2,* http://referenceworks.brillonline.com/entries/encyclopaedia-of-islam-2/derebey-SIM_1798 (accessed July 6, 2015).

Morimoto, Kazuo. *Sayyids and Sharifs in Muslim Societies: The Living Links to the Prophet.* London: Routledge, 2012.

Mottahedeh, Roy. *Loyalty and Leadership in an Early Islamic Society.* Princeton, NJ: Princeton University Press, 1980.

Mouravieff, Boris. *L'alliance russo-turque au milieu des guerres napoléoniennes.* Neuchâtel: Éditions de la Baconnière, 1954.

Muço, Entela. *Yanya valisi Tepedelenli Ali Paşa ve emlakı.* Istanbul: Eser Kitap, 2010.

Mumcu, Ahmet. *Osmanlı devletinde siyaseten katl.* Ankara: n.p., 1963.

———. *Osmanlı devletinde rüşvet.* Ankara: Ankara Üniversitesi, Hukuk Fakültesi 1969.

———. *Divan-ı Hümayun.* 2nd ed. Ankara: Phoenix, 2007.

Mundy, Martha, and Richard Saumarez Smith. *Governing Property, Making the*

Modern State: Law, Administration and Production in Ottoman Syria. London: I. B. Tauris, 2007.

Murphey, Rhoads. *Ottoman Warfare, 1500–1700*. London: Routledge, 1999.

———. *Exploring Ottoman Sovereignty: Tradition, Image and Practice in the Ottoman Imperial Household, 1400–1800*. New York: Continuum, 2008.

Mutafčieva, Vera. "L'institution de l'*ayanlik* pendant les dernières décennies du XVIII siècle." *EB* 2–3 (1965): 233–47.

———. *Agrarian Relations in the Ottoman Empire in the 16th Century*. Boulder, CO: East European Monographs, 1988.

———. *L'anarchie dans les Balkans à la fin du XVIIIe siècle*. Istanbul: Isis, 2005.

Mutafčieva, Vera, and Strashimir Dimitrov. *Sur l'état du système des timars des XVII–XVIII ss*. Sofia: Éditions de l'Academie bulgare des sciences, 1968.

Myers, A. R. *Parliaments and Estates in Europe to 1789*. London: Thames & Hudson, 1975.

Myl'nikov, A. S. "Die slawischen Kulturen in den Beschreibungen ausländischer Beobachter im 18. und zu Beginn des 19. Jahrhunderts." In *Reisen und Reisebeschreibungen im 18. und 19. Jahrhundert als Quellen der Kulturbeziehungsforschung*, ed. B. I. Krasnobaev and Gert Robel, 143–64. Berlin: U. Camen, 1980.

Naff, Thomas. "Reform and the Conduct of Ottoman Diplomacy in the Reign of Selim III, 1789–1807." *Journal of the American Oriental Society* 83, no. 3 (1963): 295–315.

Nagata, Yuzo. *Some Documents on the Big Farms (Çiftliks) of the Notables in Western Anatolia*. Tokyo: Institute for the Study of Languages and Cultures of Asia and Africa, 1976.

———. *Materials on the Bosnian Notables*. Tokyo: Institute for the Study of Languages and Cultures of Asia and Africa, 1979.

———. "Notes on the Managerial System of a Big Farm (*Çiftlik*) in the Mid-18th Century Turkey." *Annals of the Japan Association for Middle East Studies* 2 (1987): 319–41.

———. "Greek Rebellion of 1770 in the Morea Peninsula: Some Remarks Through Turkish Historical Sources." In *Memoirs of the Research Department of the Toyo Bunko (The Oriental Library)*, 46. Tokyo: Toyo Bunko, 1988.

———. "Karaosmanoğulu Hacı Hüseyin Ağa'ya ait bir tereke defteri." In *IX. Türk Tarih Kongresi*, 2: 1052–65. Ankara: Türk Tarih Kurmu, 1988.

———. "The Role of Ayans in Regional Development During the Pre-Tanzimat Period in Turkey: A Case Study of the Karaosmanoğlu Family." In *Urbanism in Islam: The Proceedings of the International Conference on Urbanism in Islam, October 22–28, 1989*, 1: 161–99. Tokyo: Daisan-Shokan, 1989.

———. *Tarihte âyânlar: Karaosmanoğulları üzerinde bir inceleme*. Ankara: Türk Tarih Kurumu, 1997.

———. *Muhzinzade Mehmed Paşa ve âyânlık müessesesi. 1976*. Izmir: Akademi Kitabevi, 1999.

———. "*Ayan* in Anatolia and the Balkans During [the] Eighteenth and Nineteenth Centuries: A Case Study of the Karaosmanoğlu Family." In *Provincial Elites in the Ottoman Empire*, ed. Antonis Anastasopoulos, 269–94. Rethymnon, Greece: Crete University Press, 2005.

Nagata, Yuza, and Feridun Emecan. "Bir ayanın doğuşu: Karaosmanoğlu Hacı Mustafa Ağa'ya ait belgeler." *B* 25, no. 29 (2004): 1–72.

Necipoğlu, Gülru. *Architecture, Ceremonial, and Power: The Topkapi Palace in the Fifteenth and Sixteenth Centuries.* Cambridge, MA: MIT Press, 1991.

Neumann, Christoph K. *Das indirekte Argument: Ein Plädoyer für die Tanzīmāt vermittels der Historie: Die geschichtliche Bedeutung von Aḥmed Cevdet Paşas Tārīḫ.* Münster: Lit, 1994.

――――. "19uncu yüzyıla girerken Konya Mevlevî asitanesi ile devlet arasındaki ilişkiler." In *II. Milletlerarası Osmanlı devleti'nde Mevlevîhaneler kongresi* [= *Türkiyat araştırmaları dergisi* II, 2], 167–79. Konya, Turkey: Selçuk Üniversitesi, 1996.

――――. "Selanik'te onsekizinci yüzyılın sonunda mesârif-i vilayet defteri: Merkezi hükümet, taşra idaresi ve şehir yönetimi üçgeninde mali işlemler." *TED* 16 (1998): 69–97.

――――. *Araç tarih amaç Tanzimat: Tarih-i Cevdet'in siyasi anlamı.* Istanbul: Tarih Vakfı Yurt Yayınları, 1999.

――――. "Ottoman Provincial Towns from the Eighteenth to the Nineteenth Century: A Reassessment of Their Place in the Transformation of the Empire." In *The Empire in the City: Arab Provincial Capitals in the Late Ottoman Empire*, ed. Jens Hanssen, Thomas Philipp, and Stefan Weber, 131–44. Würzburg: Ergon, 2002.

――――. "Political and Diplomatic Developments." In *The Cambridge History of Turkey*, vol. 3: *The Later Ottoman Empire, 1603–1839*, ed. Suraiya Faroqhi, 44–63. Cambridge: Cambridge University Press, 2006.

――――. "Birey olmanın alameti olarak tüketim kalıpları: 18. Yüzyılda Osmanlı Meta Evreninden Örnekler." *Tarih ve Toplum* 8 (2009): 7–47.

――――. "Çapanoğulları." In *EI3*, http://referenceworks.brillonline.com/entries/encyclopaedia-of-islam-3/capanogullar-COM_24380 (accessed July 15, 2015).

Neumeier, Emily. "'There is a Çapanoğlu behind this': Transformation in Patronage, Architecture and Urbanism in the Ottoman Provinces, 1779–1804." Conference paper, Middle Eastern Studies Association of North America, 2013 Annual Meeting.

Nieuwenhuis, Tom. *Politics and Society in Early Modern Iraq: Mamlūk Pashas, Tribal Shayks and Local Rule Between 1802 and 1831.* The Hague: M. Nijhoff, 1982.

North, Douglass C., John Joseph Wallis, and Barry R. Weingast. *Violence and Social Orders: A Conceptual Framework for Interpreting Recorded Human History.* Cambridge: Cambridge Univeristy Press, 2009.

Nussbaum, Felicity, ed. *The Global Eighteenth Century.* Baltimore, MD: Johns Hopkins University Press, 2003.

Ocak, A. Yaşar. "Milli mücadele'de Çapanoğlu isyanı." *Türk Kültürü Araştırmaları* 6 (1973): 83–149.

Öğreten, Ahmet. *Nizâm-ı Cedîde dâir askerî lâyihalar.* Ankara: Türk Tarih Kurumu, 2014.

Öğün, T. "Müsadere; Osmanlılarda." *DİA* 32 (2006): 67–68.

Onar, Mustafa. "Kozanoğulları (Kozandağlılar)." In *III. uluslararası Çukurova kültürü bilgi şöleni* 541–42. Adana: T. C. Adana Valiliği-Çukrova Üniversitesi, 1999.

Onar, Siddik Sami. *İdare hukukunun umumi esasları.* Istanbul: I. Akgün, 1969.

Öksüz, Melek. *Onsekizinci yüzyılın ikinci yarısında Trabzon: Toplum-kültür-ekonomi.* Trabzon, Turkey: Serander, 2006.

Okumuş, Okumuş. "Benlizâde İzzet Mehmed Bey'in Sâkînâmesi." *Turkish Studies* 4, no. 2 (2009): 900–910.

Orhonlu, Cengiz. *Osmanlı İmparatorluğu'nda derbend teşkilâtı.* 2nd ed. rev. Istanbul: Eren, 1990.

Ortaylı, İlber. *Tanzimattan sonra mahalli idareler, 1840–1878.* Ankara: Sevinç Matbaası, 1974.

———. *Tanzimattan Cumhuriyete yerel yönetim geleneği.* Istanbul: Hil Yayın, 1985.

———. *Hukuk ve idare adamı olarak Osmanlı devletinde kadı.* Ankara: Turhan Kitabevi, 1994.

———. *İmparatorluğun en uzun yüzyılı.* Istanbul: Hil, 1995.

Osterhammel, Jürgen. *The Transformation of the World: A Global History of the Nineteenth Century.* Princeton, NJ: Princeton University Press, 2014.

Osterhammel, Jürgen, and Niels P. Petersson. *Globalization: A Short History.* Princeton, NJ: Princeton University Press, 2005.

Owen, Roger. "The Middle East in the Eighteenth Century—an 'Islamic' Society in Decline: A Critique of Gibb and Bowen's *Islamic Society and the West.*" *Review of Middle East Studies* 1 (1975): 101–12.

———, ed. *New Perspectives on Property and Land in the Middle East* Cambridge, MA: Harvard Center for Middle Eastern Studies, 2000.

Öz, Mehmet. "Kânûn-i Kadîm: Osmanlı gelenekçi söyleminin dayanağı mı, islahat girişimlerinin meşrulaştırma racı mı?" In *Nizam-ı Kadimden Nizam-ı Cedide: III.Selim ve dönemi,* ed. Seyfi Kenan, 59–78. Istanbul: İSAM, 2010.

———. *Kanun-ı Kadîmin peşinde: Osmanlı'da çözülme ve gelenekçi yorumcuları.* Istanbul: Dergâh, 2013.

Özçelik, Selçuk. "Sened-i İttifak." *İstanbul Üniversitesi Hukuk Fakültesi mecmuası* 224, no. 14 (1956): 1–12.

Özel, Oktay. "Avarız ve cizye defterleri." In *Osmanlı devleti'nda bilgi ve istatistik,* ed. Halil İnalcık and Şevket Pamuk, 35–50. Ankara: DİE, 2001.

———. "The Reign of Violence: The *Celalis,* c. 1550–1700." In *The Ottoman World,* ed. Christine Woodhead, 184–202. London: Routledge, 2012.

Özkaya, Yücel. "III. Selim devrinde Nizâm-ı Cedîd'in Anadolu'da karşılaştığı zorluklar." *TAD* 1, no. 1 (1963): 145–56.

———. "XVIII. yüzyılın ikinci yarısında Anadolu'da ayanlık iddeaları." *Ankara Üniversitesi Dil Tarih-Coğrafya Fakültesi dergisi* 24, nos. 3–4 (1969): 195–231.

———. "XVIII. yüzyılda mütesellimlik müessesesi." *Ankara Üniversitesi Dil Tarih-Coğrafya Fakültesi dergisi* 28, nos. 3–4 (1970): 368–85.

———. "XVIII. yüzyılın ikinci yarısında Anadolu'da yerli ailelerin Ayanlıkları ele geçirişleri ve Büyük Hanedanların Ortaya Çıkışı." *B* 168 (1978): 667–723.

———. "XVIII. yüzyılın sonlarında tımar ve zeametlerin düzeni konusunda alınan tedbirler ve sonuçları." *TD* 32 (1979): 219–54.

———. "Rumeli Ayanları hakkında bilgiler." In *VIII. Türk Tarih Kongresi,* 102–3. Ankara: Türk Tarih Kurumu Basımevi, 1981.

———. *Osmanlı İmparatorluğu'ndaderbend ve dağlı isyanları (1791–1808)*. Ankara: Dil ve Tarih-Coğrafya Fakültesi, 1983.

———. *XVIII. yüzyılda Osmanlı kurumları ve Osmanlı toplum yaşantısı*. Ankara: Kültür ve Turizm Bakanlığı, 1985.

———. "Anadolu'da Büyük Hanedanlıklar." *B* 127 (1992): 809–45.

———. *Osmanlı İmparatorluğu'nda ayanlık*. Ankara: Türk Tarih Kurumu Basımevi, 1994.

———. *XVIII. yüzyılda Osmanlı toplumu*. Istanbul: YKY, 2008.

Özoğlu, Hakan. *Kurdish Notables and the Ottoman State: Evolving Identities, Competing Loyalties, and Shifting Boundaries*. Albany: State University of New York Press, 2004.

Özvar, Erol. *Osmanlı maliyesinde malikâne uygulaması*. Istanbul: Kitabevi, 2003.

Palmer, Robert Roswell. *The Age of the Democratic Revolution: A Political History of Europe and America, 1760–1800*. 2 vols. Princeton, NJ: Princeton University Press, 1959–64.

Pamuk, Şevket. *A Monetary History of the Ottoman Empire*. Cambridge: Cambridge University Press, 2000.

Pantazopoulos, Nikolaos J. *Church and Law in the Balkan Peninsula During the Ottoman Rule*. Thessaloníki, Greece: Institute for Balkan Studies, 1967.

Panzac, Daniel. *La marine ottomane: De l'apogée à la chute de l'Empire (1572–1923)*. Paris: CNRS éd., 2009.

Papastamatiou, D. "Tax-Farming (*iltizam*) and Collective Fiscal Responsibility (*maktu*) in the Ottoman Southern Peloponnese in the Second Half of the Eighteenth Century." In *The Ottoman Empire, the Balkans, the Greek Lands: Toward a Social and Economic History: Studies in Honor of John C. Alexander*, ed. Elias Kolovos, Phokion Kotzagiorgis, and Sophia Laiou, 289–307. Istanbul: Isis, 2007.

Pappe, Ilan. *The Rise and Fall of a Palestinian Dynasty: The Husaynis, 1700–1948*. Berkeley: University of California Press, 2010.

Parker, Charles H. *Global Interactions in the Early Modern Age*. Cambridge: Cambridge University Press, 2010.

Paskaleva, Virginia. "Osmanlı Balkan eyaletlerinin Avrupa devletlerle ticaretleri Tarihine katkı (1700–1850)." *İstanbul Üniversitesi İktisat Fakültesi mecmuası* 27, no. 1–2 (1967): 48–59.

Peacock, Andrew C. S., ed. *The Frontiers of the Ottoman World*. New York: Oxford University Press, 2009.

Peirce, Leslie P. *The Imperial Harem: Women and Sovereignty in the Ottoman Empire*. New York: Oxford University Press, 1993.

Peters, Rudolph. *Crime and Punishment in Islamic Law: Theory and Practice from the Sixteenth to the Twenty-First Century*. Cambridge: Cambridge University Press, 2005.

Petersen, Andrew. *A Gazetteer of Buildings in Muslim Palestine: Part 1*. Oxford: Oxford University Press, 2001.

Petković, Bogoljub. "Mahmud Paša Bušatlija od 1787–1796." *Istoriski zapisi* 10, nos. 1–2 (1957): 211–42.

Pezzi, Massimiliano. *Aspettando la pace: Il Levante ottomano nei documenti diplomatici napoletani: 1806–1812*. Rossano, Italy: Studio Zeta, 1992.

Philipp, Thomas. *Acre: The Rise and Fall of a Palestinian City, 1730–1831.* New York: Columbia University Press, 2001.

Petmezas, Sokrates. "Christian Communities in Eighteenth- and Early Nineteenth-Century Ottoman Greece: Their Fiscal Functions." In *Parallels Meet: New Vistas of Religious Community and Empire in Ottoman Historiography,* ed. Molly Greene, 71–116. Princeton, NJ: Markus Wiener, 2003. Reprinted in *Minorities in the Ottoman Empire* (Princeton, NJ: Markus Wiener, 2005).

Philliou, Christine. "Communities on the Verge: Unraveling the Phanariot Ascendancy in Ottoman Governanace," *Comparative Studies in Society and History* 51 (2009): 151–81.

———. *Biography of an Empire: Governing Ottomans in an Age of Revolution.* Berkeley: University of California Press, 2011.

Piterberg, Gabriel. "The Formation of the Ottoman Egyptian Elite in the 18th Century." *IJMES* 22 (1990): 257–89.

———. *An Ottoman Tragedy: History and Historiography at Play.* Berkeley: University of California Press, 2003.

Plomer, William. *Ali the Lion: Ali of Tebeleni, Pasha of Jannina, 1741–1822.* London: Jonathan Cape, 1936.

Pocock, John G. A. *The Ancient Constitution and the Feudal Law: A Study of English Historical Thought in the Seventeenth Century.* Cambridge: Cambridge University Press, 1957.

Poggi, Gianfranco. *The Development of the Modern State: A Sociological Introduction.* Stanford, CA: Stanford University Press, 1978.

Pomeranz, Kenneth. *The Great Divergence: China, Europe, and the Making of the Modern World Economy.* Princeton, NJ: Princeton University Press, 2000.

———. "Their Own Path to Crisis? Social Change, State-Building and the Limits of Qing Expansion, c. 1770–1840." In *The Age of Revolutions in Global Context c. 1760–1840,* ed. David Armitage and Sanjay Subrahmanyam, 189–208. New York: Palgrave Macmillan, 2010.

Psalidas, Athanasios. *Historia tēs poliorkias tōn Iōanninōn, 1820–1822.* Athens: n.p., 1962.

Puryear, Vernon J. *Napoleon and the Dardanelles.* Berkeley: University of California Press, 1951.

Pylia, Martha. "Les notables moréotes, fin du XVIIIe début du XIXe siècle: Fonctions et comportements." PhD diss., Université de Paris I–Panthéon Sorbonne, 2001.

Rabbat, Nasser. "A Mosque and an Imperial Dream." Series on Muhammad Ali. *Al-Ahram Weekly,* August 18–24, 2005: 18.

Radushev, Evgeni. "Les dépenses locales dans l'empire Ottoman au XVIIIe siècle selon les données des registres de cadi de Ruse, Vidin et Sofia." *EB* 16 (1980): 74–94.

———. *Agrarnite institutsii v Osmanskata imperiia prez XVII–XVIII vek.* Sofia: Marin Drinov, 1995.

Rafeq, Abdul-Karim. *The Province of Damascus, 1723–1783.* Beirut: Khayats, 1966.

Ramazanoğlu, M. Gözde. "Nizam-ı Cedid'in kentsel ölçekteki simgesi: Üsküdar Selimiye yerleşim alanı." In *II. Üsküdar sempozyumu 12–14 Mart 2004 bildiriler*, 1: 69–73. Istanbul: Üsküdar Belediyesi, 2005.

———. "Selimiye as a Town of the Nizâm-ı Cedîd." In *III. Selim: İki asrın dönemecinde İstanbul = Istanbul at a Turning Point Between Two Centuries*, ed. Çoşkun Yılmaz, 123–40. Istanbul: İstanbul Avrupa Kültür Başkenti, 2010.

Ranke, Leopold von. *Hardenberg und die Geschichte des Preussischen Staates von 1793–1813*. Leipzig: Ducker & Humblot, 1879.

Reed, Howard Alexander. "The Destruction of the Janissaries by Mahmud II in June 1826." PhD diss., Princeton University, 1951.

Reilly, James A. "Elites, Notables and Social Networks of Eighteenth-Century Hama." In *Islamic Urbanism in Human History: Political Power and Social Networks*, ed. Tsugitaka Sato, 211–32. New York: Kegan Paul International, 1997.

Reychman, J. "Les échos de la révolution polonaise de 1794 dans les pays balkaniques." *Association internationale d'études du sud-est européen* 4 (1969): 441–47.

Reynolds, Michael A. *Shattering Empires: The Clash and Collapse of the Ottoman and Russian Empires, 1908–1918*. Cambridge: Cambridge University Press, 2011.

Reynolds, Susan. *Kingdoms and Communities in Western Europe, 900–133*. Oxford: Clarendon Press, 1984.

Roider, Karl A. *Austria's Eastern Question, 1700–1790*. Princeton, NJ: Princeton University Press, 1982.

Rose, John Holland. *The Indecisiveness of Modern War and Other Essays*. London: G. Bell, 1927.

Rosenberg, Hans. *Bureaucracy, Aristocracy, and Autocracy: The Prussian Experience, 1660–1815*. Cambridge, MA: Harvard University Press, 1966.

Rosenthal, Jean-Laurent, and Roy Bin Wong. *Before and Beyond Divergence: The Politics of Economic Change in China and Europe*. Cambridge, MA: Harvard University Press, 2011.

El-Rouayheb, Khaled. "Was There a Revival of Logical Studies in Eighteenth Century Egypt?" *Die Welt des Islams* 45, no. 1 (2005): 1–19

Rudé, George F. E. *The Crowd in History: A Study of Popular Disturbances in France and England, 1730–1848*. New York: Wiley, 1981.

Runciman, Steven. *The Great Church in Captivity*. Cambridge: Cambridge University Press, 1968.

Šabanov, F. Š. "Osmanlı İmparatorluğunda hükümdarlığın hukukî esasları." In *VI. Türk Tarih Kongresi: Ankara, 20–26 Ekim 1961*, 428–30. Ankara: Türk Tarih Kurumu Basımevi, 1967.

Sabev, Orlin. *İbrahim Müteferrika ya da ilk Osmanlı matbaa serüveni, 1726–1746: Yeniden Değerlendirme*. Istanbul: Yeditepe, 2006.

Sack, Dorothee. *Damaskus: Entwicklung und Struktur einer orientalisch-islamischen Stadt*. Mainz: Philipp von Zabern, 1989.

Sadat, Deena R. "Urban Notables in the Ottoman Empire: The Ayan." Ph.D. diss., Rutgers University, 1969.

———. "Rumeli ayanları: The Eighteenth Century." *Journal of Modern History* 44 (1972): 346–63.

———. "Ayan and Aga: The Transformation of the Bektashi Corps in the 18th century." *Muslim World* 63, no. 3 (1973): 206–19.

Şahin, Canay. "The Rise and Fall of an *Ayan* Family in Eighteenth-Century Anatolia: The Caniklizades (1737–1808)." PhD diss., Bilkent University, Ankara, 2003.

———. "The Economic Power of Anatolian *Ayans* in the late Eighteenth Century: The Case of the Caniklizades." *IJTS* 11, nos. 1–2 (2005): 29–48.

Şahin, Kaya. *Empire and Power in the Reign of Süleyman: Narrating the Sixteenth-Century Ottoman World.* Cambridge: Cambridge University Press, 2013.

Sajdi, Dana. *The Barber of Damascus: Nouveau Literacy in the Eighteenth-Century Ottoman Levant.* Stanford, CA: Stanford University Press, 2013.

Sajdi, Dana, ed. *Ottoman Tulips, Ottoman Coffee: Leisure and Lifestyle in the Eighteenth Century.* New York: Tauris Academic Studies, 2007.

Sakaoğlu, Necdet. *Anadolu derebeyi ocaklarından Köse Paşa Hanedanı.* Ankara: Yurt Yayınevi, 1984.

———. "Ayan Mehmed Ağa ve konağı." *TT* 15, no. 90 (1991): 23–29.

———. *Bir mülkün kadın sultanları: Vâlide sultanlar, hâtunlar, hasekiler, kadınefendiler, sultanefendiler.* Istanbul: Oğlak Yayınları, 2008.

Şakiroğlu, Mahmud. "Çukurova tarihinden sayfalar 1: Payas ayanı Küçük Ali Oğulları." *TAD* 15, no. 26 (1991): 103–39.

———. "Çukurova tarihinden sayfalar I: Payas ayanı Küçük Ali Oğulları." *Tarih araştırmaları dergisi* 15, no. 26 (1992): 103–41.

Şakul, Kahraman. "Ottoman Attempts to Control the Adriatic Frontier in the Napoleonic Wars." In *The Frontiers of the Ottoman World*, ed. Andrew C. S. Peacock, 253–71. New York: Oxford University Press, 2009.

———. "Adriyatik'te Yakobinler: Mehmed Şakir Efendi'nin '*Takrir-gûne*' Tahriri." *Kebikeç* 33 (2012): 231–50.

Salih, Ayhan. "Bilecik ayan ve voyvodası Kalyoncu Ali Ağa." Seminar essay no. 5,999, Department of History, Istanbul University, 1960.

Salih, Münir Paşa [Çorlulu]. *Louis XVI et le Sultan Selim III.* Reprinted from *Revue d'histoire diplomatique.* Paris: Plon-Nourrit, 1912

Salihlioğlu, Halil. "Emin." *DİA*, 11 (1995): 111–12.

Salzmann, Ariel. "An Ancien Régime Revisited: 'Privatization' and Political Economy in the Eighteenth-Century Ottoman Empire." *Politics & Society* 21, no. 4 (1993): 393–424.

———. "Citizens in Search of a State: The Limits of Political Participation in the Late Ottoman Empire." In *Extending Citizenship, Reconfiguring States*, ed. Michael Hanagan and Charles Tilly, 37–66. New York: Rowman & Littlefield, 1999.

———. "İmparatorluğu özelleştirmek: Osmanlı XVIII. yüzyılında paşalar ve ayanlar." In *Osmanlı*, vol. 3: *İktisat*, ed. Güler Eren, 132–39. Ankara: Yeni Türkiye, 1999.

———. "The Age of Tulips: Confluence and Conflict in Early Modern Consumer Culture (1500–1730)." In *Consumption Studies and the History of the Ottoman Empire*, ed. Donald Quataert, 83–106. Albany: State University of New York Press, 2000.

———. *Tocqueville in the Ottoman Empire: Rival Paths to the Modern State.* Leiden: Brill, 2004.

Sarıcaoğlu, Fikret. *Kendi kaleminden bir padişahın portresi: Sultan I. Abdülhamid (1774–1789).* Istanbul: Tatav, Tarih ve Tabiat Vakfı, 2001.

Sariyannis, Marinos. "Ruler and State, State and Society in Ottoman Political Thought." *Turkish Historical Review* 4 (2013): 92–126.

Saul, Norman E. *Russia and the Mediterranean, 1797–1807.* Chicago: University of Chicago Press, 1970.

Savcı, Bahri. "Osmanlı-Türk reformlarının (ıslahat hareketlerinin) bir batı demokrasisi doğurma çabaları." *Ankara Üniversitesi Siyasal Bilgiler Fakültesi Dergisi* 21, no. 1 (1966): 114.

———. "Batılı ilkeler altında demokratikleşme." *Ankara Üniversitesi Siyasal Bilgiler Fakültesi Dergisi* 29, nos. 1–2 (1974): 1–25.

Sayyid-Marsot, Afaf Lutfi. *Egypt in the Reign of Muhammad Ali.* Cambridge: Cambridge University Press, 1984.

Schatkowski-Schilcher, Linda. *Families in Politics: Damascene Factions and Estates of the 18th and 19th Centuries.* Wiesbaden: F. Steiner, 1985.

———. "Lore and Reality in Middle Eastern Patriarchy." *Die Welt des Islams,* n.s., 28, nos. 1–4 (1988): 496–512.

Schlechta-Wssehrd, Ottokar-Maria von. *Die Revolutionen in Constantinopel in den Jahren 1807 und 1808.* Vienna: Carl Gerold's Sohn, 1882.

Schmitt, Carl. *Constitutional Theory.* Translated by Jeffrey Seitzer. Durham, NC: Duke University Press, 2008.

Schur, Nathan. *A History of Acre.* Tel Aviv: Dvir, 1990. In Hebrew.

Scott, James C. *Seeing Like a State: How Certain Schemes to Improve the Human Condition Have Failed.* New Haven, CT: Yale University Press, 1998.

Şeker, Fatih M. *Osmanlılar ve Vehhâbîlik: Hüseyin Kâzım Kadri'nin Vehhâbîlik risâlesi.* Istanbul: Dergâh Yayınları, 2007.

Sel, Fatma Turhan. *The Ottoman Empire and the Bosnian Uprising: Janissaries, Modernisation and Rebellion in the Nineteenth Century.* London: I. B. Tauris, 2014.

Şen, Adil. *Osmanlı'da dönüm noktası, III. Selim hayatı ve ıslahatları.* Ankara: Fecr Yayınları, 2003.

Şener, Abdüllatif. *Tanzimat dönemi Osmanlı vergi sistemi.* Istanbul: İşaret, 1990.

Serbestoğlu, İbrahim. "Trabzon valisi Canikli Tayyar Mahmud Paşa Isyanı ve Caniklizadelerin sonu, 1805–1808." *Uluslararası Karadeniz incelemeleri dergisi* 1 (2006): 89–106.

Sezer, Hamiyet. "Tepedelenli Ali Paşa isyanı." PhD diss., Ankara University, 1995.

———. "Tepedelenli Ali Paşa'nin oğulları" *TAD* 28 (1995): 155–64.

———. "Tepedelenli Ali Paşa'nın çiftlikleri üzerine bir araştırma." *B* 62, no. 233 (1998): 75–105.

———. "Tepedelenli Ali Paşa ve oğullarının çiftlik ve gelirlerine ilişkin yeni bilgi-bulgular." *OTAM* 18 (2005): 333–57.

Shaw, Stanford J. "The Established Ottoman Army Corps under Sultan Selim III (1789–1807)." *Der Islam* 40 (1965): 142–84.

———. "The Origins of Ottoman Military Reform: The Nizam-ı Cedid Army of Sultan Selim III." *Journal of Modern History* 37 (1965): 291–306.

———. "The Nizam-i Cedid Army under Sultan Selim III, 1789–1807." *Oriens* 18 (1965–66): 168–84.

———. *Between Old and New: The Ottoman Empire under Sultan Selim III, 1789–1807.* Cambridge, MA: Harvard University Press, 1971.

———. "The Ottoman Empire and the Serbian Uprising, 1804–1807." In *The First Serbian Uprising, 1804–1813*, ed. Wayne S. Vucinich, 71–94. Boulder, CO: Social Science Monographs, 1982.

Shupp, Paul Frederic. *The European Powers and the Near Eastern Question, 1806–1807.* New York: Columbia University Press, 1931.

Schulze, Reinhardt. "Was ist die islamische Aufklärung?" *Die Welt des Islams* 36, no. 3 (1996): 276–325

Sigalas, Nikos. "Devlet et État: Du glissement sémantique d'un ancien concept du pouvoir au début du XVIIIe siècle ottoman." In *Byzantina et moderna: Mélanges en l'honneur d'Hélène Antoniadis-Bibicou*, ed. G. Grivaud and S. Petmezas, 385–415. Athens: Alexandreia, 2007.

———. "Des histoires des Sultans à l'histoire de l'État: Une enquête sur le temps du pouvoir ottoman (XVIe–XVIIIe siècles)." In *Les Ottomans et le temps*, ed. F. Georgeon and F. Hitzel, 99–127. Leiden: Brill, 2011.

Singer, Amy. *Palestinian Peasants and Ottoman Officials: Rural Administration Around Sixteenth-Century Jerusalem.* Cambridge: Cambridge University Press, 1994.

Sinoué, Gilbert. *Le dernier pharaon: Méhémet-Ali, 1770–1849.* Paris: Pygmalion, 1997.

Siruni, H. Dj. "Ramiz Pacha et son activité." *Studia et Acta Orientalia* 8 (1971): 103–24.

———. "Bairakdar Moustapha Pascha et Manouk Bey 'Prince de Moldavie.'" *Balcania* 6 (1989): 50–76.

Skerović, N. P. "'Pjesen': Crnogorska pobjeda nad Skadarskim pašom Mahmutom Bušatliom kao istoriski dokument." *Istoriski Časopis* 1, nos. 1–2 (1948): 167–80.

Skiotis, Dennis N. "From Bandit to Pasha: First Steps in the Rise to Power of Ali of Tepelen, 1750–1784." *IJMES* 2 (1971): 219–44.

Smail, Daniel Lord. *The Consumption of Justice: Emotions, Publicity, and Legal Culture in Marseille, 1264–1423.* Ithaca, NY: Cornell University Press, 2003.

Sohrabi, Nader. *Revolution and Constitutionalism in the Ottoman Empire and Iran.* New York: Cambridge University Press, 2011.

Sönmez, Erdem. "From 'Kanun-ı Kadim' (Ancient Law) to 'Umum-ı Kuvvet' (Force of the People): Historical Context of the Ottoman Constitutionalism." MS.

Sorel, Albert. *The Eastern Question in the Eighteenth Century: The Partition of Poland and the Treaty of Kainardji.* 1898. Reprint. New York: H. Fertig, 1969.

Sorkin, David. *The Religious Enlightenment: Protestants, Jews, and Catholics from London to Vienna.* Princeton, NJ: Princeton University Press, 2011.

Söylemez, Faruk. *Osmanlı devletinde aşiret yönetimi: Rişvan aşireti örneği.* Istanbul: Kitabevi, 2007.

Soysal, İsmail. *Fransız ihtilali ve Türk-Fransız diplomasi münasebetleri (1789–1802).* Ankara: Türk Tarih Kurumu Basımevi, 1964.

Stanislavskaia, M. A. *Russko-angliiskie otnosheniia i problemy Sredizemnomoria, 1798–1807.* Moscow: Izd. Akademii nauk SSSR, 1962.

Stavrianos, L. S. *The Balkans since 1453.* New York: Rinehart, 1958.

Subrahmanyam, Sanjay, and Christopher A. Bayly. "Portfolio Capitalist and the Political Economy of Early Modern India." *Indian Economy and Social History Review* 25, no. 4 (December 1988): 401–24.

Sućeska, Avdo. "Taksit: Prilog izučavanju dažbinskog sistema u našim zemljama pod turskom vlašću." *Year Book of the Faculty of Law in Sarajevo* 7 (1960): 339–62.

———. *Ajani: Prilog i zučavanju lokalne vlasti u našim zemljama za vrijeme turaka.* Sarajevo: Naučno društvo SR Bosne i Hercegovine, 1965.

———. "Bedeutung und Entwicklung des Begriffes A'yān im Osmanischen Reich." *Südostforschungen* 25 (1966): 3–21.

———. "Die Entwicklung der Besteuerung durch die Avariż-i dîvanîye und Tekalîf-i 'örfîye im Osmanischen Reich während des 17. und 18. Jh." *Südostforschungen* 27 (1968): 89–130.

———. "Malikane." *Prilozi za orijentalnu filologiju* 36 (1986): 197–229.

———. "Malikane (Lifelong Lease of Government Estates in the Ottoman State)." *Prilozi za orijentalnu filologiju* 36 (1987): 197–230.

———. "Osmanlı yönetimi altında Yugoslavya ulus ve halklarının tarihteki bazı ayırıcı nitelikleri." *X. Türk Tarih Kongresi,* 1: 1169–72. Ankara: Türk Tarih Kurumu, 1993.

Svoronos, Nicolas. *Le commerce de Salonique au XVIIIe siècle.* Paris: Presses universitaires de France, 1956.

Swann, Julian. "The French Nobility, 1715–1789." In *The European Nobilities in the Seventeenth and Eighteenth Centuries,* ed. H. M. Scott, vol. 1: *Western Europe,* 142–73. New York: Palgrave Macmillan, 1995.

———. *Provincial Power and Absolute Monarchy: The Estates General of Burgundy, 1661–1790.* Cambridge: Cambridge University Press, 2003.

Tabakoğlu, Ahmet. *Gerileme dönemine girerken Osmanlı maliyesi.* Istanbul: Dergâh, 1985.

Tamdoğan, Işık. "Le Nezir, ou les relations des bandits et des nomades avec l'état dans la Cukurova du XVIIIe siècle." In *Sociétés rurales ottomanes = Ottoman rural societies,* ed. Mohammad Afifi, 259–69. Cairo: Institut français d'archéologie orientale, 2005.

Tankut, Gönül. "Urban Transformation in the Eighteenth Century Ottoman City." [Middle East Technical University, Ankara] *M.E.T.Ü. Journal of the Faculty of Architecture* 1, no. 2 (1975): 247–62.

Tanör, Bülent. *Osmanlı-Türk anayasal gelişmeleri.* Istanbul: YKY, 1992.

———. *Türkiye'de kongre iktidarları, 1918–1920.* Istanbul: YKY, 1998.

Tanpınar, Ahmet Hamdi. *XIX. Asır Türk Edebiyatı tarihi.* 1949. Istanbul: YKY, 2006.

———. *Beş şehir* [Five Cities]. 6th ed. Istanbul: YKY, 2006.

Taş, Hülya. *Ankara'nın bütüncül tarihine katkı: XVII. yüzyılda Ankara.* Ankara:

Atatürk Kültür, Dil ve Tarih Yüksek Kurumu, Türk Tarih Kurumu Yayınları, 2006.

Tekindağ, Şehabeddin. "Cezzar'ın Mısır'daki hayatı hakkında bir araştırma." *TD* 26 (1972): 123–28.

Telci, Cahit. "Osmanlı devletinde 18. yüzyılda muhallefat ve müsadere süreci." *Tarih İncelemeleri dergisi* 22, no. 2 (December 2007): 145–66.

Tezcan, Baki. "The Politics of Early Modern Ottoman Historiography." In *The Early Modern Ottomans: Remapping the Empire*, ed. Virginia H. Aksan and Daniel Goffman, 167–98. Cambridge, 2007.

———. *The Second Ottoman Empire: Political and Social Transformation in the Early Modern World*. Cambridge: Cambridge University Press, 2010.

Theophilowa, Marie Jliewa. *Die Rebellion des Pascha Paswan-Oglou und ihre Bedeutung für die bulgarische Befreiungsbewegung im XIX. Jahrhundert: Ein Beitrag zur Vorgeschichte der bulgarischen Befreiungsbewegung*. Zurich: Leemann, 1913.

Thompson, E. P. *The Making of the English Working Class*. Harmondsworth, England: Penguin Books, 1972.

———. *Customs in Common*. New York: New Press, 1991.

Tilly, Charles, ed. *The Formation of National States in Western Europe*. Princeton, NJ: Princeton University Press, 1975.

———. "Parliamentarization of Popular Contention in Great Britain, 1758–1834." *Theory and Society* 26, nos. 2–3 (1997): 245–73.

Todorova, Maria N. *Balkan Family Structure and the European Pattern: Demographic Developments in Ottoman Bulgaria*. Washington, D.C.: American University Press, 1993.

[Tökin], İsmail Hüsrev. "Şark vilayetlerinde derebeylik." *Kadro* 11 (1932): 22–29.

———. "Türkiye'de derebeylik rejimi." *Kadro* 7 (1932); 8 (1932): 16–23.

———. "Türkiye'de toprak ağalığı (Türkiye'de derebeylik rejimi)." *Kadro* 9 (1932): 23–29.

Toledano, Ehud R. *State and Society in Mid-Nineteenth-Century Egypt*. Cambridge: Cambridge University Press, 1990.

Travers, Robert. *Ideology and Empire in Eighteenth-Century India: The British in Bengal*. Cambridge: Cambridge University Press, 2007.

———. "Imperial Revolutions and Global Repercussions: South Asia and the World, c. 1750–1850." In *The Age of Revolutions in Global Context, c. 1760–1840*, ed. David Armitage and Sanjay Subrahmanyam, 144–66. New York: Palgrave Macmillan, 2010.

Trivellato, Francesca. *The Familiarity of Strangers: The Sephardic Diaspora, Livorno, and Cross-Cultural Trade in the Early Modern Period*. New Haven, CT: Yale University Press, 2009.

Tucker, Ernest. *Nadir Shah's Quest for Legitimacy in Post-Safavid Iran*. Gainesville: University Press of Florida, 2006.

Tunaya, Zafer Tarık. *Türkiye'nin siyasi hayatında batılılaşma hareketleri*. Istanbul: Arba, 1996.

Uluçay, Çağatay. "Karaosmanoğullarına ait bazı düşünceler." In *III. Türk Tarih Kongresi*, 243–60. Ankara: Türk Tarih Kurumu, 1943.

———. "Karaosmanoğlullarına ait bazı vesikalar." *TV* 2, no. 9 (1942): 193–207; 2, no. 10 (1942): 300–308; 2, no. 12 (1943): 434–40; 3, no. 14 (1944): 117–26.

———. *XVII. asırda Saruhan'da eşkiyalık ve halk hareketleri.* Istanbul: Resimli Ay, 1944.

———. *Manisa ünlüleri.* Manisa, Turkey: Lise, 1946.

———. *18. ve 19. yüzyıllarda Saruhan'da eşkiyalık ve halk hareketleri.* Istanbul: Berksoy, 1955.

Ünal, Mehmet Ali. "Osmanlı İmparatorluğu'nda müsadere." *Türk dünyası araştırmaları dergisi* 49 (1987): 95–112.

Unat, Faik Reşit, and Bekir Sıtkı Baykal. *Osmanlı sefirleri ve sefaretnameleri.* 3rd ed. Ankara: Türk Tarih Kurumu Basımevi, 1992.

Urquhart, David. *Sultan Mahmoud and Mehemet Ali Pasha.* London: J. Ridgway, 1835.

Ursinus, Michael. "'*Avarız Hanesi*' und '*Tevzi Hanesi*' in der Lokalverwaltung des Kaza Manastır (Bitola) im 17. Jh." *Prizoli za orijentalnu filologiyu i istorija jugoslavenskih naroda po vladavinom* 30 (1980): 481–93.

———. *Regionale Reformen im Osmanischen Reich am Vorabend der Tanzimat: Reformen der rumelischen Provinzialgouverneure im Gerichtssprengel von Manastir (Bitola) zur Zeit der Herrschaft Sultan Mahmuds II. (1808–39).* Berlin: K. Schwarz, 1982.

———. "Zur Geschichte des Patrons: Patrocinium, *himaya* und der *'uhdecilik.*" *Die Welt des Islams* 13–14, nos. 1–4 (1984): 476–97.

———. "The Çiftlik Sahibleri of Manastır as a Local Elite, Late Seventeenth to Early Nineteenth Century." In *Provincial Elites in the Ottoman Empire,* ed. Antonis Anastasopoulos, 247–58. Rethymnon, Greece: Crete University Press, 2005.

———. *Grievance Administration (şikayet) in an Ottoman Province: The Kaymakam of Rumelia's 'Record Book of Complaints' of 1781–1783.* London: Routledge, 2005.

———. "The Transformation of the Ottoman Fiscal Regime, c. 1600–1800." In *The Ottoman World,* ed. Christine Woodhead, 423–35. London: Routledge, 2012.

Urvoy, Dominique. "Le monde musulman selon les idéaux de la Révolution française." *Revue du monde musulman et de la Méditerranée,* nos. 52–53: *Les Arabes, les Turcs et la Révolution française* (1989): 35–48.

Uzunçarşılı, İsmail Hakkı. "Sadrazam Halil Hamid Paşa." *TM* 5 (1935): 213–68.

———. "Halil Hamid Paşa." *TM* 5 (1936): 213–68.

———. "Vezir Hakkı Mehmed Paşa (1747–1811)." *TM* 6 (1936–39): 177–284.

———. "Arşiv vesikalarına göre Yedi Ada Cumhuriyeti." *B* 1 (1937): 627–39.

———. "Cezayirli Gazi Hasan Paşa'ya dair." *TM* 7–8 (1942): 17–40.

———. *Meşhur Rumeli âyânlarından Tirsinikli İsmail, Yıllıkoğlu Süleyman Ağalar ve Alemdar Mustafa Paşa.* Istanbul: Maarif Matbaası, 1942.

———. *Osmanlı devleti teşkilatından: Kapukulu ocakları.* 2 vols. Ankara: Türk Tarih Kurumu, 1943–44.

———. "Âyân." *İA,* 2 (1944): 40–43.

———. *Osmanlı Devletinin saray teşkilatı.* Ankara: Türk Tarih Kurumu, 1945.

———. *Osmanlı Devletinin merkez ve Bahriye teşkilatı.* Ankara: Türk Tarih Kurumu, 1948.

———. *Osmanlı Tarihi,* vol. 4: *Karlofça antlaşmasından XVIII. yüzyılın sonlarına kadar.* Ankara: Türk Tarih Kurumu, 1956.

———. "Nizâm-ı Cedid ricâlinden Vâlide Sultan kethüdası meşhur Yusuf Ağa ve Kethüdazâde Arif Efendi." *B* 20, no. 79 (1956): 485–524.

———. "Kabakçı vakasına dair bir mektub." *B* 29, no. 116 (1965): 253–61.

———. "Nizam-ı Cedid ricalinden Kadı Abdurrahman Paşa." *B* 35, no. 138 (1971): 245–303.

———. "Çapanoğulları." *B* 150 (1974): 215–61.

———. "Sultan III. Selim ve Koca Yusuf Paşa." *B* 39, no. 154 (1975): 233–56.

Vacalopoulos, Apostolos Evangelou. *History of Macedonia, 1354–1833.* Translated by Peter Megann. Thessaloníki, Greece: Institute for Balkan Studies, 1973.

Van Leeuwen, Richard. *Notables and Clergy in Mount Lebanon: The Khazin Sheikhs and the Maronite Church, 1736–1840.* Leiden: Brill, 1994.

Vandal, Albert. *Napoléon et Alexandre Ier: L'alliance russe sous le premier empire.* 3 vols. Paris: Plon, 1897–1918.

Veinstein, Gilles. "*Ayan* de la région d'Izmir et le commerce du Levant (deuxième moitié du XVIIIe siècle)." *Revue de l'occident musulman et de la Méditerranée* 20, no. 2 (1975): 131–47.

———. "Le patrimoine foncier de Panayote Benakis, kocabaşı de Kalamata." *JTS* 19 (1987): 211–33.

———. "Les provinces balkaniques (1606–1774)." In *Histoire de l'Empire ottoman,* ed. Robert Mantran, 287–315. Paris: Fayard, 1989.

———. "On the *Çiftlik* Debate." In *Landholding and Commercial Agriculture in the Middle East,* ed. Çağlar Keyder and Faruk Tabak, 35–53. Albany, NY: State University of New York Press, 1991.

———. "Inalcik's Views on the Ottoman Eighteenth Century and the Fiscal Problem." *Oriente moderno,* n.s., 18 (1999): 1–10.

Venturi, Franco. *The End of the Old Regime in Europe, 1768–1776.* Translated by R. Burr Litchfield. Princeton, NJ: Princeton University Press, 1989.

———. *The End of the Old Regime in Europe, 1776–1789.* Translated by R. Burr Litchfield. Princeton, NJ: Princeton University Press, 1991.

Veselá-Přenosilová, Zdenka. "Contribution à la question du combat du gouvernement ottoman contre Tepedelenli Ali Paşa." *Archiv Orientální* 31 (1963): 401–22.

———. "Quelques examples de la résignation (*ferağat*) de la solde et la pension dans l'Egypte ottomane vers le milieu du XVIIIe siècle." *Archiv Orientální* 35, no. 2 (1967): 183–96.

Wagner, Wenceslas. "Some Comments on Old 'Privileges' and the 'Liberum Veto.'" In *Constitution and Reform in Eighteenth-Century Poland,* ed. S. Fiszman, 65–85. Bloomington: Indiana University Press, 1997.

Wasserstein, David J., and Ami Ayalon, eds. *Mamluks and Ottomans: Studies in Honour of Michael Winter.* London: Routledge, 2006.

Whitcomb, Edward A. *Napoleon's Diplomatic Service.* Durham, NC: Duke University Press, 1979.

White, Joshua. "Shifting Winds: Piracy, Diplomacy, and Trade in the Ottoman

Mediterranean, 1624–1626." In *Well-Connected Domains: Towards an Entangled Ottoman History*, ed. Pascal Firges, Tobias Graf, Christian Roth, and Gülay Tulasoğlu, 37–53. Leiden: Brill, 2014.

White, Sam. *The Climate of Rebellion in the Early Modern Ottoman Empire.* New York: Cambridge University Press, 2011.

Wilkins, Charles L. *Forging Urban Solidarities: Ottoman Aleppo, 1640–1700.* Leiden: Brill, 2010.

Winter, Stefan. *The Shiites of Lebanon under Ottoman Rule, 1516–1788.* Cambridge: Cambridge University Press, 2010.

Wolf, John. *The Barbary Coast: Algeria under the Turks 1500 to 1830.* New York: Norton, 1979.

Woodhead, Christine. "Ottoman Languages." In *The Ottoman World*, ed. id., 143–58. London: Routledge, 2012.

———, ed. *The Ottoman World.* London: Routledge, 2012.

Woods, Gordon S. "The American Revolution." In *The Cambridge History of Eighteenth-Century Political Thought*, ed. M. Goldie and R. Wolker, 601–25. Cambridge: Cambridge University Press, 2006.

Woods, John E. *The Aqquyunlu: Clan, Confederation, Empire: A Study in 15th/9th Century Turko-Iranian Politics.* Minneapolis: Bibliotheca Islamica, 1976.

Yakschitch, Grégoire. "Notes sur Passvan-Oglu, 1759–1807, par l'adjudant-commandant Mériage." *Revue slave* 1 (1906): 261–79, 418–29; 2 (1906): 139–44, 436–88; 3 (1907): 138–44, 278–88.

———. *L'Europe et la résurrection de la Serbie, 1804–1883.* Paris: Hachette, 1907.

Yalçınkaya, Alaaddin. "Osmanlı Devleti'nin modernleşme sürecinde Avrupalıla'ın istihdam edilmesi (1774–1807)." In *Erken klasik dönemden XVIII yüzyıl sonuna kadar Osmanlılar ve Avrupa: Seyahat, karşılaşma ve etkileşim*, ed. Seyfi Kenan, 421–48. Istanbul: İSAM, 2010.

———. "III. Selim döneminde dış temsilciliklerin kurulması." In *Nizâm-ı Kadîmden Nizâm-ı Cedîde: III.Selim ve dönemi*, ed. Seyfi Kenan, 593–624. Istanbul: İSAM, 2010.

Yaman, Talat Mümtaz. "Osmanlı imparatorluğu teşkilatında mütesellimlik müessesesine dair." *Türk hukuk tarihi dergisi* 1 (1941): 75–105.

———. "Nizam-ı Cedîd'in lağvına dair bir vesika." *TV* 2, no. 12 (1943): 433.

Yaycıoğlu, Ali. "Sened-i İttifak (1808): Bir entegrasyon ve ortaklık denemesi." In *Nizâm-ı Kadîmden Nizâm-ı Cedîde: III.Selim ve dönemi*, ed. Seyfi Kenan, 667–709. Istanbul: İSAM, 2010.

———. "Provincial Elites and the Empire in the Late Ottoman World: Conflict or Partnership?" In *The Ottoman World*, ed. Christine Woodhead, 436–52. London: Routledge, 2012.

———. "Rahova 1784: 18. yüzyıl Osmanlı Balkanlarında katılım, bilgi ve güç." In *Özer Ergenç'e armağan*, ed. Ümit Ekin, 458–76. Istanbul: Bilge Kültür Sanat, 2013.

———. "*Révolutions de Constantinople*: The French and the Ottoman Worlds in the Age of Revolutions." In *French Mediterraneans: Transnational and Imperial Histories*, ed. Patricia M. E. Lorcin and Todd Shepard. Lincoln: University of Nebraska Press, forthcoming [2016].

———. "Space, Place and Territory in the Ottoman Empire." In *Ottoman Topologies: Production of Space in an Early Modern Empire*, eds. Cemal Kafadar and Ali Yaycıoğlu. Work in progress.

———. "Wealth, Power and Death: Capital Accumulations and Imperial Confiscations in the Ottoman Empire, 1450–1830." Work in progress.

Yazar, İlyas. "Ebû Beklir Kânî'nin (1712–1791) şiirinde İstanbul." *Uluslararası Sosyal Araştırmalar 3* 2, no. 6 (2009): 699–704.

Yediyıldız, Bahaeddin. *Institution du vaqf au XVIIIe siècle en Turquie: Étude socio-historique*. Ankara: Société d'histoire turque, 1975.

———. "Vakıf müessesesinin XVIII. asırda kültür üzerindeki etkileri." In *Social and Economic History of Turkey (1071–1920)*, ed. Osman Okyar and Halil İnalcık, 157–61. Ankara: Meteksan, 1980.

———. "Müessese-toplum çerçevesinde XVIII. asır Türk toplumu ve vakıf müessesesi." *VD* 15 (1982): 23–53.

———. "Vakıf müessesesinin XVIII. asır Türk toplumundaki rolü." *VD* 14 (1982): 1–27.

Yenişehirlioğlu, Filiz. "Architectural Patronage of Ayan Families in Anatolia." In *Provincial Elites in the Ottoman Empire*, ed. Antonis Anastasopoulos, 321–43. Rethymnon, Greece: Crete University Press, 2005.

Yeşil, Fatih. "İstanbul'un iaşesinde Nizâm-ı Cedid: Zahire Nezâreti'nin kuruluşu ve iş leyişi (1793–1839)." *Türklük araştırmaları* 15 (2004): 113–42.

———. "Looking at the French Revolution Through Ottoman Eyes: Ebûbekir Râtib Efendi's Observations." *Bulletin of the School of Oriental and African Studies* 70 (2007): 283–304.

———. "Nizam-Cedid'ten yeniçeriliğin kaldırılmasına kadar Osmanlı kara ordusunda değişim, 1793–1826." PhD diss., Hacettepe University, Ankara, 2009.

———. *Aydınlanma çağında bir Osmanlı Ebûbekir Râtib Efendi (1750–1799)*. Istanbul: Tarih Vakfı Yurt Yayınları, 2010.

———. "İstanbul önlerinde bir İngiliz filosu: Uluslararası bir krizin siyasi ve askeri anatomisi." In *Nizâm-ı Kadîmden Nizâm-ı Cedîde: III. Selim ve dönemi*, ed. Seyfi Kenan, 391–493. Istanbul: İSAM, 2010.

———. "III. Selim devri siyasî literatürüne bir katkı: Yeni bir lâyiha üzerine notlar." *B* 76 (2012): 75–146.

Yi, Eunjeong. *Guild Dynamics in Seventeenth-Century Istanbul: Fluidity and Leverage*. Leiden: Brill, 2004.

Yıldız, Aysel. "Vaka-yı Selimiyye, or the Selimiyye Incident: A Study of the May 1807 Rebellion." PhD diss., Sabancı University, Istanbul, 2008.

———. "Şehzadeye öğütler: Ebûbekir Râtıb Efendi'nin Şehzade Selim'e (III) bir mektubu." *Osmanlı araştırmaları / Journal of Ottoman Studies* 42 (2013): 233–74.

Yıldız, Gültekin. *Neferin adı yok: Zorunlu askerliğe geçiş sürecinde Osmanlı devleti'nde siyaset, ordu ve toplum, 1826–1839*. Istanbul: Kitabevi, 2009.

Yılmaz, Fikret. "Kara Osman-oğlu Ataullah Ağa'ya ait malların müsaderesi ve bir kira defteri." *Tarih İncelemeleri dergisi* 5 (1995): 239–52.

———. "Siyaset, isyan ve İstanbul, 1453–1808." In *İstanbul Tarihi Ansiklopesi*. Istanbul: İstanbul Büyükşehir Belediyesi, forthcoming.

Yılmaz, Gülay. "The Economic and Social Roles of Janissaries in a Seventeenth-

Century Ottoman City: The Case of Istanbul." PhD diss., McGill University, 2011.

———. "Blurred Boundaries Between Soldiers and Civilians: Artisan Janissaries in Seventeenth-Century Istanbul." In *Bread from the Lion's Mouth: Artisans Struggling for a Livelihood in Ottoman Cities*, ed. Suraiya Faroqhi, 175–93. New York: Berghahn, 2015.

Yılmaz, Hüseyin. "Osmanlı tarihçiliğinde Tanzimat öncesi siyaset düşüncesine yaklaşımlar." *Türkiye araştırmaları literatür dergisi* 1, no. 2 (2003): 231–98.

———. "The Sultan and the Sultanate: Envisioning Rulership in the Age of Süleymān the Lawgiver (1520–1566)." Ph.D. diss., Harvard University, 2005.

Yılmazçelik, İbrahim. *XIX. yüzyılın ilk yarısında Diyarbakır, 1790–1840: Fizikî, idarî, ve sosyo-ekonomik yapı*. Ankara: Türk Tarih Kurumu Basımevi, 1995.

Yosmaoğlu, İpek. *Blood Ties: Religion, Violence, and the Politics of Nationhood in Ottoman Macedonia, 1878–1908*. Ithaca, NY: Cornell University Press, 2014.

Ypsilanti, Helene. "Die Fürsten Alexander und Konstantin Ypsilanti als Hospodaren der Moldau und Walachei (Mit Benützung des Familienarchivs Ypsilanti)." *Revue internationale des études balkaniques* 3 (1937–38): 225–28.

Zandi-Sayek, Sibel. *Ottoman Izmir: The Rise of a Cosmpolitan Port, 1840–1880*. Minneapolis: University of Minnesota Press, 2012.

Zarinebaf, Fariba. *Crime and Punishment in Istanbul, 1700–1800*. Berkeley: University of California Press, 2010.

Zeeden, Ernst Walter. *Hardenberg und der Gedanke einer Volksvertretung in Preussen, 1807–1812*. Vaduz, Liechtenstein: Kraus, 1965.

Zens, Robert. "Pasvanoğlu Osman Paşa and the Paşalık of Belgrade, 1791–1807." *IJTS* 8, nos. 1–2 (2002): 89–104.

———. "The *ayanlık* and Pazvantoğlu Osman Paşa of Vidin in the Age of Ottoman Social Change, 1791–1815." PhD diss., University of Wisconsin, 2004.

Zilfi, Madeline C. "Elite Circulation in the Ottoman Empire: Great Mollas of the Eighteenth Century." *Journal of the Economic and Social History of the Orient* 26, no. 3 (1983): 318–64.

———. *The Politics of Piety: The Ottoman Ulema in the Postclassical Age (1600–1800)*. Minneapolis: Biblioteca Islamica, 1988.

———. *Women and Slavery in the Late Ottoman Empire*. Cambridge: Cambridge University Press, 2010.

Zinkeisen, J. W. *Geschichte des Osmanischen Reiches in Europa*. 7 vols. Hamburg: F. Perthes, 1859–63.

Žižek, Slavoj. *For They Know Not What They Do: Enjoyment as a Political Factor*. London: Verso, 1991.

Zürcher, Erik J. *Turkey: A Modern History*. London: I. B. Tauris, 1993.

———. *The Young Turk Legacy and Nation Building: From the Ottoman Empire to Atatürk's Turkey*. London: I. B. Tauris, 2010.

Notes

PREFACE

1. Pamuk, *Monetary History*, 191.

INTRODUCTION

1. Pioneering writings on the period that set the paradigm until recently include Lewis, *Emergence of Modern Turkey*, 75–127; Shaw, *Old and New*, 71–211; Berkes, *Developments of Secularism in Turkey*, 72–89; Karal, *Osmanlı tarihi*, 5; and Akçura, *Osmanlı devleti'nin dağılma devri*, 1–57. For two earlier studies, see Iorga, *Geschichte des Osmanischen Reiches*, 5, and Zinkeisen, *Geschichte des Staaten*, vols. 6 and 7.

2. Palmer, *Age of the Democratic Revolution*.

3. See, e.g., Lewis, "Impact of the French Revolution on Turkey."

4. Lewis, *Emergence of Modern Turkey*, 129–72. For a new synthetic history of the Ottoman Empire in the nineteenth century, see Hanioğlu, *Brief History*.

5. For a recent study of the Young Turk Revolution of 1908 and the Iranian Constitutional Revolution of 1906, see Sohrabi, *Revolution and Constitutionalism*. On historiographies of revolutions, see Haynes and Wolfreys, eds., *History and Revolution*.

6. Baker, "Revolution 1.0"; Armitage, *Declaration of Independence*.

7. Venturi, *End of the Old Regime in Europe, 1768–1776*, 3–72.

8. Armitage and Subrahmanyam, eds., *Age of Revolutions in Global Context*; Desan, Hunt, and Nelson, eds., *French Revolution in Global Perspective*; Osterhammel, *Transformation of the World*.

9. Bayly, *Birth of the Modern World*, 86–120.

10. Ibid., 23–120; Bayly, "Age of Revolutions in Global Context"; Osterhammel and Petersson, *Globalization*, 57–81; Parker, *Global Interactions*; Liberman, "Transcending East-West Dichotomies," 82–94; Armitage and Subrahmanyam, "Introduction: The Age of Revolutions"; Kooster, *Revolutions in the Atlantic World*, 158–73; Nussbaum, ed., *Global Eighteenth Century*; Hobsbawm, *Age of Revolution*, 7–26; Travers, "Imperial Revolutions and Global Repercussions"; Jasanoff, "Revolutionary Exiles"; Hunt, "French Revolution in Global Context";

Pomeranz, "Their Own Path to Crisis"; Pincus, *1688*, 2–47; DuRivage, *Revolution Against Empire*.

11. Pomerans, *Great Divergence*, 3–28; Rosenthal and Wong, *Before and Beyond Divergence*, 12–34; North, Wallis, and Weingast, *Violence and Social Orders*, 251–72; Acemoglu and Robinson, *Why Nations Fail*, 183–212; Fukuyama, *Origins of Political Order*, 290–302; Kuran, *Long Divergence*, 63–116, 279–302.

12. Adanır and Faroqhi, eds., *Ottomans and the Balkans*, 1–56.

13. Hourani, "Ottoman Reform and the Politics of Notables"; Gelvin, "'Politics of Notables' Forty Years After."

14. İnalcık, "Nature of Traditional Society"; id., "Military and Fiscal Transformation"; id., "Centralization and Decentralization."

15. Sućeska, *Ajani*.

16. Rafeq, *Province of Damascus*; Barbir, *Ottoman Rule in Damascus*; Schatkowski-Schilcher, *Families in Politics*; Cohen, *Palestine*; Philipp, *Acre*; Marcus, *Middle East on the Eve of Modernity*; Meriwether, *Kin Who Count*; Hathaway, *Politics of Households*; Akarlı, "Provincial Power Magnates."

17. For the most comprehensive studies of regional notables in Ottoman Anatolia, see Özkaya, *Osmanlı İmparatorluğu'nda ayanlık*; for case studies, see Sakaoğlu, *Anadolu derebeyi ocaklarından Köşe Paşa hanedanı*; Nagata, *Tarihte ayanlar*; Gökhan and Bal, *Osmanlı dönemi Maraş'ın idari tarihinde Dulkadirli ve Beyazidli idareciler*; Söylemez, *Osmanlı devletinde aşiret yönetimi*; Karataş, *Bayezid sancağı ve idarecileri*; Maden, *XVIII. yüzyılın sonlarında Kastamonu*; Rıza Karagöz, *Canikli Ali Paşa*; id., *Karadeniz'de bir Hanedan Kurucusu*; Yılmazçelik, *XIX. yüzyılın ilk yarısında Diyarbakır*; Bilgin, *Doğu Karadeniz'de bir derebeyi ailesi*; Öksüz *Onsekizinci yüzyılın ikinci yarısında Trabzon*.

18. Mutafčieva, *Anarchie dans les Balkans*; Sadat, "Rumeli ayanları"; id., "Ayan and Ağa"; Radushev, *Agrarnite institutsii v Osmanskata imperiia*; id., "Dépenses locales"; Gradeva, "Osman Pazvantoglu"; id., "War and Peace along the Danube"; Esmer, "Culture of Rebellion"; ead., "Economies of Violence"; Zens, "*Ayanlık* and Pazvantoğlu"; id., "Pasvanoğlu Osman Paşa"; Bakardjieva, "Between Anarchy and Creativity."

19. Kontogiorgis, *Koinoniki dynamiki*; Anastasopoulos, "Mixed Elite of a Balkan Town; id., "Lighting the Flame of Disorder"; Petmezas, "Christian Communities"; Papastamatiou, "Tax-Farming"; Kostantaras, "Christian Elites"; Pylia, "Notables moréotes."

20. Dina Rizk Khoury, *State and Provincial Society*; Doumani, *Rediscovering Palestine*; Fahmy, *All the Pasha's Men*; Mikhail, *Nature and Empire*. Aymes, *Un grand progrés—sur le papier*; id., *A Provincial History of the Ottoman Empire*.

21. Genç, "Osmanlı maliyesinde malikâne sistemi"; id., "Study of the Feasibility."

22. McGowan, *Economic Life in Ottoman Europe*, 121–69.

23. Cezar, *Osmanlı maliyesinde bunalım*; Özvar, *Osmanlı maliyesinde malikane uygulaması*.

24. Salzmann, "Ancien Régime Revisited."

25. Karaman and Pamuk, "Ottoman State Finances."

26. Itzkowitz, "Eighteenth-Century Ottoman Realties"; Abou-El-Haj, *Formation*.

27. Kafadar, "Janissaries and Other Riffraff "; Tezcan, *Second Ottoman Empire*.
28. Shaw, *Old and New*; Karal, *Osmanlı İmparatorluğu*, 5.
29. Berkes, *Development of Secularism in Turkey*, 23–89; Tanpınar, *XIX. asır Türk edebiyatı*, 61–69.
30. Mitchell, *Colonizing Egypt*; Fahmy, *All the Pasha's Men*, Yeşil, "Nizâm-ı Cedîd'ten yeniçeriliğin kaldırılışına."
31. Zilfi, *Politics of Piety*; Hamadeh, *City's Pleasures*.
32. Tezcan, *Second Ottoman Empire*, 191–244.
33. Barkey, *Empire of Difference*, 197–262.

CHAPTER 1: EMPIRE

1. Chapter epigraph:
   Lâyık olursa cihânda, taht ü şevket
   Eylemek mahz-ı safâdır bana nâsa hizmet
   Din-i İslam'a Hudâ ide i'ânet-hürmet
   Geh yıkılur-yapulur geh buna derler devrân.
   Yılmaz, *III. Selim (İlhâmî)*, 222–23.
2. Eren, *Selim III*.
3. Bianchi and Kieffer, *Dictionnaire*, 868; Steingass, *Comprehensive Persian-English Dictionary*, 449.
4. Halm, "Dawr."
5. On the changing meaning of the term "revolution" see Baker, *Inventing the French Revolution*, 204–7.
6. Shaw, *Between Old and New*, 3–67.
7. Fleischer, *Bureaucrat and Intellectual*, 154, 182.
8. Dilçin, "Şeyh Galib'in şiirlerinde III. Selim."
9. Woods, *Aqquyunlu*, 103–5; Donzel, "Mudjaddid"; Algar, "Naqshibandi Order," 142–51.
10. Gölpınarlı, *Mevlânâ'dan sonra Mevlevilik*, 148–74; Neumann, "19uncu yüzyıla girerken Konya Mevlevî asitanesi."
11. Uzunçarşılı, "Selim III'ün veliaht iken Fransa kralı Louis XVI ile Muhabereleri"; Salih Münir [Çorlulu], "Louis XVI et le Sultan Selim III"; Beydilli, "İshak Bey"; Yıldız, "Şehzadeye Öğütler."
12. "*Cümle dünya yıkılub, kurula bir gün mizân.*"
13. McGowan, "Age of the Ayans," 646.
14. Boyar and Fleet, *Social History of Ottoman Istanbul*; Lewis, *Istanbul*.
15. Woodhead, "Ottoman Languages," 143–50; Tezcan, "Ethnicity, Race, Religion and Social Class."
16. See, e.g., Woodhead, ed., *Ottoman World*. For a recent compilation on the Ottoman World in the seventeenth, eighteenth, and early nineteenth centuries, see Faroqhi, ed., *Cambridge History of Turkey*, 3; also see McGowan, "Age of the Ayans."
17. Birken, *Provinzen des Osmanischen Reiches*; Göyünç, "Osmanlı devleti'nde taşra teşkilatı"; Veinstein, "Provinces balkaniques"; Kármán and Kunčević, eds., *European Tributary States*.

18. Orhonlu, *Osmanlı İmparatorluğunda derbend teşkilâtı*, 129–37; Heywood, "Ottoman *Menzilhane* and *Ulak* System"; Halaçoğlu, *Osmanlılarda ulaşım ve haberleşme*.

19. İnalcık, ed., *Economic and Social History of the Ottoman Empire*, 1: 179–377; Greene, "Ottomans in the Mediterranean"; Panzac, *Marine ottomane*, 183–266.

20. On the Ottoman borderlands, see Peacock, ed., *Frontiers of the Ottoman World*. On piracy, see Göyünç, "Kapudan-ı Deryâ Küçük Hüseyin Paşa," 37–38; Greene, *Catholic Pirates and Greek Merchants*, 78–108; Joshua White, "Shifting Winds."

21. Maier, *Among Empires*, 24–45.

22. Barkey, *Empire of Difference*, 67–107; Murphey, *Exploring Ottoman Sovereignty*, 99–115; Peirce, *Imperial Harem*, 15–27; Kunt, "Royal and Other Households."

23. İnalcık, "Osmanlı Padişahı"; id. "Comments on 'Sultanism'"; Murphey, *Exploring Ottoman Sovereignty*; Kolodziejczyk, "Khan, Caliph, Tsar and Emperor."

24. Fleischer, *Bureaucrat and Intellectual*, 289–91.

25. Kafadar, "Osmanlı siyasal düşüncesinin kaynakları"; Peirce, *Imperial Harem*, 229–66; Tezcan, *Second Ottoman Empire*, 19–29; Yılmaz, "Osmanlı tarihçiliğinde Tanzimat öncesi siyaset düşüncesine yaklaşımlar."

26. Section epigraph: Özkaya, "Canikli Ali Paşa'nın risalesi 'Tedâbirü'l-gazavât,'" 154.

27. Kunt, *Sultan's Servants*, 31–94

28. Sariyannis, "Ruler and State"; Sigalas, "Devlet et État"; id., "Des histoires des Sultans."

29. On the Ottoman imperial elite, see Fleischer, *Bureaucrat and Intellectual*, 214–33; Şahin, *Empire and Power*, 15–19; Kunt, *Sultan's Servants*, 31–76; id., "Royal and Other Households"; Zilfi, *Politics of Piety*, 43–80; Philliou, *Biography*, 5–36; Findley, *Bureaucratic Reform*, 3–43; Yeşil, *Aydınlanma çağında bir Osmanlı*, 13–31

30. İnalcık, "Stedan Dušan'dan Osmanlı İmparatorluğuna."

31. Akdağ, *Celali isyanları*; White, *Climate of Rebellion*, 163–85; Özel, "Reign of Violence."

32. See pp. 76–95.

33. Kılıç, *Osmanlıda seyyidler ve şerifler*, 62–110; Canbakal, "On the 'Nobility' of Provincial Notables"; Kırımlı and Yaycıoğlu, "Heir of Chingis Khan."

34. İnalcık, *Ottoman Empire*, 65–103; id., "Comments on Sultanism"; Mumcu, *Osmanlı devleti'nde siyaseten katl*, 23–47, 49–65; Kunt, *Sultan's Servants*, 31–76. At the highest level, 44 of 188 grand viziers between 1453 and 1821 lost their lives at the sultan's order. The wealth of many more holders of offices and contracts was seized after their natural deaths or dismissal and exile. These conventions were not abolished entirely until the Tanzimat edict in 1839. See Yaycıoğlu, "Wealth, Power and Death."

35. Section epigraph: MK ŞS: Malatya 3, p. 39.

36. İnalcık, ed., *Economic and Social History of the Ottoman Empire*, 1: 103–

77; McGowan, "Age of the Ayans," 689–94; Adanır, "Ottoman Peasantries," 269–98.

37. Howard, "Ottoman Timar System"; Murphey, *Ottoman Warfare*, 36–43; Aksan, *Ottoman Wars*, 54–55; Ágoston, "Military Transformation in the Ottoman Empire and Russia."

38. Özkaya, "XVIII. yüzyılda mütesellimlik"; Yaman, "Osmanlı İmparatorluğu teşkilatında mütesellimlik"; İnalcık "Military and Fiscal Transformation"; Cezar, *Levendler*, 256–343.

39. İnalcık, ed., *Economic and Social History of the Ottoman Empire*, 1: 55–75; Çakır, *Osmanlı Mukataa Sistemi*, 31–60; Matuz, "Contributions to the Ottoman Institution of *iltizam*"; Cvetkova, "Otkupnata sistema (*iltizam*)."

40. Papademetriou, *Render unto the Sultan*, 107–37.

41. Cezar, *Osmanlı maliyesinde bunalım*, 34–74; Ağır, "Evolution of Grain Policy."

42. İnalcık, "Military and Fiscal Transformation"; Pamuk, *Monetary History*, 112–47; Karaman and Pamuk, "Ottoman State Finances," 598–603; Genç, "Osmanlı maliyesinde malikane sistemi"; Çızakça, *Comparative Evolution*, 135–77; Sućeska, "Malikane," 197–230; Özvar, *Osmanlı maliyesinde malikane uygulaması*; Ursinus, "Transformation"; Darling, "Public Finances."

43. İnalcık, "Emergence of Big Farms"; Veinstein, "On the Çiftlik Debate"; McGowan, *Economic Life in Ottoman Europe*, 121–70. For a classical Marxist interpretation of the *çiftlik* formation, see Gandev, "Apparition des rapports capitalistes," 207–13.

44. BOA: HAT 8301.

45. McGowan, "Age of the Ayans," 696–709; Genç, "17–19. yüzyıllarda sanayi ve ticaret merkezi olarak Tokat"; id., "XVIII. yüzyılda Osmanlı sanayii." For a private initiative to establish a broadcloth factory in Moldavia, see BOA: HAT 45539.

46. Kafadar, "Yeniçeri-Esnaf Relations"; id., "Janissaries and Other Riffraff"; id., "On the Purity and Corruption of the Janissaries"; Yılmaz, "Economic and Social Roles of the Janissaries," 175–242; Tezcan, *Second Ottoman Empire*, 191–226.

47. Uzunçarşılı, *Kapukulu ocakları*, 144–707; Kafadar, "Yeniçeriler"; Beydilli, *Yeniçeriler*, 7–68; Ágoston, "Firearms and Military Adaption." From the late sixteenth century on, the Ottoman Empire was engaged in long wars against the Hapsburgs on the western front (1578–1611, 1684–99) and Safavid Iran on the eastern front (1678–90, 1603–11). We should add to this the Celali revolts (1590s–1650s) and the conquest of Crete (1645–69).

48. According to an Ottoman bureaucrat, the number of janissaries throughout the empire totalled about 400,000 in the late eighteenth century. Raif, *Tableau des nouveaux règlements de l'Empire ottoman*, 16–17.

49. Kadić, *Tārīḫ-i Anvarī*, 126–30.

50. *Kavanin-i Yeniçeriyan*, 87.

51. Ibid., 82.

52. Janissary rebellions occurred in 1589, 1600, 1622, 1632, 1648, 1651, 1655, 1656, 1687, 1703, 1730, 1807, and 1808. See Kafadar, "Janissaries and Other Riffraff," 122–25; Abou-el-Haj, *1703 Rebellion*, 16–39; Aktepe, *Patrona*

Halil isyanı; Tezcan, *Second Ottoman Empire,* 115–53; Konrad "Coping with the Riffraff and the Mob"; Yılmaz, "Economic and Social Roles of the Janissaries," 135–70; Karahasanoğlu, *Politics and Governance.* For a recent analysis of the tradition of the urban rebellions, see Yılmaz, "Siyaset, isyan ve İstanbul."

53. Conventionally, Ottoman historians associated janissary revolts with violence committed by the corrupt, undisciplined janissary corps, often in alliance with reactionary forces. This approach, which coalesced in the political atmosphere after the destruction of the janissary corps in 1826, persisted until recently. But following Abou-el-Haj's and Cemal Kafadar's work on the social and economic roles of the janissaries and janissary revolts, historians have revisited the subject (see Abou-el-Haj, *1703 Rebellion;* Kafadar, "Janissaries and Other Riffraff", id., "*Yeniçeri-Esnaf* Relations"). Thorough analyses of janissary revolts illustrate that these were much more complex than merely violence committed by corrupt janissaries who were only after their own corporate interests against legitimate authorities. Each revolt had a complex socioeconomic and political context, and the janissaries often acted as part of or led larger coalitions of competing factions and unhappy or threatened segments of Ottoman society. Janissary revolts assumed a rather constitutional character, as seen in their discourses on rights and moral economies. Baki Tezcan in his *Second Ottoman Empire* (191–226) and Gabriel Piterberg in *Ottoman Tragedy* (163–84) argue that the janissary revolts in the seventeenth century, starting with the murder of Osman II in 1622, profoundly altered the empire's political and social formation, as well as the nature of the Ottoman state and political discourse. Still, some Ottoman historians argue that there is no basis for regarding janissary revolts as social protest. Recently, Kemal Beydilli, a prominent historian of the Ottoman eighteenth century, has argued that janissary revolts were in fact similar to the periodic coups of modern armies in Turkey and elsewhere with their group interest in mind (Beydilli, *Yeniçeriler,* 21).

54. Başaran, *Selim III,* 158.

55. On eighteenth-century urban life in the Ottoman Empire, see Sajdi, ed., *Ottoman Tulips, Ottoman Coffee;* Salzmann, "Age of Tulips."

56. Başaran, *Selim III,* 148–57; Sajdi, *Barber of Damascus,* 14–38; Sabev, *İlk Osmanlı matbaa serüveni,* 269–77; Ghobrial, *Whispers of Cities,* 67–86; Akın, "Existing Performances."

57. BOA: C D 5220.

58. "In every *kaza,* the kadis, the Muslim and Christian notables [ayans and *kocabaşı*], behaved like a republic [*cumhur*]," the observant intellectual Ottoman bureaucrat Penah Efendi complains (Berker, "Mora ihtilali tarihçesi veya Penah Efendi mecmuası, 1769," 318).

59. Eldem, *French Trade,* 203–26.

60. Gorceix, *Bonneval Pacha;* Tott, *Mémoires du baron de Tott;* Aksan, "Breaking the Spell of the Baron de Tott."

61. Coller, "East of Enlightenment."

62. Kitromilides, *Enlightenment and Revolution;* id. "Enlightenment East and West"; Hovannisian and Myers, eds., *Enlightenment and Diaspora.*

63. Sabev, *İbrahim Müteferrika;* Karışman, *Erzurumlu İbrahim Hakkı,* 466–525; Küçük, "Case for the Ottoman Enlightenment"; id., "Natural Philosophy and Politics in the Eighteenth Century"; Schulze, "Was ist die islamische

Aufklärung?"; el-Rouayheb, "Was There a Revival of Logical Studies in Eighteenth Century Egypt?"

64. Sorkin, *Religious Enlightenment*.

65. McGowan, *Economic Life in Ottoman Europe*, 1–44; id., "Age of the Ayans," 724–42; Eldem, *French Trade in Istanbul*, 13–34; Kadı, *Ottoman and Dutch Merchants*, 145–69; Paskaleva, "Osmanlı Balkan Eyaletlerinin Avrupa Devletlerle Ticaretleri Tarihine Katkı"; Doumani, *Rediscovering Palestine*, 95–103; Trivellato, *Familiarity of Strangers*, 102–31; Aslanian, *From the Indian Ocean to the Mediterranean*, 73–77; Chénier, "Révolutions," 331–72. For a rich collection of documents, inclding correspondance, decrees, and petitions between merchants of the Republic of Dubrovnik and the Ottoman authorities in Bosnia, see Miović, *Dubrovačka Republika*, 129–212.

66. Genç, "Économie ottomane," 177–96; id., 18. "Yüzyıda Osmanlı Sanayii"; Karaman and Pamuk, "Ottoman State Finances"; McGowan, "Age of the Ayans," 724–42. Recently, historians working on case studies on wealth accumulation, such as Ergene, Kaygun, Coşgel, and Canbakal, have been skeptical about the argument that there was general economic growth in the Ottoman world in the first part of the eighteenth century. Nevertheless, there is agreement that certain segments of Ottoman society accumulated noticeable wealth through various activities, including tax-farming and trade in the eighteenth century; see Ergene, Kaygun, and Coşgel "Temporal Analysis of Wealth"; Coşgel and Ergene, "Inequality of Wealth"; Canbakal, "Reflections on the Distribution of Wealth." On the tulip period, see Hamadeh, *City's Pleasures*; Grehan, *Everyday Life and Consumer Culture*, 94–155. On the new cities of the eighteenth century, see Aktuğ, *Nevşehir İbrahim Paşa Külliyesi*, 1–40; Faroqhi, "Newshehir"; Acun, *Bozok Sancağı*; Minorsky, "Sulaymāniyya"; Longrigg, "Bābān."

67. Aksan, *Ottoman Wars*, 129–258; Genç, "Économie ottomane," 177–96.

68. Cezar, *Osmanlı maliyesinde bunalım*, 73–76.

69. BOA: C ML 14979.

70. *Tarih-i Vasıf*, 2: 239.

71. BOA: C ML 27398.

72. BOA: C ML 23161; BOA: C S 6353.

73. Davison, *Essays*, 29–59; Köse, *1774 Küçük Kaynarca anlaşması*, 107–32.

74. Uzunçarşılı, "Cezayirli Gazi Hasan Paşa'ya dair"; Beydilli, "Halil Hamid Paşa."

75. Cezar, *Osmanlı maliyesinde bunalım*, 86–103; BOA: HAT 11379; Ahmed Vasıf Efendi, *Mehasinü'l-asar*, 190.

76. Cezar, *Osmanlı maliyesinde bunalım*, 79–105; id., "Osmanlı mali tarihinde 'esham'"; Genç, "Eshâm: İç Borçlanma"; Çizakça, *Comparative Evolution*, 180.

77. Akyıldız, "Osmanlı'da idari sorumluluğun paylaşımı"; Findley, "Madjlis-i Shūrā"; Mumcu, *Divan-ı humayun*; Erken, "Osmanlı Devleti'nde bir danışman organı."

78. Beydilli, "Küçük Kaynarca'dan Tanzimat'a," 31; *Tarih-i Cevdet*, 5: 122–25.

79. Shaw, *Between Old and New*, 72–74.

80. Öğreten, *Nizâm-ı Cedîd'e dâir askerî lâyihalar*, 104–9; Çağman, *Lâyihaları*, 12.

81. TSA, E 447.

82. Unat, *Osmanlı sefirleri ve sefaretnameleri*; Yalçınkaya, "III. Selim döneminde dış temsilciliklerin kurulması"; Yeşil, *Aydınlanma çağında bir Osmanlı Ebubekir Râtıb Efendi*, 205–365; Naff, "Reform and the Conduct of Ottoman Diplomacy."

83. Kafadar, "Myth of the Golden Age"; Öz, *Kanun-ı Kadîmin peşinde*, 63–108; id., "Kânûn-ı Kadîm." 65–76; Howard, "Ottoman Historiography"; Abou-el-Haj, *Formation*, 35–45; Fleischer, *Bureaucrat and Intellectual*, 101–3, 154, 182, 299–305.

84. Hamadeh, *City's Pleasures*, 236. For two important articles on political writing during the reign of Selim, see Beydilli, "Küçük Kaynarca'dan Tanzimat'a"; Aksan, "Ottoman Political Writing." Also see Artan, "Composite Universe," 754–57.

85. Karal, "Nizam-ı Cedid," 107.

86. Çağman, *Lâyihaları*, 32. For Hacı İbrahim Efendi, who was nicknamed Gizli Sıtma (Hidden Malaria) by the public owing to his draconian decisions as a fiscal bureaucrat, see Öğreten, *Nizâm-ı Cedîd'e*, 85–90.

87. Ibid., 8.

88. Ibid., 61, 77.

89. Ibid., 73.

90. Yeşil, *Aydınlanma çağında bir Osmanlı*, 275.

91. BOA, HAT 9783; Findley, "Writer and Subject"; Beydilli, "Ignatius Mouradgea d'Ohsson"; Ohsson, *Tableau général*.

92. Çağman, *Lâyihaları*, 49–50; Öğreten, *Nizâm-ı Cedîd'e dâir askerî lâyihalar*, 91–97; Uzunçarşılı, "Vezir Hakkı Mehmed Paşa."

93. Yeşil, *Aydınlanma çağında bir Osmanlı*, 189.

94. Özkaya, "Canikli Ali Paşa'nın risalesi," 159–60.

95. Çağman, *Lâyihaları*, 16–17.

96. Ermiş, *History of Ottoman Economic Thought*, 141.

97. Ibid., 81.

98. Behiç, "Sevânihü'l-levâyih," 61; Genç, "Osmanlı iktisadî dünya görüşünün ilkeri." For a through analysis on the ideas of Ottoman intellectuals over trade and monetary policy, see Ermiş, *History of Ottoman Economic Thought*, 140–57.

99. Çağman, *Lâyihaları*, 12.

100. Ibid., 39.

101. Ibid., 63.

102. Ibid., 61.

103. Berker, "Mora ihtilali tarihçesi veya Penah Efendi mecmuası," 473.

104. Çağman, *Lâyihaları*, 19–22.

105. Ibid., 53, 72, and 39.

106. Berker, "Mora ihtilali tarihçesi veya Penah Efendi mecmuası, 1769," 158.

107. Çağman, *Lâyihaları*, 16.

108. Başaran, *Selim III*, 218. Also see Akarlı, "*Maslaha*."

109. BOA: HAT 16130. I would like to thank Fatih Yeşil for providing me with Atıf's report. Also see Şakul, "Adriyatik'te Yakobinler," 237; Yeşil, "Looking at the French Revolution," 283–304; Yaycıoğlu, "*Révolutions*."

110. Behiç, "Sevânihü'l-levâyih," 51–58.

111. *Nizâm-ı Cedîd kanunları*, Koç and Yeşil, eds.

112. Shaw, *Between Old and New*, 132.

113. BOA: C A 1985.

114. BOA: C ZB 4148.

115. For a comprehensive analysis of the drills of the New Army, see Yeşil, "Nizam- Cedid'ten yeniçeriliğin kaldırılmasına kadar," 35–87; also see Fahmy, *All the Pasha's Men*, 112–58.

116. Seyyid Mustafa, *Diatribe*, 20–21.

117. Yeşil, "Nizam- Cedid'ten yeniçeriliğin kaldırılmasına kadar," 82–84.

118. Ibid., 83.

119. *Nizâm-ı Cedîd kanunları*, Koç and Yeşil, eds., 96.

120. Beydilli, *Türk bilim ve matbaacılık tarihinde Mühendishâne*, 97–150; Hitzel, "Les écoles de mathématiques turques"; Yalçınkaya, "Osmanlı Devleti'nin modernleşme sürecinde Avrupalılar'ın istihdam edilmesi."

121. Juchereau de Saint-Denys, *Révolutions*, 2: 53–57.

122. Beydilli and Şahin, eds., *Mahmud Râif Efendi ve Nizam-ı Cedid'e dair eseri*, 159–245.

123. Seyyid Mustafa, *Diatribe*, 11.

124. Mitchell, *Colonising Egypt*, 34–62; Scott, *Seeing Like a State*, 9–86.

125. Ramazanoğlu, "Nizam-ı Cedid'in kentsel ölçekteki simgesi"; id., "Selimiye."

126. Bardakçı, ed., *Üçüncü Selim devrine ait bir bostancıbaşı defteri*, 1–64.

127. Zilfi, *Women and Slavery*, 82–85.

128. Artan, "Composite Universe," 775– 77; Hitzel, *Hadice Sultan ve Melling Kalfa*; *Voyage pittoresque de Constantinople . . . d'après les dessins de M. Melling*.

129. On the regulation (*niẓāmnāme*) of the new imperial Treasury, see BOA: C ML 23134 and BOA: KK 2380.

130. Initially, units worth 5,000 *ġuruş* were gradually transferred to the Treasury, but this was later raised to 10,000 *ġuruş* (Cezar, *Osmanlı maliyesinde bunalım*, 165–69).

131. Ibid., 180–85.

132. Ibid., 183.

133. Dimitrov, "Timars," 194–251.

134. Ibid., 48–49. For an interpretation of the document, see Barkan, "Timar," 299–333.

135. Shaw, *Between Old and New*, 86–98, 368–77; also see Uzunçarşılı, "Nizâm-i Cedîd ricalinden valide sultan kethüdasi meşhur Yusuf Ağa"; Göyünç, "Kapudan-ı deryâ Küçük Hüseyin Paşa"; Algar, "Political Aspects of Naqshibendi History," 137–39; Abu-Manneh, "Naqshibandiyya in the Early Nineteenth-Century"; id., "Naqshibandi-Mujaddidi and the Bektashi Orders," 18–21; Gölpınarlı, *Mevlâna'dan sonra Mevlevilik*, 250–51. For a detailed analysis of the policies and the elites of the New Order, see Danacı Yıldız, "Vaka-yı Selimiye," 109–201.

136. Shaw, *Between Old and New*, 37–72.

137. Şakul, "Ottoman Attempts to Control the Adriatic Frontier," 253–70; Saul, *Russia and the Mediterranean*, 65–101; Puryear, *Napoleon and the Dardanelles*, 23–40; Yaycıoğlu, "*Révolutions*."

138. See Koca Sekbanbaşı, *Koca Sekbanbaşı Risâlesi*; Wilkinson, *Account of the Principalities of Wallachia and Moldavia*, 7: 265–355; Beydilli, "Evreka, Evreka"; Birinci, "Koca Sekbanbaşı Risalesinin müellifi."

139. Koca Sekbanbaşı, *Koca Sekbanbaşı Risâlesi*, 35.

140. Ibid, 66–72.

141. Ibid., 76, 94–95.

142. İşbilir, "Dihkânîzâde Ubeydullah Kuşmânî," 290–91.

143. Danacı Yıldız, ed., *Asiler ve gaziler*, 16–17.

144. Kuşmânî, *Zebîre*, 27, 55, 68, 71.

145. Ibid., 25–28, 47, 64, 81.

146. Ibid., 33, 40–41.

147. Ibid., 74–75

148. Ibid., 73. For the qur'anic citation of Kuşmânî, see Qur'an 2/216.

149. Ibid., 33, 40, 65, 72–75

150. Karpat, *Politicization of Islam*, 68–116.

151. Foucault, *Discipline and Punish*, 168.

152. Mitchell, *Colonising Egypt*; Fahmy, *All the Pasha's Men*.

153. *Tarih-i Cevdet*, 8: 143.

154. Ebû Bekir Efendi, *Vaka-i cedid*, in Danacı Yıldız, ed., *Asiler ve gaziler*, 112.

CHAPTER 2: THE NOTABLES

1. Chapter epigraph: Berker, "Mora ihtilali tarihçesi veya Penah Efendi mecmuası," 473.

2. On the issue of clan names ending in -*oğlu* or -*zāde*, see p. 69.

3. BOA: HAT 42074.

4. Meriwether, *Kin Who Count*, 51; Findley, *Bureaucratic Reform*, 31–32; Zilfi, "Elite Circulation in the Ottoman Empire," 320; Schatkowski-Schilcher, "Lore and Reality in Middle Eastern Patriarchy," 497–98.

5. Doumani, ed., *Family History in the Middle East*; Todorova, *Balkan Family Structure*; Gerber, "Anthropology and Family History"; Duben, "Turkish Families and Households."

6. Hathaway, *Politics of Households in Ottoman Egypt*, 17–31; also see Lier, *Haushalte und Haushaltspolitik*, 32–64; Neumann, "18. yüzyılda Osmanlı meta evreninden örnekler," 38–44; Abou-El-Haj, "Ottoman Vezir and Paşa Households."

7. Necipoğlu, *Architecture, Ceremonial and Power*, 242–58.

8. Kırımlı and Kançal-Ferrari, *Kırım'daki Kırım Tatar (Türk-İslam) mimari eserleri*, 178–90.

9. Bingöl, *İshak Paşa Sarayı*; Karataş, *Bayezid sancağı ve idarecileri*, 23–40; Riza Karagöz, *Karadeniz'de bir Hanedan Kurucusu*, 137–42; Konstantios, *Kastro of Ioannina*; Marino, "Constructions d'Isma'il Pacha"; Keenan, *Damascus*, 144–55; Yenişehirlioğlu, "Architecture Patronage of Ayan Families"; Arel, "Aydın ve Yöresinde bir Ayan Ailesi."

10. Kinneir, *Journey*, 90–91.

11. Acun, *Bozok Sancağı (Yozgat İli)'nda Türk mimarisi*, 5–50; Duru, "Yozgat Çapanoğlu Camii ve vakfiyeleri," 71–89. Members of larger households who were not part of the central family but operated within the administrative body of the household at different levels also participated in the architectural vitalization

of the city and surrounding areas. Various members of the Çapanoğlu house-hold commissioned mosques and mansions in different neighborhoods of the city. Later, Armenian merchant families under the protection of the Çapanoğlu house built an Armenian church across from the family mosque. In the early nineteenth century, Yozgat was a city of the Çapanoğlus, not only as a center of a politi-cal enterprise, but also in its scenery; see Neumeier, "'There is a Çapanoğlu be-hind this.'" For an inventory and analysis of the architectural patronage of the Karaosmanoğlu family in western Anatolia, see Kuyulu, *Kara Osmanoğlu ailesine ait mimari eserler.*

12. Dupré, *Voyage à Athènes et à Constantinopole.*

13. For the vivid description of Ali Pasha's palace by John Cam Hobhouse, Lord. Broughton, during his visit to Ioannina with Byron, see Hobhouse, *Travels,* 49–50.

14. For various languages spoken and written in the Ottoman Empire, see Woodhead, "Ottoman Languages."

15. Yenişehirlioğlu, "Architectural Patronage."

16. For the register of the kadi documents related to the activities of the waqfs of İsmail of Ruse, see Orientalski Otdel kim Narodnata Biblioteka "Kiril i Metodii," Sofia (hereafter KM): R 11. Also see Radushev et al., eds., *Inventory of Ottoman Turkish Documents,* no. 471; Bakardjieva, "Between Anarchy and Creativity."

17. *Vekâyi'-i Baba Paşa,* 144–45.

18. *Takrir-i Mütesellim-i Cezzar Ahmed Paşa,* f. 2–3. For the construction ac-tivities of Jazzar Ahmad Pasha, see Dichter et al., *Akko,* 108–17, 216–19; Lurie, *Acre* (in Hebrew), 28–49; Petersen, *Gazetteer,* 73–76; Schur, *History of Acre* (in Hebrew), 207–16.

19. Yazar, ed., *Kânî dîvânı,* 404–5; id., "Ebû Beklir Kânî'nin," 702.

20. Duygu, *Yozgat tarihi ve Çapanoğulları,* 2–25.

21. Barbir, *Ottoman Rule in Damascus,* 67–88; Schatkowski-Schilcher, *Fami-lies in Politics,* 107–32; for the relationship between the urban literary culture and the notables, see Sajdi, *Barber of Damascus,* 77–114. On how the 'Azms and other families constituted a social network in Hama, see Reilly, "Elites."

22. Fahmy, *All the Pasha's Men,* 1–9; Güler, *Cezzar Ahmed Paşa,* 1–7; Lier, *Haushalte und Haushaltspolitik,* 32–64; Philliou, *Biography,* 5–40; Kırımlı and Yaycıoğlu, "Heir of Chinghis Khan"; Piterberg, "Formation of an Ottoman Egyp-tian Elite"; Hathaway, *Politics of Households,* 32–51.

23. Meriwether, *Kin Who Count,* 153–76.

24. Yediyıldız, *Institution du vaqf,* 35–54, 207–10; Doumani, "Endowing Family"; Duru, "Yozgat Çapanoğlu Camii ve Vakfiyeleri."

25. Doumani, *Rediscovering Palestine,* 61–68.

26. Özkaya, "XVIII. yüzyılın ikinci yarısında Anadolu'da yerli ailelerin ayanlıkları ele geçirişleri"; id., "Anadolu'da büyük hanedanlıklar"; *Şanizade tarihi,* 1: 74–75; Also see chapter 5 of this book.

27. Philliou, *Biography,* 58–60.

28. Emecen, "Osmanlı hanedanına alternatif arayışlar."

29. İnalcık, "Kırım Hanlığının Osmanlı tabiliğine girmesi"; id., "Power Rela-tionships," 195–202.

30. On titles such as steward of the chiefs of the Sublime Abode and chief of the

imperial stable, see BOA: HAT 53753 (1807); Pakalın, *Osmanlı tarih deyimleri ve terimleri sözlüğü*, 1: 426; 2: 542.

31. İnalcık, "Centralization and Decentralization," 40.

32. Morimoto, ed., *Sayyids and Sharifs*, 1–12; Kılıç, *Osmanlıda Seyyidler ve Şerifler*, 62–134; Canbakal, "On the 'Nobility' of Provincial Notables," 47–50.

33. Özkaya, "XVIII yüzyılın ikinci yarısına ait sosyal yaşantıyı ortaya koyan bir belge," 307.

34. On the Ottoman state's complex office and contract system, see Özkaya, *XVIII. yüzyılda Osmanlı toplumu*, 189–243.

35. See chapter 3 of this book.

36. Genç, "Osmanlı maliyesinde malikane sistemi"; Çızakça, *Comparative Evolution*, 135–177; Sućeska, "Malikane," 197–230; Özvar, *Osmanlı maliyesinde malikane uygulaması*, 19–27.

37. Özvar, *Osmanlı maliyesinde malikâne uygulaması*, 97–162.

38. Özkaya, "XVIII. yüzyılda mütesellimlik müessesesi," 386.

39. Özkaya, *XVIII. yüzyılda Osmanlı toplumu*, 204–5.

40. On the transformation of the governorship and provincial administration, see Kunt, *Sultan's Servants*; Göyünç, "Osmanlı devleti'nde taşra teşkilatı"; Kılıç, "XVII yüzyılın ilk yarısında Osmanlı devleti'nin eyalet ve sancak teşkilatlanması"; Halaçoğlu, *XIV–XVII. yüzyıllarda Osmanlılarda devlet teşkilatı ve sosyal yapı*, 83–87; Kılıç, *18. yüzyılın ilk yarısında Osmanlı devletinin idari taksimatı-eyalet ve sancak tevcihatı*; Özkaya, *XVIII. yüzyılda Osmanlı toplumu*, 189–204; Ursinus, *Grievance Administration*, 1–47; Georgieva, "Administrative Structure and Government of Rumelia."

41. Gökhan and Bal, *Dulkadirli ve Bayezidli idareciler*, 113–16; Karataş, *Bayezid sancağı ve idarecileri*, 17–49.

42. Clayer, "Ali Paşa Tepedelenli."

43. Güler, *Cezzar Ahmed Paşa*, 53–63.

44. Fahmy, *All the Pasha's Men*, 10–39.

45. Zens, "Pasvanoğlu Osman Paşa."

46. Akarlı, "Provincial Power Magnates."

47. Salzmann, "*Ancien Régime* Revisited."

48. Özkaya, "XVIII. Yüzyılın ikinci yarısında Anadolu'da yerli ailelerin ayanlıkları ele geçirişleri"; Erdoğan et al., *Rusçuk ayanı*, 35–62; Mert, *Çapanoğulları*, 17–45; Nagata, *Tarihte ayanlar*, 59–88; Fleming, *Muslim Bonaparte*, 36–55; Fahmy, *All the Pasha's Men*, 27–38.

49. Pakalın, *Osmanlı tarih deyimleri ve terimleri sözlüğü*, 2: 172–73.

50. For negotiation between Suleiman and the central government about the appointment of a Porte-steward for Süleyman Çapanoğlu, see BOA: HAT 53979.

51. For a note on Şevki Efendi, a former professor who became a Porte-steward in Istanbul, see BOA: HAT 51481 (1811).

52. For a case of revenue remittance by the Porte-stewards of Mehmed Ali of Egypt, see BOA: HAT 16270 (1808).

53. Şahin, "Rise and Fall of an Ayan Family," 85–93.

54. Jamgocyan, *Banquiers des sultans*, 33–144; Cezar, "Role of the sarrafs"; Koyuncu, "Osmanlı Devleti'nde Sarrafların Mültezimlere Kefilliği"; Şahin,

"Rise and Fall of an Ayan Family," 93–100. On the relations between money-men and landowners in the seventeenth century, see Gara, "Moneylenders and Landowners."

55. Siruni, "Bairakdar Moustapha Pacha et Manouk Bey."

56. On negotiations between Mustafa and the central government, see Uzunçarşılı, *Alemdar Mustafa Paşa*, 44–62.

57. BOA: HAT 2036 and 2036-A.

58. BOA: HAT 895, 966, and 1208. Also see Güler, *Cezar Ahmed Paşa*, 64–65.

59. BOA: C D 16590.

60. BOA: C A 7587.

61. Söylemez, *Osmanlı devletinde aşiret yönetimi*, 276–77; Sakaoğlu, *Anadolu derebey ocaklarından Kösa Paşa hanedanı*, 201–7; BOA: HAT 16700.

62. Mert, *XVIII. ve XIX yüzyıllarda Çapanoğulları*, 47–72; Uzunçarşılı, "Çapanoğlulları"; Duygu, *Yozgat tarihi ve Çapanoğulları*, 21–31; Neumann, "Çapanoğulları."

63. Mert, *XVIII. ve XIX yüzyıllarda Çapanoğulları*, 47–72.

64. Uzunçarşılı, "Nizam-ı Cedid ricalinden Kadı Abdurrahman Paşa," 245–302.

65. Dimitrov, "Timars," 33–56, 194–251.

66. BOA: HAT 11887.

67. BOA: HAT 2037.

68. BOA: C D 11831.

69. TSA: E8 465.

70. Menemencioğlu Ahmed Bey, *Menemencioğulları tarihi*, 18–36.

71. Mert, *XVIII. ve XIX Yüzyıllarda Çapanoğulları*, 47–72.

72. Fleming, *Muslim Bonaparte*, 36–69; Skiotis, "From Bandit to Pasha"; Muço, *Yanya Valisi Tepedelenli Ali Paşa ve emlakı*.

73. After changing hands many times following Ali Pasha's death fighting Otto-man troops in 1822, his collection ended up in the Gennadius Library in Athens. See Panagiotopoulos et al. eds., *Archeio Ali Pasa*.

74. Ibid., vol. 1, nos. 100 and 101.

75. Ibid., nos. 39 and 221.

76 Ibid., p. 37, no. 21. I would like to thank Antonis Hadjikyriacou for trans-lating this document.

77. BOA: C D 17018

78. Panagiotopoulos et al. eds., *Archeio Ali Pasa*, vol. 1, no. 9.

79. Ibid., nos. 131, 142.

80. Ibid., no. 149.

81. Ibid., nos. 192–96.

82. Ibid., no. 132.

83. BOA: HAT 52507-A

84. Panagiotopoulos et al. eds., *Archeio Ali Pasa*, vol. 1, no. 54.

85. Ibid., no. 29.

86. Ibid., nos. 27, 30, 180.

87. Uzunçarşılı, *Alemdar Mustafa Paşa*, 8–32; Erdoğan et al., *Rusçuk ayanı*, 35–62; Bakardjieva, "Between Anarchy and Creativity."

88. *Vekâyi'-i Baba Paşa*, 141.

89. BOA: HAT 2620. See BOA: A AMD 52/2 for a similiar case in which İsmail of Ruse was accused of installing his men as ayan in the surrounding towns without their having been elected.

90. BOA: HAT 3207.

91. BOA: HAT 2580.

92. Salzmann, *Tocqueville in the Ottoman Empire*, 123–75.

93. Söylemez, *Osmanlı devletinde aşiret yönetimi*, 52–104.

94. Özoğlu, *Kurdish Notables and the Ottoman State*, 43–68.

95. Pylia, "Notables moréotes"; Kostantaras, "Christian Elites," 631–39; Veinstein, "Patrimoine foncier de Panayote Benakis."

96. Winter, *Shiites of Lebanon under Ottoman Rule*, 117–45.

97. For a discussion on multifaceted spatial structures of different polities, see Brenner, *New State Spaces*, 27–68. Overlapping zone formations in the Ottoman world are discussed in Yaycıoğlu, "Space, Place and Territory" (work in progress).

98. In the summer of 1805, İsmail of Ruse was appointed purchasing officer (*mübaya'a me'mūru*) and was asked to buy wheat and barley for Istanbul from several districts in eastern Bulgaria (BOA: C B 6168). Around the same time, he received 25,000 *ğuruş* from Ahmed Şakir Efendi, the chief of the provisioning of Istanbul, to be used for purchases and for his services (BOA: C B 3915). Ali Pasha of Ioannina and Hüseyin of the Karaosmanoğlus acquired the contract for provisioning Istanbul in 1805 and 1806 (BOA: C B 2173; BOA C B 1824). In 1793, İbrahim Pasha, the governor of Niğde and Kayseri, was executed. The Çapanoğlus were asked to carry out the confiscation process and seize and register İbrahim's inheritance (BOA: C ADL 521). That year, when the intendant of Bayındır, Mehmed Karayılanoğlu died, the imperial Treasury asked Mehmed Karaosmanoğlu to administer the confiscation process. Kasaosmanoğlu supervised the sale of Karayılanoğlu's inheritance, which his family bought for 20,000 *ğuruş* (BOA: C ML 3108).

99. In 1795 and 1804, extensive inspections targeted agricultural units that had been assigned to members of the now-shrinking provincial cavalry units. According to the 1804 inspection, 3,575 such units were registered throughout the empire, but 2,047 appeared to be vacant, that is to say, their holders did not appear at inspections (Cezar, *Osmanlı maliyesinde bunalım ve değişim*, 183; Dimitrov, "Timars," 33–56, entire list at 48–49).

100. İnalcık, "Emergence of Big Farms," 24–34; Veinstein, "On the *Çiftlik* Debate," 47–53; Ergenç, "XVIII. yüzyılda Osmanlı Anadolu'sunda tarım üretiminde yeni boyutlar"; McGowan, *Economic Life in Ottoman Empire*, 121–69; Frangakis-Sytrett, "Trade of Cotton and Cloth"; Dina Rizk Khoury, "Introduction of Commercial Agriculture."

101. Cezar, "Role of the *sarraf*s."

102. Kinneir, *Journey*, 80–93. For trade routes in central Anatolia, see Faroqhi, *Towns and Townsmen of Ottoman Anatolia*, 56–57. On the Armenian merchants of Yozgat, see Darean and Erkanean, eds., *Patmagirk' Eozkati ew shrjakayits' (Gamirk') Hayots'*.

103. Vacalopoulos, *History of Macedonia*, 515–25; Beaujour, *Tableau du*

commerce de la Grèce, 1: 55–58; Katardžiev, *Serskata oblast;* Leake, *Travels,* 3: 202–10; Cousinéry, *Voyage,* 163–64.

104. Frangakis-Syrett, *Commerce in Smyrna,* 39–40, 116–18; Veinstein, "*Ayân* de la région d'Izmir"; Kadı, *Ottoman and Dutch Merchants,* 179–82.

105. Ionescu, *Manuc Bei,* 23–30; Bakardjieva, "Between Anarchy and Creativity."

106. Philipp, *Acre,* 94–134; Doumani, *Rediscovering Palestine,* 95–104.

107. See chapter 4.

108. BOA: HAT 1730 details negotiations between Mustafa/Manuk and the central state for the inheritance of late Ismail of Ruse; Siruni, "Bairakdar Moustafa Pacha et Manouk Bey," 54–86; Ionescu, *Manuc Bei,* 31–38.

109. Ionescu, *Manuc Bei,* 38–39. Also see note 108 above.

110. Bayrak-Ferlibaş, "Alemdar Mustafa Paşa'nın Muhallefatı," 85–94; BOA: MAD 9726.

111. Subrahmanyam and Bayly, "Portfolio Capitalist"; also see Travers, *Ideology and Empire,* 85–97.

112. Esmer, "Culture of Rebellion"; id., "Economies of Violence"; Koller, *Bosnien an der Schwelle,* 72–85; Mutafčieva, *Anarchie dans les Balkans;* Özkaya, *Osmanlı İmparatorluğunda dağlı isyanları;* Şeker, *Osmanlılar ve Vehâbîlik,* 196–223; Shaw, *Between Old and New,* 211–45, 283–326.

113. Shaw, "Nizam-ı Cedid Army."

114. The most significant example was Mehmed Ali of Egypt, who regularized and systematized the mass conscription of young Egyptian peasants into a new army in the 1820s, similarly to what Selim III tried but failed to achieve on an imperial scale between 1792 and 1807. See Fahmy, *All the Pasha's Men,* 76–111.

115. İnalcık, "Military and Fiscal Transformation"; Cezar, *Osmanlı tarihinde levendler,* 235–56.

116. According to a report prepared by French experts, Ismail of Ruse claimed to be able to assemble eighty thousand men from his region with the help of subordinate strongmen acting with him. AMAE: CP Turquie 212: 88 (dispatch from General Sébastiani concerning the developments in Ottoman Rumelia, August 25, 1806). See, too, Hurmuzaki, ed., *Documente,* suppl. 1, vol. 2, no. 483, pp. 348–49; Driault, *Études napoléoniennes: La politique orientale,* 37. In 1804, when a sizeable army, consisting of several Balkan magnates, was established to subdue brigands in eastern Bulgaria, most of the ayans and intendants (voyvodas) of Rumelia were asked to unite their forces under the leadership of Ismail of Serres. See BOA: C A 27990, which lists troops arriving in Sofia under the command of provincial leaders in January 1804. We must add to this list the enduring Mamluk system, or recruitment through networks that enslaved young men and marketed them as soldiers. Such mechanisms, though in decline, persisted in Egypt and Baghdad, through networks operating from Caucasia to some of the Arab provinces in the late eighteenth century.

117. Şahin, "Rise and Fall of an Ayan Family"; Riza Karagöz, *Canikli Ali Paşa,* 146–54.

118. BOA: C D 4372.

119. BOA: HAT 4051-D.

120. BOA: C ADL 3109.
121. BOA: C D 6092.
122. BOA: HAT 4048-G.
123. BOA: HAT 4048-İ.
124. BOA: HAT 4048-B, HAT 4079-B.
125. BOA: HAT 4072-E, HAT 4075.
126. BOA: HAT 4045-D.
127. BOA: HAT 53363, 53421.
128. BOA: HAT 53472.
129. BOA: HAT 53700.
130. Barkey, *Bandits and Bureaucrats*, 195–242. For a theoretical discussion on the relationship between law and rebellion in Islamic legal context, see Abou El Fadl, *Rebellion and Violence in Islamic Law*, 320–42.
131. Zens, "Pasvanoğlu Osman Paşa"; Gradeva, "Osman Pazvantoğlu of Vidin," Sadat, "Ayan and Aga"; Mutafčieva, *Anarchie dans les Balkans*, 127–249; Theophilowa, *Rebellion des Pascha Paswan-Oglou*; Yakschitch, "Notes sur Passvan Oglou."
132. BOA: HAT 12581-A.
133. Hurmuzaki, ed., *Documente*, suppl. 1, vol. 2, no. 264, p. 189.
134. HHStA, Türkei V, carton 23.
135. Sofroni, *Osmanlı'da bir Papaz*, 34–35.
136. BOA: HAT 12581-A.
137. Pouqueville, *Travels*, 234.
138. BOA: HAT 16147-C.
139. BOA: HAT 16147-B.
140. BOA: HAT 45557, 45558, 45559.
141. Zens, "*Ayanlık* and Pazvantoğlu."
142. The Gerays were the khans of Crimea. They accepted the suzerainty of the Ottomans in the fifteenth century, becoming semi-independent rulers of Crimea. After Catherine II annexed Crimea in 1782, most of the members of the family immigrated to the Ottoman Balkans, where they settled on estates (*çiftliks*) granted by the Ottoman central government. Discussed in Kırımlı and Yaycıoğlu, "Heir of Chinghis Khan."
143. Ibid.; *Spomenik II. Ispisi iz frantsuskikh arkhiva*, 121–22.
144. DeWeese, "Fusing Islam and Chinggisid Charisma."
145. BOA: HAT 6362.
146. BOA: HAT 47888.
147. During his long exile in Russia, Tayyar Mahmud Bey of Canik established relations with the Russian court and met Tsar Alexander I; he returned to the Ottoman empire with a request from Alexander to the sultan (BOA: HAT 53809, a memorandum submitted to Mustafa IV concerning Tayyar's meeting with the Russian emperor, ca. February 1807).
148. Fleming, *Muslim Bonaparte*, 70–178; Boppe, *Albanie et Napoléon*.
149. Hughes, *Travels*, 183.
150. Miller, *Mustapha Pacha Bairaktar*, 268–77.
151. Mumcu, *Osmanlı devleti'nde siyaseten katl*; Yaycıoğlu, "Wealth, Power and Death"; Karataş, "18–19. yüzyıllarda Osmanlı devleti'nde bazı müsadere

uygulamaları"; Ünal, "Osmanlı İmparatorluğu'nda müsadere"; Öğün, "Müsadere"; Esen, "İslam hukuku açısından müsadere"; Baysun, "Müsadere"; Telci, "Osmanlı devletinde 18. yüzyılda muhallefat ve müsadere süreci"; Cezar "Bir Ayanın Muhallefatı." Göçek, "Muṣādara"; Barbir, "One Marker of Ottomanism."; Fikret Yılmaz, "Kara Osman-oğlu Ataullah Ağa'ya."

152. BOA: C ML 6959.

153. Yaycıoğlu, "Wealth, Power and Death"; BOA: C ML 5068, C ADL 5445, C ML 6959, HAT 53309, C ADL 3041, and C ML 9301.

154. When Mehmed Pasha 'Azm died in 1784, Osman Agha, a confiscator sent by the center to Damascus, brought six hundred troops with him to handle possible resistance from the family or the people of Damascus. After the confiscation, Mehmed Pasha's heirs came to Istanbul to renegotiate the confiscation process and offered new deals to get back the inheritance. See Ahmed Vasıf Efendi, *Mehâsinü'l-âsâr ve hakāikü'l-ahbâr*, 43–44, 136–37.

155. When Halil Agha, the overseer of Yeni Zağra, a town in Ottoman Bulgaria, was executed in 1796, his property was confiscated by the state, but it was reported that his family had concealed his movable property, including a lot of gold, in the houses of his wives (BOA: C ML 3125).

156. In 1807, Ali Pasha of Ioannina asked the state to allow him to buy the inheritance of a certain Tahir Pasha. Ali had joined in the war against Russia, and he implied that this inheritance would help to finance his expenditures on it. Sultan Selim was advised to leave the inheritance to Ali Pasha, but refused, saying: "How can we allow him to appropriate this inheritance, when its value has not been substantiated yet" (BOA: HAT 56308).

157. In the summer of 1793, when the intendant (voyvoda) of Bayındır in western Anatolia, Karayılanoğlu Mehmed Agha, died, the family offered 20,000 *guruş* to the Porte in return for the inheritance. The central government asked Mehmed Karaosmanoğlu, a leading regional strongman, to report on the real value of the inheritance. After receiving his report, the state accepted the family's proposal (BOA: C ML 3108).

158. When İsmail of Ruse died, Mustafa Bayraktar offered 800 *kīse* (400,000 *guruş*) for his estate. However, Hasan Ağa, the customs chief at Ruse, claimed that it was worth at least 1,000 *kīse* (500,000 *guruş*), part of which, he said, was due to him in repayment of expenditures incurred on the Treasury's behalf. The case was submitted to Sultan Selim III, who wrote: "The value of the inheritance is to be set at 800 *kīse*. Of this, take 500 *kīse* in cash for [immediate military] expenditures. The remaining 300 *kīse* (150,000 *guruş*) is to be granted to the customs chief against what he claims from the Porte." Istanbul accepted Bayraktar's estimate and left İsmail's property in his possession, but a few months later, after he was appointed commander of the Danubian army, Bayraktar renegotiated the payment, and the Porte reduced the amount due from him by 300 *kīse*, provided that Bayraktar used this amount for military purposes. BOA: HAT 1730; BOA: C ML 2889.

159. Cohen, *Palestine*, 53–77; Philipp, *Acre*, 136–68; Akarlı, "Provincial Power Magnates," 47–50; Güler, *Cezar Ahmed Paşa*.

160. BOA: C A 11391-1.

161. Danacı Yıldız, ed., *Âsiler ve gâziler*, 65, 128.

162. BOA: HAT 4155.

163. Güler, *Cezzar Ahmed Paşa*, 16–25.
164. Inalcik, "Arnavutluk'ta Osmanlı Hakimiyetinin Yerleşmesi"; id. "İskender Beg."
165. Clayer, *Aux origines du nationalisme albanais*, 441–45.
166. Tezcan, *Second Ottoman Empire*, 140–52; Barkey, *Bandits and Bureaucrats*, 141–87.
167. North et al., *Violence and Social Order*, 251–72.
168. *Şanizade tarihi*, 1: 74–75.

CHAPTER 3: COMMUNITIES

1. On popular revolts in the Ottoman world, see Akdağ, *Celâlî isyanları*; Gara et al., *Popular Protest and Political Participation*.
2. Lewis, *Emergence of Modern Turkey*, 75–127; Devereux, *First Ottoman Constitutional Period*, 21–33; Ortaylı, *Tanzimattan sonra mahalli idareler*; Çadırcı, *Tanzimat döneminde Anadolu kentleri'nin sosyal ve ekonomik yapıları*.
3. KM: Ruse court record (*Rusçuk şeriye sicili*), no. 53, pp. 4–6ff.
4. Uzunçarşılı, *Alemdar Mustafa Paşa*, 44–46; Erdoğan et al., *Rusçuk ayanı*; Bakardjiava, "Between Anarchy and Creativity"; Bakardjieva and Yordanov, *Ruse*; Meral Bayrak-Ferlibaş, ed., *Osmanlı İdaresinde bir Balkan Şehri: Rusçuk*.
5. These records were also called the *maṣraf defteri* (book of expenses) or *salyāne defteri* (book of dues).
6. For earlier studies of *tevzî'* practices, see İnalcık, "Centralization and Decentralization"; Ursinus, "'Avarız Hanesi' und 'Tevzi Hanesi'"; Cezar, "18. ve 19. yüzyıllarda Osmanlı taşrasında oluşan mali sektörün mahiyeti ve büyüklüğü üzerine"; Veinstein, "İnalcık's Views"; Neumann, "Selanik'te onsekizinci yüzyılın sonunda masarif-i vilayet defterleri"; Günay, "Yerel kayıtlar ışığında XVIII. yüzyıl sonlarında İzmir"; Çelikel and Sağırlı, "Tokat şer'iyye sicillerine göre salyane defterleri"; McGowan, *Economic Life in Ottoman Europe*, 159–64; Wilkins, *Forging Urban Solidarities*, 36–43.
7. For a comprehensive survey of the Ottoman tax system in the fifteenth and sixteenth centuries, see İnalcık, ed., *Economic and Social History*, 1: 11–177.
8. İnalcık, "Military and Fiscal Transformation"; Faroqhi, "Crisis and Change"; Darling, *Revenue-Raising and Legitimacy*, 49–79; Cezar, "Osmanlı maliyesinde XVII. yüzyılın ikinci yarısında 'İmdadiye' uygulaması"; Suceska, "Taksit"; Radushev, "Dépenses locales"; Adanır, "Ottoman Peasantries"; Ursinus, "Transformation."
9. Goffman, "Jews of Safed," 81–90.
10. For lump-sum tax collection, see İnalcık, ed., *Economic and Social History*, 145–53; Adanır, "Semi-autonomous Forces," 162, 166; Darling, *Revenue-Raising and Legitimacy*, 103–5.
11. Ergenç, *XVI. yüzyılın sonlarında Bursa*, 141–49.
12. *Defter-i ḳażā' ve livā.*, 13–29ff.
13. Ergene, *Local Court, Provincial Society, and Justice*; Anıl, *Osmanlı'da kadılık*; Jennings, "Kadi, Court and Legal Procedure." For a recent edited volume on kadis and kadi courts in Islamic legal culture, see Masud, Peters, and Powers, eds., *Dispensing Justice in Islam*.

14. Orhonlu, "Osmanlı teşkilatına aid küçük bir risale, *Risale-yi terceme*," 45.
15. BOA: HAT 2056-A.
16. For a discussion on why the larger provincial units lost their fiscal signifi-cance and the districts were becoming the main focal units for fiscal administra-tions in the eighteenth century, see Neumann, "Selanik'te Onsekizinci Yüzyılın Sonunda Mesarif-i Vilayet Defterleri," 90.
17. On the collective identities of local communities, see Ergenç, "Toplumsal düşünce açıklama kanalı olarak: Cemm-i Gafir ve Cem'-i Kesir"; Neumann, "Ot-toman Provincial Towns," 137–39; Gara, "In Search of Communities."
18. Canbakal, *Society and Politics in an Ottoman Town*, 150–78; Ergenç, "'Ayân ve eşrâf' diye anılan seçkinler grubunun XVIII yüzyılda Osmanlı toplu-mundaki rolü"; Wilkins, *Forging Urban Solidarities*, 94–108.
19. If the community consisted entirely of non-Muslims, as in parts of the Peloponnese and some Aegean islands, no Muslim notable was listed. See Konto-giorgis, *Koinoniki dynamiki*, 78–79.
20. Hallaq, *Origins and Evolution of Islamic Law*, 110–13, 138–40.
21. Susan Reynolds, *Kingdoms and Communities*, 23–33, 51–58.
22. This meaning of the term *ayan* accords with its usage in classical Arabic. *A'yān* in Arabic, is the plural form of *'ayn*, which means "eye." *A'yān*, then, refers not only to eyes but also to notable individuals, with the connotation of the eyes of the community or group. In Ottoman political discourse, as in clas-sical Arabic, the term was used in its plural form to signify a collectivity of no-tables. Ayans, in this sense, were the notables of a community or any grouping. Ayanhood was, therefore, collective, natural leadership, which came into being in accordance with the specific social, political, and cultural circumstances of each community. For ayanhood in the medieval context, see Mottahedeh, *Loyalty and Leadership*, 120–30. For ayanhood in the pre-eighteenth century Ottoman context, see Ergenç, "Osmanlı klasik dönemindeki eşrâf ve ayân üzerine bazı bilgiler"; Canbakal, *Society and Politics*, 150–78; Sućeska, *Ajani*, 28–30.
23. The term *ayan* referred exclusively to Muslim administrators who acted at the district level on behalf of both Muslim and non-Muslim communities. As for exclusively Christian or Jewish communities, there was no empirewide standard procedure to appoint community administrators. Each community designated its administrator according to communal practices and conventions. However, in Greek-speaking lands, rules similar to the ones applied to ayans guided some community leaders who exclusively managed Greek communities' affairs on or below district level; the Ottomans called these individuals generically *kocabaşıs* (literally, big heads), or *re'āyā vekīli*, i.e., the representatives of non-Muslim com-munities. See Kontogiorgis, *Koinoniki dynamiki*, 68–98; Mert, "XVIII. ve XIX. Yüzyıllarda Osmanlı İmparatorluğu'nda Kocabaş deyimi, seçimleri ve Kocabaşılık iddiaları"; Nagata, *Muhsinzade Mehmed Paşa ve ayanlık müessesesi*, 42–45, 58–59; Hadjikyriacou, "Society and Economy," 177–80, 261–73.
24. Often regular direct taxes (*'avārız* and *nüzūl*), which were paid to the cen-tral government, were collected with a similar apportionment method, but they were registered separately; see Wilkins, *Forging Urban Solidarities*, 36–43.
25. Occasionally, communities were ordered to supply grain, livestock, or other goods at less than the market value. The communities either delivered the

demanded items and services at the price stated or offered a subsidy instead. The costs of these obligatory sales or subsidies were also apportioned to the communities in the apportionment registers. On such practices, see Ağır, "Grain Redistribution."

26. See, e.g., BOA: C D 3149, C D 7309, and C ADL 2847.

27. In the Edirne *tevzî'* registers for September 1802, for example, in addition to imperial taxes and dues related to imperial services, such as financing the postal service or accommodating imperial officeholders, we see outlays for construction of fortifications; fixing water pumps; supplying clothes and food to prostitutes in the city jail; hospitality to three sheikhs visiting from the Holy Cities; restoration of public buildings and functionaries' residences; renting houses used by public figures; the wages of firefighters, city-wall guards, and mercenaries protecting the districts against bandits; and compensating people whose property had been damaged by bandits (MK ŞS: Edirne 270, no. 108).

28. Ibid. For the register of the kadi documents related to the activities of the waqfs of Ismail of Ruse, see KM: R 11. See, too, Radushev et al. eds., *Inventory of Ottoman Turkish Documents*, no. 471; Bakardjieva, "Between Anarchy and Creativity."

29. Singer, *Charity in Islamic Societies.*

30. İbrahim Efendi, "Muhasebe-i Evvel el-Hac İbrahim Efendi Layihası," 36–37.

31. *'Sabıkı muktezasınca'* MK ŞS: Manisa 242, p. 39, no. 76. And see, too, MK ŞS, Trabzon 110, f. 63B, no. 302.

32. "Erbab-ı Sühen," MK ŞS: Tokat 3, p. 14.

33. MK ŞS: Denizli 671, 27.

34. In Ruse, as in most of districts, the main units to which the aggregate burden was allocated were the neighborhoods in the town and villages in the hinterland. However, in Sivas, a major district in central Anatolia, the city community's burden was allocated among professional organizations (*esnâf*) rather than neighborhoods. MK ŞS: Sivas 6, no. 63; see also Özdemir, "Sivas'ın iki yılı," 82–87.

35. Molla Mustafa, *XVIII. yüzyıl günlük hayatına dair Saraybosnalı Molla Mustafa'nın mecmuası*, 130.

36. Cezar, "18. ve 19. yüzyıllarda Osmanlı taşrasında oluşan yeni mali sektörün mahiyeti ve büyüklüğü üzerine," 93.

37. Although in principle all property holders were subject to the apportionment, there were always cases in which certain groups had different fiscal statuses, because they were tax exempt for their collective services, or because they were immune (*serbest*), since they were under the jurisdiction of various holders or imperial waqfs. In such a situation, there were often conflicts among different groups in the district community. I examine such cases in the section in this chapter titled "Communities and Immunities." In 1786, Amasya, an immune community living in the woods was included into the Amasya *tevzî'* registers. This triggered a conflict between the forest dwellers and Amasya officials. Eventually, the Porte decreed that since they delivered other services and their imperial dues were collected under a different arrangement, the forest communities in the region were immune from apportionment, and administrators were instructed not to ask them for *tevzi* shares. MK ŞS: Amasya 62, p. 28.

38. Molla Mustafa, *XVIII. yüzyıl günlük hayatına dair Saraybosnalı Molla Mustafa'nın mecmuası,* 107. On *taksit* collection in Bosnia, see Sućeska, "Taksit."

39. In Ruse, İsmail Agha claimed 10 percent interest for his expenses. In Skopje (Üsküp), a register dated July 1792 indicates that the ayan received a fixed allowance called *a'yāniye* for his services, not interest (Kurz, *Sicill,* 255–57). We find a similar fixed manager's fee in Edirne in 1802 (MK ŞS: Edirne 270, no. 108) and an *ikrāmiye* (gratuity) in Kastamonu in 1797 (MK ŞS: Kastamonu 692, no. 199).

40. Smail, *Consumption of Justice,*147.

41. BOA: C D 7309.

42. BOA: C D 7309.

43. BOA: C ML 6108 (C 1218 / October 1803); BOA: HAT 52126-A (n.d.); For the role of moneylenders in the eighteenth and early nineteenth centuries, see Cezar, "Role of the *sarrafs*"; Minoglou, "Ethnic Minority Groups."

44. Sućeska, *Ajani,* 122.

45. Kontogiorgis, *Koinoniki dynamiki,* 87–96; Petmezas, "Christian Communities"; Papastamatiou, "Tax-Farming *(iltizam)* and Collective Fiscal Responsibility," 289–305. Also see Pylia, "Notables moréotes"; Kostantaras, "Christian Elites."

46. Petmezas, "Christian Communities," 80–83.

47. Nenadović, *Memoirs,* 12–13.

48. McGowan, *Economic Life in Ottoman Europe,* 66.

49. Erdoğan et al., *Rusçuk ayanı,* 126–32.

50. At such a tribunal between the community and the ayan in the Nevrekop court in 1783, more than two hundred individuals, as representatives of the community, asked their ayan, Bönlü Paşo, to settle the accounts under the supervision of the imperial inspector. BOA: C ADL 1930.

51. MK ŞS: Bursa, 375, p. 18a–b.

52. BOA: C ML 4273; also see BOA: C D 1391. In another decree, it was ordered that accounts be drawn up twice a year through a "unanimous vote" *(ittifāk-ı ārā)* of the participants in the meeting and then sent to the Porte for possible "discounts and revisions" *(tenkīḥ ve temyīz)*; see BOA: C D 5898.

53. Based on Salonika's apportionment registers, Christoph Neumann argues that fiscal experts in Istanbul examined the account books along four parameters: 1. The expenses might be contrary to Sharia or sultanic law. If so, experts could omit the item on the basis of falsehood *(ḥilāf)* or mischievousness *(fāsid).* 2. Items could be considered too high *(fāhiş)* when compared with their equivalents in earlier books. 3. There was the possibility of accounting mistakes, such as repetition *(mükerrer).* 4. There might be obscure *(meşkūk)* items. Neumann, "Selanik'te onsekizinci yüzyılın sonunda mesarif-i vilayet defteri," 91.

54. BOA: C D 7794.

55. Neumann, "Selanik'te onsekizinci yüzyılın sonunda mesarif-i vilayet defteri," 94; Cezar, "18. ve 19. yüzyıllarda Osmanlı taşrasında oluşan yeni mali sektörün mahiyeti ve büyüklüğü üzerine," 106.

56. MK ŞS: Sivas 6, no. 43; see also Özdemir, "Sivas'ın iki yılı," 66.

57. For a discussion of the apportionment system and *mālikāne* units in Mosul, see Dina Rizk Khoury, *State and Provincial Society,* 190–96.

58. Cezar, "18. ve 19. yüzyıllarda Osmanlı taşrasında oluşan yeni mali sektörün mahiyeti ve büyüklüğü üzerine," 115.

59. Nagata, *Muhsin-zade Mehmed Paşa ve ayanlık müessesesi*, 44–50.
For two major surveys on the ayan institution, see also Özkaya, *Osmanlı
İmparatorluğunda Ayanlık*; Sućeska, *Ajani*, 53–75; For a discussion on ayanship
in the Balkans, see Mutafčieva, "Institution de l'ayanlik"; Mert, "Ayan"
60. MK ŞS: Konya 58, p. 155. Also see Baykal, "A'yânlık müessesesinin düzeni
hakkında belgeler," no. 1.
61. MK ŞS: Ankara.155, no. 147; MK ŞS: Karaman 284, p. 52. Baykal,
"A'yânlık müessesesininin düzeni," no. 2. For a discussion of the document, see
Sućeska, *Ajani*, 93n400; İnalcık, "Centralization and Decentralization," 49–50.
62. Baykal, "A'yânlık müessesesininin düzeni," no. 3; Sućeska, *Ajani* 93n400;
İnalcık, "Centralization and Decentralization," 49–50; see also BOA: C D 15934,
C D 8275, and Müh, 175, p. 392.
63. MK ŞS: Karaman 284, p. 52. Baykal, "A'yânlık müessesesininin düzeni,"
no. 3.
64. BOA: C D 16599 (report concerning the notes from the kadis of the districts in Anadolu province, stating that the edict about the new arrangement of
the ayanship had been received and the edicts had been announced to the communities, B 1198 / June 1784); Sućeska, *Ajani*, 93n400; İnalcık, "Centralization and
Decentralization," 49–50; Ergenç, "Ayân ve eşrâf diye anılan seçkinler"; Mert,
"Ayan." I have used the edict available in MK ŞS: Bursa 375, p. 18a–b. Also see
MK ŞS: Kayseri 163, p. 14; MK ŞS: Çankırı 17, s. 107; MK ŞS: Afyon 57, no. 13.
65. MK ŞS: Bursa 375, p. 18a–b
66. Ibid.
67. Ibid.
68. Ibid.
69. Sućeska, *Ajani*, 95; Osman Nuri Ergin, *Mecelle-yi umur-ı belediye*, 1:
1664–66. BOA: C D 12669.
70. BOA: C D 3661 (a petition from the community of Kandiye [Heraklion] in
Crete concerning the abolition of ayanship and institution of urban stewardship,
September 1786). Also see MK ŞS: Kayseri 164, p. 101; BOA: Müh, 183, p. 675,
no. 735; BOA: C D 1409; BOA: C D 13416, C S 3661, and C D 13416.
71. İnalcık, "Appointment Procedure of a Guild Warden (*kethüda*)," 135–
42. For the nature of *kethüda*ship, see İnalcık, "Comments on 'Sultanism,'"
62–63; Yi, *Guild Dynamics*, 70–81; Ergenç, "Osmanlı şehirlerindeki yönetim
kurumlarının niteliği."
72. In Tokat in 1755, for example, both the *şehir kethüdası* and the ayan oversaw the city's affairs simultaneously. BOA: C D 3447.
73. Sućeska, *Ajani*, 95.
74. BOA: C D 12669 (petitions concerning the complaints on the manager in
Nevrekop, March 1786).
75. BOA: C D 12370 (note of kadi and the petition of the community of Pravishta district concerning the estate of former ayan Halil Agha and the urban
stewardship, August 1786).
76. Sućeska, *Ajani*, 140–45; Mert, "Ayan."
77. BOA: C D 3935; for a notification dated January 1791 from the Söğütçük
district stating that the court received the new decree from Istanbul about the
annulment of city stewardship and the new arrangement of ayanship; and the

decree was read aloud in the presence of the community of the district; see BOA: C D 10969.

78. BOA: C D 3935.

79. BOA: C ZB 3564.

80. BOA: C D 5161.

81. BOA: C D 3149.

82. BOA: C D 7309

83. BOA: C ZB 3231.

84. BOA: HAT 12094.

85. BOA: HAT 3207.

86. BOA: C D 13317.

87. BOA: C D 12232. Also see Yaycıoğlu, "Rahova 1784."

88. Ivanova, "Widdin"; Atanasov, V Osmanskata periferiia, 240–62; Radushev, "Dépenses locales."

89. Yaycıoğlu, "Rahova 1784," 474–77.

90. BOA: HAT 12001.

91. For a similar case study, see Anastasopoulos, "Lighting the Flame of Disorder."

92. Genç, "Osmanlı maliyesinde malikane sistemi"; Çızakça, Comparative Evolution, 135–77; Sućeska, "Malikane," 197–230; Özvar, Osmanlı maliyesinde malikane uygulaması; Ursinus, "Transformation." For a spatial analysis of the administrative units, see Başarır, "XVIII. yüzyılda Diyerbakır voyvodalığı'nın mekansal örgütlenmesi."

93. BOA: C D 7309.

94. BOA: C D 3541.

95. İbrahim Efendi, "Muhasebe-i evvel el-Hac İbrahim Efendi layihası," 37.

96. BOA: C ML 19165.

97. TSA: 31/18, 46/15, 107/39, 131/18.

98. BOA: C D 6365. For the petition of the community see BOA: C D 1655.

99. For a similar case in 1806 in which Tirsinikli İsmail Agha was asked to resolve a conflict between local contractors and the Kazanlık community, mālikāne of Yusuf Agha, an Istanbul grandee who was the sultan's mother's steward, see BOA: C ML 1131.

100. BOA: A. AMD 50/65.

101. BOA: C D 3965.

102. BOA: A. AMD 49/11.

103. For an example of a massive apportionment process carried out by the kocabaşıs in the Peloponnese, see BOA: C M 660.

104. BOA: C D 5220.

105. BOA: C D 14219; BOA: C D 1655.

106. Anastasopoulos, "Albanians."

107. BOA: A. DVN 2402/55.

108. BOA: C D 3375. For a similar case in which the community dismissed its ayan and invited in another ayan from outside, see BOA: C D 13317.

109. Canbakal, "Vows as Contract"; Faroqhi, "Räuber, Rebellen und Obrigkeit"; Tamdoğan, "Nezir"; Anastasopoulos, "Political Participation, Public Order, and Monetary Pledges (Nezir) in Ottoman Crete."

110. BOA: C ZB 3564.
111. BOA: A. DVN D 842.
112. Hochstrasser, "Physiocracy," 432.
113. Ergenç, "Osmanlı'da *Enfâ'* kuralının devlet ve reaya arasındaki mali ilişkiler açısından anlamı."
114. İbrahim Efendi, "Muhasebe-i evvel el-Hac İbrahim Efendi layihası," 37; Also see Sućeska, *Ajani*, 104–5.
115. Yeşil, "III. Selim devri siyasî literatürüne bir katkı," 86–92, and text, 4a.
116. Mehmed Şerif Efendi, "Defterdar Mehmed Şerif Efendi layihası," 20.
117. Legay, *États provinciaux*; Swann, *Provincial Power and Absolute Monarchy*.
118. Kuhn, *Origins of the Modern Chinese State*, 65–66.
119. Grindle, *Going Local*, 181.
120. Kaynar, *Mustafa Reşit Paşa*, 237–50; Çadırcı, *Tanzimat döneminde Anadolu*, 203–23.
121. Çadırcı, *Tanzimat döneminde Anadolu*, 249–72; Moaz, *Ottoman Reform*. For an important synthetic work on municipal reform in the nineteenth-century Ottoman Empire, see Ortaylı, *Tanzimattan Cumhuriyete yerel yönetim geleneği*.

CHAPTER 4: CRISIS

1. BOA: HAT 2056-A.
2. Uzunçarşılı, *Alemdar Mustafa Paşa*, 208–11.
3. Ibid., 46.
4. Ibid.
5. Ibid., "Seni dahi çünkü Ruscuklu istemiş, Rusçuğa ayan olasın," 51.
6. Ebû Bekir Efendi, *Vaka-i cedid*; Mustafa Necip, *Mustafa Necip Efendi tarihi* (also known as *Veka-yi Selimiyye*); *Yayla İmamı risalesi* (also known as *Tarih-i vekayi-i selimiyye*); Arapyan, *Rusçuk âyânı Mustafa Paşa'nın hayatı ve kahramanlıkları*; Oğulukian, *Georg Oğulukyan'ın ruznamesi*.
7. *Asım tarihi*, 1: 102–19, 2: 26–36, 182–208; *Câbî tarihi*, 1: 102–398; *Şanizade tarihi*, 1: 55–78.
8. *Tarih-i Cevdet*; see, too, Neumann, *Araç tarih, amaç Tanzimat*.
9. *Tarih-i Cevdet*, 8: 139–54.
10. Ibid., 9: 35.
11. Juchereau de Saint-Denys, *Révolutions*; Yaycıoğlu, "*Révolutions*."
12. Juchereau de Saint-Denys, *Révolutions*, 1: 1.
13. Baker, *Inventing the French Revolution*, 202–23; id., "Revolution 1.0."
14. Following Juchereau, the Austrian Orientalist Ottokar-Maria Schlechta-Wsserhd (1825–94) published his *Die Revolutionen in Konstantinopel in den Jahren 1807 und 1808* in 1882, a revised version of Juchereau's narrative in light of the interpretations of Ottoman historians, particularly Cevdet's. See *Meyers Großes Konversations-Lexikon*, 17: 833, "Schlechta-Wssehrd, Ottokar."
15. Altınay, "Sultan Selim-i Salisde halk ve millet muhabbeti."

16. Akçura, *Osmanlı devleti'nin dağılma devri*; Karal, *Fransa-Mısır ve Osmanlı İmparatorluğu.*

17. Shaw, *Between Old and New.*

18. Gökçe, "Edirne ayanı Dağdeviren-oğlu Mehmed Ağa."

19. HHStH: Türkei II—139, no. 20, 60–62ff.; no. 21, 1–10ff.: Türkei 140, nos. 17–19; PRO: FO 78–51; BOA: HAT 2787.

20. BOA: HAT 3366.

21. Ibid.

22. *Câbî tarihi*, 1: 62.

23. *Asım tarihi*, 1: 112.

24. PRO, FO 78–50: 29–33.

25. AMAE CP Turquie 212: 88.

26. BOA: HAT 2345.

27. Ibid.

28. BOA: HAT 3350.

29. BOA: A. AMD 50/3.

30. BOA: HAT 1819.

31. Djuvara, *Pays roumain*, 45–97; Hitchins, *Romanians*, 19–24; Panaitescu, *Corespondenţa lui Constantin Ypsilanti*, 1–24.

32. Shupp, *European Powers*, 146.

33. BOA: HAT 2482.

34. Driault, *Études napoléoniennes: La politique orientale de Napoléon*; id., *Napoléon et l'Europe; Tilsitt, France et Russie*; Tatistcheff, *Alexandre Ier et Napoléon*; Shupp, *European Powers*, 66–79.

35. Shupp, *European Powers*, 146–48; Driault, *Études napoléoniennes: La politique orientale de Napoléon*, 55–61; Puryear, *Napoleon and the Dardanelles*, 141–54; Stanislavskaia, *Russko-angliiskie otnosheniia*, 442–47.

36. Scudamore, *France in the East*, 91–92.

37. Bradisteanu, *Beziehungen*, 100–101.

38. BOA: HAT 12618.

39. Mikhailovskii-Danilevskii, *Russo-Turkish War of 1806–1812*; BOA: HAT 43758; Eclisiarhul, *Cronograful Tarii Românesti*, 137.

40. Ahmed Osmanzade Taib, *Hadikat ül-Vüzera*, 301–5; Miller, *Mustapha Pacha Bairaktar*, 124–231; Uzunçarşılı, *Alemdar Mustafa Paşa*, 40–81.

41. Uzunçarşılı, *Alemdar Mustafa Paşa*, 42.

42. BOA: HAT 2482. The document is published in Uzunçarşılı, *Alemdar Mustafa Paşa*, 21–22. See, too, Ypsilanti, "Fürsten Alexander und Konstantin Ypsilanti," 225–35.

43. Uzunçarşılı, *Alemdar Mustafa Paşa*, 43–44.

44. BOA: HAT 2056, 2056-A.

45. Uzunçarşılı, *Alemdar Mustafa Paşa*, 46.

46. BOA: HAT 2580.

47. BOA: HAT 2580; Uzunçarşılı, *Alemdar Mustafa Paşa*, 45–48.

48. Uzunçarşılı, *Alemdar Mustafa Paşa*, 51.

49. Stratford Canning, "Account of the Three Last Insurrections at Constantinople and the Present State of the Turkish Empire," March 25, 1809, in PRO: FO 78/63: 182–96.

50. Uzunçarşılı, *Alemdar Mustafa Paşa*, 54.

51. Ibid., 48.

52. BOA: C ML 8723.

53. For biographies of Manuk Bey, see Hovnanean, *Mirzayean Manuk Pēyin*, and Ionescu, *Manuc Bei*. For the documents concerning business between Tirsinikli İsmail Ağa and Manuk Bey in Romanian archives, see Guboglu, *Catalogul documentelor turceşti*, vol. 1, nos. 568, 692–95, 726, 727, 773, 777, 783, 800, 817, 824, 835, 841, 862, 870, 871, 874, 888, 892, 896, 897, and 898; Mehmed, *Documente turceşti*, vol. 3, no. 124.

54. AMAE: CP Turquie 217: 29 (a report from Mériage in Ruse to Paris on the Ottoman-Russian negotiations, May 1808); Hurmuzaki, ed., *Documente*, suppl. 1, vol. 2, no. 672: 517.

55. Siruni, "Bairakdar Moustapha Pascha et Manouk Bey," 68; Ionescu, *Manuc Bei*, 33–38; Guboglu, *Catalogul documentelor turceşti*, vol. 1: no. 745, 746, 747; BOA: HAT 1730.

56. "Pour préserver la Cour et les Etats de S. H. du danger de devenir la proie de l'ambition démesurée de Bonaparte" (Hurmuzaki, ed., *Documente*, suppl. 1, vol. 2, no. 506, 366–67).

57. Ibid., no. 504, 365–66. Also see KM: 112 (Ruse) 64/5.

58. BOA: HAT 54094.

59. BOA: C A 35129, C A 44857, C A 10296.

60. BOA: HAT 1569. "Dans le court séjour qu'a fait le Prince Moruzzi à Ruschiuk, il est parvenu à réconcilier le dit ayan de Ruschiuk avec Passavan-Oglou" (Mehmed, *Documente turceşti*, vol. 3, no. 131, 214–17). See, too, AMAE: CP Turquie 213: 1; Hurmuzaki, ed., *Documente*, suppl. 1, vol. 2, no. 514, 371–72, and no. 520, 377–78; *Journal politique*, no. 9 (January 30, 1807), suppl.; Bradisteanu, *Beziehungen*, 115.

61. AMAE: CP Turquie 213: 11; Hurmuzaki, ed., *Documente*, suppl. 1, vol. 2: no. 517, 374.

62. *Journal politique*, no. 9 (January 30, 1807), suppl.

63. BOA: A.AMD, no. 52; CA 38938.

64. BOA: HAT 6362; KM: OAK 10–64.

65. AMAE: CP Turquie 213: 132 (report by Mériage in Vidin to Talleyrand concerning the governership of Molla İdris, March 20, 1807); Hurmuzaki, ed., *Documente*, suppl. 1, vol. 2, no. 553, 403.

66. AMAE: CP Turquie 213: 114 (report by Mériage to Talleyrand concerning the military activities of Molla İdris and Mustafa Pasha in February and March, March 9, 1807); Hurmuzaki, ed., *Documente*, suppl. 1, vol. 2, no. 547, 397–98; AMAE: CP Turquie 213: 86 (report from Mériage in Vidin on military preparations in the Danubian region, February 26, 1807); AMAE: CP Turquie 213: 86 (report from Mériage in Vidin on military activities in the Danubian region, February 15, 1807); Hurmuzaki, ed., *Documente*, suppl. 1, vol. 2, no. 543, 394; AMAE: CP Turquie 213: 86 (report from Lamare in Ruse on the campaigns organized by Mustafa Ağa and Molla İdris Pasha, February 16, 1807); Hurmuzaki, ed., *Documente*, suppl. 1, vol. 2, no. 541, 393.

67. *Asım tarihi*, 2: 21, 180–81; *Tarih-i Cevdet*, 8: 89.

68. *Asım tarihi*, 1: 215; Uzunçarşılı, *Alemdar Mustafa Paşa*, 57.

69. BOA: HAT 641, C A 1298.

70. BOA: HAT 6411.

71. BOA: HAT 15039.

72. BOA: HAT 5965, CA 32118.

73. Shupp, *European Powers*, 327–53.

74. Ibid., 234–67.

75. Danacı Yıldız, ed., *Asiler ve gaziler*, 98.

76. BOA: C A 15901.

77. Hafız Mehmed b. Süleyman, *Ceride* (SK, Zühtü Bey, no. 453: 2a–3b), published by Beydilli, *Osmanlı Döneminde imamlar ve bir imamın günlüğü*, 103–236; *Câbî tarihi*, 1: 102–10. For a detailed narrative of the British incident, see Yeşil, "İstanbul önlerinde bir İngiliz filosu"; Danacı Yıldız, "Vaka-yı Selimiyye," 268–329.

78. Juchereau de Saint-Denys, *Révolutions*, 2: 75.

79. Ibid., 70–9; Driault, *Études napoléoniennes: La politique orientale de Napoléon*, 80–110.

80. Driault, *Études napoléoniennes: La politique orientale de Napoléon*, 98–105; AMAE: CP Turquie 213; AMAE: Corresp. de Turquie, no. 24 (1806–10), suppl.

81. Juchereau de Saint-Denys, *Révolutions*, 2: 74.

82. PRO: FO 78-55 (February 25, 1807).

83. Driault, *Études napoléoniennes: La politique orientale de Napoléon*, 105–10; PRO: FO 78-55 (reports between February 24 and March 6, 1808). For evaluations of the crisis between the Porte and the British ambassador and the failure of the military operation, see James, *Naval History*, 210–20; Arbuthnot, *Correspondence*, 1–5.

84. Yeşil, "İstanbul önlerinde bir İngiliz filosu," 455–66.

85. *Câbî tarihi*, 1: 105–6.

86. Yeşil, "İstanbul önlerinde bir İngiliz filosu," 465.

87. BOA: HAT 56092; HAT 57208.

88. BOA: C A 36907 (September 1806).

89. *Mustafa Necib Efendi tarihi*, 26. The breakdown of Ottoman troops on the Danubian frontier was:
Western front: 40,000 (İsmail of Serres, İdris of Vidin, Mehmed Hüsrev
    Pasha of Bosnia)
Crajova: 8,000 (Mustafa Bayraktar)
Ruse: 25,000 (Mustafa Bayraktar)
Silistra: 22,000 (grand vizier's army, janissaries, and the Karaosmanoğlus'
    and Çapanoğlus' divisions)
Izmail: 30,000 (Pehlivan Agha and Bayraktar)
Bräila (Ibrail): 15,000 (Celal Pasha)
Total: 140,000
Some 60,000 Russian troops were deployed on the other side of the Danube
AMAE: CP Turquie 214: 145 (report by Boutin from Silistre concerning the composition of the Ottoman forces, June 26, 1807); Hurmuzaki, ed., *Documente*, suppl. 1, vol. 2, no. 594, 442.

90. On the characteristics of the Ottoman army, see AMAE: CP Turquie 213: 30 (report concerning the military structure of the Ottoman army, January 1807);

Hurmuzaki, ed., *Documente*, suppl. 1, vol. 2, no. 525, 380; AMAE: CP Turquie 214: 72 (June, 13 1807); Hurmuzaki, ed., *Documente*, suppl. 1, vol. 2, no. 583, 428; AMAE: CP 211 (January 27, 1806). For a report on the composition of an army formed by regional and local strongmen, see BOA: C A 27990. Also see Juchereau de Saint-Denys, *Révolutions*, 1: 92–96.

91. *Asım tarihi*, 1: 139. For the constant deterioration of the quality of the bread and the rise of prices in the time of the New Order, see Yeşil, "Zâhire nâzareti'nin kuruluşu," 141; Ağır, "Evolution of the Grain Policy," 585–87.

92. For the Ottoman sources about the revolt, *Asım tarihi*, 2: 20–53; *Câbî tarihi*, 1: 126–38; *Mustafa Necip Efendi tarihi*, 84–85; *Tarih-i Cevdet*, 8: 155–86; Derin, "Kabakçı Mustafa ayaklanmasına dair bir tarihçe"; id., "Yayla İmamı risalesi"; id., "Tüfengçi-başı Arif Efendi Tarihçesi"; Uzunçarşılı, "Kabakçı Mustafa İsyanına Dair Yazılmış Bir Tarihçe"; *Vaka-i cedid*; Ebû Bekir Efendi, *Vaka-i cedid*; Arapyan, *Rusçuk âyânı Mustafa paşa'nın hayatı ve kahramanlıkları*; *Sultan Selim-i Salisin Hal'ine dair risale*; Oğulukian, *Georg Oğulukyan'ın ruznamesi*; Andreasyan, "III. Selim ve IV. Mustafa devirlerine ait Georg Oğulukyan'ın ruznamesi"; Kethüda Said Efendi, "Tarih." For sources in European languages, see Juchereau de Saint-Denys, *Révolutions*; Prévost, "Constantinople en 1806 et 1807" and "Constantinople en 1808"; Canning, "Account of the Three Last Insurrections at Constantinople and the Present State of the Turkish Empire," 182–96; Franz Freiherr von Ottenfels, "Historische Schilderung der am 28ten July 1808 in Konstantinopel vorgefallenen Thronveränderung," HHStA, Türkei VII-2; *Relazione della catastrofe di Selim III. ed elevazione al trono di Constantinopoli di Mustafa' IV*; Schlechta-Wssehrd, *Revolutionen*; Krasnokutskii, *Dnevnye zapiski poezdki v Konstantinopl' v 1808 godu*. For a detailed study of the fall of the New Order in 1807, see Yıldız, "Vaka-yı Selimiyye," esp. 330–450.

93. *Mustafa Necib Efendi tarihi*, 28–29; Ebû Bekir Efendi, *Vaka-i cedid*, 113.

94. *Mustafa Necib Efendi tarihi*, 27; *Tarih-i Cevdet*, 8, 170–83.

95. For a modern novella on Kabakçı Mustafa, see Koçu, *Kabakçı Mustafa*.

96. *Câbî tarihi*, 1, 125–30; *Asım tarihi*, 2: 20–26; *Tarih-i Cevdet*, 8: 155–59; *Mustafa Necib Efendi tarihi*, 27–28.

97. Oğulukian, *Georg Oğulukyan'ın ruznamesi*, 5; *Câbî tarihi*, 1: 130; *Asım tarihi*, 2: 29–32; *Tarih-i Cevdet*, 8: 159–61; *Mustafa Necib Efendi tarihi*, 28–29.

98. *Mustafa Necib Efendi tarihi*, 46.

99. *Câbî tarihi*, 1: 130.

100. Ibid., 128–32.

101. *Tarih-i Cevdet*, 8: 167.

102. *Asım tarihi*, 2: 32–50; *Tarih-i Cevdet*, 8: 170–75; *Mustafa Necib Efendi tarihi*, 28–29.

103. BOA: HAT 7537.

104. Oğulukian, *Georg Oğulukyan'ın ruznamesi*, 5–6.

105. *Tarih-i Cevdet*, 8: 175.

106. For a critical edition of the contract, see Beydilli, "Kabakçı isyanı."

107. *Asım tarihi*, 2: 46–52; *Tarih-i Cevdet*, 8: 180–85; *Mustafa Necip Efendi tarihi*, 55–57; *Câbî tarihi*, 1: 145–46; Danacı Yıldız, ed., *Asiler ve gaziler*, 123–25; Beydilli, "Kabakçı isyanı"; Schlechta-Wsserhd, *Revolutionen*, 127–29.

108. Kafadar, "Janissaries and Other Riffraff," 119–25; Piterberg, *Ottoman Tragedy*, 163–83.

109. *Asım tarihi*, 2: 51.

110. İnalcık, "Military and Fiscal Transformation," 300–303.

111. Canbakal, "Vows as Contract in Ottoman Public Life"; Tamdoğan, "Nezir," 259–69.

112. *Asım tarihi*, 2, 98–100; *Mustafa Necib Efendi tarihi*, 70–74; *Tarih-i Cevdet*, 8: 213–14; AMAE: CP Turquie 214: 145 (report by Boutin from Silistre on the deployment of Ottoman forces, July 26, 1807); Hurmuzaki, ed., *Documente*, suppl. 1, vol. 2, no. 594, 442–44.

113. *Mustafa Necib Efendi tarihi*, 65–69, 73; *Tarih-i Cevdet*, 8: 186–92, 212–13; Uzunçarşılı, *Alemdar Mustafa Paşa*, 64–69. For an account of Pehlivan's assassination by Alemdar Mustafa Pasha, see BOA: HAT 54144 (July 1807).

114. BOA: C A 21112 (February 1808).

115. BOA: HAT 59055 (ca. July 1807).

116. *Tarih-i Cevdet*, 8: 192– 202.

117. For observations about the security and economy of the city after the revolution, see Oğulukian, *Georg Oğulukyan'ın ruznamesi*, 18–24.

118. Kırımlı and Yaycıoğlu, "Heir of Chinghis Khan."

119. BOA: HAT 53809 (February 1807).

120. BOA: HAT 53657 (Summer 1807).

121. Ibid.

122. Oğulukian, *Georg Oğulukyan'ın ruznamesi*, 19–21.

123. Miller, *Mustapha Pacha Baïraktar*, 256–57.

124. Uzunçarşılı, *Alemdar Mustafa Paşa*, 93–94.

125. *Mustafa Necib Efendi tarihi*, 78–79.

126. For the Prussiasn partition plan, see Ranke, *Hardenberg*, 3: 460–62; Zeeden, *Hardenberg*.

127. On the impact of the news from Istanbul on the Tilsit negotiations, see Butterfield, *Peace Tactics*, 221–25; Shupp, *European Powers*, 544–50.

128. Napoleon I, *Correspondance*, 15: 12819.

129. Vandal, *Napoléon et Alexandre Ier*, 1: 499–507.

130. Shupp, *European Powers*, 544–50; Driault, *Napoléon et l'Europe*, 113–289.

131. AMAE: CP Turquie 215: 29 (report from Ruse on the negotiations between Ottoman and Russian officers, September 16, 1807). BOA: C H 5444 (letter concerning the negotiations, C 1222 / June 1807).

132. Ionescu, *Manuc Bei*, 81–84.

133. For the negotiations of the ceasefire, see AMAE: CP Turquie 215: 17, 19, 21, 23, 29, 33, 36, 41 (report from Ruse on the negotiations between the Ottoman and Russian officers, September 1807); BOA: C H 5444 (letter concerning the negotiations, C 1222 / June 1807); Miller, *Mustapha Pacha Baïraktar*, 200–204.

134. Driault, *Études napoléoniennes: La politique orientale de Napoléon*, 215–54; Miller, *Mustapha Pacha Baïraktar*, 256–57.

135. Boppe, *Albanie et Napléon*, 125–73.

136. Driault, Études napoléoniennes: La politique orientale de Napoléon: 255–308.

137. Tarih-i Cevdet, 6: 135.

138. Juchereau de Saint-Denys, Révolutions, 2: 192.

139. Köprülü, "Asım Efendi," 669–70.

140. Asım tarihi, 2: 182–208.

141. Schlechta-Wsserhd, Revolutionen; Ali Seydi, Alemdar Mustafa Paşa; [Mehmed] Efdalüddin [Tekiner], "Alemdar Mustafa Paşa."

142. Uzunçarşılı, Alemdar Mustafa Paşa.

143. Mustafa Necib Efendi tarihi, 70–100; Arapyan, Rusçuk âyânı Mustafa Paşa'nın hayatı ve kahramanlıkları, 7.

144. Juchereau de Saint-Denys, Révolutions, 2: 165–88; Prévost, "Constantinople en 1808," 487. Juchereau de Saint-Denys was a military adviser to the Ottoman State and Achille Félicité Prévost was secretary in the French Embassy during the Revolution. For the French foreign service in the age of Napoleon, see Whitcomb, Napoleon's Diplomatic Service; Dehérain, Vie de Pierre Ruffin, in id., Orientalistes et antiquaires, 1, pt. 2: 92–93.

145. Miller, Mustapha Pacha Baïraktar, 211–27, 268–76.

146. BOA: HAT 54094.

147. Asım tarihi, 2: 180–81.

148. Juchereau de Saint-Denys, Révolutions, 2: 164.

149. Siruni, "Ramiz Pacha"; Alexandrescu-Dersca-Bulgaru, "Contribution," 77–94.

150. Behiç, "Sevânihü'l-levayıh."

151. SO, 3: 615–16.

152. Ionescu, Manuc Bei.

153. Yıldız, "Vaka-yı selimiyye" 611–67.

154. Mustafa Necib Efendi, 75.

155. Asım tarihi, 2: 114; Tarih-i Cevdet, 8: 217; Uzunçarşılı, Alemdar Mustafa Paşa, 86.

156. Uzunçarşılı, Alemdar Mustafa Paşa, 85.

157. BOA: C A 8023 (October 1808).

158. BOA: HAT 52643-B (March 1808).

159. Miller, Mustapha Pacha Baïraktar, 272.

160. Ibid., 268–277.

161. BOA: HAT 53682.

162. Asım tarihi, 2: 191; Mustafa Necib Efendi tarihi, 85.

163. BOA: HAT 32139.

164. Mustafa Necib Efendi tarihi, 85.

165. Uzunçarsılı, Alemdar Mustafa Paşa, 102–11.

166. Asım tarihi, 2: 193.

167. Uzunçarşılı, Alemdar Mustafa Paşa, 115.

168. Asım tarihi, 2: 195–202; Tarih-i Cevdet, 8: 298–305; Uzunçarşılı, Alemdar Mustafa Paşa, 118–23; "Historische Schilderung der am 28ten July 1808 in Konstantinopel vorgefallenen Thronveränderung," HHStA, Türkei VII-2 (1808).

169. Derin, "Yayla İmamı risalesi," 213–72.

170. Mustafa Necib Efendi tarihi, 90.

171. *Asım tarihi*, 2: 195–202; *Tarih-i Cevdet*, 8: 298–305.
172. BOA: Milli Emlaktan devrolunan defterler, no. 11, *Ruzname*; *Şanizade tarihi*, 1: 21–23.
173. TSA: E 1025/2 (September 1808).
174. *Şanizade tarihi*, 1: 24.
175. *Tarih-i Cevdet*, 8: 324–28; *Câbî tarihi*, 1: 181–87; *Yayla İmamı risalesi*, 247–29; Oğulukian, *Georg Oğulukyan ruznamesi*, 34–36.
176. *Asım tarihi*, 2: 140–42, 162, 174–75; *Câbî tarihi*, 1: 236. For a comment on Tayyar Pasha's execution, see HHStA: Türkei VII-2, no. 33, 209–14ff. (September 1808).
177. A report from Ludolf a Circello, the representative of Naples to Istanbul, August 18, 1808, Archivio di Stato di Napoli: Esteri-fasc. 241, inc. 117, 9r–10. See also Pezzi, *Aspettando la pace*, 88–89. On the price regulations, see *Câbî tarihi*, 1: 204–17.
178. *Bastı İstanbul'u dağ civanları*
   Alemdar Paşa'nın pehlivanları
   Kuruldu siyaset çün Divanları
   Kırcalı askeri cebken poturlu
   Gitmez buralardan artık bir türlü.
as published in Koçu, *Türk giyim, kuşam ve süslenme sözlüğü*, 194. For another version of the ode, see Öztelli, *Uyan padişahım*, 203–4.
179. BOA: HAT 23559, 23562.
180. Kadić, *Tarih–i Anwarî*, 147–48.
181. HHStA: Türkei, VII-2 (1808), no. 33, 225–28ff.
182. *Şanizade tarihi*, 1: 62.
183. *Câbî tarihi*, 1: 169.
184. BOA: C S 559 (September 1808).
185. *Câbî tarihi*, 1: 232.
186. Oğulukian, *Georg Oğulukyan ruznamesi*, 36.
187. HHStA: Türkei, VII-2, no. 34, 232–35ff.
188. *Câbî tarihi*, 1: 218.
189. Ibid., 229.
190. HHStA: Türkei VII-2, no. 30, 159–185ff. (September 10, 1808).
191. *Câbî tarihi*, 1: 224–25.
192. Beyhan, ed., *Saray günlüğü*, 246–47.
193. *Câbî tarihi*, 1: 228.
194. *Sanizade tarihi*, 1: 66–68; *Tarih-i Cevdet*, 9: 5–6; Uzunçarşılı, *Alemdar Mustafa Paşa*, 141–42.
195. BOA: C A 15925.
196. *Câbî tarihi*, 1: 233–34.
197. Khoury, *State and Provincial Society*, 166.
198. KM: Hacıoğlu Pazarı şeriye sicili (court record) (1213–24), no. 337.
199. HHStA: Türkei, VII-2, no. 31, 186–90ff. (September 1808).
200. Ibid., no. 35, 252–55ff. (November 1808).
201. Yeşil, "Nizâm-ı Cedîd'ten yeniçeriliğin kaldırılmasına kadar," 179–81.
202. *Yayla İmamı risalesi*, 215–72.
203. *Câbî tarihi*, 1: 241.

204. Pakalın, *Osmanlı tarih deyimleri ve terimleri sözlüğü*, 1: 546–47.
205. *Documente Turceşti Privind Istoria României*, vol. 3, nos. 159, 162.
206. Krasnokutskii, *Dnevnye zapiski poezdki v Konstantinopol' v 1808 godu*, 1–20.
207. *Câbî tarihi*, 1: 214, 224, 225.
208. Ibid., 257, 239.
209. Ibid., 240–47.
210. *Şanizade tarihi*, 1: 98–99; *Câbî tarihi*, 1: 246–51.
211. Sakaoğlu, *Bir mülkün kadın sultanları*, 367.
212. Franz Freiherr von Ottenfels, "Schilderung der letzten Hälfte des Novembers 1808, in Costantinopel vorgefallenen Angelegenheiten," HHStA: Türkei VII-2 (November 1808).
213. Krasnokutskii, *Dnevnye zapiski poezdki v Konstantinopol' v 1808 godu*, 18–20.
214. Beydilli, "Baba Paşa."
215. Russia, Foreign Ministry, *Vneshniaia politika Rossii XIX i nachala XX veka*, 4: 408.
216. BOA: C A 16171.
217. BOA: C A 34844.
218. BOA: A. DVN 2403/61.
219. BOA: C A 8189; C A 37666; HAT 15701; KM: 112 - (Ruse) 64/5; BOA: A.DVN 2404/20.
220. *SO*, 4: 513.
221. Franz Freiherr von Ottenfels, "Schilderung der letzten Hälfte des Novembers 1808, in Constantinopel vorgefallenen Angelegenheiten," HHStA Türkei VII-2 (November 1808).
222. Ibid.
223. *Şanizade tarihi*, 1: 102.
224. Tanpınar, *Beş şehir*, 226.
225. BOA: HAT 15783.
226. BOA: HAT 15783.

CHAPTER 5: SETTLEMENT

1. *Vekayi'-i Baba Paşa*, 211.
2. *Şanizade tarihi*, 82.
3. For a copy of the Deed of Agreement made for Hüsrev Pasha, a leading member of the imperial elite and governor, who was not in Istanbul during the meeting, see SK: Hüsrev Paşa, no. 863.
4. Prior to the recent discovery in the Ottoman Archives of a copy of the imperial writ, BOA: HAT 35242, historians had access to neither the original Deed nor the contracting parties' copies. They thus had to rely on the versions published by Şanizade and Ahmed Cevdet Pasha. HAT 35242, found in neither *Şanizade tarihi*, 1: 75–82, nor *Tarih-i Cevdet*, 9: 278–83, is now, however, available in Akyıldız, "Sened-i İttifak'ın ilk tam metni," 215–22, with an English translation in Akyıldız and Hanioğlu, "Negotiating the Power of the Sultan," 23–30.

5. The English translation of the Deed of Alliance provided in this chapter is based on the translation in Akyıldız and Hanioğlu, "Negotiating the Power of the Sultan," with some modifications.

6. TSA: E 8393-1 (October 1809).

7. See chapter 3 above.

8. On the transformation of the office of the grand vizier, see Yılmaz, "Sultan and the Sultanate."

9. TSA: E 8393/1.

10. TSA: E 1479/2. See above, p. 177.

11. BOA: HAT 15783.

12. On the scribal bureau, see Findley, *Bureaucratic Reform*, 51–91.

13. Mehmed Tahsin is not included in the list of the signatories in HAT 35242. However, he was included in *Şanizade tarihi*, 81–82, *Tarih-i Cevdet*, 282–83, and SK: Hüsrev Paşa, no. 863.

14. Uzunçarşılı, "Nizam-ı Cedid ricalinden Kadı Abdurrahman Paşa"; Alexandrescu-Dersca-Bulgaru, "Contribution."

15. *SO*, 2: 679. On the province of Rumelia, see Georgieva, "Administrative Structure and Government of Rumelia."

16. İpşirli, "Esad Efendi, Salihzâde."

17. Kılıç, *Osmanlıda seyyidler ve şerifler*, 79–86; Morimoto, ed., *Sayyids and Sharifs*.

18. Mehmed İzzet came from a bureaucratic family. His father was a leading official in the imperial Treasury, Arif Efendi (d. 1797); *SO*, 3: 847; Okumuş, "Benlizâde İzzet Mehmed Bey'in sâkînâmesi," 900–910.

19. Panagiotopoulos et al. eds., *Arkheio Ali Pasa*, 1, no. 431.

20. *Câbî tarihi*, 1: 234.

21. *Vekâyi'-i Baba Paşa*, 211.

22. Ahmed Vasıf Efendi, *Mehâsinü'l-âsâr ve hakâikü'l-ahbâr*, 91.

23. In this sequential system, *ta'ahhüd*, *kafâla*, and *żemān/ḍamān*, or promise and commitment, surety, and liability—and their derivatives *müte'ahhid*, *kefîl*, and *żāmin/ḍāmin*—were the essence of the Deed.

24. Hallaq, *Sharī'a*, 258–60, 553.

25. Ahmed Cevdet Paşa, *Mecelle-yi ahkam-ı adliye*, 190, no. 612.

26. Ibid., 193, nos. 626 and 627.

27. Canbakal, "Vows as Contract in Ottoman Public Life"; Faroqhi, "Räuber, Rebellen und Obrigkeit im osmanischen Anatolien"; Tamdoğan, "Nezir"; Başaran, *Selim III*.

28. For the procedural matters in Islamic Criminal law, see Peters, *Crime and Punishment in Islamic Law*, 79–91.

29. Schmitt, *Constitutional Theory*, 75.

30. See chapter 4 above.

31. Žižek, *For They Know Not What They Do*, 182–97, 205–9.

32. *Şanizade tarihi*, 1: 74–80.

33. Ibid., 74–75.

34. *Tarih-i Cevdet*, 9: 5–8, 278–83. Also see Neumann, *Araç tarih, amaç Tanzimat*, 48–49, 188–89, 204–7.

35. On nineteenth-century Ottoman historiography, see Kütükoğlu, "Sultan II.

Mahmud devri Osmanlı tarihçiliği"; Kafadar and Karateke, "Late Ottoman and Early Republican Historical Writing."

36. For Ahmed Cevdet Pasha's accounts pertaining to the marginalization of the some provincial dyansties, see *Tarih-i Cevdet*, 10: 117–18 (the Serezli family after the death of İsmail Bey of Serres), 194 (execution of several notables in Thrace), 197 (the intendant of Drama), 198 (notables in Trabzon); 209–19 (various orders for the executions of some notables in Anatolia and the Balkans), 11: 23, 48, 87–88; for an interpretation of Mahmud's policy of eliminating the provincial dynasties, see Hanioğlu, *Brief History*, 60–61; Neumann, "Ottoman Provincial Towns," 142–44; Zürcher, *Turkey*, 33, 41.

37. *Vekâyi'-i Baba Paşa*, 268–69.

38. Philliou, *Biography*, 56–60.

39. *Tarih-i Cevdet*, 12: 166–88; Reed, "Destruction of the Janissaries"; Levy, "Ottoman Ulema"; Yıldız, *Neferin Adı Yok*, 139–221.

40. Ursinus, *Regionale Reformen*; Çadırcı, *Tanzimat döneminde Anadolu kentleri'nin sosyal ve ekonomik yapısı*; Findley, *Bureaucratic Reform*, 140–50; Ortaylı, *Mahalli idareler*, 22–24; Kornrumpf, "Zur Rolle des Osmanischen Meclis."

41. BOA: C D 6239.

42. Kaynar, *Mustafa Reşit Paşa*, 295–301.

43. Namık Kemal, "Usul-ı meşverete dair mektubun birincisi," *Hürriyet* 12 (27 Cemaziye'l-evvel 1285 / September 14, 1868), 6. Quoted from Sönmez, "From 'Kanun-ı Kadim' (Ancient Law) to 'Umum-ı Kuvvet' (Force of the People)."

44. Also see Mardin, "Freedom."

45. Menekşe, *İstanbul Camileri*, 41–42; Açıkgözoğlu, "Zeyneb Sultan Külliyesi."

46. Tanör, *Türkiye'de kongre iktidarları*, 1918–1920, 270–85; Kendirici, *Meclis-i Mebusan'dan Türkiye Büyük Millet Meclisine*, 60–100.

47. Ocak, "Milli mücadele'de Çapanoğlu isyanı."

48. Tökin, "Türkiye'de toprak ağalığı"; id., "Türkiye'de derebeylik rejimi."

49. Meeker, *Nation of Empire*, 285–317.

50. Fleming, *Muslim Bonaparte*, 18–34; Güthenke, *Placing Modern Greece*, 200; Clayer, "Myth of Ali Pasha," 132–33.

51. Gradeva, "Osman Pazvantoğlu," 135–40.

52. Philip Khoury, *Urban Notables and Arab Nationalism*, 8–52.

53. Di-Capua, *Gatekeepers*, 30–35.

54. Ionescu, *Manuc Bei*, 1–30; Hovnanean, *Mirzayean Manuk Pēyin varuts' patmut'iwně*.

55. Onar, *İdare hukukunun umumi esasları*, 147–48; Kubalı, *Türk esas teşkilat hukuku dersleri*, 50; Savcı, "Batılı ilkeler altında demokratikleşme," 10; id., "Osmanlı-Türk reformlarının (ıslahat hareketlerinin) bir batı demokrasisi doğurma çabaları," 114; Abadan and Savcı, *Türkiye'de Anayasa Gelişmelerine bir Bakış*, 19; İlhan Akın, *Kamu hukuku*, 301; Tunaya, *Türkiye'nin siyasi hayatında batılılaşma hareketleri*, 25; Özçelik, "Sened-i İttifak," 1–12; Akşin, "Sened-i İttifak ile Magna Carta'nın karşılaştırılması," 115–23; Küçükömer, *Düzenin yabancılaşması*, 56–57.

56. This model was inspired by the liberal European legal historians of the late nineteenth and early twentieth centuries, who argued that the modern democratic state was the product of centuries of struggle between the state and civil society,

king and parliament, might and right, center and periphery, public and private. See Pollock and Maitland, *History of English Law*; Maine, *Ancient Law*; Pocock, *Ancient Constitution*, 256–58.

57. Lewis et al., "Dustur."

58. Itzkowitz, "Men and Ideas," 12–26.

59. İnalcık, "Sened-i İttifak ve Gülhane Hatt-ı Hümâyûnu," 603–22.

60. Berkes, *Development of Secularism*, 90–92; id., *Türkiye'de çağdaşlaşma*, 509–10. For a similar view, see Tanör, *Osmanlı-Türk anayasal gelişmeleri*, 41–64.

61. Sućeska, *Ajani*, 152–53.

62. Mardin, *Genesis*, 148.

63. *Journal politique* (Leiden), cited in Salzmann, "Ancien Régime Revisited," 408; Barkey, *Empire of Difference*, 218–24.

64. Kili and Gözübüyük, *Türk anayasa metinleri*, 11–73; Tanör, *Osmanlı-Türk anayasal gelişmeleri*, 117–20, 164–65.

65. İnalcık, "Adaletnameler."

66. Palmer, *Age of the Democratic Revolution*, 1: 503–28.

67. Lewis, "Mashwara"; Erken, "Osmanlı devleti'nde bir danışma organı," 13–29.

68. Kaminsky, "Estate, Nobility, and the Exhibition of Estate"; Myers, *Parliaments and Estates*; Poggi, *Development*, 36–85; Swan, "French Nobility," 143–46; Madariaga, "Russian Nobility," 225–27; Frost "Nobility of Poland-Lithuania," 184–85.

69. Baker, "Fixing the French Constitution;" 301–4; id., "Political Language," 648–53; Gordon S. Woods, "American Revolution," 610–16.

70. Grześkowiak-Krawawics, "Anti-Monarchism," 53–4; Wagner, "Some Comments."

71. Davies, *God's Playground*, 2: 3–130; Sorel, *Eastern Question*, 120–49, 261–2.

CONCLUSION

1. Chapter epigraph: Yaşar Kemal, *İnce Memed*, vol. 3: 310.

2. Brewer, *Sinews of Power*, 167–218.

3. DuRivage, *Revolution Against Empire*.

4. Tucker, *Nadir Shah's Quest for Legitimacy*; Jos J. L. Gommans, *The Rise of the Indo-Afghan Empire*.

5. Avrich, *Russian Rebels*, 180–255.

6. Erefe, "Bread and Provisioning."

7. Heyd, "Ottoman *ulema*," 80–96.

8. Hanioğlu, *Brief History*, 55–71.

9. Çelik, *Şeyhü'l-vüzera Koca Hüsrev Paşa*, 415–46.

10. *Vekâyi'-i Baba Paşa*.

11. BOA: HAT 17249.

12. Acun, *Çapanoğulları ve eserleri*, 38–65; Karaca, *Anadolu islahatı*, 17.

13. Aravantinos, *Historia Ali Pasha*; Kardam, *Cizre-Bohtan beyi Bedirhan*; Kamberović, *Husein-kapetan Gradaščević*.

14. Sezer, "Tepedelenli Ali Paşa'nin oğulları"; Kuneralp, *Son dönem Osmanlı erkân ve ricali*, 85.

15. İslamoğlu, "Property as a Contested Domain"; Barkan, "Türk toprak hukuku tarihi tarihinde Tanzimat." See also the articles in Owen, ed., *New Perspectives*.

16. İnalcik, *Tanizamat ve Bulgar meselesi*; Turhan, *Ottoman Empire*. For a new interpretation on the Tanzimat reforms in the Balkans, see Blumi, *Reinstating the Ottomans*, 31–95.

17. See, e.g., Doumani, *Rediscovering Palestine*, 118–30.

18. Tugay, *Three Centuries: Family Chronicles of Turkey and Egypt*; Hunter, *Egypt under the Khedives*.

19. Osterhammel, *Transformation*, 404.

20. Armitage, *Foundations*, 215–32.

21. Zens, "Pasvanoğlu Osman Paşa"; Fleming, *Muslim Bonaparte*, 57–69; Güner, *Vehhâbî-Suûdîler*, 201–14.

22. Brown, *Rise of Western Christendom*, 21.

23. For a recent book on the transition from empire to nation, see Anscombe, *State, Faith and Nation*, 121–218. Also see Kayalı, *Arabs and Young Turks*, 30–51; Yosmaoğlu, *Blood Ties*, 48–77; M. A. Reynolds, *Shattering Empires*, 140–66.

24. Zandi-Sayek, *Ottoman Izmir*, 75–114; Ursinus, *Regionale Reformen*, 189–233; Çadırcı, *Tanzimat döneminde Anadolu kentleri'nin sosyal ve ekonomik yapıları*; Ortaylı, *Tanzimattan cumhuriyete yerel yönetim geleneği*.

25. Hanioğlu, *Brief History*, 72–149.

26. For the Albanian nationalist Ottoman nobles, see Birecikli, *Political Activities of Ismail Kemal Bej Vlora*; Avlonyalı Ekrem Bey, *Osmanlı Arnavutluk'undan anılar*. On the role of the Ottoman notables in Syrian nation-building, see Philip Khoury, *Urban Notables*, 58–74; Campos, *Ottoman Brothers*, 224–44; Pappe, *Rise and Fall*, 246–82; Gelvin, *Divided Loyalties*, 82–85.

27. Güthenke, *Placing Modern Greece*, 200; Clogg, *Concise History of Greece*, 29, 39, 41–42.

28. Clayer, "Myth of Ali Pasha"; id., *Aux origines du nationalisme albanais*, 442–43; Di-Capua, *Gatekeepers*, 30–35.

29. Tanör, *Türkiye'de kongre iktidarları*, 93–155, 252–83; Findley, *Turkey, Islam, Nationalism and Modernity*, 192–305; Zürcher, *Young Turk Legacy*, 137–38; Ocak, "Milli Mücadele'de Çapanoğlu isyanı"; Kendirci, *Meclis-i Mebusan'dan Türkiye Büyük Millet Meclisine*, 51–100; Frey, *Turkish Political Elite*, 184–91.

Index